AF780488

Time Series Analysis in Earthquake Complex Networks

Time Series Analysis in Earthquake Complex Networks

Guest Editors

Tamaz Chelidze
Luciano Telesca
Filippos Vallianatos

MDPI

Basel • Beijing • Wuhan • Barcelona • Belgrade • Novi Sad • Cluj • Manchester

Guest Editors

Tamaz Chelidze
Mikheil Nodia Institute of Geophysics
Ivane Javakhishvili Tbilisi State University
Tbilisi
Georgia

Luciano Telesca
Institute of Methodologies for Environmental Analysis
National Research Council
Tito
Italy

Filippos Vallianatos
Department of Geology and Geoenvironment
National and Kapodistrian University of Athens
Athens
Greece

Editorial Office

MDPI AG
Grosspeteranlage 5
4052 Basel, Switzerland

This is a reprint of the Special Issue, published open access by the journal *Entropy* (ISSN 1099-4300), freely accessible at: https://www.mdpi.com/journal/entropy/special_issues/IW4QPHRP50.

For citation purposes, cite each article independently as indicated on the article page online and as indicated below:

Lastname, A.A.; Lastname, B.B. Article Title. *Journal Name* **Year**, *Volume Number*, Page Range.

ISBN 978-3-7258-6500-0 (Hbk)
ISBN 978-3-7258-6501-7 (PDF)
https://doi.org/10.3390/books978-3-7258-6501-7

© 2026 by the authors. Articles in this book are Open Access and distributed under the Creative Commons Attribution (CC BY) license. The book as a whole is distributed by MDPI under the terms and conditions of the Creative Commons Attribution-NonCommercial-NoDerivs (CC BY-NC-ND) license (https://creativecommons.org/licenses/by-nc-nd/4.0/).

Contents

entropy

MDPI

Article

Prognostic Properties of Instantaneous Amplitudes Maxima of Earth Surface Tremor

Alexey Lyubushin * and Eugeny Rodionov

Institute of Physics of the Earth RAS, Moscow 123242, Russia; evgeny_980@list.ru
* Correspondence: lyubushin@yandex.ru

Abstract: A method is proposed for analyzing the tremor of the earth's surface, measured by GPS, in order to highlight prognostic effects. The method is applied to the analysis of daily time series of vertical displacements in Japan. The network of 1047 stations is divided into 15 clusters. The Huang Empirical Mode Decomposition (EMD) is applied to the time series of the principal components from the clusters, with subsequent calculation of instantaneous amplitudes using the Hilbert transform. To ensure the stability of estimates of the waveforms of the EMD decomposition, 1000 independent additive realizations of white noise of limited amplitude were averaged before the Hilbert transform. Using a parametric model of the intensities of point processes, we analyze the connections between the instants of sequences of times of the largest local maxima of instantaneous amplitudes, averaged over the number of clusters and the times of earthquakes in the vicinity of Japan with minimum magnitude thresholds of 5.5 for the time interval 2012–2023. It is shown that the sequence of the largest local maxima of instantaneous amplitudes significantly more often precedes the moments of time of earthquakes (roughly speaking, has an "influence") than the reverse "influence" of earthquakes on the maxima of amplitudes.

Keywords: earth surface tremor; cluster analysis; principal components; Hilbert–Huang decomposition; seismic process; event sequence intensity model

1. Introduction

This article presents the further development of methods for analyzing ground surface tremor proposed in [1–3]. The coherence of the tremor of the earth's surface was analyzed in [4,5]. In [6,7], coherent analysis of GPS time series was used to assess seismic hazard in Japan and California.

In this case, the main emphasis is on the use of the Hilbert–Huang expansion, which is well suited to take into account the effects of nonstationarity and nonlinearity in time series [8,9]. This method has been successfully used to analyze geodetic time series [10,11], when processing hydrological [12], financial [13], biological [14,15] and seismic [16] data.

The main purpose of the article is to clarify common hypotheses that movements of the earth's crust recorded by GNSS may contain predictive information. That displacements recorded by geodetic methods respond to the effects of earthquakes is widely known and has been demonstrated many times. But extracting geodetic effects that predict seismic events is much more challenging. In our paper, we propose one method for detecting predictive effects in space geodesy data.

The works [17–20] analyzed the composition of GPS time series—both their high-frequency part and low-frequency seasonal components—in connection with the estimates of the velocities of tectonic plates. In [21–27], using multivariate statistical methods, the influence of hydrological loads on tectonic displacements of sections of the earth's crust was studied. The influence of time delays on the sensitivity of GPS solutions due to the impact of ionospheric and tropospheric factors was analyzed in [28]. The causes of the occurrence of "anomalous harmonics" in the spectral decomposition of GPS time series were considered in [29].

The detailed structure of earth surface displacements presented in GPS time series has been analyzed in the works of a large number of scientists. One of the most popular approaches is the use of the maximum likelihood method for estimating the parameters of GPS time series models [30–33]. This method was used in [34–36] to estimate the parameters of the power spectrum shape and noise amplitude for data from different regions of the world, and the error estimates are discussed in [37,38]. The influence of the spectrum shape and noise amplitude on the errors of displacement velocity estimates was investigated in [39,40]. Phase correlations of GPS time series were studied in [41,42] using parametric models for a number of tectonically active regions.

In [43,44], principal component analysis, empirical orthogonal function analysis, and singular spectrum analysis were used to determine the most common spatial and temporal components of GPS time series. In [45], a joint analysis of accelerometer readings and the noise component of GPS time series was performed. The influence of non-stationary effects on the estimates of relative displacements of crustal blocks and station positions was studied in [46–48].

2. Data

GPS data of daily earth displacements are taken from the Nevada Geodetic Laboratory website [49] at: http://geodesy.unr.edu/gps_timeseries/tenv3/IGS14/, access at 19 August 2024.

The set of 1047 GPS stations within domain $30^\circ \leq \text{Lat} \leq 46^\circ$, $128^\circ \leq \text{Lon} \leq 146^\circ$, were chosen. These stations presented in Figure 1a have daily time series from the beginning of 2009 to the end of 2023 (15 years), with a total number of gaps of less than 365 samples, and the longest gap less than 182 samples. The vertical components of ground displacement are investigated. The choice of only the vertical component for Japan is due to the fact that it does not contain the catastrophic jump and subsequent long-term relaxation due to the impact of the mega-earthquake of 11 March 2011. Gaps in the GPS time series are filled in using information from the left and right neighborhoods of the gap of the same length as the gap length [4].

The set of stations was previously divided into 15 clusters (Figure 1). The number 15 was chosen as the number of clusters, which optimally splits their "cloud". Let us split the set of station position vectors $\vec{\zeta}$ into a given number q of clusters using the k-means clustering method [50]. Let C_r, $r = 1, \ldots, q$ be clusters, let $\vec{z}_r = \sum_{\vec{\zeta} \in C_r} \vec{\zeta} / n_r$ be the vector of the center of mass of the cluster C_r, and let n_r be the number of vectors in the cluster, $\sum_{r=1}^{q} n_r = N$. Vector $\vec{\zeta} \in C_r$ if the distance $\left| \vec{\zeta} - \vec{z}_r \right|$ is the minimum among the positions of all cluster centers. The k-means method minimizes the sum of squared distances:

$$G(\vec{z}_1, \ldots, \vec{z}_q) = \sum_{r=1}^{q} \sum_{\vec{\zeta} \in C_r} \left| \vec{\zeta} - \vec{z}_r \right|^2 \rightarrow \min_{\vec{z}_1, \ldots, \vec{z}_q} \tag{1}$$

relative to the position of the cluster centers $\vec{z}_r$. Let $\Phi(q) = \min_{\vec{z}_1, \ldots, \vec{z}_q} G(\vec{z}_1, \ldots, \vec{z}_q)$. We used a trial number of clusters in the range $2 \leq q \leq 50$. The problem of choosing the best number q^* of clusters was solved using the maximum pseudo-F-statistic criterion [51]

$$PFS(q) = \sigma_1^2(q) / \sigma_0^2(q) \rightarrow \max_{2 \leq q \leq 50} \tag{2}$$

where

$$\sigma_0^2(q) = \frac{\Phi(q)}{N - q}, \ \sigma_1^2(q) = \sum_{r=1}^{q} \frac{n_r}{N} \cdot \left| \vec{z}_r - \vec{z}_0 \right|^2, \ \vec{z}_0 = \frac{1}{N} \sum_{1}^{N} \vec{\zeta} \tag{3}$$

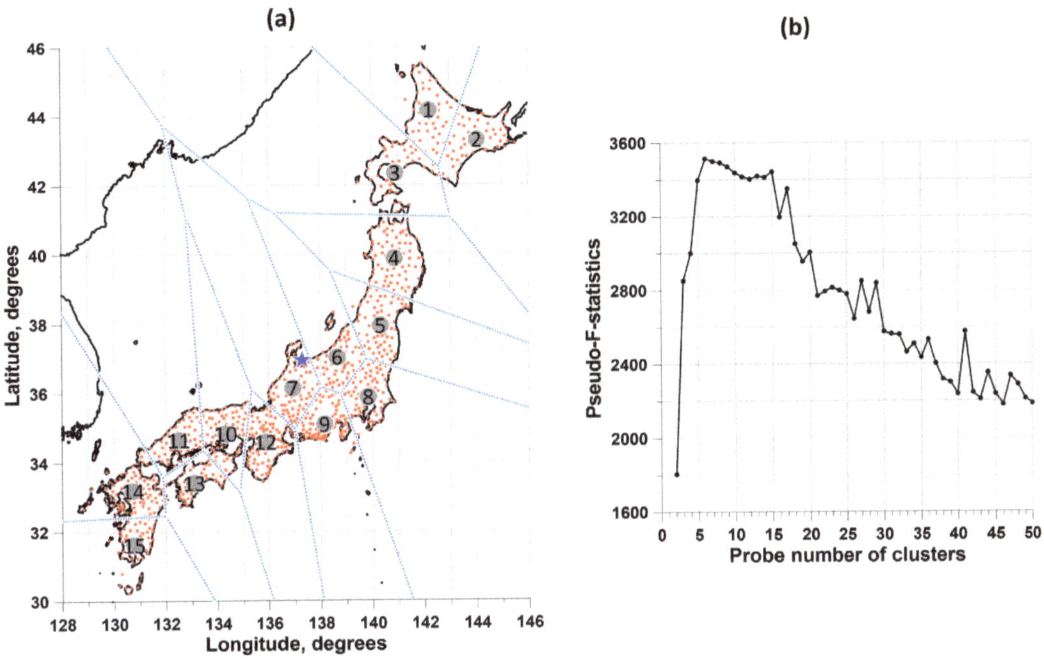

Figure 1. (**a**) shows the positions of 1047 GPS stations and their division into 15 clusters. The numbered circles indicate the centers of gravity of the clusters, and the blue lines indicate the boundaries between Voronoi cells. The blue star shows the position of the center of mass of all cluster centers. (**b**) shows a plot of the pseudo-F-statistic that allowed us to select 15 as the number of clusters.

The plot in Figure 1b presents the pseudo-F-statistic values as a function of the trial number of clusters. The number 15 on the pseudo-F-statistics graph is the inflection point of the dependence on the trial number of clusters and realizes one of the largest local maxima for the number of clusters from 2 to 50. On the pseudo-F-statistics graph, they represent two local maxima with close values of the number of clusters 6 and 15. Of these two values, 15 was chosen as the largest in order to provide the most detailed breakdown of the set of stations. Figure 1a shows the division of a set of stations into 15 clusters along with Voronoi cells, which indicate that the stations belong to a particular cluster.

Clusters of stations are ordered by increasing latitude of the position of their centers of gravity. Table 1 shows for each cluster (first row) the number of stations in the cluster (second row).

Table 1. Number of N_{sta} stations in each Clust# cluster.

Clust#.	1	2	3	4	5	6	7	8	9	10	11	12	13	14	15
N_{sta}	57	56	54	83	69	61	78	77	91	76	57	95	48	88	57

3. Principal Components of Increments in a Moving Time Window

Since the goal is to study the tremor of the earth's surface, that is, the high-frequency part of the earth's surface displacements, the analysis was carried out for increments of time series. Switching to increments reduces the dominant influence of low frequencies in the daily GPS time series and ensures stationarity of time series fragments within the 365-day time windows that are used further.

The division of a set of stations into 15 clusters is used for the subsequent application of the principal component method [52]. For each cluster of stations, the first principal component of the time series of increments of vertical displacements of the earth's surface was calculated in a sliding adaptation time window of 365 days in length.

Let there be a p-dimensional cloud of similar N-dimensional signals $\{y_j(k),\, k = 1, \ldots, N\}$, $j = 1, \ldots, p$. Let us choose the size of the sliding window w and center the signals,

$$x_j(k) = y_j(k) - \overline{y_j(k)},\ j = 1, \ldots, p,\ k = w, \ldots, N, \tag{4}$$

$$\overline{y_j(k)} = \frac{1}{w}\sum_{i=1}^{w} y_j(k - w + i),\ k = w, \ldots, N. \tag{5}$$

The next step is to calculate the sample estimate of the covariance $(p \times p)$-dimensional matrix in a sliding window:

$$r_{XX}^{(m,n)} = \frac{1}{w}\sum_{i=1}^{w} x_m(i - w + k)x_n(i - w + k),\ k, j = 1, \ldots, p,\ k = w, \ldots, N. \tag{6}$$

Let $\phi^{(s)} = \left(\phi_1^{(s)}, \ldots, \phi_p^{(s)}\right)^T$ be the eigenvector of this matrix corresponding to the maximum eigenvalue. Let us put

$$\xi_s(k) = \sum_{j=1}^{p} \left(\phi_j^{(k)}\right)^2 x_j(k),\ k = w, \ldots, N. \tag{7}$$

Having generalized Formulas (4)–(7) with understandable changes to the case $k = 1, \ldots, w - 1$, let us determine the weighted average in a sliding time window of length w using the formula

$$\xi(k) = \begin{cases} \xi_{w-1}(k),\ k < w, \\ \xi_k(k),\ k \geq w. \end{cases} \tag{8}$$

Thus, Formulas (7) and (8) determine the values of the weighted average increments of vertical time series of displacements of the earth's surface. The squared values of the eigenvector of the covariance matrix in the sliding time window corresponding to the largest eigenvalue are taken as weights. The sum of these weights is equal to one.

Within each of the 15 clusters, a transition to a weighted average was made using the method described above; the length w of the sliding time window was taken as equal to 365 samples, i.e., 1 year. At the same time, in order to eliminate the influence of large outliers, before calculating the weighted average, the so-called winsorization procedure was carried out [53], which consists in eliminating outliers falling beyond the level $\mu \pm 4\sigma$ by cutting off the values of the time series in a sliding time window (μ and σ are sample estimates of the mathematical expectation and standard deviation for the current time window). The procedure is repeated iteratively until the values μ and σ stop changing.

Figure 2 shows graphs of the first principal components of increments (in the form of weighted averages) of vertical displacements of the earth's surface in each of the identified 15 clusters.

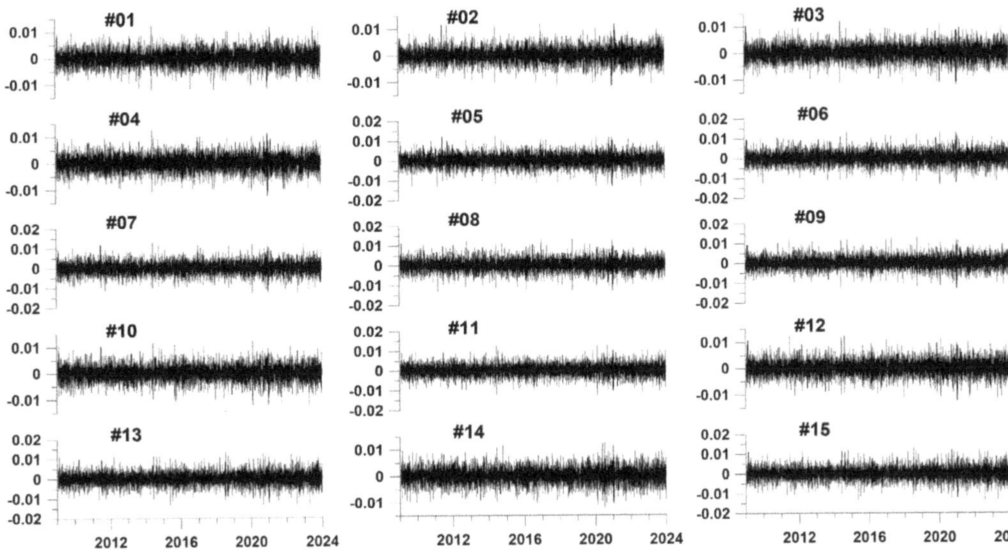

Figure 2. Graphs of weighted average vertical displacements of the earth's surface in each of the selected 15 clusters in a sliding time window of 365 days. The Y axes represent displacement increments in mm.

4. Empirical Mode Decomposition

Let $x(k)$ be the analyzed discrete signal. Empirical mode decomposition (EMD) [8,9] represents the decomposition of the signal into modes of oscillation:

$$x(k) = \sum_{j=1}^{n} h_j(k) + r_n(k) \tag{9}$$

where $h_j(k)$ is the j-th empirical mode, $r_n(k)$ is the remainder, n is the number of empirical modes.

The algorithm for decomposing into a sequence of empirical modes is iterative for each level j. Let us denote by m, $m = 0, 1, \ldots, M_j$ the index of iterations, where M_j is the maximum number of iterations for level j. The iterations are described by the formula

$$h_j^{(m+1)}(k) = h_j^{(m)}(k) - z_j^{(m)}(k), \tag{10}$$

Here $z_j^{(m)}(k) = \left(p_j^{(m)}(k) + q_j^{(m)}(k)\right)/2$, where $p_j^{(m)}(k)$ and $q_j^{(m)}(k)$ are both the upper and lower envelopes for the signal, which are constructed using spline interpolation (usually a third order spline) over all local maxima and minima of the signal $h_j^{(m)}(k)$.

Iterations (10) are initialized with step zero for the first level ($j = 1$) of the expansion $h_1^{(0)}(k) = x(k)$. Next, the upper $p_1^{(0)}(k)$ and lower $q_1^{(0)}(k)$ envelopes are found, and the middle line $z_1^{(0)}(k)$ is calculated and found $h_1^{(2)}(k)$ using Formula (10). For $h_1^{(1)}(k)$, the upper $p_1^{(1)}(k)$ and lower $q_1^{(1)}(k)$ envelopes are determined, and the middle line $z_1^{(1)}(k)$ is found, and so on, until the last iteration index M_1, after which it is considered that the first empirical mode $h_1(k)$ has been found.

The condition for stopping iterations is usually chosen in the form of the following inequality:

$$\sum_k \left(h_j^{(m+1)}(k) - h_j^{(m)}(k)\right)^2 \Big/ \sum_k \left(h_j^{(m)}(k)\right)^2 \leq \delta, \tag{11}$$

where δ is some small number, for example 0.01. After the mode $h_j(k)$ is found, the iterative process of determining the empirical mode $h_{j+1}(k)$ of the next level is started. This process is initialized by the formula for the initial iteration index $m = 0$:

$$h_{j+1}^{(0)}(k) = x(k) - h_j(k), \quad (12)$$

According to formula (12), the high-frequency part is subtracted from the original signal and a new, lower-frequency signal is considered as a new signal for subsequent decomposition. The construction of empirical oscillation modes continues until the number of local extrema becomes too small for envelopes to be constructed from them. As the number j of the empirical mode level increases, the signals become increasingly low-frequency and tend towards an unchanging form. The sequence $h_1(k), h_2(k), \ldots, h_n(k)$ is constructed in such a way that its sum gives an approximation to the original signal $x(k)$, which can be represented in formula (9) [8,9]. Empirical modes are orthogonal to each other, thus constituting a certain empirical basis for the decomposition of the original signal.

In the practical implementation of the method, technical difficulties arise due to edge effects, since the continuation of the envelopes beyond the first and last points of local extrema is ambiguous. To overcome this difficulty, there are several approaches, in particular mirror continuation [8,13] of the analyzed sample back and forth for a sufficiently long period of time. It was this approach that was used in this work.

5. Ensemble Empirical Mode Decomposition

One of the key disadvantages of the EMD method is the problem of mode mixing, which occurs when one empirical mode includes signals of different scales or when signals of the same scale are distributed over different empirical modes. For example, if "intermittency" is observed in the signal, that is, against the background of a smooth signal, short-term sections of higher frequency behavior appear, then with EMD decomposition behavior modes with different frequencies are mixed, since relatively rare points of local extrema of smooth behavior are interspersed with much more frequent points of local extrema of the high-frequency component.

To combat this effect, ref. [9] proposed the ensemble empirical mode decomposition (EEMD) method. This is a regularization of the EMD method in which white noise of finite amplitude is added to the original data. This allows the true empirical modes to be determined as the average over an ensemble of trials, each of which is the sum of signal and white noise.

The EEMD algorithm includes the following steps:

1. Add a white noise implementation to the original data.
2. Decomposition of data with the addition of white noise into empirical modes.
3. Repeat steps 1 and 2 quite a large number of times with different implementations of white noise.
4. Obtain the ensemble average for the corresponding empirical modes.

Thus, numerous "artificial" observations are simulated:

$$x^{(i)}(k) = x(k) + \varepsilon_i(k), \quad (13)$$

where $\varepsilon_i(k)$ is the i-th realization of white noise.

The true component, according to the EEMD definition, for a sequence of all levels of empirical modes is calculated as the average value of the expansions of the noisy modes (13). It is important to note that EEMD largely eliminates this mixing problem [9]. Adding independent white noise to the sample has a regularizing effect, since it simplifies the construction of envelopes (after adding a small amount of white noise, many local extrema are immediately created). The operation of averaging over a sufficiently large number of independent implementations of white noise makes it possible to eliminate the influence of the noise component and to isolate the true internal modes of oscillations.

For each of the resulting 15 time series, EEMD waveforms of principal components were calculated. EEMD waveforms are obtained by averaging 1000 decompositions of the original signals, to which are added independent Gaussian white noises with a standard deviation of 0.1 from the standard deviation of the weighted average from each cluster. Figure 3 shows EEMD waveform plots for the first 6 expansion levels for three of the 15 clusters.

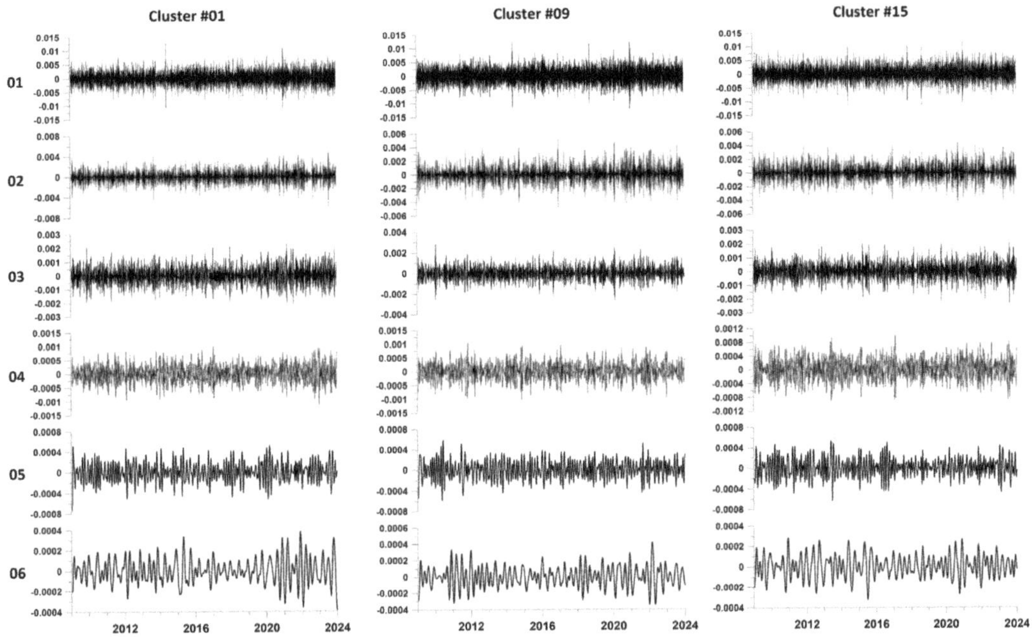

Figure 3. EEMD waveform plots for the first 6 decomposition levels for 3 clusters (numbers 1, 9 and 15). Decomposition level numbers are indicated on the left.

6. Hilbert Transform

The Hilbert transform of the signal is determined by the formula [54]:

$$H_X(t) = \int_{-\infty}^{+\infty} \frac{X(u)}{\pi(t-u)}\, du = X(t) * \left(\frac{1}{\pi t}\right) \tag{14}$$

where $f(t) * g(t) = \int_{-\infty}^{+\infty} f(u) \cdot g(t-u)\, du$ is the convolution of two functions. If $\widetilde{f}(\omega)$ and $\widetilde{g}(\omega)$ are the Fourier transforms of convolutional functions $\widetilde{f}(\omega) = \int_{-\infty}^{+\infty} f(t) \cdot e^{-i\omega t}\, dt$, then, as is known, the Fourier transform of convolution is equal to the product of the Fourier transforms of convolutional functions. Fourier transform from $1/(\pi t)$ equals:

$$\int_{-\infty}^{+\infty} \frac{e^{-i\omega t}}{\pi t}\, dt = -i \cdot sign(\omega) = \begin{cases} -i, & \omega > 0 \\ 0, & \omega = 0 \\ i, & \omega < 0 \end{cases} \tag{15}$$

Thus, if $\widetilde{X}(\omega)$ there is a Fourier transform of $X(t)$, then

$$\widetilde{H}_X(\omega) = -i \cdot sign(\omega) \cdot \widetilde{X}(\omega) = \begin{cases} -i \cdot \widetilde{X}(\omega), & \omega > 0 \\ 0, & \omega = 0 \\ i \cdot \widetilde{X}(\omega), & \omega < 0 \end{cases} \tag{16}$$

If you present $\widetilde{X}(\omega) = \left|\widetilde{X}(\omega)\right| e^{-i\varphi(\omega)}$, then

$$\widetilde{H}_X(\omega) = \begin{cases} \left|\widetilde{X}(\omega)\right| e^{-i(\varphi(\omega)+\pi/2)}, & \omega > 0 \\ 0, & \omega = 0 \\ \left|\widetilde{X}(\omega)\right| e^{-i(\varphi(\omega)-\pi/2)}, & \omega < 0 \end{cases} \tag{17}$$

In practice, it is more convenient to calculate the Hilbert transform using the concepts of an analytical signal:

$$Z_X(t) = X(t) + i \cdot H_X(t) = \left|Z_X(t)\right| \cdot e^{i\vartheta(t)} \equiv A_X(t) \cdot e^{i\vartheta(t)} \tag{18}$$

where $A_X(t) = \sqrt{X^2(t) + H_X^2(t)}$ are the amplitudes of the signal $X(t)$ envelope, and $\vartheta(t)$ is the instantaneous phase. The derivative $\nu(t) = d\vartheta(t)/dt$ is called instantaneous frequency. The Fourier transform of the analytical signal $\widetilde{Z}_X(\omega) = \widetilde{X}(\omega) + i \cdot \widetilde{H}_X(\omega) = \widetilde{X}(\omega) \cdot (1 + sign(\omega))$ or:

$$\widetilde{Z}_X(\omega) = \begin{cases} 2\widetilde{X}(\omega), & \omega > 0 \\ \widetilde{X}(0), & \omega = 0 \\ 0, & \omega < 0 \end{cases} \tag{19}$$

after which the Hilbert transform is equal to the imaginary part of the result of the inverse Fourier transform of $\widetilde{Z}_X(\omega)$

$$H_X(t) = \mathrm{Im}\left(\frac{1}{2\pi} \int_{-\infty}^{+\infty} \widetilde{Z}_X(\omega) e^{i\omega t} d\omega\right) \tag{20}$$

For each of the resulting 15 time series, EEMD waveforms of principal components were calculated. EEMD waveforms are obtained by averaging 1000 decompositions of the original signals, to which are added independent Gaussian white noises with a standard deviation of 0.1 from the standard deviation of the weighted average from each cluster. Figure 4 shows EEMD waveform plots for the first 6 expansion levels for three of the 15 clusters.

For a discrete-time signal $X(t)$, $t = 0, \ldots, (N-1)$, this transformation can be calculated using the discrete Fourier transform:

$$d_X^{(N)}(\omega_k) = \sum_{t=0}^{N-1} X(t) \cdot \exp(-i\omega_k t),\ \omega_k = \frac{2\pi}{N}(k-1),\ k = 0, 1, \ldots, (N-1) \tag{21}$$

after which the second part of the Fourier coefficients (corresponding to negative frequencies) should be reset to zero: $h_X^{(N)}(\omega_k) = 0$, $k = N/2 + 1, \ldots, (N-1)$ while the 1st part should be doubled: $h_X^{(N)}(\omega_k) = 2 \cdot d_X^{(N)}(\omega_k)$, $k = 1, \ldots, N/2$. The Hilbert transform is then calculated as the imaginary part of the inverse discrete Fourier transform:

$$H_X(t) = \mathrm{Im}\left(\sum_{k=0}^{N-1} h_X^{(N)}(\omega_k) \cdot \exp(i\omega_k t)/N\right),\ t = 0, 1, \ldots, (N-1) \tag{22}$$

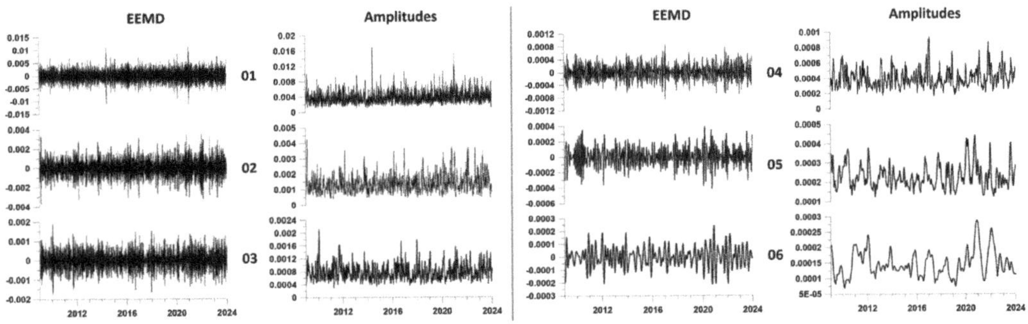

Figure 4. Plots of mean EEMD waveforms and mean instantaneous amplitudes averaged over all 15 station clusters for the first 6 decomposition levels. The left side of the figure, separated by a vertical blue line, shows pairs of graphs (waveforms—their amplitudes) for levels 1–3, and the right side shows graphs for levels 4–6. The decomposition level numbers are indicated between the waveform and amplitude graphs.

Thus, after determining the instantaneous amplitudes and frequencies of the EEMD, the Hilbert–Huang decomposition can be represented as follows:

$$x(t) = \sum_{j=1}^{n} h_j(t) + r_n(t),\ h_j(t) = \mathrm{Re}\left\{ A_j(t) \cdot \exp\left(i \cdot \int \nu_j(s)\, ds \right) \right\} \tag{23}$$

7. Influence Matrix

To solve the problem of estimating the connection between two sequences of random events, a parametric intensity model is used. In [55–57] this method was used to test the hypotheses that local extrema of the average values of certain properties of seismic noise and magnetic field precede the instants of strong earthquakes.

Let $t_j^{(\alpha)}$, $j = 1, \ldots, N_\alpha;\ \alpha = 1, 2$ represent the moments in time of 2 streams of events. In our case it is:

(1) a sequence of moments in time corresponding to the largest local maxima of the amplitudes of the envelopes at certain levels of the EEMD Huang decomposition
(2) a sequence of times of seismic events with a magnitude not less than a given value.

Let us present their intensities in the form:

$$\lambda^{(\alpha)}(t) = b_0^{(\alpha)} + \sum_{\beta=1}^{2} b_\beta^{(\alpha)} \cdot g^{(\beta)}(t) \tag{24}$$

where $b_0^{(\alpha)} \geq 0, b_\beta^{(\alpha)} \geq 0$ are parameters, and $g^{(\beta)}(t)$ is the influence function of flow events $t_j^{(\beta)}$ with number β:

$$g^{(\beta)}(t) = \sum_{t_j^{(\beta)} < t} \exp(-(t - t_j^{(\beta)})/\tau) \tag{25}$$

According to formula (25), the weight of an event with number j becomes non-zero for times $t > t_j^{(\beta)}$ and decays with a characteristic time τ. The parameter $b_\beta^{(\alpha)}$ determines the degree of influence of the sequence β on the sequence α. The parameter $b_\alpha^{(\alpha)}$ determines the degree of self-excitation to which the flow α influences itself, and the parameter $b_0^{(\alpha)}$ reflects the purely random (Poisson) intensity component. Let us fix the parameter τ and consider the problem of estimating the parameters $b_0^{(\alpha)}, b_\beta^{(\alpha)}$.

The log-likelihood function for a non-stationary Poisson process within the time interval $[0, T]$ equals [58]:

$$\ln(L_\alpha) = \sum_{j=1}^{N_\alpha} \ln(\lambda^{(\alpha)}(t_j^{(\alpha)})) - \int_0^T \lambda^{(\alpha)}(s)ds, \ \alpha = 1,2 \tag{26}$$

We need to find parameters $b_0^{(\alpha)}, b_\beta^{(\alpha)}$ from maximum of functions (26). It is easy to obtain the following expression:

$$b_0^{(\alpha)} \frac{\partial \ln(L_\alpha)}{\partial b_0^{(\alpha)}} + \sum_{\beta=1}^{2} b_\beta^{(\alpha)} \frac{\partial \ln(L_\alpha)}{\partial b_\beta^{(\alpha)}} = N_\alpha - \int_0^T \lambda^{(\alpha)}(s)ds \tag{27}$$

The parameters $b_0^{(\alpha)}, b_\beta^{(\alpha)}$ are non-negative. It means that each term on the left side of (27) equals to zero at point of maximum of function (26)—either due to the necessary conditions for the extremum (if the parameters are positive), or, if the maximum is reached at the boundary, then the parameters themselves are equal to zero. Therefore, at the maximum point of the likelihood function the equality holds:

$$\int_0^T \lambda^{(\alpha)}(s)ds = N_\alpha \tag{28}$$

Let us substitute the expression $g^{(\beta)}(t)$ from (28) into (27) and divide by T. Then we get another form of formula (28):

$$b_0^{(\alpha)} + \sum_{\beta=1}^{m} b_\beta^{(\alpha)} \cdot \overline{g}^{(\beta)} = \lambda_0^{(\alpha)} \equiv N_\alpha / T \tag{29}$$

where

$$\overline{g}^{(\beta)} = \int_0^T g^{(\beta)}(s)ds/T \tag{30}$$

average value of the influence function. Substituting $b_0^{(\alpha)}$ from (29) into (26), we obtain the following maximum problem:

$$\Phi^{(\alpha)}(b_1^{(\alpha)}, b_2^{(\alpha)}) = \sum_{j=1}^{N_\alpha} \ln(\lambda_0^{(\alpha)} + \sum_{\beta=1}^{2} b_\beta^{(\alpha)} \cdot \Delta g^{(\beta)}(t_j^{(\alpha)})) \to \max \tag{31}$$

where $\Delta g^{(\beta)}(t) = g^{(\beta)}(t) - \overline{g}^{(\beta)}$, under restrictions:

$$b_1^{(\alpha)} \geq 0, b_2^{(\alpha)} \geq 0, \sum_{\beta-1}^{2} b_\beta^{(\alpha)} \overline{g}^{(\beta)} \leq \lambda_0^{(\alpha)} \tag{32}$$

It could be shown that function (31) is convex with a negative definite Hessian. Therefore, problem (31) and (32) has a unique solution. The problem (31) and (32) is solved numerically for a given relaxation parameter τ. After this step we can define the influence matrix with elements $\kappa_\beta^{(\alpha)}, \alpha = 1,2;\ \beta = 0,1,2$ using the formulas:

$$\kappa_0^{(\alpha)} = \frac{b_0^{(\alpha)}}{\lambda_0^{(\alpha)}} \geq 0, \ \kappa_\beta^{(\alpha)} = \frac{b_\beta^{(\alpha)} \cdot \overline{g}^{(\beta)}}{\lambda_0^{(\alpha)}} \geq 0 \tag{33}$$

The value $\kappa_0^{(\alpha)}$ is the share of the average intensity $\lambda_0^{(\alpha)}$ of the process with number α, which is purely random, part $\kappa_\alpha^{(\alpha)}$ is caused by the influence of self-excitation $\alpha \rightarrow \alpha$, and $\kappa_\beta^{(\alpha)}$, $\beta \neq \alpha$ is due to external influence $\beta \rightarrow \alpha$. From Formula (29) the normalization condition follows:

$$\kappa_0^{(\alpha)} + \sum_{\beta=1}^{2} \kappa_\beta^{(\alpha)} = 1, \ \alpha = 1,2 \tag{34}$$

As a result, the influence matrix can be determined:

$$\left(\left\| \begin{matrix} \kappa_0^{(1)} \\ \kappa_0^{(2)} \end{matrix} \right\| \left\| \begin{matrix} \kappa_1^{(1)} & \kappa_2^{(1)} \\ \kappa_1^{(2)} & \kappa_2^{(2)} \end{matrix} \right\| \right) \tag{35}$$

The first column of matrix (35) is composed of Poisson shares of average intensities. The diagonal elements of the right submatrix of size 2 × 2 consist of self-exciting elements of mean intensity, while the off-diagonal elements correspond to mutual excitation. The sums of the component rows of the influence matrix (34) equal 1. The influence matrices are estimated in a certain moving time window of length L with an offset ΔL and with a given value of the relaxation parameter τ.

8. Estimation of Connections between the Times of Local Amplitude Maxima and Seismic Events

The further plan of the article is to use the apparatus of influence matrices to assess the relationship between the times of maximum average amplitudes of the envelopes and the times of sufficiently strong earthquakes. A magnitude threshold of 5.5 was chosen. There were 673 such seismic events in the vicinity of the Japanese islands during the period of time 2009–2023—see Figure 5a. However, the mega-earthquake of 11 March 2011 with a magnitude of 9 gave rise to a surge in aftershock activity, as a result of which, if we consider the time interval 2012–2023, when the intensity of aftershocks had already decreased, the number of earthquakes with a magnitude of at least 5.5 will decrease by almost 2 times to 349—see Figure 5b. It should be noted that accurately estimating the time of the end of the Tohoku earthquake aftershocks is a difficult task [59] and in this case we used a rough estimate based on the visual perception of the intensity of seismic events.

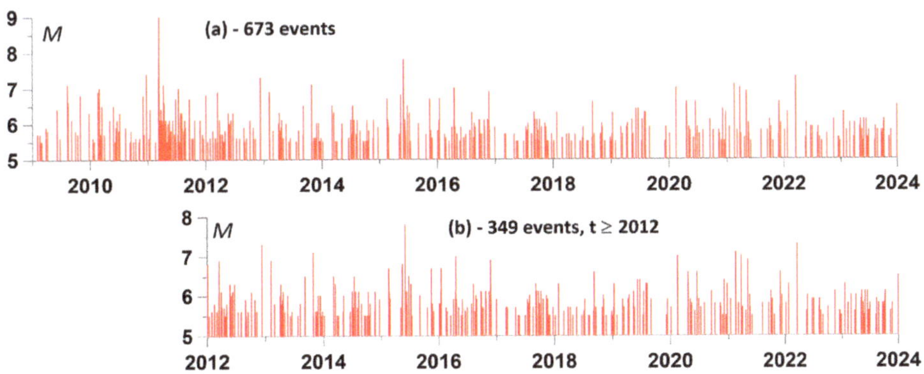

Figure 5. Time sequence of earthquakes with a magnitude of at least 5.5 in the vicinity of the Japanese Islands: (**a**) in the time period 2009–2023; (**b**) in the period of time 2012–2023.

The working hypothesis is that for certain levels of EEMD decomposition, the times of the largest local maxima of the average amplitudes of the envelopes precedes the times of earthquakes. For a correct comparison of two streams of events, it is necessary that their average intensity be approximately equal. This means that the number of the largest local maxima of the amplitudes of the envelopes during the time period under study should be equal to the number of earthquakes. From these considerations, it becomes clear that for a correct analysis of the connections between the time instants of local maximum amplitudes of envelopes and seismic events, the time interval of aftershock activity must be excluded. Therefore, further analysis is carried out for the time period 2012–2023 lasting 12 years.

Figure 6 shows the distribution of epicenters of earthquakes with a magnitude of at least 5.5.

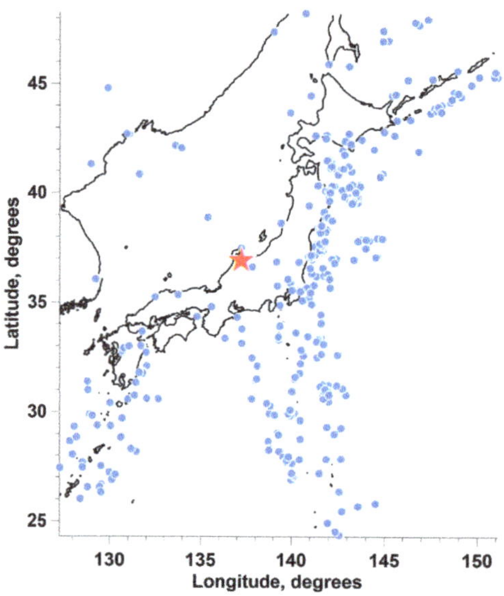

Figure 6. Distribution of epicenters of 349 earthquakes with a magnitude of at least 5.5 in the vicinity of the Japanese Islands in the time period 2012–2023. The red asterisk marks the center of gravity of the centers of 15 clusters of GPS stations (Figure 1a), which is chosen as the center of a circle with a radius of 1500 km.

It should be taken into account that as the number of the decomposition level increases, both the waveforms of the levels themselves and the amplitudes of their envelopes become increasingly low-frequency. As a result, it is possible to select the 349 largest local maxima of average amplitudes in the interval 2012–2023 only for a certain number of lower expansion levels. For the time interval 2012–2023, only the first two levels are suitable for selecting 349 local maxima of amplitudes, since the number of local extrema already at the third level is 242, that is, less than 349. From the first two levels, it was decided to choose the second as the lower frequency, and for which the results of mutual influence assessments are more expressive.

In Figure 7, the red dots represent the selected 349 largest local maxima of the average amplitude of the envelopes at the second level of decomposition.

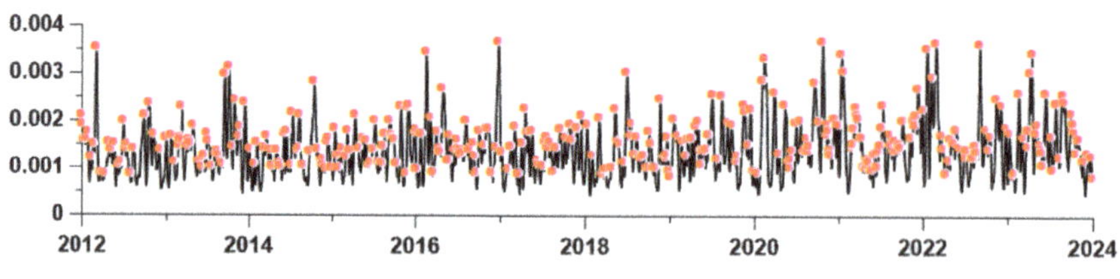

Figure 7. Average instantaneous amplitudes of the second level of EEMD decomposition and the 349 largest local maxima (red dots).

Let us call the "direct" influence of the moments of time of earthquakes on the occurrence of local maxima of the average amplitudes of the envelopes, and the "reverse" —correspondingly, the advance of the moments of time of local maxima of amplitudes relative to the times of earthquakes. Figure 8 shows graphs of changes in the components of the matrix of "direct" and "reverse" influence for level 2 when assessed in a sliding window of 2 years.

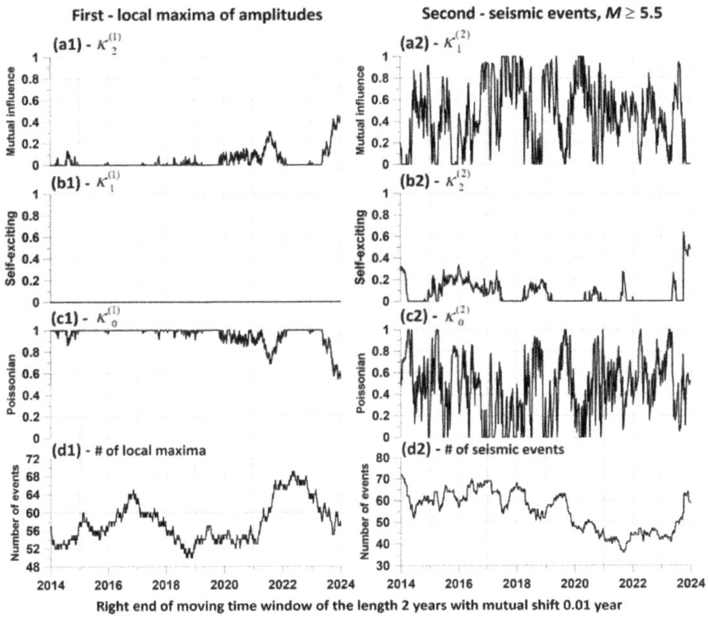

Figure 8. Graphs of changes in the components of the influence matrix between sequences of seismic events with a magnitude of at least 5.5 and the sequence of moments in time of 349 of the largest local maxima of the average amplitudes at the second level of EEMD decomposition. The estimates were made in a sliding time window of length 2 years with a shift of 0.01 year for a relaxation time τ of the model (24, 25) of 0.1 year. The graphs (**a1–c1**) refer to the components of the influence matrix (35), which refers to the intensity fractions of the sequence of the largest local amplitude maxima, while the graphs (**a2–c2**) refer to the intensity fractions of the sequence of seismic events. Plots (**d1**) and (**d2**) present the numbers of local maxima of amplitudes (**d1**) and the number of seismic events (**d2**) within moving time window. Other explanations are in the text.

Of these graphs, the pair (a1, a2) is of greatest importance: a1 represents the change in the components of the direct influence of seismic events on the positions of local amplitude maxima, while a2 represents the inverse influence of the times of local amplitude maxima on seismic events. From a comparison of these two graphs, it is clear that the reverse influence significantly exceeds the direct influence; that is, there is a delay effect of seismic events relative to the maximum amplitudes. In other words, there is a predictive effect. Graphs (b1, b2) represent changes in the self-exciting component of average intensities, while graphs (c1, c2) represent changes in the purely random (Poisson) component. Finally, the pair of plots (d1, d2) represents the change in the number of jointly analyzed time points in each time window. Let us recall once again that the sum of the components (a1, b1, c1) and (a2, b2, c2) is equal to 1 for any position of the time window.

Figure 8 presents the results of estimates of the mutual influence of two sequences of events only for a time window of 2 years. In order to increase the representativeness of this result, we will carry out similar estimates for a sufficiently large set of time lengths varying within specified limits. In this case, for each value of the length of the time window, we will identify local maxima of the components of the influence matrix, which are responsible for the mutual influence of sequences of events when the time windows are shifted. Let us describe a method for constructing a set of maximum components of mutual influence matrices in the form of numbered points.

1. The minimum $L_{\min}$ and maximum $L_{\max}$ lengths of time windows and N_L—the number of lengths of time windows in this interval are selected. Thus, the lengths of the time windows took on the values $L_k = L_{\min} + (k-1)\Delta L$, $k = 1, \ldots, N_L$, $\Delta L = (L_{\max} - L_{\min})/(N_L - 1)$. In our calculations, we took $L_{\min}$ as equal to 1 year, and $L_{\max}$—3 years, $N_L = 100$.
2. Each time window of length L_k was shifted from left to right along the time axis with some offset Δt. Let us denote by $t_j(L_k)$, $j = 1, \ldots, M(L_k)$ the sequence of moments in time of the positions of the right windows with length L_k. The number $M(L_k)$ of time windows in length L_k is determined by their time offset Δt. We used a time window offset Δt of 0.01 year.
3. For each position of a time window of length L_k, the elements of the influence matrix (35) are estimated for a given relaxation time τ of the model (26–27), corresponding to the mutual influence of the two processes being analyzed. We took a value τ equal to 0.1 year. For definiteness, we will consider one influence, for example, of the first process on the second. As a result of such estimates, we obtain their values in the form $(t_j(L_k), c_j(L_k))$, where $c_j(L_k)$ is the corresponding element of the influence matrix for a position with a time window number j of length L_k.
4. In the sequence $(t_j(L_k), c_j(L_k))$, we select elements $(t_j^*(L_k), c_j^*(L_k))$ corresponding to local maxima of values $c_j(L_k)$, that is, from the condition $c_{j-1}(L_k) < c_j^*(L_k) < c_{j+1}(L_k)$. Let us present each element $(t_j^*(L_k), c_j^*(L_k))$ as a vertical segment of length $c_j^*(L_k)$ located at a time point $t_j^*(L_k)$. The combination of such vertical graphic elements for all $k = 1, \ldots, N_L$, $j = 1, \ldots, M(L_k)$ visualizes the "strength" of the mutual influence of processes on each other.

So, the full set of free parameters of the method: τ, $L_{\min}$, $L_{\max}$, N_L, Δt. The result of such estimates is presented in Figure 9.

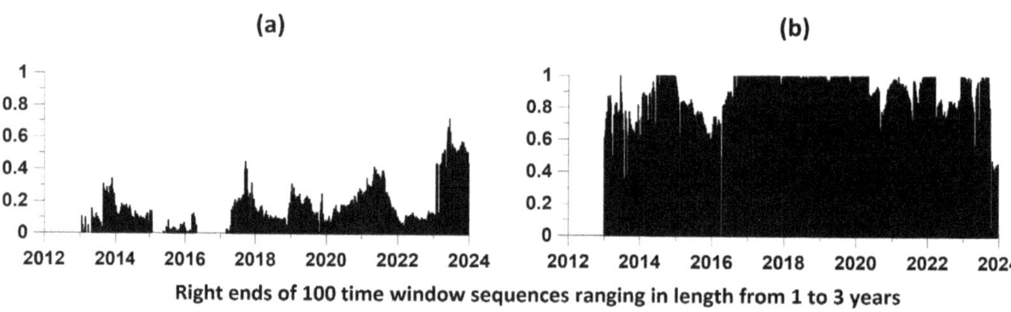

Figure 9. Maximum values of the elements of the influence matrices in a sequence of 100 time windows of length from 1 to 3 years, taken with an offset of 0.01 year: (**a**) for the "direct" influence of the time points of seismic events on the positions of the largest local maxima of average amplitudes on the second EEMD level of decomposition; (**b**) for the "reverse" influence of the positions of amplitude maxima on earthquakes. The relaxation time of the model is 0.1 year.

The results presented in Figure 9 confirm the conclusions made earlier based on the graphs in Figure 8: the "reverse" influence of the time instants of local maxima of envelope amplitudes at the second level on the time instants of earthquakes is significantly greater (Figure 9b) than the "direct" influence of earthquakes on the occurrence of local maxima in the amplitudes of the envelopes (Figure 9a).

9. Conclusions

Traditional methods of analyzing data on crustal movements obtained using space geodesy are focused on identifying systematic low-frequency components that can be interpreted as manifestations of slow tectonic movements. The high-frequency component of these time series, which can be called the "tremor" of the earth's surface, is most often interpreted as a manifestation of noise arising from atmospheric and ionospheric fluctuations. Our point is that, despite the presence of this process noise, it is in the high-frequency component of GPS data that there is hidden prognostic information. In this article, the joint use of cluster analysis, principal component analysis, Hilbert–Huang decomposition and evaluation of parametric models of the mutual influence of sequences of events allowed us to obtain a result confirming the presence of predictive information in high-frequency tremor of the earth's surface.

The authors used software which was written by them using programming languages Fortran and Python.

Author Contributions: A.L.—idea, programming, paper preparation; E.R.—programming, data preparation. All authors have read and agreed to the published version of the manuscript.

Funding: This research received no external funding.

Institutional Review Board Statement: Not applicable.

Data Availability Statement: The open access data from the source: http://geodesy.unr.edu/gps_timeseries/tenv3/IGS14/ (accessed on 15 January 2024) were used.

Acknowledgments: The work was carried out within the framework of the state assignment of the Institute of Physics of the Earth of the Russian Academy of Sciences (topic FMWU-2022-0018).

Conflicts of Interest: The authors declare that the research was conducted in the absence of any commercial or financial relationships that could be construed as a potential conflict of interest.

References

1. Lyubushin, A. Identification of Areas of Anomalous Tremor of the Earth's Surface on the Japanese Islands According to GPS Data. *Appl. Sci.* **2022**, *12*, 7297. [CrossRef]
2. Lyubushin, A. Singular Points of the Tremor of the Earth's Surface. *Appl. Sci.* **2023**, *13*, 10060. [CrossRef]
3. Lyubushin, A. Entropy of GPS-measured Earth tremor. In *Revolutionizing Earth Observation—New Technologies and Insights;* Abdalla, R.M., Ed.; IntechOpen: Rijeka, Croatia, 2024. [CrossRef]
4. Lyubushin, A. Global coherence of GPS-measured high-frequency surface tremor motions. *GPS Solut.* **2018**, *22*, 116. [CrossRef]
5. Lyubushin, A. Field of coherence of GPS-measured earth tremors. *GPS Solut.* **2019**, *23*, 120. [CrossRef]
6. Filatov, D.M.; Lyubushin, A.A. Fractal analysis of GPS time series for early detection of disastrous seismic events. *Phys. A Stat. Mech. Its Appl.* **2017**, *469*, 718–730. [CrossRef]
7. Filatov, D.M.; Lyubushin, A.A. Precursory Analysis of GPS Time Series for Seismic Hazard Assessment. *Pure Appl. Geophys.* **2019**, *177*, 509–530. [CrossRef]
8. Huang, N.E.; Shen, Z.; Long, S.R.; Wu, V.C.; Shih, H.H.; Zheng, Q.; Yen, N.C.; Tung, C.C.; Liv, H.H. The empirical mode decomposition and the Hilbert spectrum for nonlinear and non-stationary time series analysis. *Proc. R. Soc. Lond. Ser. A* **1998**, *454*, 903–995. [CrossRef]
9. Huang, N.E.; Wu, Z. A review on Hilbert-Huang transform: Method and its applications to geophysical studies. *Rev. Geophys.* **2008**, *46*, RG2006. [CrossRef]
10. Pan, Y.; Shen, W.-B.; Ding, H.; Hwang, C.; Li, J.; Zhang, T. The Quasi-Biennial Vertical Oscillations at Ghlobal GPS Stations: Identification by Ensemble Empirical Mode Decomposition. *Sensors* **2015**, *15*, 26096–26114. [CrossRef]
11. Li, W.; Guo, J. Extraction of periodic signals in Global Navigation Satellite System (GNSS) vertical coordinate time series using the adaptive ensemble empirical modal decomposition method. *Nonlin. Process. Geophys.* **2024**, *31*, 99–113. [CrossRef]
12. Huang, Y.; Schmitt, F.G.; Lu, Z.; Liu, Y. Analysis of daily river flow fluctuations using empirical mode decomposition and arbitrary order Hilbert spectral analysis. *J. Hydrol.* **2009**, *373*, 103–111. [CrossRef]
13. Huang, N.E.; Wu, M.; Qu, W.; Long, S.R.; Shen, S.S.P. Applications of Hilbert–Huang transform to non-stationary financial time series analysis. *Appl. Stoch. Models Bus. Ind.* **2003**, *19*, 245–268. [CrossRef]
14. Li, H.; Kwong, S.; Yang, L.; Huang, D.; Xiao, D. Hilbert-Huang Transform for Analysis of Heart Rate Variability in Cardiac Health. *IEEE/ACM Trans. Comput. Biol. Bioinform.* **2011**, *8*, 1557–1567. [CrossRef]

15. Wei, H.-C.; Xiao, M.-X.; Chen, H.-Y.; Li, Y.-Q.; Wu, H.-T.; Sun, C.-K. Instantaneous frequency from Hilbert-Huang transformation of digital volume pulse as indicator of diabetes and arterial stiffness in upper-middle-aged subjects. *Sci. Rep.* **2018**, *8*, 15771. [CrossRef] [PubMed]
16. Sarlis, N.V.; Skordas, E.S.; Mintzelas, A.; Papadopoulou, K.A. Micro-scale, mid-scale, and macro-scale in global seismicity identified by empirical mode decomposition and their multifractal characteristics. *Sci. Rep.* **2018**, *8*, 9206. [CrossRef]
17. Beavan, J. Noise properties of continuous GPS data from concrete pillar geodetic monuments in New Zealand and comparison with data from U.S. deep drilled braced monuments. *J. Geophys. Res.* **2005**, *110*, B08. [CrossRef]
18. Langbein, J. Noise in GPS displacement measurements from Southern California and Southern Nevada. *J. Geophys. Res.* **2008**, *113*, B05405. [CrossRef]
19. Blewitt, G.; Lavallee, D. Effects of annual signal on geodetic velocity. *J. Geophys. Res.* **2002**, *107*, 2145. [CrossRef]
20. Bos, M.S.; Fernandes, R.M.S.; Williams, S.D.P.; Bastos, L. Fast error analysis of continuous GPS observations. *J. Geod.* **2008**, *82*, 157–166. [CrossRef]
21. Liu, B.; Xing, X.; Tan, J.; Xia, Q. Modeling Seasonal Variations in Vertical GPS Coordinate Time Series Using Independent Component Analysis and Varying Coefficient Regression. *Sensors* **2020**, *20*, 5627. [CrossRef]
22. Liu, B.; Dai, W.; Liu, N. Extracting seasonal deformations of the Nepal Himalaya region from vertical GPS position time series using Independent Component Analysis. *Adv. Space Res.* **2017**, *60*, 2910–2917. [CrossRef]
23. Tesmer, V.; Steigenberger, P.; van Dam, T.; Mayer-Gurr, T. Vertical deformations from homogeneously processed GRACE and global GPS long-term series. *J. Geod.* **2011**, *85*, 291–310. [CrossRef]
24. Yan, J.; Dong, D.; Burgmann, R.; Materna, K.; Tan, W.; Peng, Y.; Chen, J. Separation of Sources of Seasonal Uplift in China Using Independent Component Analysis of GNSS Time Series. *J. Geophys. Res. Solid Earth* **2019**, *124*, 11951–11971. [CrossRef]
25. Santamaría-Gómez, A.; Memin, A. Geodetic secular velocity errors due to interannual surface loading deformation. *Geophys. J. Int.* **2015**, *202*, 763–767. [CrossRef]
26. Fu, Y.; Argus, D.F.; Freymueller, J.T.; Heflin, M.B. Horizontal motion in elastic response to seasonal loading of rain water in the Amazon Basin and monsoon water in Southeast Asia observed by GPS and inferred from GRACE. *Geophys. Res. Lett.* **2013**, *40*, 6048–6053. [CrossRef]
27. Chanard, K.; Avouac, J.P.; Ramillien, G.; Genrich, J. Modeling deformation induced by seasonal variations of continental water in the Himalaya region: Sensitivity to Earth elastic structure. *J. Geophys. Res. Solid Earth* **2014**, *119*, 5097–5113. [CrossRef]
28. He, X.; Montillet, J.P.; Fernandes, R.; Bos, M.; Yu, K.; Hua, X.; Jiang, W. Review of current GPS methodologies for producing accurate time series and their error sources. *J. Geodyn.* **2017**, *106*, 12–29. [CrossRef]
29. Ray, J.; Altamimi, Z.; Collilieux, X.; van Dam, T. Anomalous harmonics in the spectra of GPS position estimates. *GPS Solut.* **2008**, *12*, 55–64. [CrossRef]
30. Roncagliolo, P.A.; García, J.G.; Mercader, P.I.; Fuhrmann, D.R.; Muravchik, C.H. Maximum-likelihood attitude estimation using GPS signals. *Digit. Signal Process.* **2007**, *17*, 1089–1100. [CrossRef]
31. Wang, F.; Li, H.; Lu, M. GNSS Spoofing Detection and Mitigation Based on Maximum Likelihood Estimation. *Sensors* **2017**, *17*, 1532. [CrossRef]
32. Parkinson, B.W. *Global Positioning System: Theory and Applications*; AIAA: Reston, VA, USA, 1996; p. 781.
33. Xu, J.; He, J.; Zhang, Y.; Xu, F.; Cai, F. A Distance-Based Maximum Likelihood Estimation Method for Sensor Localization in Wireless Sensor Networks. *Int. J. Distrib. Sens. Netw.* **2016**, *12*, 2080536. [CrossRef]
34. Langbein, J.; Johnson, H. Correlated errors in geodetic time series, Implications for time-dependent deformation. *J. Geophys. Res.* **1997**, *102*, 591–603. [CrossRef]
35. Williams, S.D.P.; Bock, Y.; Fang, P.; Jamason, P.; Nikolaidis, R.M.; Prawirodirdjo, L.; Miller, M.; Johnson, D.J. Error analysis of continuous GPS time series. *J. Geophys. Res.* **2004**, *109*, B03412. [CrossRef]
36. Wang, W.; Zhao, B.; Wang, Q.; Yang, S. Noise analysis of continuous GPS coordinate time series for CMONOC. *Adv. Space Res.* **2012**, *49*, 943–956. [CrossRef]
37. Agnew, D. The time domain behavior of power law noises. *Geophys. Res. Lett.* **1992**, *19*, 333–336. [CrossRef]
38. Amiri-Simkooei, A.R.; Tiberius, C.C.J.M.; Teunissen, P.J.G. Teunissen Assessment of noise in GPS coordinate time series: Methodology and results. *J. Geophys. Res.* **2007**, *112*, B07413. [CrossRef]
39. Caporali, A. Average strain rate in the Italian crust inferred from a permanent GPS network—I. Statistical analysis of the time-series of permanent GPS stations. *Geophys. J. Int.* **2003**, *155*, 241–253. [CrossRef]
40. Zhang, J.; Bock, Y.; Johnson, H.; Fang, P.; Williams, S.; Genrich, J.; Wdowinski, S.; Behr, J. Southern California permanent GPS geodetic array: Error analysis of daily position estimates and site velocities. *J. Geophys. Res.* **1997**, *102*, 18035–18055. [CrossRef]
41. Li, J.; Miyashita, K.; Kato, T.; Miyazaki, S. GPS time series modeling by autoregressive moving average method, Application to the crustal deformation in central Japan. *Earth Planets Space* **2000**, *52*, 155–162. [CrossRef]
42. Kermarrec, G.; Schon, S. On modelling GPS phase correlations: A parametric model. *Acta Geod. Geophys.* **2018**, *53*, 139–156. [CrossRef]
43. Teferle, F.N.; Williams, S.D.P.; Kierulf, H.P.; Bingley, R.M.; Plag, H.P. A continuous GPS coordinate time series analysis strategy for high-accuracy vertical land movements. *Phys. Chem. Earth Parts A/B/C* **2008**, *33*, 205–216. [CrossRef]
44. Chen, Q.; van Dam, T.; Sneeuw, N.; Collilieux, X.; Weigelt, M.; Rebischung, P. Singular spectrum analysis for modeling seasonal signals from GPS time series. *J. Geodyn.* **2013**, *72*, 25–35. [CrossRef]

45. Bock, Y.; Melgar, D.; Crowell, B.W. Real-Time Strong-Motion Broadband Displacements from Collocated GPS and Accelerometers. *Bull. Seismol. Soc. Am.* **2011**, *101*, 2904–2925. [CrossRef]
46. Goudarzi, M.A.; Cocard, M.; Santerre, R.; Woldai, T. GPS interactive time series analysis software. *GPS Solut.* **2013**, *17*, 595–603. [CrossRef]
47. Hackl, M.; Malservisi, R.; Hugentobler, U.; Jiang, Y. Velocity covariance in the presence of anisotropic time correlated noise and transient events in GPS time series. *J. Geodyn.* **2013**, *72*, 36–45. [CrossRef]
48. Khelif, S.; Kahlouche, S.; Belbachir, M.F. Analysis of position time series of GPS-DORIS co-located stations. *Int. J. Appl. Earth Observ. Geoinf.* **2013**, *20*, 67–76. [CrossRef]
49. Blewitt, G.; Hammond, W.C.; Kreemer, C. Harnessing the GPS data explosion for interdisciplinary science. *Eos* **2018**, *99*, 485. [CrossRef]
50. Duda, R.O.; Hart, P.E.; Stork, D.G. *Pattern Classification*; Wiley: Hoboken, NJ, USA, 2000.
51. Vogel, M.A.; Wong, A.K.C. PFS clustering method. *IEEE Trans. Pattern Anal. Mach. Intell.* **1979**, *1*, 237–245. [CrossRef] [PubMed]
52. Jolliffe, I.T. *Principal Component Analysis*; Springer: Berlin/Heidelberg, Germany, 1986.
53. Huber, P.J. *Robust Statistics*; Wiley: Toronto, ON, Canada; Chichester, UK; New York, NY, USA, 1981.
54. Bendat, J.S.; Piersol, A.G. *Random Data. Analysis and Measurement Procedures*, 4th ed.; Wiley & Sons: Hoboken, NJ, USA, 2010.
55. Lyubushin, A. Investigation of the Global Seismic Noise Properties in Connection to Strong Earthquakes. *Front. Earth Sci.* **2022**, *10*, 905663. [CrossRef]
56. Lyubushin, A. Seismic Hazard Indicators in Japan based on Seismic Noise Properties. *J. Earth Environ. Sci. Res.* **2023**, *5*, 1–8. [CrossRef]
57. Lyubushin, A.; Rodionov, E. Wavelet-based correlations of the global magnetic field in connection to strongest earthquakes. *Adv. Space Res.* **2024**. [CrossRef]
58. Cox, D.R.; Lewis, P.A.W. *The Statistical Analysis of Series of Events*; Methuen: London, UK, 1966.
59. Varotsos, P.A.; Sarlis, N.V.; Skordas, E.S.; Toshiyasu, N.; Masashi, K. The unusual case of the ultra-deep 2015 Ogasawara earthquake (Mw7.9): Natural time analysis. *EPL* **2021**, *135*, 49002. [CrossRef]

Disclaimer/Publisher's Note: The statements, opinions and data contained in all publications are solely those of the individual author(s) and contributor(s) and not of MDPI and/or the editor(s). MDPI and/or the editor(s) disclaim responsibility for any injury to people or property resulting from any ideas, methods, instructions or products referred to in the content.

entropy

MDPI

Article

Visibility Graph Investigation of the Shallow Seismicity of Lai Chau Area (Vietnam)

Luciano Telesca [1,*], Anh Tuan Thai [2,*], Dinh Trong Cao [2] and Thanh Hai Dang [2]

[1] Institute of Methodologies for Environmental Analysis, National Research Council, 85050 Tito, Italy
[2] Institute of Geophysics, Vietnam Academy of Science and Technology, Hanoi 100000, Vietnam; cdtrong@igp.vast.vn (D.T.C.); dthai@igp.vast.vn (T.H.D.)
* Correspondence: luciano.telesca@cnr.it (L.T.); tatuan@igp.vast.vn (A.T.T.)

Abstract: In this study, the topological properties of the shallow seismicity occurring in the area around the Lai Chau hydropower plant (Vietnam) are investigated by using visibility graph (VG) analysis, a well-known method to convert time series into networks or graphs. The relationship between the seismicity and reservoir water level was analyzed using Interlayer Mutual Information (IMI) and the Frobenius norm, both applied to the corresponding VG networks. IMI was used to assess the correlation between the two variables, while the Frobenius norm was employed to estimate the time delay between them. The total seismicity, which resulted in an $M \geq 0.8$ with a *b*-value of 0.86, is characterized by a *k-M* slope of ≈9.1. Analyzing the variation of the seismological and topological parameters of the seismicity relative to the distance from the center of the Lai Chau reservoir revealed the following features: (1) the *b*-value fluctuates around a mean value of 1.21 at distances of up to 10–11 km, while, for distances larger than 25–30 km, it tends to the value of 0.86 ; (2) the maximum IMI between the monthly number of earthquakes and the monthly mean water level occurs at a distance of 9–11 km, showing a distance evolution similar to that of the *b*-value; (3) at these distances from the center of the reservoir, the time lag between the earthquake monthly counts and the monthly water level mean is 9–10 months; (4) the relationship between the *b*-value and the *k-M* slope suggests that the *k-M* slope depends on the number of earthquakes within a 22 km radius from the center of the dam. Our study's findings offer new insights into the complex dynamics of seismicity occurring around reservoirs.

Keywords: reservoir-triggered seismicity; fractal; spectral; time clustering

1. Introduction

Visibility graph (VG) analysis has become an increasingly popular statistical method for characterizing the time-dynamic properties of series across various research fields. It has been applied in economics [1–4], meteorology [5–7], and oceanography [8], among other fields.

By the VG method, initially introduced by Lacasa et al. [9], time series are transformed into graphs where nodes represent the values of the series, and the links or connections between nodes indicate the relationships between them. In the VG method, these connections are determined by the mutual 'visibility' between the values of the series. The graphs obtained by the VG exhibit various parameters, with one of the most crucial being the degree, which quantifies the number of links connecting a node to others within the same graph.

In recent years, the VG method has been employed for analyzing the complexity of seismicity. Due to its ability to describe and characterize complex systems, VG analysis serves as a valuable tool for uncovering the intricate features of seismic processes. A sequence of earthquakes can be modeled as a discrete time series, where magnitudes occurring at specific times represent its values. By applying the VG to this series, the time series of magnitudes is converted into a graph.

The first analysis of the topological properties of earthquakes through the VG method was focused on the behavior of the distribution of the degree of earthquakes, whose magnitudes represented the nodes of the graph [10]. For the particular case of seismicity in Italy, it was found that this distribution was magnitude threshold independent. The relationship between the seismological and topological properties of earthquakes was firstly investigated in [11], where the b-value of the Gutenberg–Richter law, which approximates the frequency–magnitude distribution, was linked with the slope of the line fitting the degree versus magnitude (called the k-M slope). Successive studies performed on the real seismicity of various seismo-tectonic areas and on synthetic seismicity produced by laboratory stick–slip-type experiments reinforced such a relationship, suggesting that a certain universality might exist between the b-value and the k-M slope [12–14]. Very recently, in [15], on the basis of synthetic seismic catalogs obeying various probability distributions, it was demonstrated that the relationship between the b-value and the k-M slope is universal and stable, and that an estimate of the k-M slope can perform better than the commonly used b-value estimation methods, especially in cases with incomplete catalogs or affected by variations in the magnitude–frequency relations.

2. Seismo-Tectonic Settings

The collision between the Indian and Eurasian plates, which began approximately 45 million years ago, led to the formation of numerous strike–slip faults between Myanmar and the Red River fault during the early Cenozoic [16,17]. Northwestern Vietnam is a mountainous region with a complex geological structure dominated by several active faults, including the Lai Chau–Dien Bien fault zone, the Son La fault, the Ma River fault, the Da River fault, and the Red River fault. This region is the most seismically active in Vietnam, bounded by the Lai Chau–Dien Bien fault zone to the west, the Red River fault to the northeast, and the Ma River fault to the southwest. The present tectonic characteristics of these faults are determined based on surface geological investigations and studies of deep crustal structures [17–21]. Lai Chau Hydroelectric Reservoir is located in the northwest, with a total capacity of 1215 million m^3. Construction of the dam began on 5 November 2011, at the uppermost section of the Da River's mainstream in Vietnam, near the border with China. The Lai Chau hydropower reservoir area has high mountainous terrain, strong cleavage, and large slopes and is strongly affected by the Muong Te fault and Dien Bien–Lai Chau fault. The geology of the area belongs to the Dien Bien Phu complex and formations such as the Da River, Nam Ma, and Nam Po (Figure 1) [18,21]. The reservoir began impounding in May 2015, and, shortly afterward, earthquakes started occurring around the dam and its vicinity. Since then, earthquakes have continued to occur, with approximately 1500 recorded to date. There are four main faults in the region under study, the Lai Chau–Dien Bien, Muong Te, Nam Nho, and Nam Nhe, with all other faults being branches of these main ones. The Lai Chau–Dien Bien fault zone is one of the most seismically active zones in Indochina, beginning in southern Yunnan Province (China) and extending over 150 km in Vietnam from the north of Chieng Chai (at the Vietnam–China border), through Lai Chau and Dien Bien Phu, to Tay Trang (near the Vietnam–Laos border). The strongest earthquakes ($M > 5$) have been recorded along this fault zone. The northern section follows a nearly north–south strike, while the southern section gradually shifts from a southward to a southwestward strike. The main fault, along with its associated subsidiary faults, is characterized by both strike–slip and oblique–slip movements, with the principal fault plane dipping westward at angles of 60–70° in the northern part and 70–80° (sometimes up to 90°) in the southern part of the fault zone [17,18,21]. During the Cenozoic, the Lai Chau–Dien Bien fault zone underwent two main phases of tectonic development, marked by dextral (right-lateral) and sinistral (left-lateral) shear activities. The shift from right-lateral to left-lateral motion occurred over 5 million years ago, during the Pliocene. The Muong Te fault zone, near to which the Lai Chau reservoir is located, is a fairly large fault running in the NW-SE direction from Chinese territory through Vietnam, with a length within Vietnamese territory of about 120 km. In the Neo-Tectonic period, the fault had two phases of deformations: the early phase of left-lateral strike–slip motion and the late phase of right-lateral strike–slip motion. Moderate earthquakes ($4 < M \leq 4.8$) were observed on this fault zone. The Nam Nhe fault zone is a branch of the Muong Te fault zone that has a length < 50 km and the width of the rupture zone reaches > 1 km. Moderate earthquakes ($4.1 < M \leq 4.6$) have been observed in this fault zone (Figure 1) [17,18,21]. The Muong Nhe fault zone had two phases of deformations, the same as the Muong Te fault zone.

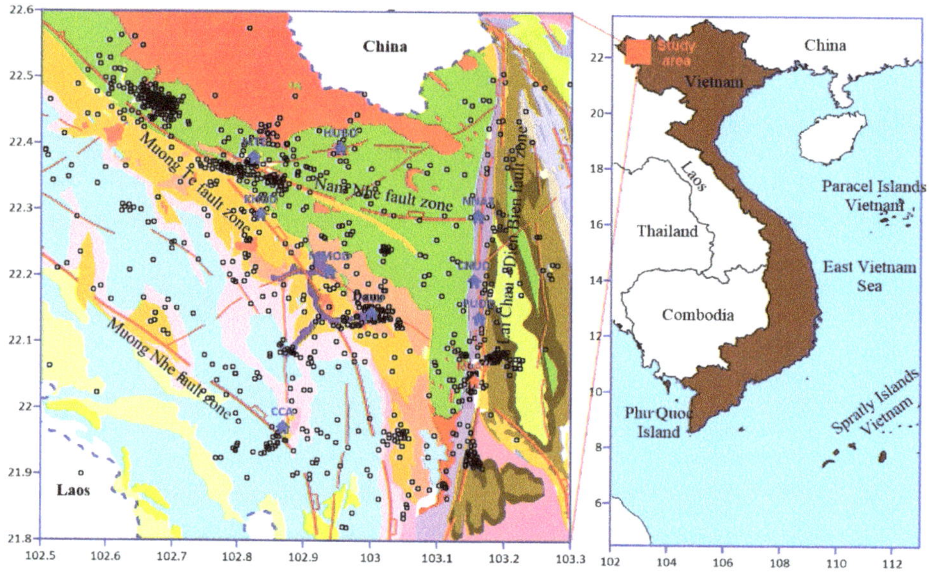

Figure 1. Spatial distribution of earthquake epicenters during the period of September 2014 to June 2021 (dark circles). Lai Chau reservoir is in light blue. The blue and red building symbols indicate the local seismic stations and national seismic stations, respectively. Geology and identified geologically mapped faults (red) with dip and slip direction as given by [18]. (Modified from [22]).

3. The Frequency–Magnitude Distribution

The Gutenberg–Richter (GR) law [23] represents the relationship between the number N of earthquakes with magnitude $M \geq M_{th}$ and the threshold magnitude M_{th}. The function $log_{10}N = a - bM_{th}$ is utilized to fit the frequency–magnitude distribution of earthquakes. The parameters a and b indicate, respectively, the level of seismicity and the proportion of small events compared to large ones. The b-value is crucial for reliably assessing the seismic hazard of an area [24,25]. In this paper, the estimate of b is performed by using the maximum likelihood method (MLE) [26]:

$$b = \frac{log_{10}(e)}{< M > -(M_c - \frac{\Delta M_{bin}}{2})} \tag{1}$$

where $< M >$ is the mean magnitude of the earthquakes with magnitude $M \geq M_c$, ΔM_{bin} is the binning width of the catalog (generally 0.1), and M_c is the completeness magnitude, defined as the smallest magnitude detectable by a seismic network [27].

The estimate of the b-value depends on the calculation of the completeness magnitude M_c. Two common methods for estimating M_c are the goodness-of-fit (GFT) test and the maximum curvature (MAXC) method [28]. In the GFT method, M_c is calculated by comparing the observed frequency–magnitude distribution with synthetic distributions. These synthetic distributions are generated using the values of a and b estimated from the observed data for magnitudes $M \geq M_{co}$ as a function of increasing cutoff magnitude M_{co}.

Let R represent the absolute difference in the number of earthquakes in each magnitude bin between the observed and synthetic distributions. The completeness magnitude, M_c, is determined at the first cutoff magnitude, M_{co}, where the observed data for $M \geq M_{co}$ can be modeled by a straight line (in a log–linear plot) for a fixed confidence level $R = R_c$. In the maximum curvature (MAXC) method [28], M_c is identified as the magnitude corresponding to the largest bin in the non-cumulative frequency–magnitude distribution.

In our paper, we utilize both the MAXC and GFT methods, estimating the completeness magnitude with each. Subsequently, we determine the M_c by selecting the maximum value between the two methods, opting for the more conservative approach.

4. Methods

In this study, we employed the visibility graph (VG) method, which converts a time series into a graph or network. Two arbitrary data values (t_a, y_a) and (t_b, y_b) have visibility, and, consequently, become two connected nodes of the associated graph, if any other data (t_c, y_c) placed between them fulfill the following [9]:

$$y(t_c) < y(t_b) + (y(t_a) - y(t_b))\frac{t_b - t_c}{t_b - t_a}, \tag{2}$$

for the so-called Natural Visibility Graph (NVG), or

$$y(t_a), y(t_b) > y(t_c), \tag{3}$$

for the so-called Horizontal Visibility Graph (HVG), where $t_a < t_c < t_b$.

The VG method has been applied in several research fields, like economics [1–3], weather forecasting [5,6], medicine [29], etc. One of the most relevant parameters of the VG method is the degree that is the number of links departing from a node; generally, the higher values of the series behave as hubs of the graph, since they "attract" more links than those converging to the lower ones.

After constructing the network associated with the time series using the visibility graph, the adjacency matrix is an $N \times N$ matrix, where N is the length of the time series. The element a_{ij} of this matrix is equal to 1 if the nodes i and j are linked; otherwise, it is 0.

An earthquake sequence can be analyzed using the VG method by considering the magnitudes as the nodes of the graph and "drawing" links between two magnitudes fulfilling the "visibility" rule (Equation (2)). Thus, a seismic sequence can also be converted into a graph using the VG method. Figure 2a shows an example of an earthquake sequence with the links drawn by applying Equation (2), while Figure 2b shows the resulting graph.

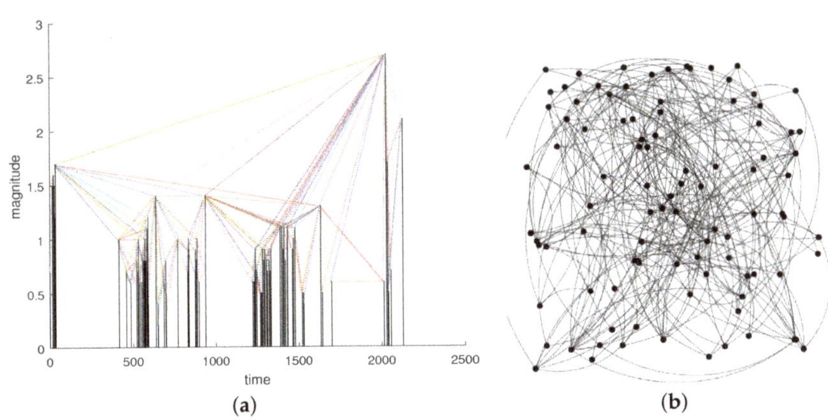

Figure 2. (**a**) Earthquake sequence and the links among the magnitudes defined by the VG. (**b**) Graph of the links among the nodes defined by the VG.

The VG can also be utilized to explore the relationship between two time series by employing the *Interlayer Mutual Information* (IMI), $I_{\alpha\beta}$. Consider two time series $x_\alpha(t)$ and $x_\beta(t)$ and their VG (VG_α and VG_β). Let k_α and k_β denote their respective degree sequences. The IMI is defined as follows [30]:

$$I_{\alpha\beta} = \sum_{k_\alpha}\sum_{k_\beta} P(k_\alpha, k_\beta) \log\left(\frac{P(k_\alpha, k_\beta)}{P(k_\alpha)P(k_\beta)}\right), \quad (4)$$

where $P(k_\alpha, k_\beta)$ is the joint probability of finding a node with a degree of k_α in VG_α and k_β in VG_β. This joint probability is computed as follows:

$$P(k_\alpha, k_\beta) = \frac{N_{k_\alpha,k_\beta}}{N}, \quad (5)$$

with N_{k_α,k_β} being the number of nodes that have the corresponding degree of k_α and k_β in VG_α and VG_β, respectively. Since N is the total number of nodes, it must hold that it is equal to the sum over all possible N_{k_α,k_β} values.

By definition, $I_{\alpha\beta}$ describes the the average statistical dependency between the degree sequences, which can be used to characterize the nature of the time series [9,31]. From this, it can be inferred that the higher this parameter is, the more similarly the signals underlying the VGs are expected to behave.

Recently, ref. [32] proposed a method to compare two series and identify the time lag between them using the visibility graph algorithm, which has been shown to be more effective than cross-correlogram techniques. If A_α and A_β are the adjacency matrices of the VGs of time series $x_\alpha(t)$ and $x_\beta(t)$, respectively, we can define their "distance", the quantity $||A_\alpha - A_\beta||_2$, where $||\cdot||_2$, called the Frobenius norm of a matrix, is the square root of the sum of the squares of the elements of the matrix, that is, the square root of the trace of the product of the matrix with itself. In mathematical notation, if D denotes the matrix $A_\alpha - A_\beta$ and D_{ij} the (i, j)th element of D (with $i, j = 1, \ldots, T$), then

$$||A_\alpha - A_\beta||_2 = ||D||_2 = \sqrt{\mathrm{Trace}(DD^T)} = \sqrt{\sum_{i=1}^{T}\sum_{j=1}^{T} D_{ij}^2}. \quad (6)$$

To calculate the time lag between $x_\alpha(t)$ and $x_\beta(t)$, convert x_β(t) into its corresponding adjacency matrix, A_β. Consider time-shifted copies of the $x_\alpha(t)$, $(x_{\alpha,\tau_1}(t), \ldots, x_{\alpha,\tau_k}(t)$, each shifted in time by a lag from the set $\{\tau_1, \ldots, \tau_k\}$. Convert these time-shifted copies of x_α into their visibility graphs and obtain the corresponding adjacency matrices $A_{\alpha,\tau_1}, \ldots, A_{\alpha,\tau_K}$. We determine the copy A_{α,τ_s} for which the Frobenius norm $||A_\beta - A_{\alpha,\tau_s}||_2$ is minimized. The time lag between the two original series is then taken as τ_s.

As an example, consider two sinusoids, $y(t) = \sin\left(\frac{2\pi t}{10}\right)$ and $y_d(t) = \sin\left(\frac{2\pi(t-3)}{10}\right)$. Both have a period of $T = 10$, while the second one is delayed by $d = 3$ (Figure 3). Plotting $||A_y - A_{y_d}||_2$ between the two sinusoids, the minimum is at $\tau = 3$, which is exactly the delay of the second sinusoid with respect to the first one (Figure 4).

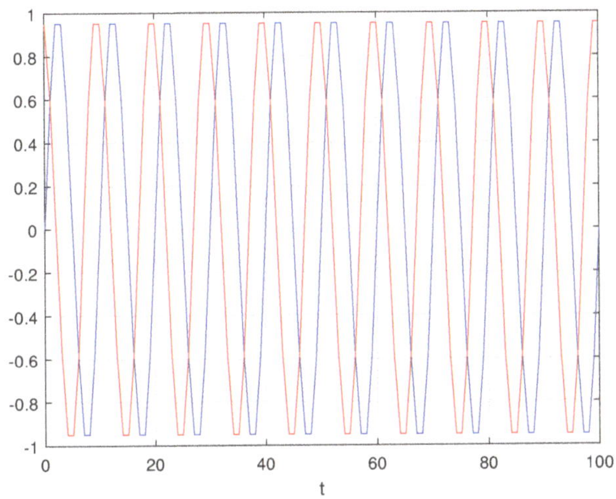

Figure 3. Comparison between two sinusoids, $y(t) = \sin\left(\frac{2\pi t}{10}\right)$ (blue) and $y_d(t) = \sin\left(\frac{2\pi(t-3)}{10}\right)$ (red), both with period $T = 10$ and the second one delayed by $d = 3$.

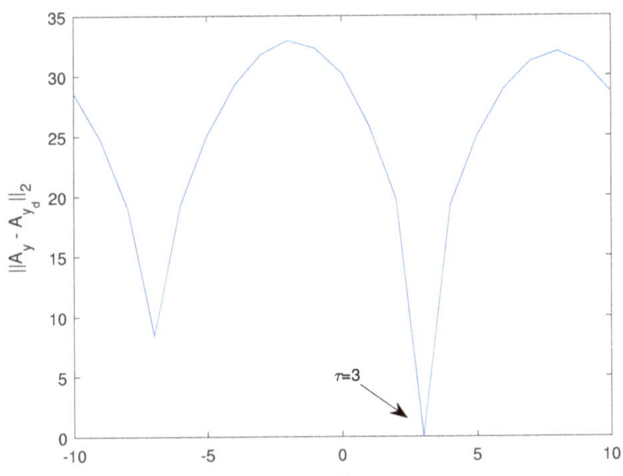

Figure 4. Froebenius norm $\|A_y - A_{y_d}\|_2$ between the two sinusoids plotted in Figure 3.

5. Results

5.1. Analysis of the Whole Seismic Dataset

In our study, we analyzed the shallow (depth $\leq$ 10 km) seismicity that occurred around the Lai Chau reservoir, up to 40 km from the center of the dam, from 2015 to 2021, and its relationship with the water level. The seismic catalog contains 805 events. Figure 5 shows the cumulative and non-cumulative frequency–magnitude distribution of the earthquakes occurring at depths of up to 10 km and within a 40 km radius from the center of the dam. Applying the MAXC and GFT methods with a confidence level of 90%, we obtained M_c values of 0.8 and 0.7, respectively. Therefore, we selected 0.8 as the completeness magnitude for the seismic dataset. With this value of M_c, the complete seismic catalog contains 533 events. Applying Equation (1), the value of b is 0.86 $\pm$ 0.03.

We applied the VG method to this seismic dataset. Figure 6 shows the NVG and HVG applied to the seismic dataset. At each magnitude, M is associated with a degree k that represents the number of links of that magnitude (Figure 7).

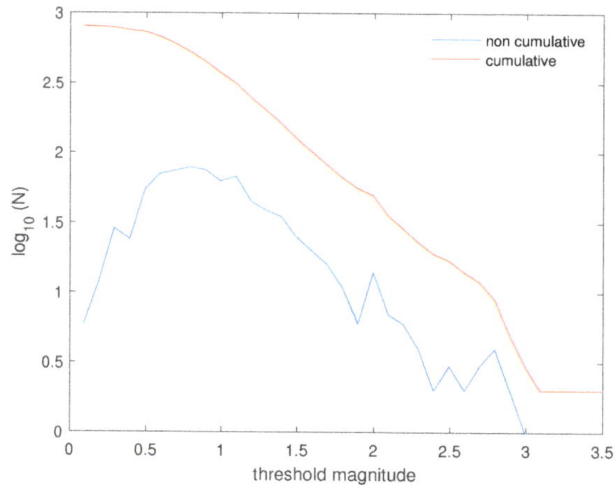

Figure 5. Frequency–magnitude distribution of earthquakes occurring at depths of up to 10 km and within a 40 km radius from the center of the dam.

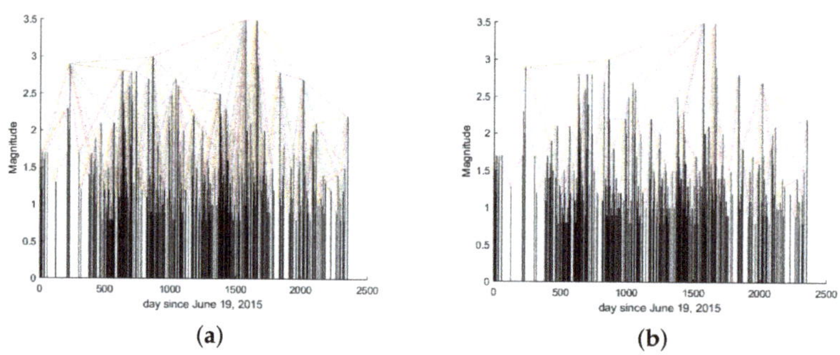

Figure 6. Sequence of earthquakes occurring within 40 km of the center of Lai Chau reservoir. The links among the magnitudes are defined by the NVG (**a**) and HVG (**b**).

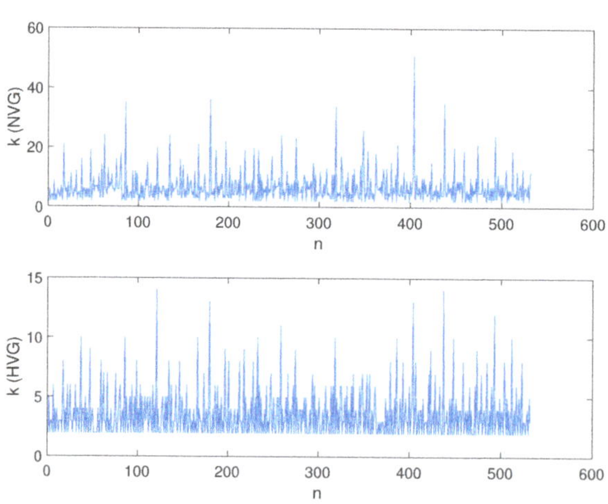

Figure 7. Sequences of degree k for the NVG and HVG applied to the seismic dataset shown in Figure 6.

In a study by Telesca et al. [11], an interesting relationship was found between the degree k(NVG) of a seismic sequence and magnitude. The slope of the linear fit of such a relationship is called the k-M slope. Several studies of observational [13], experimental [33], and physics-based synthetic [14] seismic catalogs have shown a positive correlation between the k-M slope and the b-value. Recently, ref. [15] demonstrated that the relationship between the k-M slope and b is universal and stable, and that their ratio depends on the size of the catalog.

The relationship between the k(NVG) and M of our seismic dataset is illustrated in Figure 8, along with the fitting regression line, whose slope is the k-M slope. The k-M slope is positive (9.07 ± 0.30), and this indicates that the degree and the magnitude are positively correlated; thus, the larger the magnitude, the higher the degree. In fact, the more intense events behave as "hubs" of the seismic sequence, attracting more connections than the smaller events and being made visible by more earthquakes than the smaller ones. We generated 1000 randomize earthquake sequences by shuffling the magnitudes while preserving the original times of occurrence. For each random sequence, we calculated the k-M slope. Figure 9 illustrates the distribution of the k-M slopes from the randomized sequences, alongside the k-M slope derived from the original seismic series. It is evident that the randomization does not significantly alter the k-M slope of the original sequence. This is due to the dominant role of the largest events, which continue to act as 'hubs' of the sequence even after shuffling the magnitudes, thereby driving the structure of the seismic network. This suggests that the k-M relationship is primarily influenced by the presence of these large events.

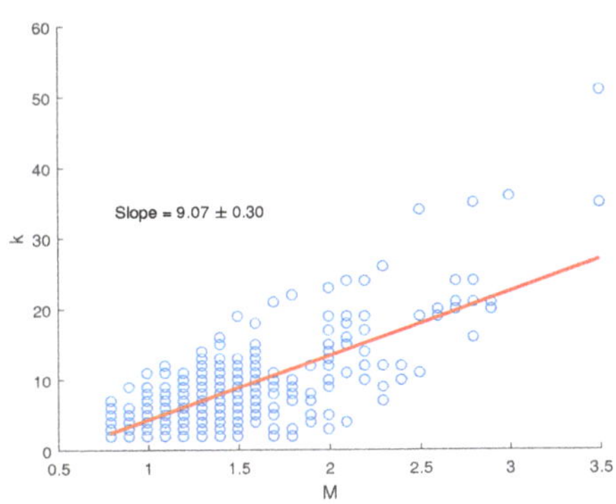

Figure 8. k-M relationship between the degree and the magnitude for the whole seismic dataset. The slope of the regression line is 9.07.

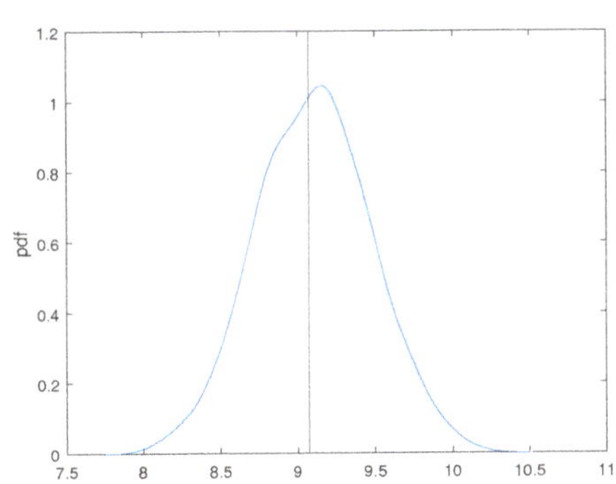

Figure 9. Distribution of the k-M slope for the randomized earthquake sequences. The vertical line indicates the k-M slope of the original sequence.

Figure 10 illustrates the monthly variations in the number of earthquakes (with $M \geq M_c$) alongside the mean water level of the Lai Chau reservoir. Applying Equation (4), the IMI calculated by using the NVG is ~1.07 and that calculated by using the HVG is ~0.41.

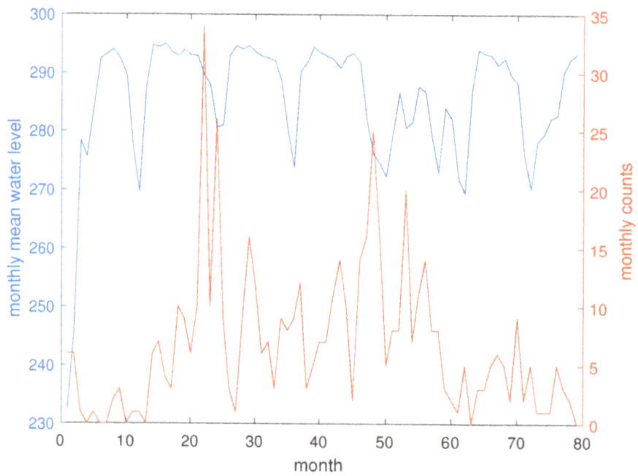

Figure 10. Monthly earthquake counts (red) and mean water level (blue) during the investigation period.

5.2. Distance-Dependent Analysis of Seismicity

To investigate the changes in the seismological and topological properties of the seismicity relative to the distance from the center of the dam, we analyzed seismic events occurring within a range of 6 to 40 km from the center.

Figure 11 shows the variation with the distance from the center of the completeness magnitude (Figure 11b) and the number of earthquakes with magnitude greater than or equal to M_c (Figure 11a).

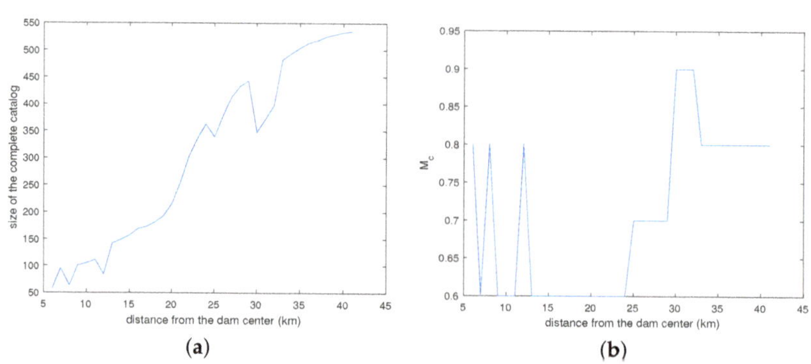

Figure 11. Number of earthquakes in the complete seismic catalog (**a**,**b**) showing completeness magnitude versus distance from the center of the reservoir.

Figure 12 illustrates the variation of the *b*-value with distance from the dam center. The red horizontal line represents the *b*-value calculated for the tectonic seismicity observed prior to the reservoir impoundment, corresponding to the completeness magnitude $M_c = 0.7$, as indicated by Lizurek et al. [34]. Three distinct regimes can be observed in the variation of the *b*-value with distance from the center of the dam:

1. Up to approximately 10–11 km, the *b*-value ranges around a mean value of ~1.21.
2. Between approximately 10–11 km and 24–25 km from the center of the dam, the *b*-value decreases with the distance from the center of the dam.

3. For distances greater than approximately 25–30 km from the dam center, the calculated b-value closely matches the value reported by Lizurek et al. [34].

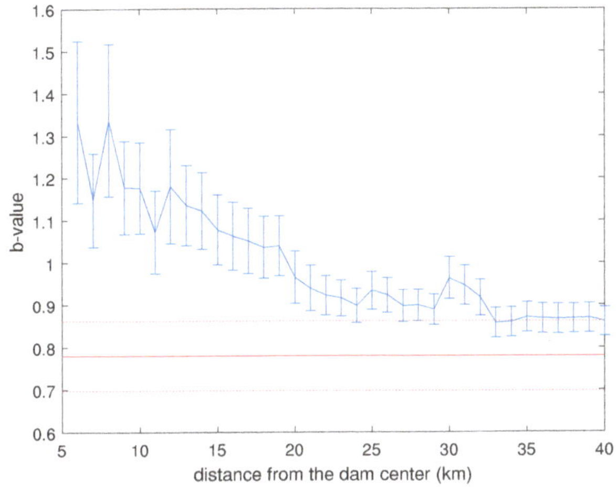

Figure 12. Variation of the b-value with the distance from the center of the dam (blue). The red horizontal line represents the b-value calculated for the tectonic seismicity observed prior to the reservoir impoundment, corresponding to a completeness magnitude of 0.7, as indicated in [34]. The error on b is indicated by the vertical bars, while the red dotted horizontal lines delimit the error band on b calculated in [34].

Since Lizurek et al. [34] calculated the b-value for the background seismicity that occurred before the impoundment of the reservoir, the events occurring more than ~24–25 km from the dam are likely tectonic in nature. In the first regime (up to approximately 10–11 km), the b-value is significantly larger than that of the regional seismicity, which could provide additional evidence that the earthquakes occurring near the dam are likely reservoir triggered [35]. In the regime of intermediate distances from the dam center, the decrease in the b-value could suggest a mixture of tectonic and reservoir-triggered earthquakes, with seismicity tending to be dominated by tectonic earthquakes as the distance from the dam increases.

We calculated the IMI between the monthly number of earthquakes and the monthly mean water level (Figure 13). The variation of the IMI with the distance from the center of the dam is quite similar to that of the b-value; for small distances, it increases, reaching a maximum at 9–11 km, then it decreases up to approximately 25 km. For larger distances, it fluctuates around mean values of approximately 0.99 (NVG) and 0.39 (HVG).

The similarity in the distance-related variation of both the b-value and IMI is very striking; three distance regimes are identified in the b-value variation, which closely match those identified in the IMI variation. The distance of 9–11 km, at which the IMI reaches its maximum, could be considered the furthest distance from the dam where the water level fluctuations impact on seismicity.

Considering the distance from the center of the dam corresponding to the peak of IMI, we computed the time lag between the monthly number of earthquakes and the monthly mean water level shifted by lag τ ranging from -12 to 12 months (Figure 14). In both cases, the time lag between the two variables is 9–10 months, showing that the occurrence of earthquakes follows water level fluctuations with a delay of 9–10 months.

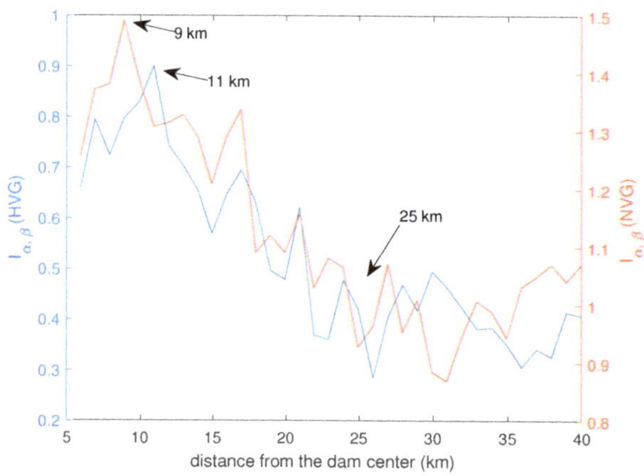

Figure 13. IMI between monthly number of earthquakes and monthly mean water level calculated by NVG (red) and HVG (blue).

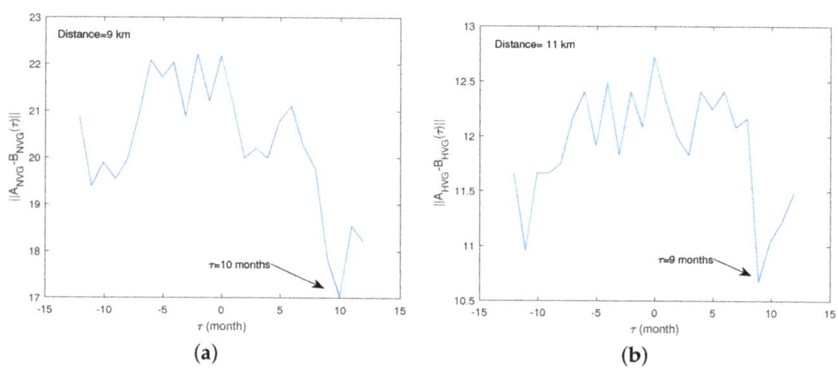

Figure 14. Variation with the time lag τ of the Frobenius norm of the difference between the adjacency matrix of the monthly number of earthquakes and that of the τ-shifted monthly mean of water calculated by using the NVG (**a**) and the HVG (**b**).

Figure 15 shows the variation of the *k-M* slope with the distance from the dam center. This topological parameter exhibits an increasing trend followed by an approximately constant or weakly decreasing one. In order to more precisely identify the breakpoint between these two trends, we applied the segmented regression method [36]. The found breakpoint is at 22 km. Figure 16 shows the relationship between the *b*-value and the *k-M* slope for the Lai Chau seismic sequence compared with that of seismic datasets analyzed in previous studies [11,12,37]. For distances from the center of the dam greater than or equal to 22 km, the Lai Chau seismic dataset aligns with the general relationship found for the other seismic datasets, while, for smaller distances, the seismic sequences in the Lai Chau area deviate from this general relationship. Focusing only on the Lai Chau dataset, the relationship between the *k-M* slope and the *b*-value (Figure 17) is characterized by two distinct behaviors. For distances from the dam center less than 22 km, the relationship is negative, while for distances greater than or equal to 22 km, the relationship is positive. To explain the negative relationship for distances less than 22 km, we analyzed the *k-M* slope in relation to the number of events for each distance. We found that, up to about 22 km from the center of the dam, the *k-M* slope increases with the number of events, whereas, for distances greater than 22 km, the *k-M* slope appears to be independent of the number of events (Figure 18).

Recently, Li et al. [15] found that the ratio between the *k-M* slope and the *b*-value can be influenced by the catalog size and, for Poissonian catalogs, derived the following relationship between this ratio and the number N of earthquakes:

$$\frac{k\text{-}M\ \text{slope}}{b} = -15.15(\log_{10}N)^{-2.14} + 11.85. \tag{7}$$

We calculated the ratio between the *k-M* slope and the *b*-value for the Lai Chau data and related it to the number of earthquakes, changing the distance from the dam center. The results are shown in Figure 19 and compared with Equation (7). Although the two curves do not perfectly overlap (Equation (7) is derived from Poissonian catalogs), their trends are almost identical. There is a clear increase in the ratio with the size of the catalog, which tends to stabilize as the catalog size grows. For the Lai Chau dataset, the saturation of the ratio starts for distances from the dam center larger than 22 km.

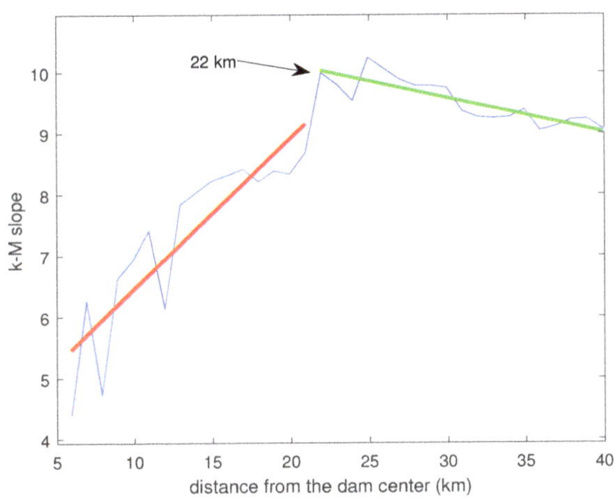

Figure 15. Variation of the *k-M* slope with the distance from the center of the dam.

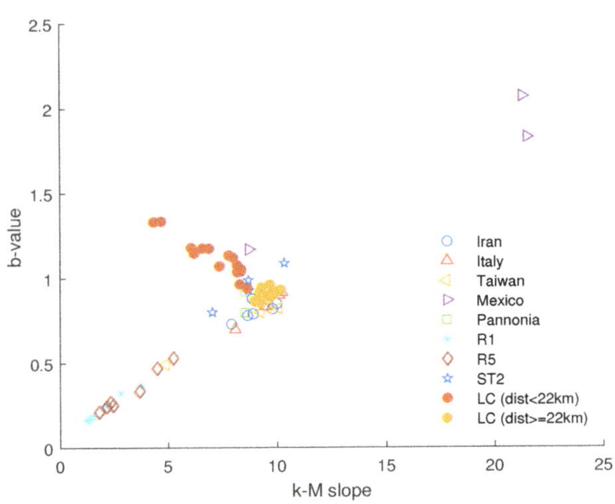

Figure 16. Relationship between the *k-M* slope and the *b*-value for the Lai Chau dataset (for distances from the dam center less than, larger than, or equal to 22 km) compared with that of the seismic datasets analyzed in previous studies (Iran [12], Italy and Taiwan [33], Mexico [11], Pannonia [38], R1 and R2 [39], and ST2 [37]).

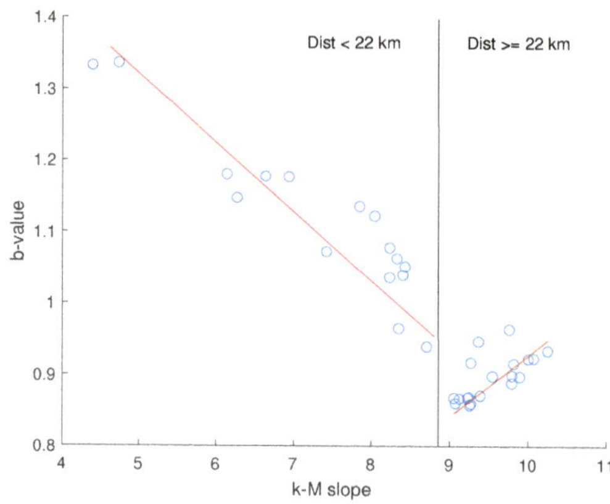

Figure 17. Relationship between the *k-M* slope and the *b*-value for the seismic datasets extracted at distances from the center varying from 6 to 40 km. The vertical black line separates the values relative to distances less than, greater than, or equal to 22 km from the center of the dam.

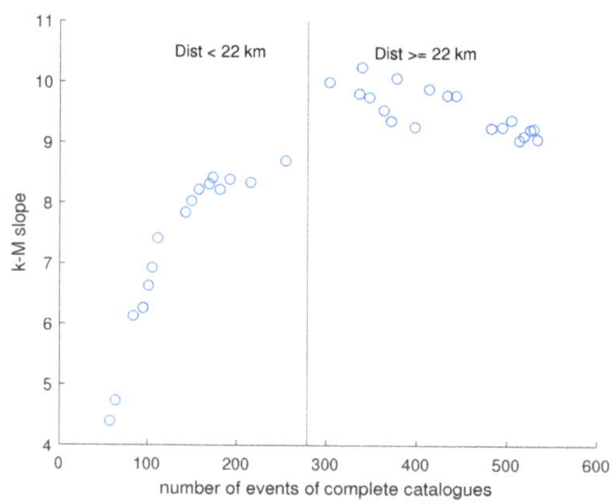

Figure 18. Relationship between the *k-M* slope and the number of events for the seismic datasets extracted at distances from the center varying from 6 to 40 km. The vertical black line separates the values relative to distances less than, greater than, or equal to 22 km from the center of the dam.

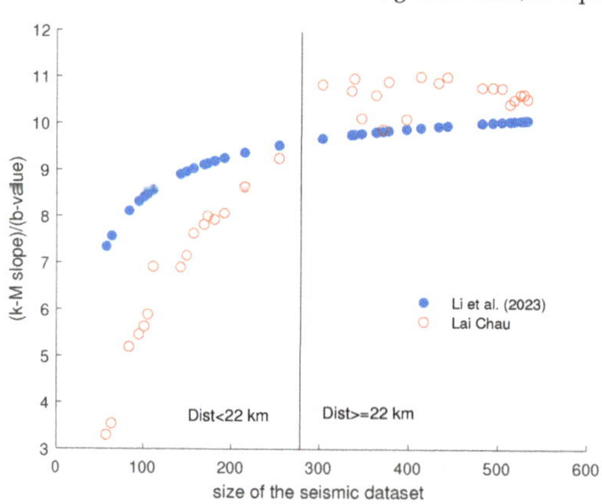

Figure 19. Variation of the ratio between *k-M* slope and the *b*-value with catalog size for Lai Chau dataset (red circles) compared with the relationship proposed in [15] (blue filled circles).

6. Conclusions

In this study, we analyzed the time dynamics of the shallow seismicity occurring in the vicinity of the Lai Chau reservoir (Vietnam), focusing on its seismological and topological properties, along with their mutual relationship. We employed the VG method to convert the investigated series into networks and analyzed a variety of network quantities (degree, *k-M* slope, IMI, and Frobenius norm) related to the earthquake series and also to the reservoir water level. The total seismicity, whose completeness magnitude is 0.8 and *b*-value is 0.86, is characterized by a *k-M* slope of $\approx$9.1. The positive value of the *k-M* slope indicates a positive correlation between degree and magnitude, which means that the higher the magnitude, the larger the degree. Thus, the larger events behave as "hubs" of the VG seismic network, being made visible by more earthquakes than the smaller ones. The *b*-value shows a non-trivial pattern as the distance from the dam's center increases. For distances up to 10–11 km, it ranges around a mean value of 1.21, while, for distances larger than 25–30 km, it aligns with the background value found by [34]; for intermediate distances, the *b*-value decreases with the distance from the dam's center. The IMI between the monthly number of earthquakes and the monthly mean water level is at its maximum at a distance of 9–11 km, and, at these distances, the time lag between the two variables is 9–10 months. The relationship between the *b*-value and the *k-M* slope seems to suggest that the *k-M* slope depends on the number of earthquakes within a 22 km radius from the center of the dam.

Author Contributions: Conceptualization, L.T.; methodology, L.T.; software, L.T.; formal analysis, L.T.; investigation, L.T. and A.T.T.; resources, L.T. and D.T.C.; data curation, A.T.T. and T.H.D.; writing—original draft preparation, L.T.; writing—review and editing, L.T. and A.T.T.; visualization, L.T. and A.T.T.; project administration, L.T. and D.T.C.; funding acquisition, L.T. and D.T.C. All authors have read and agreed to the published version of the manuscript.

Funding: This research was carried out thanks to funding under the CNR (Italy)/VAST (Vietnam) bilateral agreement, project "Investigation of space-time dynamics of seismicity triggered by Lai Chauhy-dropower reservoir, Vietnam", for the period 2023–2024. This research was funded by the Vietnam Academy of Science and Technology (VAST) under grant number VAST05.02/23-24.

Data Availability Statement: IS EPOS (2018), Episode: LAI CHAU, https://episodesplatform.eu/#episode:LAI_CHAU, (accessed on 2 April 2024) https://doi.org/10.25171/InstGeoph_PAS_ISEPOS-2018-012, (accessed on 2 April 2024).

Conflicts of Interest: The authors declare no conflicts of interest.

References

1. Zhang, R.; Ashuri, B.; Shyr, Y.; Deng, Y. Forecasting construction cost index based on visibility graph: A network approach. *Phys. A Stat. Mech. Its Appl.* **2018**, *493*, 239–252. [CrossRef]
2. Long, Y. Visibility graph network analysis of gold price time series. *Phys. A Stat. Mech. Its Appl.* **2013**, *392*, 3374–3384. [CrossRef]
3. Wang, N.; Li, D.; Wang, Q. Visibility graph analysis on quarterly macroeconomic series of China based on complex network theory. *Phys. A Stat. Mech. Its Appl.* **2012**, *391*, 6543–6555. [CrossRef]
4. Qian, M.C.; Jiang, Z.Q.; Zhou, W.X. Universal and nonuniversal allometric scaling behaviors in the visibility graphs of world stock market indices. *J. Phys. A Math. Theor.* **2010**, *43*, 335002. [CrossRef]
5. Jiang, W.; Wei, B.; Zhan, J.; Xie, C.; Zhou, D. A visibility graph power averaging aggregation operator: A methodology based on network analysis. *Comput. Ind. Eng.* **2016**, *101*, 260–268. [CrossRef]
6. Chen, S.; Hu, Y.; Mahadevan, S.; Deng, Y. A visibility graph averaging aggregation operator. *Phys. A Stat. Mech. Its Appl.* **2014**, *403*, 1–12. [CrossRef]
7. Elsner, J.; Jagger, T.; Fogarty, E. Visibility network of United States hurricanes. *Geophys. Res. Lett.* **2009**, *36*, L16702. [CrossRef]
8. Pierini, J.; Lovallo, M.; Telesca, L. Visibility graph analysis of wind speed records measured in central Argentina. *Phys. A Stat. Mech. Its Appl.* **2012**, *391*, 5041–5048. [CrossRef]
9. Lacasa, L.; Luque, B.; Ballesteros, F.; Luque, J.; Nuno, J.C. From time series to complex networks: The visibility graph. *Proc. Natl. Acad. Sci. USA* **2008**, *105*, 4972–4975. [CrossRef]

10. Telesca, L.; Lovallo, M. Analysis of seismic sequences by using the method of visibility graph. *Europhys. Lett.* **2012**, *97*, 50002. [CrossRef]
11. Telesca, L.; Lovallo, M.; Ramirez-Rojas, A.; Flores-Marquez, L. Investigating the time dynamics of seismicity by using the visibility graph approach: Application to seismicity of Mexican subduction zone. *Phys. A Stat. Mech. Its Appl.* **2013**, *391*, 1553–1562. [CrossRef]
12. Khoshnevis, N.; Taborda, R.; Azizzadeh-Roodpish, S.; Telesca, L. Analysis of the 2005–2016 earthquake sequence in Northern Iran using the visibility graph method. *Pure Appl. Geophys.* **2017**, *174*, 4003–4019. [CrossRef]
13. Azizzadeh-Roodpish, S.; Cramer, C.H. Visibility graph analysis of Alaska crustal and Aleutian subduction zone seismicity: An investigation of the correlation between b value and k–M slope. *Pure Appl. Geophys.* **2018**, *175*, 4241–4252. [CrossRef]
14. Perez-Oregon, J.; Lovallo, M.; Telesca, L. Visibility graph analysis of synthetic earthquakes generated by the Olami–Feder–Christensen spring-block model. *Chaos* **2020**, *30*, 093111. [CrossRef]
15. Li, L.; Luo, G.; Liu, M. The *k-M* Slope: A Potential Supplement for b-Value. *Seismol. Soc. Am.* **2023**, *94*, 1892–1899. [CrossRef]
16. Tapponnier, P.; Lacassin, R.; Leloup, P.; Scharer, U.; Zhong, D.; Wu, H.; Liu, X.; Ji, S.; Zhang, L.; Zhong, J. The Ailao Shan/Red River Metamorphic Belt: Tertiary Left-Lateral Shear between Indochina and South China. *Nature* **1990**, *343*, 431–437. [CrossRef]
17. Tran, V.T.; Van, D.T. Characteristics of the Pliocene-Quaternary Neotectonics in Northwest Vietnam Region. *J. Sci. Sci. Earth* **2006**, *22*, 86–99. Vietnam National University Hanoi, 30th anniversary of establishment of the Geological Faculty.
18. Le, V.D. State-Level Independent Final Report: "Establishing the Seismological Observation Network for Reservoir Earthquake in Da River Ladder of Hydroelectric Dam". Technical Report. 2019. Available online: https://www.most.gov.vn/cchc/tin-tuc/525/15956/bao-cao-ket-qua-tu-danh-gia-nhiem-vu-khcn-cap-quoc-gia--nghien-cuu-thiet-lap-mang-tram-quan-trac-dong-dat-va-danh-gia-dong-dat-kic.aspx (accessed on 17 October 2024). (In Vietnamese, with English Abstract)
19. Nguyen, D.X. State-Level Independent Final Report: "Reservoir Triggered Seismicity in Hoa Binh Hydropower". Technical Report. 1996. (In Vietnamese, with English Abstract)
20. Nguyen, N.T. State-Level Independent Final Report: "Study on Modern Fault Tectonics and Related Earthquakes in Hoa Binh Area as a Basis for Evaluating the Stability of Hoa Binh Hydropower". Technical Report. 2008. (In Vietnamese, with English Abstract)
21. Van, D.T. Development Characteristics of the Lai Chau-Dien Bien Fault Zone. Ph.D. Thesis, Institute of Geological Sciences, Vietnam Academy of Science and Technology, Hanoi, Vietnam, 2011. (In Vietnamese, with English Abstract)
22. Telesca, L.; Thai, A.; Cao, D.; Cao, D.; Dinh, Q.; Mai, X. Fractal and Spectral Analysis of Seismicity in the Lai Chau Area (Vietnam). *Fractal Fract.* **2023**, *7*, 776. [CrossRef]
23. Gutenberg, R.; Richter, C.F. Frequency of earthquakes in California. *Bull. Seismol. Soc. Am.* **1944**, *34*, 185–188. [CrossRef]
24. Wyss, M. Towards a physical understanding of the earthquake frequency distribution. *Geophys. J. R. Astron. Soc.* **1973**, *31*, 341–359. [CrossRef]
25. Scholz, C.H. The frequency-magnitude relation of microfracturing in rock and its relation to earthquakes. *Bull. Seismol. Soc. Am.* **1968**, *58*, 399–415. [CrossRef]
26. Aki, K. Maximum likelihood estimate of b in the formula $log(N) = a - bM$ and its confidence limits. *Bull. Earthq. Res. Inst. Univ. Tokyo* **1965**, *43*, 237–239.
27. Utsu, T. Representation and analysis of the earthquake size distribution: A historical review and some new approaches. *Pageoph* **1999**, *155*, 509–535. [CrossRef]
28. Wiemer, S.; Wyss, M. Minimum magnitude of completeness in earthquake catalogs: Examples from Alaska, the Western United States, and Japan. *Bull. Seismol. Soc. Am.* **2000**, *90*, 859–869. [CrossRef]
29. Yu, M.; Hillebrand, A.; Gouw, A.A.; Stam, C.J. Horizontal visibility graph transfer entropy (HVG-TE): A novel metric to characterize directed connectivity in large-scale brain networks. *NeuroImage* **2017**, *156*, 249–264. [CrossRef] [PubMed]
30. Lacasa, L.; Nicosia, V.; Latora, V. Network structure of multivariate time series. *Sci. Rep.* **2015**, *5*, 15508. [CrossRef]
31. Mali, P.; Manna, S.; Mukhopadhyay, A.; Haldar, P.; Singh, G. Multifractal analysis of multiparticle emission data in the framework of visibility graph and sandbox algorithm. *Phys. A Stat. Mech. Its Appl.* **2018**, *493*, 253–266. [CrossRef]
32. John, R.; John, M. Adaptation of the visibility graph algorithm for detecting time lag between rainfall and water level fluctuations in Lake Okeechobee. *Adv. Water Resour.* **2019**, *134*, 103429. [CrossRef]
33. Telesca, L.; Chen, C.C.; Lovallo, M. Investigating the relationship between seismological and topological properties of seismicity in Italy and Taiwan. *Pure Appl. Geophys.* **2020**, *177*, 4119–4126. [CrossRef]
34. Lizurek, G.; Wiszniowski, J.; Nguyen, V.D.; Dinh, Q.V.; Le, V.D.; Van, D.T.; Plesiewicz, B. Background seismicity and seismic monitoring in the Lai Chau reservoir area. *J. Seismol.* **2019**, *23*, 1373–1390. [CrossRef]
35. Gupta, H.K.; Rastogi, B.K.; Narain, H. Some Discriminatory Characteristics of Earthquakes Near the Kariba, Kremasta, and Koyna Artificial Lakes. *Bull. Seismol. Soc. Am.* **1972**, *62*, 493–507. [CrossRef]
36. Muggeo, V.M.R. Estimating regression models with unknown break-points. *Stat. Med.* **2003**, *22*, 3055–3071. [CrossRef] [PubMed]
37. Telesca, L.; Thai, A.T.; Lovallo, M.; Cao, D.T.; Nguyen, L.M. Shannon Entropy Analysis of Reservoir-Triggered Seis-micity at Song Tranh 2 Hydropower Plant, Vietnam. *Appl. Sci.* **2022**, *12*, 8873. [CrossRef]

38. Telesca, L.; Lovallo, M.; Toth, L. Visibility graph analysis of 2002–2011 Pannonian seismicity. *Phys. A Stat. Mech. Its Appl.* **2014**, *416*, 219–224. [CrossRef]
39. Telesca, L.; Lovallo, M.; Ramirez-Rojas, A.; Flores-Marquez, L. Relationship between the frequency magnitude distribution and the visibility graph in the synthetic seismicity generated by a simple stick-slip system with asperities. *PLoS ONE* **2014**, *9*, e106233. [CrossRef]

Disclaimer/Publisher's Note: The statements, opinions and data contained in all publications are solely those of the individual author(s) and contributor(s) and not of MDPI and/or the editor(s). MDPI and/or the editor(s) disclaim responsibility for any injury to people or property resulting from any ideas, methods, instructions or products referred to in the content.

entropy

MDPI

Article

Multimodal Non-Extensive Frequency-Magnitude Distributions and Their Relationship to Multi-Source Seismicity

Erick de la Barra [1,†], Pedro Vega-Jorquera [2,†] and Sérgio Luiz E. F. da Silva [3,4,5,*,†]

1 School of Business, Universidad Católica del Norte, Coquimbo 1781421, CO, Chile; erick.delabarra@ucn.cl
2 Department of Physics, Universidad de La Serena, La Serena 1720169, CO, Chile; pvega@userena.cl
3 Laboratory of Parallel Architectures for Signal Processing, Universidade Federal do Rio Grande do Norte, Natal 59078-900, RN, Brazil
4 Dipartimento di Scienza Applicata e Tecnologia, Politecnico di Torino, 10129 Torino, Italy
5 Istituto dei Sistemi Complessi—Consiglio Nazionale delle Ricerche (ISC-CNR), c/o Dipartimento di Scienza Applicata e Tecnologia del Politecnico di Torino, 10129 Torino, Italy
* Correspondence: sergio.luiz.silva@ufrn.br
† These authors contributed equally to this work.

Abstract: We investigate multimodal seismicity by analyzing it as the result of multiple seismic sources. We examine three case studies: the Redoubt and Spurr regions in Alaska, where volcanic and subduction-related seismicity occur, and the Kii Peninsula in Japan, where shallow and deep earthquakes are clearly separated. To understand this phenomenon, we perform spatial, temporal, and magnitude analyses. Our application of non-extensive statistical mechanics shows that multimodal models provide a significantly better fit than unimodal ones. We identify patterns in the distributions of time between events and distances between events using multimodal Tsallis q-gamma distributions. In addition, we use the multimodal Sotolongo–Costa model to analyze the magnitude distribution, which effectively captures the complex interactions that may explain the observed lack of fractality in multimodal seismicity.

Keywords: multimodal seismicity; non-extensive statistical mechanics; q-gamma distributions

1. Introduction

Earthquakes are complex spatio-temporal phenomena that represent a catastrophic natural hazard, and their triggering mechanisms remain an open question. Indeed, it is not fully understood why earthquakes occur both in tectonically stable parts of the inner regions of tectonic plates (known as intraplate earthquakes [1,2]) and in unstable areas, such as tectonic plate boundaries [3,4] and volcanoes [5,6]. In this context, it is natural to consider various focal mechanisms in the same seismogenic area. Therefore, analyzing the distribution of earthquakes and their magnitudes is crucial for a better understanding of their occurrence and spatial and temporal distribution.

In recent decades, the Gutenberg–Richter (GR) law [7] has been used to describe the distribution of earthquakes by analyzing the number of earthquakes, $N_{>M}$, with a magnitude greater than M, as a frequency–magnitude power law. Laboratory studies provide valuable insights into the frequency–magnitude relationship, as described by the GR law, and its variability with different materials and stress conditions. For example, ref. [8] found that microfractures in rocks induced by pressure experiments follow a frequency–magnitude relationship similar to that of earthquakes, with the b-value depending primarily on the stress and the confining pressure. Extending these findings, ref. [9] conducted thermal experiments on rock samples and discovered microquakes generated by thermoelastic stress relief. They observed that the frequency–magnitude relationship of these thermal events had a higher b-value than is typical for ordinary earthquake series. Ref. [10] extended the cumulative frequency–magnitude relationship by reformulating it based on the seismic moment and introducing the b-value as an analog to the original b-value. Finally, ref. [11] investigated the rock behavior under different stress conditions, showing that the confining pressure and intermediate stress strongly influence rock strength and ductility, affecting the frequency and magnitude of seismic events.

However, the GR law exhibits local scale invariance, i.e., the minimum magnitude is not always related to the incompleteness of seismic catalogs [12]. In this respect, the self-similarity of seismic sources and their magnitudes breaks down for low-magnitude earthquakes [13]. Moreover, the statistical distribution of earthquake magnitudes in different areas exhibits multimodal behavior [14–17] due to the diversity of focal mechanisms in a seismic region. Indeed, multimodality has been associated with non-fractality and the breakdown of self-similarity. For example, multimodal seismicity patterns have been observed in mining-induced seismicity, attributed to complex geologic features associated with inhomogeneous fault planes and dikes [18]. In addition to anthropogenic cases, natural features also exhibit multimodal characteristics, as in the case of the well-known Himalayan seismicity due to the non-planar and frictional geometry of the main Himalayan thrust, which is responsible for triggering numerous earthquakes [19,20].

In addition, several studies have demonstrated the existence of long-range correlations between seismic events, i.e., earthquake sequences exhibit a significant statistical dependence between two distant events, as measured by the autocorrelation function [21–23]. Significant progress has been made in seismological modeling through the use of Tsallis q-statistics (also known as non-extensive statistical mechanics) by incorporating concepts of long-range correlation [24–26]. More specifically, the Sotolongo–Costa–Posadas (SCP) model is based on a probability distribution derived from the principle of maximum entropy applied to the Tsallis entropy. This model generalizes the GR law and physically justifies the relationship between frequency and earthquake magnitude [27–29]. Based on the theory of seismic moment scaling (see, e.g., [30]), Silva et al. [31] slightly revised the SCP model by introducing a more realistic link between seismic energy and fragment size. The SCP model provides a physically based approach that takes into account not only the rough surfaces of the fault planes but also the distribution of rock fragments between plates and the theory of seismic moment scaling. In this sense, the SCP model assumes that the physical mechanisms for triggering an earthquake are related to the distribution of fragments and the energy distribution of the earthquake, which is determined by maximizing the Tsallis q-entropy according to first principles. Subsequently, a number of studies have shown the universality of the SCP model in analyzing seismicity in various regions [32–36]. However, all these studies and related works focused on the unimodal analysis of the statistical distribution of earthquake magnitudes.

In this work, we consider a multimodal extension of the SCP model presented in [37] and multimodal versions of Tsallis q-gamma distributions to analyze three seismogenic regions that exhibit multimodal empirical distributions. In this effort, we investigate the transferability of multimodal non-extensive models to describe multimodal and non-fractal seismicity by explaining the multi-source seismic mechanisms and their characteristics in temporal and spatial terms. This paper is organized as follows. In Section 2, we present the models used in seismology and their non-extensive multimodal extensions based on the SCP and Tsallis q-distributions. In Section 3, we describe the main features of the real-world dataset used. Then, we devote Section 4 to the presentation of the results to demonstrate the robustness of our proposed model in analyzing the seismicity generated by multi-source configurations. Finally, in Section 5, we summarize the concluding remarks of this work.

2. Multi-Source Seismicity and Bimodal Distributions in the Non-Extensive Approach

In this section, we present a multimodal extension of the SCP model to describe multi-source seismicity. The bimodal extension of the SCP model has recently been successfully used to describe the anthropogenic seismicity triggered by the exploitation of underground mines [37]. Two types of earthquakes can be distinguished in anthropogenic seismicity:

one is triggered directly by human activity and is of low energy, while the other is triggered by tectonic stresses released by human activity and is stronger than quakes triggered directly by mining operations. Each type of earthquake is associated with different modes in the multimodal SCP model. In the cases to be analyzed, two groups of earthquakes are investigated, namely shallow and deep events, which are easily identified by their spatial distribution.

Our aim is to study the cumulative frequency–magnitude distribution (FMD) of earthquakes, the spacing between events, and the recurrence times. To analyze the last two objectives, we introduce bimodal extensions to the Tsallis q-distributions, which are commonly used to describe the distances and times between events.

2.1. Bimodal Non-Extensive Model for Earthquakes

Based on non-extensive statistical mechanics (or Tsallis q-statistics), Sotolongo, Costa, and Posadas [27] introduced a new fragment-asperity interaction model for modeling earthquake magnitude distributions. This model consists of two fault planes, with rough surfaces and irregular rock fragments occupying the space between them. In this regard, the statistical distribution of fragments maximizes the Tsallis q-entropy

$$\max_{p} \quad S_q[p]\,/k_B = \frac{1}{q-1}\left(1 - \int_0^{\infty} p^q(\sigma)d\sigma\right), \tag{1}$$

subject to

$$\int_0^{\infty} p(\sigma)d\sigma = 1, \tag{2}$$

$$\langle \sigma_q \rangle = \int_0^{\infty} \sigma P_q(\sigma)d\sigma, \quad \text{with,} \quad P_q(\sigma) = \frac{p^q(\sigma)}{\int_0^{\infty} p^q(\sigma)d\sigma}, \tag{3}$$

conditions, where k_B is the Boltzmann constant, $p(\sigma)$ denotes the probability density function related to the fragment size σ, and $q \in \mathbb{R}$ is the non-extensivity parameter (entropic index). The q-parameter allows the escort distribution to scan the structure of $p(\sigma)$ differently, emphasizing events with higher or lower probabilities depending on q. The constraints in Equation (2) and Equation (3) are, respectively, the normalization condition and the q-expectation value [38], in which $P_q(\cdot)$ represents the escort probability function [39,40]. Escort distributions are derived probability functions that allow a controlled modification of the original distribution $p(\sigma)$ to emphasize different aspects of the probability structure. In the context of Tsallis q-statistics, these escort probability functions arise naturally when maximizing the Tsallis q-entropy. A notable example is the q-generalized Gaussian distribution, which emerges as an equilibrium distribution from this maximization [41–43]. In the field of source coding, for instance, escort distributions are related to Campbell's coding theorem by associating generalized length measures with the Rényi–Tsallis entropy [44]. We invite the reader to refer to [45–49] for an exploration of the fundamental concepts and diverse applications of the escort probability function.

The optimization of Equation (1), subject to the constraints in (2), leads to the distribution for the following fault plane-related fragments [31]:

$$p(\sigma) = \left[1 - \left(\frac{1-q}{2-q}\right)\left(\sigma - \langle \sigma_q \rangle\right)\right]^{\frac{1}{1-q}}, \tag{4}$$

valid for $1 < q < 2$. By considering an earthquake energy ε to be proportional to r^3, where r is the linear dimension of fragments filling the gap between the sliding plates, we have that $\sigma - \langle \sigma_q \rangle = (\varepsilon/\alpha)^{2/3}$ [31], where α is a proportionality constant. Moreover, it is noteworthy that the relation between the magnitude m of a seismic event and its released seismic energy is given by [30] $m = \frac{2}{3}log_{10}(\varepsilon)$. Thus, we may write, after some algebra, the non-extensive GR law as [31,50]:

$$\log_{10}\left(N_{>M}\right) = \log_{10}\left(N\right) + \left(\frac{2-q_M}{1-q_M}\right)\log_{10}\left[\frac{1-\left(\frac{1-q_M}{2-q_M}\right)\frac{10^M}{\alpha^{2/3}}}{1-\left(\frac{1-q_M}{2-q_M}\right)\frac{10^{M_0}}{\alpha^{2/3}}}\right], \tag{5}$$

for $M \geq M_0$, or equivalently,

$$\log_{10}\left(N_{>M}\right) = a_q - b_q\left(\log_{10}\left[1 + 10^M \Big/ (b_q \cdot \alpha^{2/3})\right] - \log_{10}\left[1 + 10^{M_0} \Big/ (b_q \cdot \alpha^{2/3})\right]\right), \tag{6}$$

where $a_q = \log_{10}(N)$, $b_q = \frac{2-q_M}{q_M-1}$ is the generalized b-value, and q_M is the entropic index related to the frequency–magnitude distribution.

The multimodal behavior of the F–M distribution (FMD) is observed in natural earthquakes. It can be explained by multi-source seismicity, as in cases where many plates, the conjunction of plates, or volcanoes are present. Thus, each source generates different types of tremors, which break the self-similarity in the FMD. As in anthropogenic tremors in mining operations, the multimodal GR distribution can be used to describe multi-source natural earthquakes, that is, a piecewise linear function for the survival $\log_{10} N_{>M}$ can be proposed:

$$\log_{10}\left(N_{>M}\right) \approx \begin{cases} a_1 - b_1(M - M_0), & M_0 \leq M \leq M_T, \\ a_2 - b_2(M - M_T), & M \geq M_T, \end{cases}$$

But, the multimodal GR ignores the long-range effects, and a multimodal extension of (5) would be suitable to describe multi-source seismicity considering autocorrelation and fractality:

$$\log_{10}\left(N_{>M}\right) = \begin{cases} a_1 - b_1\left(\log_{10}\left[1 + \frac{10^M}{b_1 \cdot \alpha_1^{2/3}}\right] - \log_{10}\left[1 + \frac{10^{M_0}}{b_1 \cdot \alpha_1^{2/3}}\right]\right), & M_0 \leq M \leq M_T \\ a_2 - b_2\left(\log_{10}\left[1 + \frac{10^M}{b_2 \cdot \alpha_2^{2/3}}\right] - \log_{10}\left[1 + \frac{10^{M_T}}{b_2 \cdot \alpha_2^{2/3}}\right]\right), & M \geq M_T, \end{cases} \tag{7}$$

where the continuity conditions must be satisfied:

$$a_1 = \log_{10} N_{>M_0}, \quad \text{and} \tag{8a}$$

$$a_2 = a_1 - b_1\left(\log_{10}\left[1 + 10^{M_T} \Big/ (b_1 \cdot \alpha_1^{2/3})\right] - \log_{10}\left[1 + 10^{M_0} \Big/ (b_1 \cdot \alpha_1^{2/3})\right]\right). \tag{8b}$$

The bimodal Sotolongo–Costa density is also derived:

$$f(x) = \begin{cases} \frac{b_1 \ln 10}{b_1 \alpha_1^{2/3} + 10_0^M}\left(\frac{\left[1+\frac{10^M}{b_1 \cdot \alpha_1^{2/3}}\right]}{\left[1+\frac{10^{M_0}}{b_1 \cdot \alpha_1^{2/3}}\right]}\right)^{-b_1-1} 10^M, & M_0 \leq M \leq M_T \\ \frac{b_2 \ln 10}{b_2 \alpha_2^{2/3} + 10_0^M}\left(\frac{\left[1+\frac{10_T^M}{b_1 \cdot \alpha_1^{2/3}}\right]}{\left[1+\frac{10^{M_0}}{b_1 \cdot \alpha_1^{2/3}}\right]}\right)^{-b_1-1}\left(\frac{\left[1+\frac{10^M}{b_2 \cdot \alpha_2^{2/3}}\right]}{\left[1+\frac{10^{M_0}}{b_2 \cdot \alpha_2^{2/3}}\right]}\right)^{-b_2-1} 10^M, & M \geq M_T, \end{cases}$$

A trimodal distribution can be defined analogously.

The application of the bimodal extension to earthquake distributions assumes the existence of two modes, with each mode following a Sotolongo–Costa distribution. At the same time, the Sotolongo–Costa model describes non-linearity, long-range interactions, fractality, self-organized criticality, long memory effects, and scaling in seismicity because it is based on non-extensive statistical mechanics, providing a consistent statistical framework for the description of seismicity and its properties [33,34].

2.2. Bimodal Tsallis Distribution and Interevent Distances

The Tsallis distribution is used to model three-dimensional distances between the hypocenters of successive earthquakes. The unimodal Tsallis distribution is defined as [51]

$$p(x) = (2 - q_{TS})b(1 + b_{TS}(q_{TS} - 1)(x - x_0))^{1/(1-q_{TS})}. \tag{9}$$

The subscript TS denotes that the parameters are from the Tsallis distribution but it will be omitted when the context is clear. Here, $b > 0$, $x \in \mathbb{R}^+$ if $1 < q < 2$, $x \in (0, x_{\max})$ if $q < 1$, and $x \in C$ with $\int_C p < \infty$ if $q > 2$. Additionally, the Tsallis model appears in the interevent times modeling, that is, the elapsed time between successive tremors.

Given that, in some cases, the magnitudes behave bimodally or trimodally, we expect to observe similar behavior for the interevent distances and interevent times in these cases.

In order to model the multimodality of the interevent distances and interevent times, we define the bimodal Tsallis distribution by

$$f(x) = \begin{cases} (2-q_1)(1+(q_1-1)b_1(x-x_0))^{\frac{1}{1-q_1}}, & x_0 \le x \le x_T \\ k(2-q_2)(1+(q_2-1)b_2(x-x_T))^{\frac{1}{1-q_2}}, & x \ge x_T, \end{cases}$$

and integrating, we obtain

$$\overline{F}(x) = \begin{cases} (1+(q_1-1)b_1(x-x_0))^{\frac{2-q_1}{1-q_1}}, & x_0 \le x \le x_T \\ k(1+(q_2-1)b_2(x-x_T))^{\frac{2-q_2}{1-q_2}}, & x \ge x_T, \end{cases}$$

where $\overline{F}(x) = P(X > x)$ is the survival function and k is determined by the continuity condition at $x = x_T$:

$$k = (1+(q_1-1)b_1(x_T-x_0))^{\frac{2-q_1}{1-q_1}}.$$

As usual, it is preferable to plot $\log_{10}(N_{>x})$ instead $P(X > x)$, where $N_{>x}$ is the number of data greater than x, because the logarithm smooths out the differences along the curve $P(X > x)$:

$$\log_{10}(N_{>x}) = \begin{cases} A_1 - B_1\log_{10}(1+(q_1-1)b_1(x-x_0)), & x_0 \le x \le x_T \\ A_2 - B_2\log_{10}(1+(q_2-1)b_1(x-x_T)), & x \ge x_T, \end{cases} \tag{10}$$

where $A_1 = \log_{10} N$, $B_i = (2-q_i)/(q_i-1)$ for $i = 1,2$, N is the number of data, and $A_2 = \log_{10} Nk = A_1 - B_1\log_{10}(1+(q_1-1)b_1(x_T-x_0))$.

2.3. q-Gamma Distributions and Interevent Times

Understanding the time occurrence between successive earthquakes is vital for estimating seismic hazard. Several models have been developed to describe the interevent time distribution of earthquakes, which can be classified into Poissonian and non-Poissonian models. Non-Poissonian models include the Tsallis distribution [33] and the gamma distribution [34,52,53]. Here, we propose to characterize multimodal seismicity using the unimodal-bimodal versions of the Tsallis distribution (10) and the q-gamma distribution, a deformed version of the gamma distribution, which is given by

$$f(t) = c(t-t_0)^{\gamma_\Gamma - 1}(1+(q_\Gamma-1)b_\Gamma(t-t_0))^{\frac{1}{1-q_\Gamma}}, \quad t > t_0$$

The subscript Γ denotes that the parameters are from the q-gamma distribution, but it will be omitted when the context is clear. Here, $t \in \mathbb{R}^+$, $1 < q < 2$ is the parameter of deformation, $b, \gamma \ge 0$ are shape parameters, and c is a normalization constant given by [54]

$$c = \frac{[(q-1)b]^\gamma}{\mathrm{B}\left(\gamma, \frac{1}{q-1} - \gamma\right)}. \tag{11}$$

Since the interevent distribution follows a gamma distribution, it is reasonable to propose the non-extensive version of this distribution to model the interevent times, that is, the q-gamma distribution. It is worth noting that the q-gamma law is a generalization of the Tsallis distribution, which has been used to describe interevent time data [33]. The cumulative distribution function for $1 < q < 2$ can be expressed in terms of the incomplete beta function I [54]:

$$F(x;q,b,\gamma,x_0) = \mathrm{I}\left(\frac{(q-1)b(x-x_0)}{(q-1)b(x-x_0)+1};\gamma,\frac{1}{q-1}-\gamma\right)$$

Note that for $q \to 1$, the q-gamma distribution becomes the gamma distribution. Given that multi-source seismicity is being studied, it is reasonable to expect bimodal behavior for the interevent time distribution. Its modeling is especially important in order to properly estimate the hazard function, that is, the probability that at least one earthquake with a magnitude greater than M will occur in the next time interval ΔT, if the previous one occurred before time T [33].

For the interevent time distribution in multi-source seismicity, we propose the bimodal q-gamma distribution:

$$f(t) = \begin{cases} c_1(t-t_0)^{\gamma_1-1}(1+(q_1-1)b_1(t-t_0))^{\frac{1}{1-q_1}}, & t_0 \le t \le t_T \\ c_2(t-t_T)^{\gamma_2-1}(1+(q_2-1)b_2(t-t_T))^{\frac{1}{1-q_2}}, & t \ge t_T, \end{cases} \quad (12)$$

where $1 < q_1, q_2 < 2$, $b_1, b_2, \gamma_1, \gamma_2 \ge 0$. c_1 takes the form (11), and c_2 is such that the continuity condition is satisfied at $x = x_T$. An important form of (12) is the logarithm of the number of events whose interevent times are greater than time t:

$$\log_{10}(N_{>t}) = \begin{cases} A_1 - \log_{10}(1-F(t;q_1,b_1,\gamma_1,t_0)), & t_0 \le t \le t_T \\ A_2 - \log_{10}(1-F(t;q_2,b_2,\gamma_2,t_T))), & t \ge t_T, \end{cases}$$

where $A_1 = \log_{10} N$ and $A_2 = \log_{10} N + \log_{10}(1-F(t_T;q_1,b_1,\gamma_1,t_0))$.

According to this, the interevent times can be modeled with a very good fit using the bimodal q-gamma distribution, as we will see in Section 4 (see Table 5).

3. Data and Case Studies

To experimentally evaluate our proposal, we consider three seismogenic areas (Mount Redoubt, Mount Spurr, and the Kii Peninsula), using earthquakes from two catalogs: the United States Geological Survey (USGS) and the Japan Meteorological Agency (JMA), as shown in Table 1. Mount Redoubt (60.4852 N, 152.7431 W) and Mount Spurr (61.2997 N, 152.2514 W) are active stratovolcanoes in the Alaskan volcanic zone, while the Kii Peninsula is a large Japanese peninsula (34.1810 N, 135.5718 E). Data for the Spurr and Redoubt volcanoes were obtained from the USGS website, while data for the Kii Peninsula were obtained from the JMA. Table 1 summarizes the time periods and number of events analyzed in this study, and Figure 1 shows the locations of these regions on a map. These regions were selected because they exhibit spatially differentiated seismicity that is consistent over time, as shown in Figure 2. We hypothesize that the clustering of earthquakes in these areas follows different patterns, i.e., the FMDs differ for each cluster in a given area. Nevertheless, we need to analyze the time windows for which the degree of detection is constant, i.e., the degree of completeness must be constant. The selected volcanic areas are significantly smaller than the Kii area, as seismicity is particularly noticeable in the vicinity of the volcanoes due to volcanic activity. The selected time periods were chosen to ensure constant completeness values during the periods investigated. This criterion is intended to avoid mixing data with different degrees of completeness, which could lead to bimodal behavior. The irregularity of M_c in the volcanic areas compared to the behavior of M_c on the Kii Peninsula explains the difference in size of the selected time windows in which seismicity is analyzed. Both Mt. Redoubt and Mt. Spurr are active stratovolcanoes, but Mt.

Redoubt has shorter intervals between eruptions, producing more frequent seismological records. This difference explains why the years analyzed vary between the Redoubt and Spurr areas.

Table 1. Information on the analyzed catalogs: earthquake regions, the period covered by the datasets, and the number of events recorded for each region.

Region/Catalog	Period	Number of Events		
		Total	Shallow	Deep
Redoubt/USGS	2018–2022	1055	798	257
Spurr/USGS	2020	613	359	254
Kii/JMA	2013–2021	81,154	80,054	1100

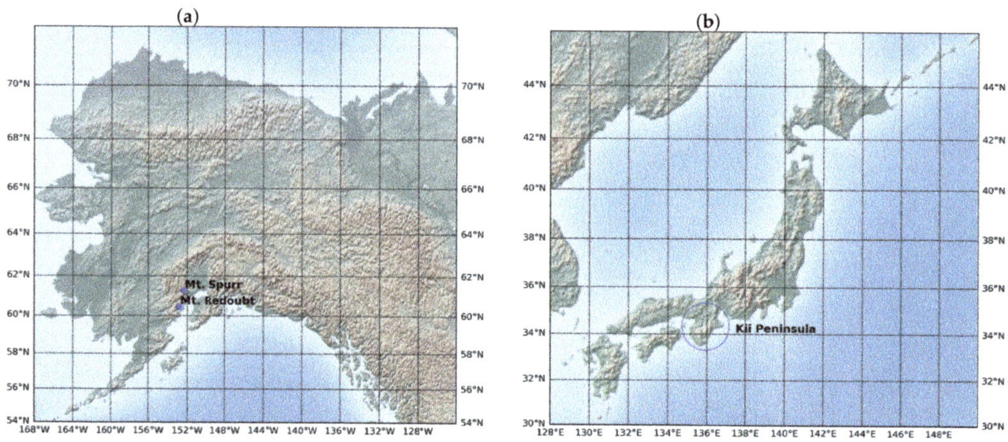

Figure 1. Geographical locations of studied seismogenic regions. In (**a**), the coordinates of the Alaskan volcanoes, Mt. Redoubt and Mt. Spurr, are marked by blue dots, and in (**b**), the Japanese Kii Peninsula is represented by a blue circle.

Figure 2a,b show 3D base maps depicting the distribution of earthquakes in Mount Redoubt, Mount Spurr, and the Kii Peninsula, in which the green points represent the hypocenters, while the colored surfaces represent the topographic maps. In these figures, we can see that deep earthquakes are spatially separated from shallow earthquakes in all seismic regions. The deep earthquakes occur at depths ranging from 80 to 150 km, 60 to 150 km, and 300 to 450 km, in the Mount Redoubt, Mount Spurr, and Kii regions, respectively, while shallow events occur at depths less than 20, 25, and 70 km. Deep hypocenters correspond to tectonic earthquakes, often large, while shallow earthquakes are generally low-magnitude events. In the figures, panels (d)–(f) show the temporal distributions of the earthquakes illustrated in panels (a)–(c), where the data points refer to all seismic events, sorted according to the occurrence time index n in ascending order, with n = 1 being the first detected earthquake, n = 2 being the second one, and so on. In fact, the existence of a region free of tremors is remarkable and separates the shallow and deep events.

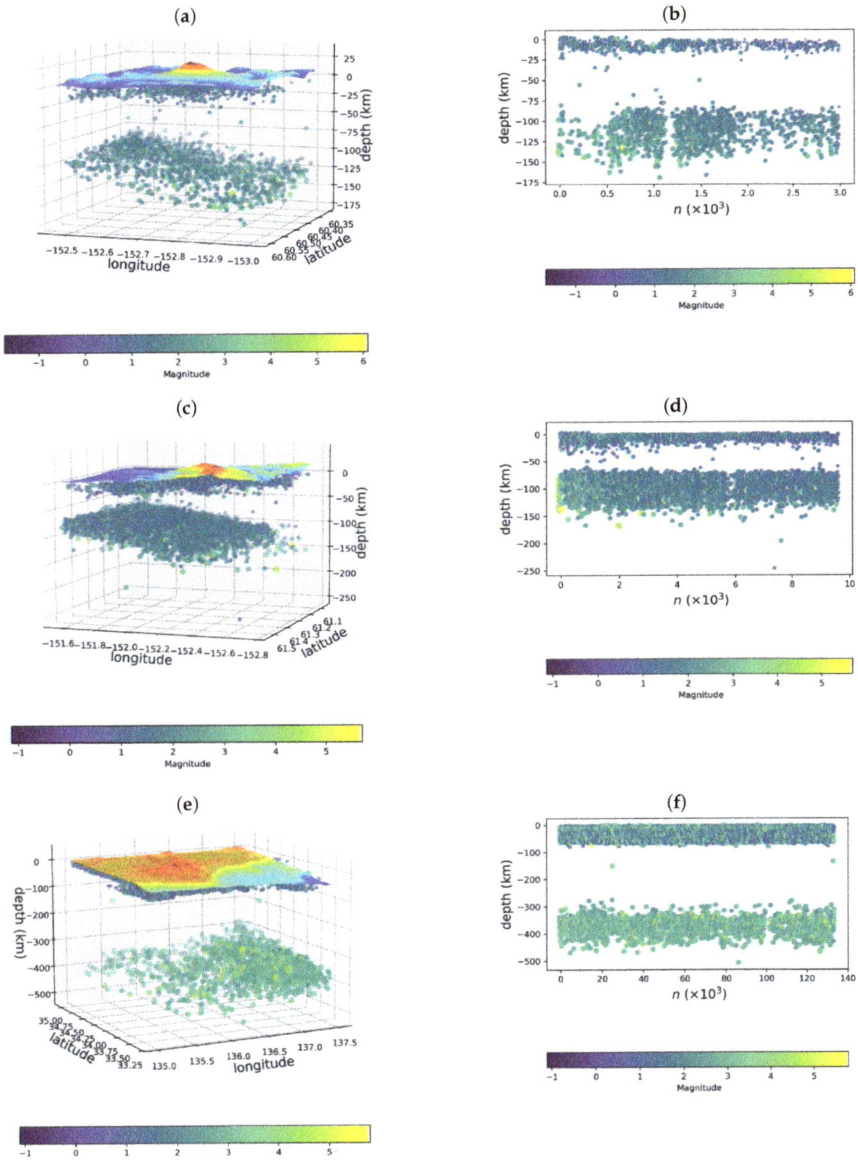

Figure 2. Three-dimensional base maps representing the distribution of earthquakes in the (**a**) Mount Redoubt, (**c**) Mount Spurr, and (**e**) Kii Peninsula regions. The green points represent the hypocenters, while the colored surfaces represent the topographic maps. Topographic data were multiplied by a factor of ten for better visualization. Panels (**b**,**d**,**f**) show the temporal development in counts of the hypocenter depth distributions associated with the Mount Redoubt (1973–2022), Mount Spurr (1970–2022), and Kii Peninsula (2009–2020) regions.

It is worth noting that these three seismogenic regions are known to experience multi-source seismic activity for different reasons, and therefore, multimodal statistical behavior is expected. For instance, Mounts Redoubt and Spurr are located at the Aleutian Arc, where the shallow events can be explained by volcanic activity close to the surface at the volcanic arc, which is induced by subduction of the Pacific Plate (oceanic crust) beneath the North American Plate (continental crust) [55]. As the oceanic plate is subducted, the pressure and temperature increase, turning the rocks into magma. The magma ascends as a result of partial melting and interaction with the mantle wedge, forming magma chambers whose contents are expelled through violent eruptions. The deep earthquakes in the Mount Redoubt and Mount Spurr regions are triggered by the subduction of the Pacific Plate beneath the North American Plate [55]. In the Kii Peninsula case, the multimodal seismicity feature results from several factors, such as a reflection of the Median Tectonic Line seismic activity, which extends 900 km in an east–west direction, and the oblique subduction of the Philippine Sea plate beneath the Southwest Japan Arc through the Nankai Trough [56]. Thus, we can observe long-continuing swarm activities of shallow, slow, and megathrust earthquakes [57]. Although our analysis considers shallow events whose hypocenters are located in the interval $[0, 70]$ km, these events can be subclassified as shallows with a focus in the interval $[0, 20]$ km and deep events with a focus in the interval $[20, 70]$ km, as discussed in [56]. But our analysis of Kii earthquakes focuses only on two groups of events: those with a hypocenter in the depth interval $[0, 70]$ km and those with a hypocenter in $[300, 450]$ km.

To visually examine the impact of shallow and deep earthquakes on the entire dataset, we analyzed the time series of earthquake magnitudes $m(n)$, sorted according to the occurrence time index n in ascending order, with $m(1)$ representing the first recorded earthquake, $m(2)$ representing the second, and so on, as depicted in Figure 3 for the Redoubt, Spurr, and Kii areas. In Figure 3, shallow events are represented by orange dots, while deep events are represented by blue dots. We can see that shallow earthquakes are concentrated at low magnitudes, while deep events significantly contribute to the concentration of events around magnitudes of 1.5, 1.5, and 3 for the Redoubt, Spurr, and Kii Peninsula regions, respectively. This contribution from deep events suggests the generation of a second statistical mode, which will be discussed later. Furthermore, at least two modes are observed in the histograms presented in Figure 4. In the magnitude distribution of shallow events (first column of Figure 4), frequencies concentrate at small magnitudes, while for deep events (second column of Figure 4), the probability accumulates at higher magnitudes. The third column of Figure 4 shows the histograms resulting from the superposition of the magnitude distributions for shallow and deep events, leading to bimodal distributions. In the histograms for the Redoubt and Spurr events (Figure 4c,f), shallow events are identified by bold bars, as they are more frequent than deep events. By observing the histograms for all events, we can visually identify at least two modes for the Redoubt region, which are barely visible for the Spurr region and not identifiable for the Kii region. The difficulty in visually observing the modes, especially for the Kii region, is explained by the small proportion of deep events (see Table 1); in this case, Figure 3 clearly shows the existence of at least two modes for that region.

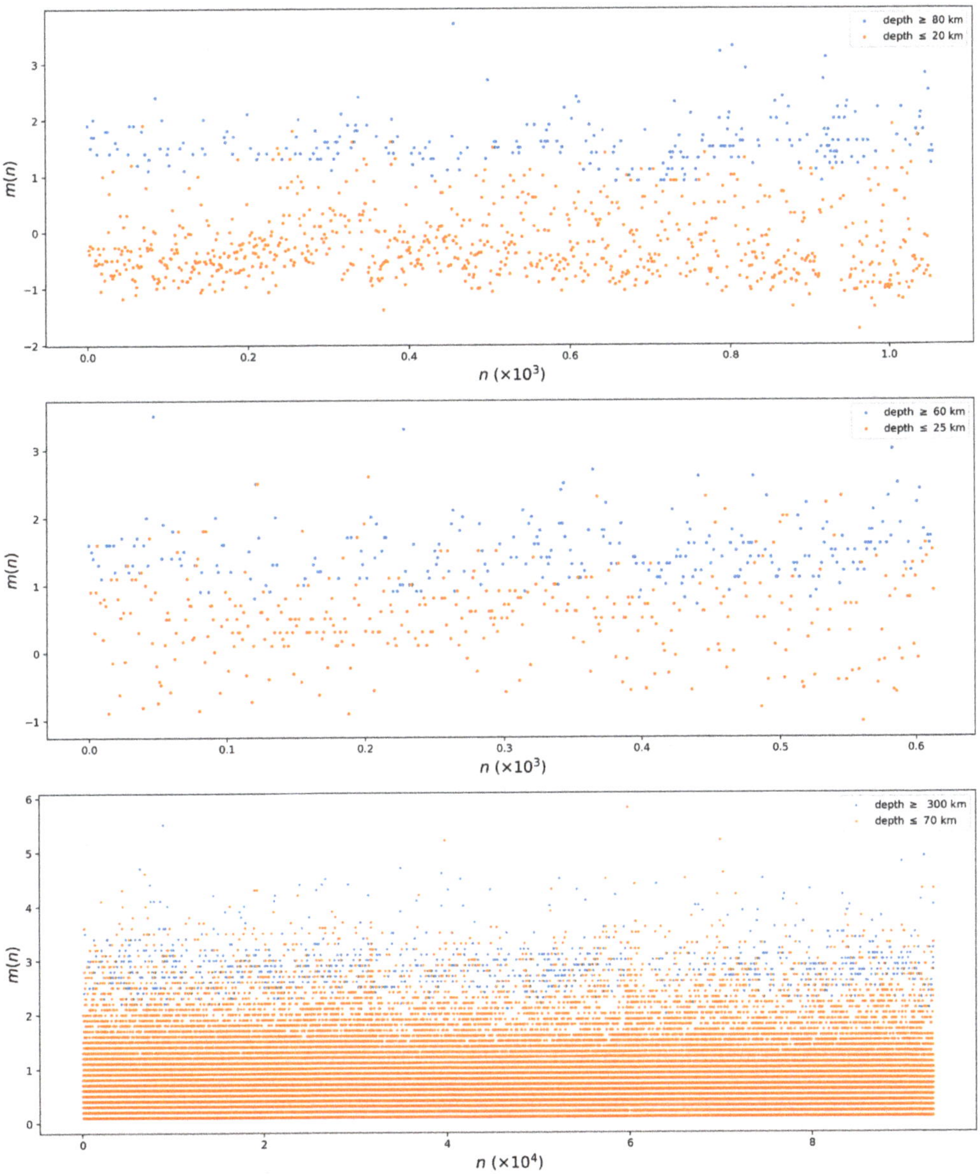

Figure 3. Earthquake time series. On the x-axis, n represents the number of events, ordered increasingly, and on the y-axis, $m(n)$ represents the magnitude of the event n. In the first, second, and third rows, we show the time series for the Redoubt, Spurr, and Kii regions, respectively. Shallow events are depicted in orange, and deep events are depicted in blue. Clearly, event magnitudes are generally larger for deep events than for shallow ones.

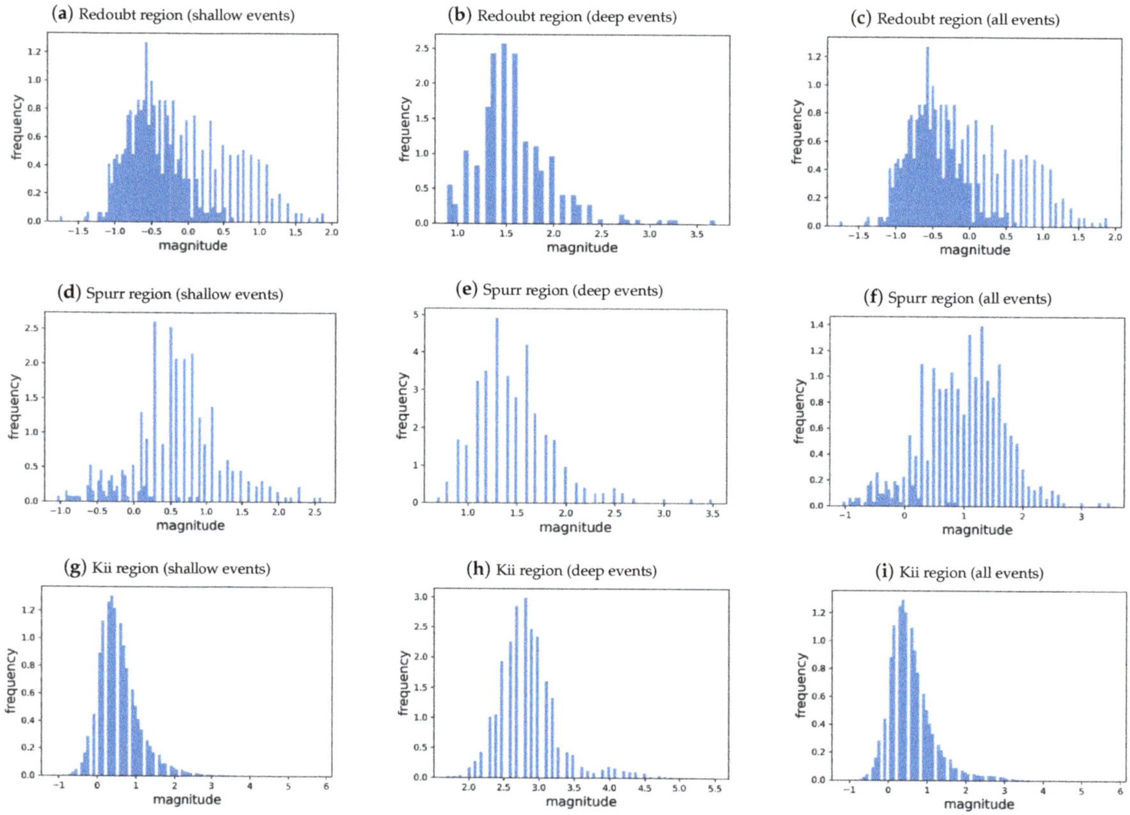

Figure 4. Histogram of the magnitudes of earthquakes. The x-axis represents the magnitude and the y-axis represents the frequency. In the first, second, and third rows, we show the histograms for the Redoubt, Spurr, and Kii regions, respectively. In the third column, the magnitude distributions for all events are shown. Histograms for shallow events are depicted in the first column, and histograms for deep events are shown in the second column.

4. Results

Before analyzing the portability of our proposed model, we examined the magnitude distributions for all seismic catalogs to explore the data consistency and completeness by determining the completeness magnitude. The completeness magnitude M_c is the minimum magnitude above which all earthquakes within a certain volume are reliably detected, avoiding inconsistency issues. Since space-differentiated earthquake clusters are present in the three regions studied in this work, we independently determined the completeness magnitude for each cluster using the method described in [54], which is based on the Maximum Curvature Method [58]. In each studied region, two clusters of earthquakes were observed: shallow events and deep ones. The completeness magnitude was determined for each cluster in a region, and the data were filtered, retaining the events whose magnitudes were above the M_c. We then obtained accurate measurements by combining the relevant data from each cluster [58]. The obtained completeness magnitudes are shown in Table 2. In this table, we observe that M_c for shallow events is less than M_c for deep quakes, which was expected because detection is more accurate for events that occur close to seismographs.

Table 2. Estimated completeness magnitudes for the three seismic areas.

Region \ Depth	Shallow	Deep
Redoubt	−0.6	1.45
Spurr	0.2	1.25
Kii	0.5	2.6

The fits of the FMD and the interevent distance and time distributions were performed using the curve_fit module in Python from the scipy.optimize package, employing the Trust Region Reflective algorithm. In addition, the confidence intervals for the estimated parameters were calculated using this function.

Figure 5 depicts the FMD as a function of the magnitudes for all regions examined. The dashed orange curve represents the best fit based on our proposed model, while the dots represent the data points. Based on a visual examination, we propose a multimodal model. The first, second, and third rows refer to the Mount Redoubt, Mount Spurr, and Kii Peninsula regions, respectively, while the first, second, and third columns correspond to shallow, deep, and all (shallow + deep) events. When examining shallow events, bimodal FMD distributions can be observed around the active volcano Mount Redoubt, but for the Mount Spurr and Kii regions, unimodal behavior of the FMD can be observed. For the Mount Redoubt region, note the high density and small α-value ($\alpha_1 = 0$) for tremors with a magnitude less than $M_T = 0.6$. and the low density and relatively large α-value ($\alpha_2 = 3.3307$) for events with a magnitude above $M_T = 0.6$. Thus, in the Mount Redoubt area, numerous low-energy events associated with swarms can be described by the first section of the SCP bimodal model. Similar behavior is observed for deep events in the three analyzed areas: the first section of the SCP bimodal distribution presents a relatively small α-value, which, in the classical SCP model, means low-energy events. In contrast, the second section exhibits a high α-value, which means high-energy events. Additionally, in the case of deep events, the α-values for the Redoubt and Spurr regions are significantly lower than the α-values corresponding to the Kii area, as expected, given that the earthquakes in the Alaskan regions are considerably smaller than those in the Kii Peninsula. We note that multimodal models arise from the presence of multiple sources of seismicity, such as anthropogenic and natural origins, or from sets of earthquakes with different characteristics (e.g., both deep and shallow earthquakes). However, our data also support the existence of multiple modes, even within sets of events that display a single characteristic. For example, the deep events shown in the second column of Figure 5 and the shallow events in the Redoubt area depicted in Figure 5a suggest that interactions between deep and shallow events can generate new modes within a set of events that otherwise share a common characteristic. This is reasonable because deep and shallow events are not independent earthquake sets.

Table 3 shows the errors of the unimodal and multimodal fits for the FMD curve. As can be seen, the fit for the multimodal models is tighter than that for the unimodal ones. Additionally, the standard error of each parameter is shown in this table.

Figure 6 depicts the interevent distance distributions, where the dashed orange curve represents the best fit, while the blue dots represent the data points. The first, second, and third rows correspond to the Mount Redoubt, Mount Spurr, and Kii Peninsula regions, respectively, while the first and second columns correspond to shallow and deep events, respectively. The results reveal that the interevent distances for shallow events present similar behavior for the Mount Redoubt and Spurr volcanic areas, while the curves for the three areas are similar when all events are considered, i.e., shallow and deep ones. When comparing Figure 6a,c, we observe that the interevent distance distribution initially exhibits a high slope, followed by a smaller slope. The α-values are similar, with an order of $\sim 10^{-1}$. Most q-values are less than one, which is usually observed in unimodal seismicity [33]. Nevertheless, for shallow events in the Kii peninsula, the behavior is different because distances less than $r_T = 23.9$ km are governed by an entropy index greater than one, while distances greater than r_T are described by a q-value less than one, as usual. The complex behavior of shallow quakes may result from the interaction between shallow and deep earthquakes. For deep events, the behavior of the interevent distance distribution is similar to the standard results found in the literature [33] for the three analyzed regions: the curves are well described by a unimodal or a bimodal Tsallis distribution, and the q-values are less than one.

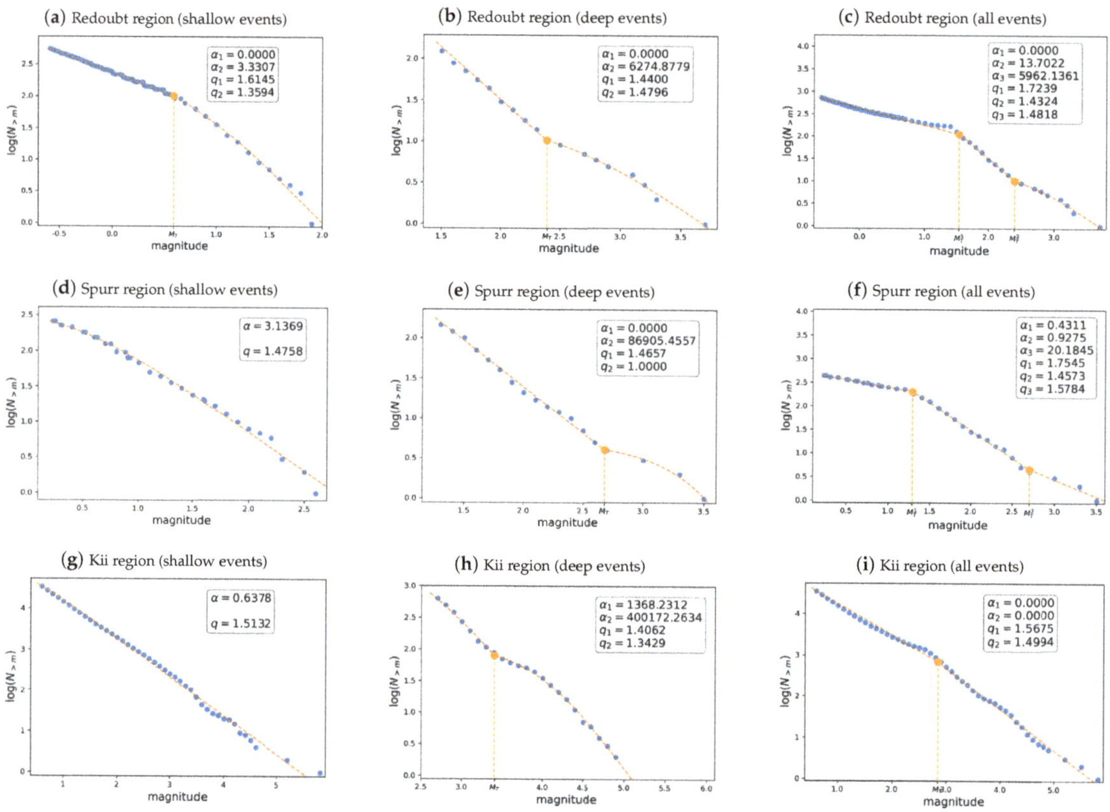

Figure 5. FMDs for the Redoubt, Spurr, and Kii regions. The first, second, and third columns correspond to shallow, deep, and all events. In each graphic, the empirical and multimodal SCP-fitted distributions are shown. The standard errors of the parameters are shown in Table 4. The main measures of goodness of fit are shown in Table 5, revealing very tight fits.

In Figure 7. we show the interevent distance distribution considering all events above $M_0 = M_c$, i.e., shallow and deep ones. A convex curve first appears in the distribution, followed by a plateau region and then a concave curve. The convex section corresponds to successive events that occur in the near field. The plateau section describes successive earthquakes occurring at different depths; that is, one is shallow and the other is deep, or both are at similar depths (i.e., both are shallow or both are deep). Note that the plateau section appears in the interval distances from 20 to 80 km, 20 to 60 km, and 60 to 300 km for the Redoubt, Spurr, and Kii regions, respectively. These intervals include the distances that separate the shallow and deep quakes, which are 60, 35, and 230 km for the Redoubt, Spurr, and Kii regions, respectively. The concave section represents successive earthquakes occurring at different depths because it starts at a distance greater than the maximum interevent distance for each cluster of earthquakes.

Table 3. Errors of the unimodal and multimodal fits for the F–M distribution. It can be observed from the root mean square error (RMSE), sum of squared errors (SSE), coefficient of determination (R^2), and mean absolute percentage error (MAPE) that, in all cases, the multimodal models fit more tightly than the unimodal ones.

Region	Events	Model	RMSE	SSE	R^2	MAPE (%)
Redoubt	All	Unimodal	0.0917	0.1223	0.9000	26.74
		Multimodal	0.0335	0.0167	0.9863	10.01
	Shallow	Unimodal	0.060	0.0507	0.9522	16.45
		Multimodal	0.0079	0.0010	0.9990	2.02
	Deep	Unimodal	0.0625	0.9265	0.9265	8.68
		Multimodal	0.0345	0.0133	0.9660	4.57
Spurr	All	Unimodal	0.0352	0.0167	0.9812	28.19
		Multimodal	0.0131	0.0021	0.9976	40.84
	Shallow	Unimodal	0.0218	0.0218	0.9944	42.94
		Multimodal	-	-	-	-
	Deep	Unimodal	0.0310	0.0310	0.0310	4.95
		Multimodal	0.0227	0.0056	0.9876	3.59
Kii	All	Unimodal	0.0452	0.0452	0.9511	4.34
		Multimodal	0.0203	0.0061	0.9907	1.83
	Shallow	Unimodal	0.0108	0.0018	0.9972	1.06
		Multimodal	-	-	-	-
	Deep	Unimodal	0.0360	0.0129	0.9762	3.31
		Multimodal	0.0134	0.0021	0.9960	1.95

Table 4. The standard deviations of the parameters shown in Figure 5.

Region	Events	σ_{α_1}	σ_{α_2}	σ_{α_3}	σ_{q_1} $\cdot 10^{-2}$	σ_{q_2} $\cdot 10^{-2}$	σ_{q_3} $\cdot 10^{-2}$	$\sigma_{M_T^1}$ $\cdot 10^{-2}$	$\sigma_{M_T^2}$ $\cdot 10^{-2}$
Redoubt	All	$1.25 \cdot 10^{-4}$	$3.61 \cdot 10$	$3.81 \cdot 10^3$	0.60	3.56	3.09	5.64	5.04
	Shallow	$6.74 \cdot 10^{-5}$	$7.51 \cdot 10^{-1}$	-	0.76	0.89	-	6.29	-
	Deep	$1.17 \cdot 10^{-2}$	$3.63 \cdot 10^3$	-	2.78	3.29	-	5.40	-
Spurr	All	3.04	3.97	$8.55 \cdot 10^3$	4.98	1.11	2.26	4.92	63.1
	Shallow	$5.90 \cdot 10^{-1}$	-	-	0.75	-	-	-	-
	Deep	$4.75 \cdot 10^{-3}$	0	-	1.24	0.027	-	3.31	-
Kii	All	$1.75 \cdot 10^{-3}$	$4.08 \cdot 10^{-1}$	-	1.14	0.78	-	29.5	-
	Shallow	$4.59 \cdot 10^{-1}$	-	-	0.35	-	-	-	-
	Deep	$1.17 \cdot 10^3$	$7.48 \cdot 10^4$	-	3.11	1.52	-	3.27	-

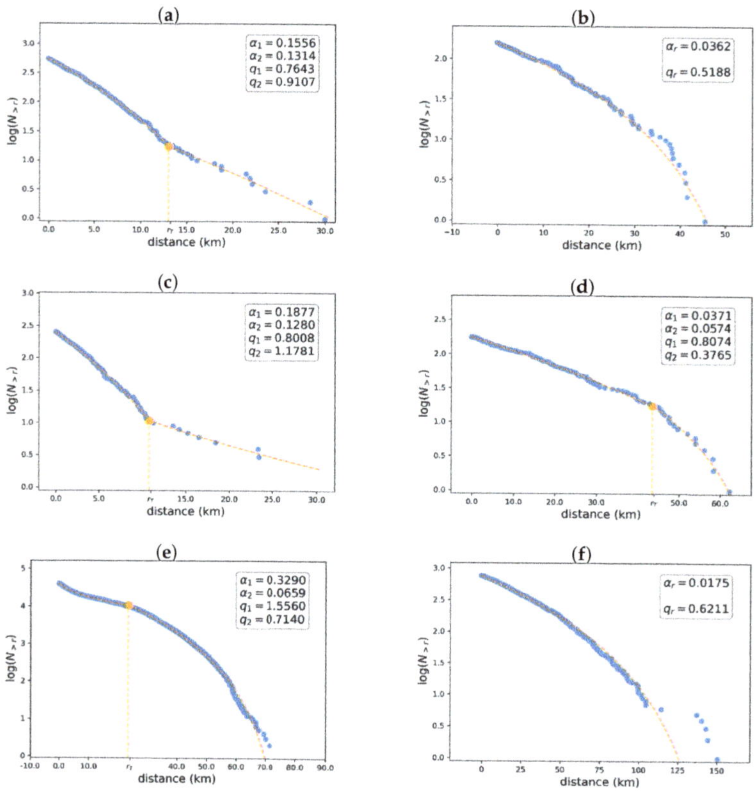

Figure 6. Interevent distance distributions. The first, second, and third rows correspond to the distributions for the Redoubt, Spurr, and Kii regions. In the first and second columns, the distributions for shallow and deep events are shown, respectively. The fitted curves are the unimodal and bimodal Tsallis distributions. The standard errors of the parameter are shown in Table 6. The main measures of goodness of fit are shown in Table 5, revealing very tight fits.

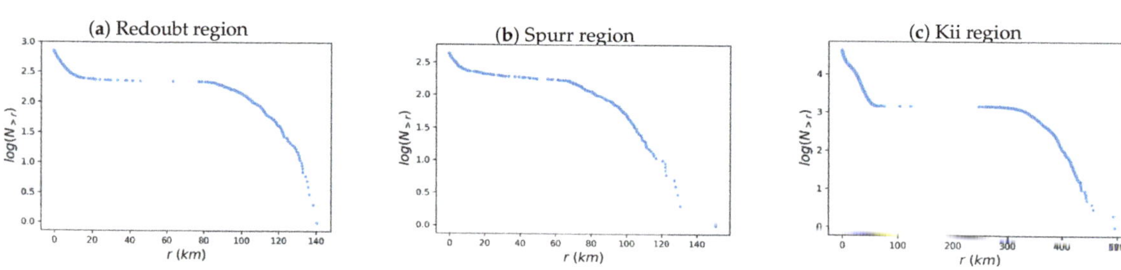

Figure 7. Interevent distance distributions considering all events (both shallow and deep ones) above the completeness magnitude. In (**a–c**), the distributions for the Redoubt, Spurr, and Kii regions are depicted.

Table 5. Errors of fits shown in Figures 6 and 8 for the interevent distances and times. It can be observed from the root mean square error (RMSE), sum of squared errors (SSE), coefficient of determination (R^2), and mean absolute percentage error (MAPE) the fits are very good.

Region	Events	Interevent	RMSE	SSE	R^2	MAPE (%)
Redoubt	All	Distances	-	-	-	-
		Times	0.0074	0.0024	0.9991	4.49
	Shallow	Distances	0.010	0.0045	0.9982	3.44
		Times	0.0088	0.0031	0.9987	5.48
	Deep	Distances	0.021	0.0083	0.9941	9.24
		Times	0.0155	0.0047	0.9966	7.52
Spurr	All	Distances	-	-	-	-
		Times	0.0101	0.0051	0.9977	6.78
	Shallow	Distances	0.0120	0.0043	0.9975	3.96
		Times	0.0845	0.1550	0.9138	19.36
	Deep	Distances	0.0182	0.0076	0.9948	6.10
		Times	0.0105	0.0025	0.9982	4.82
Kii	All	Distances	-	-	-	-
		Times	0.0193	0.1070	0.9938	6.64
	Shallow	Distances	0.0336	0.3859	0.9820	6.56
		Times	0.0203	0.1165	0.9932	6.96
	Deep	Distances	0.0136	0.0085	0.9972	7.44
		Times	0.0097	0.0048	0.9984	5.82

Table 6. The standard deviations of the parameters shown in Figure 6.

Region	Events	σ_{α_1} $\cdot 10^{-3}$	σ_{α_2} $\cdot 10^{-3}$	σ_{q_1} $\cdot 10^{-2}$	σ_{q_2} $\cdot 10^{-2}$	σ_{r_T} $\cdot 10^{-2}$
Redoubt	Shallow	1.00	7.67	0.43	3.01	7.64
	Deep	3.38	2.38	20.49	9.80	103.98
Spurr	Shallow	2.37	44.18	0.83	15.18	16.21
	Deep	1.14	7.28	2.28	9.91	103.83
Kii	Shallow	0.69	0.066	0.041	0.042	1.32
	Deep	0.10	4.02	0.48	51.28	46.55

Figure 8 depicts the interevent time distributions (waiting times) for all regions examined. The dashed orange curve represents the best fit, while the dots represent the data points. The standard deviations (measures of goodness) of the estimated parameters are summarized in Table 7. The first, second, and third rows refer to the Mount Redoubt, Mount Spurr, and Kii Peninsula regions, respectively, while the first, second, and third columns correspond to shallow, deep, and all (shallow + deep) events. We employed the q-gamma distribution to analyze the inter-occurrence times since it describes the behavior of inter-occurrence times well, as reported in [53]. This distribution is a generalization of the gamma distribution used by [59] for modeling interevent times. However, given that in the analyzed seismogenic areas, earthquakes are generated by several types of mechanisms represented by the different modes in the multimodal FMD, as previously discussed, we also expect to observe empirical multimodal distributions for the inter-occurrence time distributions. Thus, describing the interevent time distribution using the multimodal q-gamma distribution proposed in Section 2.3 is suitable. In this regard, we note that the q-values are generally greater than one, except for the Redoubt region when assessing the waiting times for shallow and deep earthquakes. In addition, the shape parameters have a similar order of magnitude for the volcanic areas, i.e., Mount Redoubt and Mount Spurr ($\sim 10^{-1}$). However, the Kii region's shape parameters are considerably greater (~ 10). Thus, the rate of events per unit of time in the Kii region is greater than that in volcanic areas. In other words, in the Kii Peninsula, waiting times are shorter than in the volcanic regions, possibly because the Kii region is larger and experiences more frequent earthquakes, as depicted in Figure 8i.

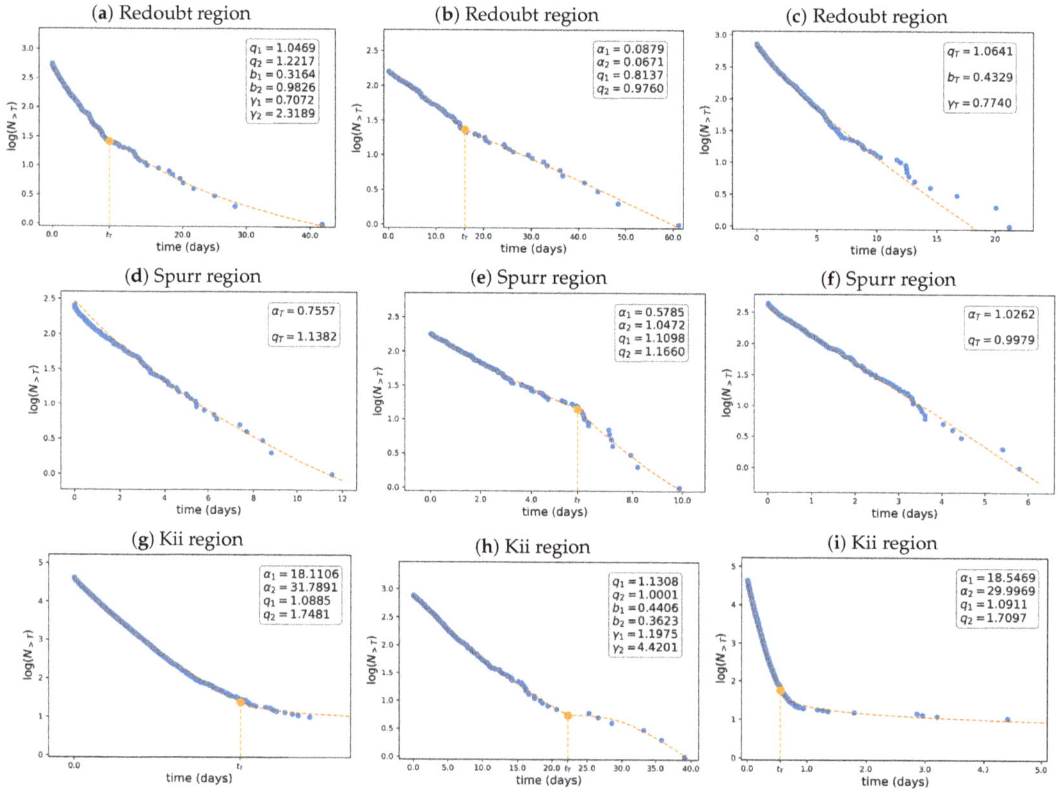

Figure 8. Interevent time distributions. The first, second, and third rows correspond to the waiting time distributions for the Redoubt, Spurr, and Kii regions, respectively. The distributions for shallow and deep events above $M_0 = M_c$ are depicted in the first and second columns, respectively. In the third column, the interevent time distributions for all events are depicted. In all cases, the unimodal-bimodal Tsallis distribution has been fitted, except in (**a**), which shows the distribution for shallow events in the Redoubt area, modeled by a unimodal q-gamma distribution; (**c**), which shows the interoccurrence times for all events occurring in the Redoubt area, modeled by the q-gamma bimodal distribution; and (**h**) which shows the interevent time distribution of deep quakes in the Kii area. The standard deviations of the estimated parameters are summarized in Table 7.

Table 7. The standard deviations of the parameters shown in Figure 8. The main measures of goodness of fit are shown in Table 5. The parameters corresponding to the fits by q-gamma distributions are not shown.

Region	Events	$\sigma_{\alpha_1} \cdot 10^{-3}$	$\sigma_{\alpha_2} \cdot 10^{-3}$	$\sigma_{q_1} \cdot 10^{-2}$	$\sigma_{q_2} \cdot 10^{-2}$	σ_{t_T}
Redoubt	Shallow	2.58	3.29	2.24	2.08	0.28
Spurr	All	10.57	-	0.37	-	-
	Shallow	20.21	-	0.80	-	-
	Deep	13.79	93.33	1.10	3.08	0.066
Kii	All	8.62	0.11	0.015	0.41	17.48
	Shallow	8.85	1.91	0.016	0.25	2.52

5. Conclusions

In this work, we proposed multimodal models in the context of non-extensive statistical mechanics to describe multi-source seismicity in terms of magnitude and spatial and temporal distribution. Our objective was to respond to the demand for new statistical models to describe multi-source seismicity, since classical models, which assume self-similarity, cannot fully explain this type of seismicity, which exhibits, at least, non-fractal behavior. Furthermore, our analysis of magnitude distributions revealed local behaviors that the Sotolongo–Costa Model, a generalization of the Gutenberg–Richter law that describes fractal phenomena, can interpret. We also observed evidence that earthquakes generated by a single source tend to present fractal behavior. Based on these considerations, we suggest that multi-source seismicity may exhibit multifractal behavior. However, this is a preliminary hypothesis that requires further investigation. Thus, provisionally, we assert that the observed behavior is at least non-fractal.

It is worth noting that the application of nonlinear and multifractal methods of analysis is of great benefit for understanding complex phenomena. For example, recent studies in mining have shown that acoustic and electromagnetic emissions in rock fractures exhibit multifractal properties and fracture propagation patterns similar to those in earthquakes. These analyses provide a refined understanding of fracture processes and fault propagation in rocks and provide indicators for predicting disasters in underground environments [60]. In addition, the use of variables such as seismic wave velocity and its gradient has been shown to be effective in detecting stress anomalies, which are essential for the assessment of risk areas [61]. Such approaches emphasize the relevance of nonlinear techniques and advanced statistical models that can provide a robust basis for monitoring seismic activity and complement traditional models, such as the Gutenberg–Richter Law, when dealing with the complexity inherent in seismological systems.

For the first time, a multimodal extension of the celebrated SCP model was applied to multi-source natural seismicity, surpassing the models found in the literature. In this context, the literature has explored the magnitude distribution in anthropogenic and natural multimodal seismicity, but there has been less focus on interevent distances and times. We found that behavior far from classical results was also observed for the interevent distance and time distributions, for which multimodal Tsallis and q-gamma distributions were successfully fitted. Real-world data analysis showed that our proposed model is workable. Further, our proposed model's outstanding agreement with field data highlights a new way to study Earth's seismicity, such as calculating earthquake recurrences. Additionally, multimodal models could be used to estimate seismic hazard, performing better than unimodal models, given that the fit of the former is tighter than that of the latter, especially for large quakes that can be underestimated or overestimated if unimodal models are employed.

In particular, the use of a multimodal model is relevant when determining the magnitude of completeness; this is because using a unimodal distribution generates inadequate values for the magnitude of completeness. Indeed, the proposed multimodal distribution, like the GR law, can help in seismic risk assessment and emergency response planning, among other applications, by more accurately estimating the expected frequency–magnitude of earthquakes, providing insights into the probability of specific magnitudes occurring. In addition, a more accurate earthquake magnitude frequency law contributes to seismic monitoring and early warning systems. Finally, this work can be complemented by future research considering earthquake source theory to improve the understanding of the various sources and their interactions. In addition, in volcanic areas, future studies should focus on the spatial delimitation between seismic sources near volcanoes (affected by magma) and the adjacent shallow crust (unaffected by magma). A detailed analysis based on focal mechanisms, for instance, would be essential to more accurately distinguish these sources, enhancing interpretation and seismic characterization at higher resolution.

Author Contributions: Conceptualization, E.d.l.B., P.V.-J. and S.L.E.F.d.S.; methodology, E.d.l.B., P.V.-J. and S.L.E.F.d.S.; software, E.d.l.B.; validation, E.d.l.B., P.V.-J. and S.L.E.F.d.S.; formal analysis, E.d.l.B., P.V.-J. and S.L.E.F.d.S.; investigation, E.d.l.B., P.V.-J. and S.L.E.F.d.S.; data curation, E.d.l.B.; writing—original draft preparation, E.d.l.B., P.V.-J. and S.L.E.F.d.S.; writing—review and editing, E.d.l.B., P.V.-J. and S.L.E.F.d.S.; visualization, E.d.l.B. All authors have read and agreed to the published version of the manuscript.

Funding: This research received no external funding.

Data Availability Statement: The data supporting the findings of this study are available from the corresponding author upon reasonable request.

Conflicts of Interest: The authors declare no conflict of interest.

References

1. Talwani, P. *Unified Model for Intraplate Earthquakes, in Intraplate Earthquakes*; Talwani, P., Ed.; Cambridge University Press: Cambridge, UK, 2014; pp. 275–302.
2. da Silva, S.L.E.F.; Julia, J.; Hilario, F. Deviatoric Moment Tensor Solutions from Spectral Amplitudes in Surface Network Recordings: Case Study in São Caetano, Pernambuco, Brazil. *Bull. Seismol. Soc. Am.* **2017**, *107*, 1495–1511. [CrossRef]
3. Frohlich, C.; Apperson, K.D. Earthquake focal mechanisms, moment tensors, and the consistency of seismic activity near plate boundaries. *Tectonics* **1992**, *11*, 279–296. [CrossRef]
4. Subarya, C.; Chlieh, M.; Prawirodirdjo, L.; Avouac, J.P.; Bock, Y.; Sieh, K.; Meltzner, A.J.; Natawidjaja, D.H.; McCaffrey, R. Plate-boundary deformation associated with the great Sumatra-Andaman earthquake. *Nature* **2006**, *406*, 46–51. [CrossRef] [PubMed]
5. Kasahara, J. Tides, Earthquakes, and Volcanoes. *Science* **2002**, *297*, 348–349. [CrossRef]
6. Gates, A.E.; Ritchie, D. *Encyclopedia of Earthquakes and Volcanoes*; Infobase Publishing: New York, NY, USA, 2006.
7. Gutenberg, B.; Richter, C.F. Frequency of earthquakes in California. *Bull. Seismol. Soc. Am.* **1944**, *34*, 185–188. [CrossRef]
8. Gutenberg, B.; Richter, C.F. The frequency-magnitude relation of microfracturing in rock and its relation to earthquakes. *Bull. Seismol. Soc. Am.* **1944**, *58*, 399–415.
9. Warren, N.W.; Latham, G.V. An experimental study of thermally induced microfracturing and its relation to volcanic seismicity. *J. Geophys. Res.* **1970**, *75*, 4455–4464. [CrossRef]
10. Wyss, M. Towards a Physical Understanding of the Earthquake Frequency Distribution. *Geophys. J. R. Astron. Soc.* **1973**, *31*, 341–359. [CrossRef]
11. Mogi, K. Fracture and flow of rocks. *Tectonophysics* **1972**, *13*, 541–568. [CrossRef]
12. da Silva, S.L.E.F. κ-generalised Gutenberg-Richter law and the self-similarity of earthquakes. *Chaos Solitons Fractals* **2021**, *143*, 110622. [CrossRef]
13. Aki, K. Magnitude-frequency relation for small earthquakes. A clue to the origin of f_{max} of large earthquakes. *J. Geophys. Res. Solid Earth* **1987**, *92*, 1349–1355. [CrossRef]
14. Finnie, G. Using Neural Networks to Discriminate between Genuine and Spurious Seismic Events in Mines. *Pure Appl. Geophys.* **1999**, *154*, 41–56. [CrossRef]
15. Zielke, O.; Arrowsmith, J.R. Depth variation of coseismic stress drop explains bimodal earthquake magnitude-frequency distribution. *Geophys. Res. Lett.* **2008**, *35*, L24301. [CrossRef]
16. Nemati, M. Seismotectonic and seismicity of Makran, a bimodal subduction zone, SE Iran. *J. Asian Earth Sci.* **2019**, *169*, 139–161. [CrossRef]
17. Sawaki, Y.; Ito, Y.; Ohta, K.; Shibutani, T.; Iwata, T. Seismological structures on bimodal distribution of deep tectonic tremor. *Geophys. Res. Lett.* **2021**, *48*, e2020GL092183. [CrossRef]
18. Gibowicz, S.J.; Kijko, A.; Dmowska, R. *An Introduction to Mining Seismology*; Elsevier Science: Amsterdam, The Netherlands, 2013.

19. Pandey, M.R.; Tandukar, R.P.; Avouac, J.; Lavé, J.P.; Massot, J.P. Interseismic strain accumulation on the Himalayan crustal ramp (Nepal). *Geophys. Res. Lett.* **1995**, *22*, 751–754. [CrossRef]
20. Dal Zilio, L.; van Dinther, Y.; Gerya, T.; Avouac, J.P. Bimodal seismicity in the Himalaya controlled by fault friction and geometry. *Nat. Commun.* **2019**, *10*, 1–11. [CrossRef]
21. Bowman, D.D.; Ouillon, G.; Sammis, C.G.; Sornette, A.; Sornette D. An observational test of the critical earthquake concept. *J. Geophys. Res. Solid Earth* **1998**, *103*, 24359–24372. [CrossRef]
22. Main, I.G.; Al-Kindy, F.H. Entropy, energy, and proximity to criticality in global earthquake populations. *Geophys. Res. Lett.* **2002**, *29*, 25-1–25-4. [CrossRef]
23. De Santis, A.; Cianchini, G.; Favali, P.; Beranzoli, L.; Boschi, E. The Gutenberg-Richter law and entropy of earthquakes: Two case studies in Central Italy. *Bull. Seismol. Soc. Am.* **2011**, *101*, 1386–1395. [CrossRef]
24. Tsallis, C. Possible generalization of Boltzmann-Gibbs statistics. *J. Stat. Phys.* **1988**, *52*, 479–487. [CrossRef]
25. Tsallis, C. *Introduction to Nonextensive Statistical Mechanics: Approaching a Complex World*, 1st ed.; Springer: New York, NY, USA, 2009; XVIII, p. 382. [CrossRef]
26. Tsallis, C. Entropy. *Encyclopedia* **2022**, *2*, 264–300. [CrossRef]
27. Sotolongo-Costa, O.; Posadas, A. Fragment-asperity interaction model for earthquakes. *Phys. Rev. Lett.* **2004**, *92*, 048501. [CrossRef] [PubMed]
28. Sotolongo-Costa, O. Non-extensive framework for earthquakes: The role of fragments. *Acta Geophys.* **2012**, *60*, 526–534. [CrossRef]
29. Posadas, A.; Sotolongo-Costa, O. Non-extensive entropy and fragment-asperity interaction model for earthquakes. *Commun. Nonlinear Sci. Numer. Simul.* **2023**, *117*, 106906. [CrossRef]
30. Lay, T.; Wallace, T.C. *Modern Global Seismology*; Academic Press: New York, NY, USA, 1995.
31. Silva, R.; Franca, G.S.; Vilar, C.S.; Alcaniz, J.S. Nonextensive models for earthquakes. *Phys. Rev. E* **2006**, *73*, 026102. [CrossRef]
32. Telesca, L. Analysis of Italian seismicity by using a nonextensive approach. *Tectonophysics* **2010**, *494*, 155–162. [CrossRef]
33. Vallianatos, F.; Papadakis, G.; Michas, G. Generalized statistical mechanics approaches to earthquakes and tectonics. *Proc. R. Soc. A Math. Phys. Eng. Sci.* **2016**, *472*, 20160497. [CrossRef]
34. Michas, G.; Vallianatos, F.; Sammonds, P. Non-extensivity and long-range correlations in the earthquake activity at the West Corinth rift (Greece). *Nonlinear Process. Geophys.* **2013**, *20*, 713–724. [CrossRef]
35. da Silva, S.L.E.F.; Corso, G. Nonextensive Gutenberg-Richter law and the connection between earthquakes and marsquakes. *Eur. Phys. J. B* **2021**, *94*, 25. [CrossRef]
36. Rotondi, R.; Bressan, G.; Varini, E. Analysis of temporal variations of seismicity through non-extensive statistical physics. *Geophys. J. Int.* **2022**, *230*, 1318–1337. [CrossRef]
37. Vega-Jorquera, P.; de la Barra, E.; da Silva, S.L.E. Antropogenic seismicity and the breakdown of the self-similarity described by nonextensive models. *Phys. A Stat. Mech. Its Appl.* **2023**, *617*, 128690. [CrossRef]
38. Abe, S.; Bagci, G.B. Necessity of q-expectation value in nonextensive statistical mechanics. *Phys. Rev. E* **2005**, *71*, 016139. [CrossRef]
39. Beck, C.; Schlogl, F. *Thermodynamics of Chaotic Systems: An Introduction*, 1st ed.; Cambridge University Press: Cambridge, UK, 1993.
40. Abe, S. Remark on the escort distribution representation of nonextensive statistical mechanics. *Phys. Lett. A* **2000**, *275*, 250–253. [CrossRef]
41. Tanaka, M. Meaning of an escort distribution and τ-transformation. *J. Phys. Conf. Ser.* **2010**, *201*, 012007. [CrossRef]
42. da Silva, S.L.E.F.; da Costa, C.A.N.; Carvalho, P.T.C.; de Araújo, J.M.; dos Santos Lucena, L.; Corso, G. Robust full-waveform inversion using q-statistics. *Phys. A Stat. Mech. Its Appl.* **2020**, *548*, 124473. [CrossRef]
43. de Lima, I.P.; da Silva, S.L.E.F.; Corso, G.; de Araújo, J.M. Tsallis Entropy, Likelihood, and the Robust Seismic Inversion. *Entropy* **2020**, *22*, 464. [CrossRef] [PubMed]
44. Bercher, J.-F. On escort distributions, q-gaussians and Fisher information. *AIP Conf. Proc.* **2011**, *1305*, 208–215.
45. Matsuzoe, H. A Sequence of Escort Distributions and Generalizations of Expectations on q-Exponential Family. *Entropy* **2017**, *19*, 7. [CrossRef]
46. Tsallis, C.; Plastino, A.R.; Alvarez-Estrada, R.F. Escort mean values and the characterization of power-law-decaying probability densities. *J. Math. Phys.* **2009**, *50*, 043303. [CrossRef]
47. Darooneh, A.H.; Naeimi, G.; Mehri, A.; Sadeghi, P. Tsallis Entropy, Escort Probability and the Incomplete Information Theory. *Entropy* **2010**, *12*, 2497–2503. [CrossRef]
48. Ilić, V.M.; Scarfone, A.M.; Wada, T. Equivalence between four versions of thermostatistics based on strongly pseudoadditive entropies. *Phys. Rev. E* **2019**, *100*, 062135. [CrossRef] [PubMed]
49. Kalogeropoulos, N. On the origin of escort distributions for q-entropies. *arXiv* **2024**, arXiv:2407.07499.
50. Telesca, L. Maximum Likelihood Estimation of the Nonextensive Parameters of the Earthquake Cumulative Magnitude Distribution. *Bull. Seismol. Soc. Am.* **2012**, *102*, 886. [CrossRef]
51. Briggs, K.; Beck, C. Modelling train delays with q-exponential functions. *Phys. A Stat. Mech. Its Appl.* **2007**, *378*, 498–504. [CrossRef]
52. Hainzl, S.; Scherbaum, F.; Beauval, C. Estimating background activity based on interevent-time distribution. *Bull. Seismol. Soc. Am.* **2006**, *96*, 313–320. [CrossRef]

53. Michas, G.; Vallianatos, F. Stochastic modeling of nonstationary earthquake time series with long-term clustering effects. *Phys. Rev. E* **2018**, *98*, 042107. [CrossRef]
54. Vega-Jorquera, P.; De la Barra, E.; Torres, H.; Vásquez, Y. Statistical Modeling of the Seismic Moments via Mathai Distribution. *Entropy* **2022**, *24*, 695. [CrossRef]
55. Wiemer, S.; Benoit, J.P. Mapping the b-value anomaly at 100 km depth in the Alaska and New Zealand subduction zones. *Geophys. Res. Lett.* **1996**, *23*, 1557–1560. [CrossRef]
56. Salah, M.K.; Zhao, D. 3-D seismic structure of Kii Peninsula in southwest Japan: evidence for slab dehydration in the forearc. *Tectonophysics* **2003**, *364*, 191–213. [CrossRef]
57. Takemura, S.; Obara, K.; Shiomi, K.; Baba, S. Spatiotemporal variations of shallow very low frequency earthquake activity southeast off the Kii Peninsula, along the Nankai Trough, Japan. *J. Geophys. Res. Solid Earth* **2022**, *127*, e2021JB023073. [CrossRef]
58. Wiemer, S.; Wyss, M. Minimum magnitude of completeness in earthquake catalogs: Examples from Alaska, the western United States, and Japan. *Bull. Seismol. Soc. Am.* **2000**, *90*, 859–869. [CrossRef]
59. Corral, Á. Long-term clustering, scaling, and universality in the temporal occurrence of earthquakes. *Phys. Rev. Lett.* **2004**, *92*, 108501. [CrossRef] [PubMed]
60. Qiu, L.; Zhu, Y.; Song, D.; He, X.; Wang, W.; Liu, Y.; Xiao, Y.; Wei, M.; Yin, S.; Liu, Q. Study on the Nonlinear Characteristics of EMR and AE during Coal Splitting Tests. *Minerals* **2022**, *12*, 108. [CrossRef]
61. Qiu, L.; Zhu, Y.; Liu, Q.; Guo, M.; Song, D.; Wang, A. Response law and indicator selection of seismic wave velocity for coal seam outburst risk. *Adv.-Geo-Energy Res.* **2022**, *9*, 198–210. [CrossRef]

Disclaimer/Publisher's Note: The statements, opinions and data contained in all publications are solely those of the individual author(s) and contributor(s) and not of MDPI and/or the editor(s). MDPI and/or the editor(s) disclaim responsibility for any injury to people or property resulting from any ideas, methods, instructions or products referred to in the content.

entropy

MDPI

Article

Relationship Between the 2019 Ridgecrest, California, M_W7.1 Earthquake and Its M_W6.4 Foreshock Sequence

Jianchang Zheng [1,2,*], Zhengshuai Zhang [2] and Xiaohan Li [2]

[1] Department of Mathematics and Statistics, University of Otago, Dunedin 9054, New Zealand
[2] Shandong Earthquake Agency, China Earthquake Administration, Jinan 250102, China; zzs@cumt.edu.cn (Z.Z.); byfeiyu@mail.ustc.edu.cn (X.L.)
* Correspondence: zjcmail@yeah.net

Abstract: The 2019 Ridgecrest M_W7.1 earthquake has received significant attention due to its complex fault activity. It is also noticeable for its M_W6.4 foreshock sequence. There are intricate dynamic relationships between earthquakes in such vigorous sequences. Based on the relocated catalogue, we adopt the nearest neighbour algorithm to analyze its foreshock and aftershock sequences. Detailed links and family structures of the sequence are obtained. The results show that a M_W5.0 event at 03:16 (UTC) on 6 July is a direct foreshock of the M_W7.1 mainshock. It is likely related to barriers on the northwest-striking fault. The M_W6.4 event on 4 July is characterized as a complex conjugate rupture. Notably, a magnitude 4.0 event occurred on the northwest-striking fault before the M_W6.4 event, establishing it as a direct foreshock. The Ridgecrest sequence is predominantly influenced by northwest fault activity. It first caused small fractures on the northwest-striking fault. Then, it triggered conjugate slips on the southwest-striking fault. Lastly, it led to larger ruptures on the northwest-striking fault.

Keywords: earthquake clusters; foreshock; aftershocks; earthquake sequence; statistical seismology

1. Introduction

The pattern and frequency of earthquake sequences can vary based on the tectonic settings, the size of the mainshock, and the characteristics of the fault system involved. Understanding earthquake sequences is important for assessing seismic hazards and preparing for potential future events. The July 2019 Ridgecrest M_W7.1 earthquake in Southern California initiated a unique sequence, resulting in numerous aftershocks as well as notable foreshocks, which highlights the intricate rupture process along conjugate structures [1–3].

Similarly to other large earthquakes (e.g., 2010 Yushu M_W7.1 [4], 2011 Tohoku M_W9.0 [5], and 2014 Chile M8.1 [6]), 2019 Ridgecrest M_W7.1 had a foreshock with M_W6.4 [7]. Foreshocks have always been the focus of seismologists, but they are still an ambiguous concept without an accurate definition [8,9]. Research into foreshocks and their role in rupture history can help us to make progress in earthquake prediction [10–12], to analyze the triggering process [13–15], and to understand the implications for earthquake nucleation [16–20].

There are many works that have studied the relationship between the mainshock and the foreshock. Researchers hope to approach earthquake forecasting through the statistical characterization of foreshocks [21]; Helmstetter et al. [22] suggest that mainshocks are aftershocks of conditional foreshocks; and Lippiello et al. [23] discuss the relevance of foreshocks in the triggering of earthquakes from a statistical viewpoint. Petrillo et al. [24] investigate the influence of the brittle–ductile transition zone on aftershock and foreshock occurrence.

Research on foreshocks is topical, especially with new technologies. For example, using the same high-resolution seismic catalog enhanced by the template matching technique, Trugman and Ross [25] suggest that foreshocks existed in 72% of the mainshocks in Southern California, whereas van den Ende and Ampuero [26] argue that this value should be less than 18%. Moutote et al. [27] use the ETAS model and find that 10/53 mainshocks were preceded by significant foreshocks in the same area. Wetzler et al. [28] systematically examine foreshocks via different approaches.

The 2019 Ridgecrest M_W7.1 earthquake sequence provides great opportunities to study foreshocks. In this paper, we focus on the relationship between the foreshock sequence and the 2019 Ridgecrest M_W7.1 mainshock. Based on the relocated catalogs, we apply the nearest neighbor distance algorithm to analyze the intrinsic spatiotemporal structure of this significant foreshock sequence. This algorithm is widely used and has proven effective in clustering analysis for earthquakes. We also examine its statistical features. This work might help us to understand the complex dynamic relationships in earthquake sequences and provide some clues and insights into the related focus mechanisms.

2. Theories and Methods

There are many cluster analysis methods in seismology [29–34]. To study the Ridgecrest sequence, we adopted the so-called "nearest neighbor distance" (NN) method [35], which was developed in recent years [36–38].

A more complex approach to distinguishing clustering events from background events involves assigning a generalized distance between the shocks. The subjective aspect in this process involves choosing a formula for distance and a threshold to define independent events. Usually, the distances in the time, space, and energy domains are considered separately. The challenge is how to put them all together with more physical meanings. The NN algorithm proposed by Zaliapin et al. [36] comprehensively considers the distribution of earthquakes in the space, time, and energy domains. It also provides a normalized parameter that makes the complex N-dimensional problem easier to handle. Based on this defined distance, we can examine the relationship between any two earthquakes and distinguish clustering events from background earthquakes.

The application of this method in various regions worldwide has demonstrated its effectiveness, e.g., Moradpour et al. [39] in Southern California, Peresan and Gentili [40] in Italy, Bayliss et al. [41] in Japan and New Zealand, Martínez-Garzón et al. [42] in Turkey, and Zaliapin and Ben-Zion [43] for the whole world.

A brief description of the NN algorithm is given below. Each event in the catalog is characterized by 5 numbers: $\{t, \lambda, \phi, h, m\}$ (time, latitude, longitude, depth, magnitude). For a given earthquake catalogue $\{t_i, \lambda_i, \phi_i, h_i, m_i\}, i = 1, \cdots, N$, the asymmetric distance n_{ij} from the event $\{t_j, \lambda_j, \phi_j, h_j, m_j\}$ to another event $\{t_i, \lambda_i, \phi_i, h_i, m_i\}$ is defined by the following formula [36]:

$$n_{ij} = \begin{cases} c\tau_{ij} r_{ij}^d 10^{-b(m_i - m_0)} & \tau_{ij} \geq 0 \\ \infty & \tau_{ij} < 0' \end{cases} \quad (1)$$

where $\tau_{ij} = t_j - t_i$, r_{ij} is the geographical distance between two events, m_0 is the magnitude of the lower threshold of the catalog, c is the constant coefficient, d is the fractal dimension of earthquake epicenters, and b is the exponent in the Gutenberg–Richter (GR) law.

Each event $\{t_i, \lambda_i, \phi_i, h_i, m_i\}$ (except for the first event in the catalog) has one closest "ancestor"—that is, among the preceding events, the one that is the shortest distance away from it. This is called its nearest neighbor. The minimum distance to the nearest neighbor is

$$\eta_j^* = \min_i n_{ij}, \tag{2}$$

We performed some numerical tests for synthetized and real catalogs, and the results proved that the NN algorithm can distinguish clustering events from background activities more physically [44]. Based on the nearest neighbor distances of events, we can classify the type of events in the whole sequence—statistically, foreshocks, mainshocks, and aftershocks.

It is possible to further define the temporal and spatial components of the magnitude-normalized NN distance [36]:

$$T_{ij} = \tau_{ij} 10^{-bm_i/2},\ R_{ij} = r_{ij}^d 10^{-bm_i/2}, \tag{3}$$

and $n = TR$ (without loss of generality, it is assumed here that $c = 1, m_0 = 0$). We therefore can analyze spatiotemporal features via distribution plots of T and R. Two-dimensional images always provide more details than 1D images, and therefore we can obtain some additional statistical information, as discussed by Li et al. [45]. This can be helpful for further analysis (see Figure 1c in this paper or, for example, Figure 4 in [37,43] and Figures 2 and 4 in [44]).

Previous works usually used images for simple statistical or qualitative evaluation, and lacked further quantitative analysis. Since the bimodal distribution of nearest neighbor distances has been confirmed by many researchers, Peresan and Gentili [40] estimated Gaussian densities for clustered and background components, and Bayliss et al. [41] applied the Markov chain Monte Carlo approach to build normal mixture models. In addition, we also used a Gaussian mixture model to fit 2D and 1D distributions [44]. Assuming that clustering and background earthquakes both satisfy the Poisson process with different parameters, we can transform the 2D superimposed Poisson process into a 1D mixture density function referring to the concept of the N-th order distance. We define the mixture density function for the nearest neighbor distance η^* as

$$PDF = \omega_1 \cdot pdf_1 + \omega_2 \cdot pdf_2 \tag{4}$$

where pdf_1 and pdf_2 are probability density functions of clustering and background events, respectively, both for a normal distribution, while ω_1 and ω_2 are proportionality coefficients, which satisfy $\omega_1 + \omega_2 = 1$. When we calculate the nearest neighbor distances η^* for a catalog, we can fit its probability distribution according to Formula (4). Then, we can distinguish clustering events from background activities.

3. Data and Study Area

At 3:19 (UTC, the same below) on 6 July 2019, an M_W7.1 earthquake occurred in the desert about 10 km northeast of Ridgecrest, Southern California, while a M_W6.4 foreshock occurred near the epicenter about 34 h before this earthquake, that is, at 17:33 on 4 July 2019. The M_W7.1 mainshock occurred in the NW–SE-trending fault zone with a dextral strike-slip trend, while the M_W6.4 foreshock occurred in the NE–SW-trending fault. The aftershocks of the M_W7.1 mainshock spread in the NW–SE direction, extending northward to China Lake and southeastward to the Garlock fault, but did not cross this fault. The mainshock was followed by more than 100,000 aftershocks. This Ridgecrest earthquake sequence was systematically observed and well documented due to the high density of instruments in California [1].

The epicenter of this earthquake was located in the Eastern California Shear Zone (ECSZ), about 150 km northeast of the San Andres Fault and about 12 km southwest of the Searles Valley in California (Figure 1a). The Eastern California Shear Zone is a seismically active region characterized by strike-slip faults, with a historical record of numerous earthquakes exceeding magnitude 7, including the Landers M_W7.1 earthquake in 1992 and the Hector Mine M_W7.1 earthquake in 1999. However, since 2000, the seismic activities in this area have been mainly composed of small and medium-scale events (only 3 events with $M \geq 5.0$).

The catalog before July 2019 is from the Southern California Seismic Network (SCSN), which is available online (https://scedc.caltech.edu/eq-catalogs/index.html, accessed on 30 October 2024). Figure 1b gives the frequency–magnitude distributions and their fitted lines, (b-1) for this catalog and (b-2) for the Ridgecrest sequence. In the first half of 2019, there were about 690 events with $M \geq 1.0$ recorded by SCSN, and the average $b = 1.118$. The higher b-value we obtained is close to the previous estimate for seismicity in the Coso Range (0.99 ± 0.08, from [46]). The lowest magnitude of completeness in this area then can be derived from the fitted line, $Mc \approx 1.5$. We then selected $M \geq 1.5$ events from the catalog and applied the NN algorithm to study its clustering features. The bimodal distribution of nearest neighbor distances is clearly shown in Figure 1c. The horizontal spreading part is for clustering events, and the skewed part on the upper right panel is for background events. The histogram and its fitted probability density function (PDF) in Figure 1d confirm the bimodal distribution. We can derive from the fitted result that $\omega_1 = 0.534$ and $\omega_2 = 0.466$, implying a higher clustering events ratio in regional seismic activities. As mentioned previously, the local seismicities in the Coso area are mainly characterized by sequences and small swarms [46]. The clustering events are independent of background events, this is in agreement with previous studies [47,48]. Here, we give the intersection point of the two PDFs, $Jx = -2.328$—that is to say, the probability for an event to be background or belong to clusters at this point is equivalent. If the nearest neighbour distance η^* of any event is smaller than Jx, the event is more likely to be clustered.

The accurate location of earthquakes is helpful for depicting the spatial and temporal distribution images in more detail for earthquakes in the source area and determining the spatial distribution of seismic faults [49]. By using data from densely deployed arrays and the Southern California Seismic Network (SCSN), White et al. [49] derived a more precise earthquake catalogue for the 2019 M_w 6.4 and M_w7.1 Ridgecrest earthquake sequence. We use this catalogue in our study for further nearest neighbor analysis. We analyze the temporal and spatial distribution characteristics of the hypocenters and discuss the intrinsic relationship among events in this sequence.

Based on White et al.'s catalog [49], we selected the events within the red rectangle in Figure 1a for our next analysis. The clusters that occurred in Garlock stepover, as well as in Coso geothermal field and Cactus Flats (see in Figure 1a), which were clearly identified as induced activities (as studied in many papers, e.g., [2,50]), were not included in the sequence. We first determined the lowest magnitude of completeness Mc of the sequence based on the GR relationship. Figure 1b shows the results of the least square method: the b-value of the Ridgecrest sequence is about 0.826, and the approximate magnitude of completeness $Mc \approx 1.5$. However, it is obvious from the fitting result in Figure 1(b-2) that the linear relationship does not match the data well. The reason for this situation, as shown in Figure 2 (and also analyzed in [1]), would be that small-magnitude events following a large earthquake are missing at the very beginning point, even when the template matching technique is performed. We thus selected events with $M \geq 2.0$ for subsequent calculations, just like the criteria in Hardebeck's study [2]. In order to reduce the amount of computation, we chose 7 days of data after the mainshock for nearest neighbor calculation, referring to Chen's study [51].

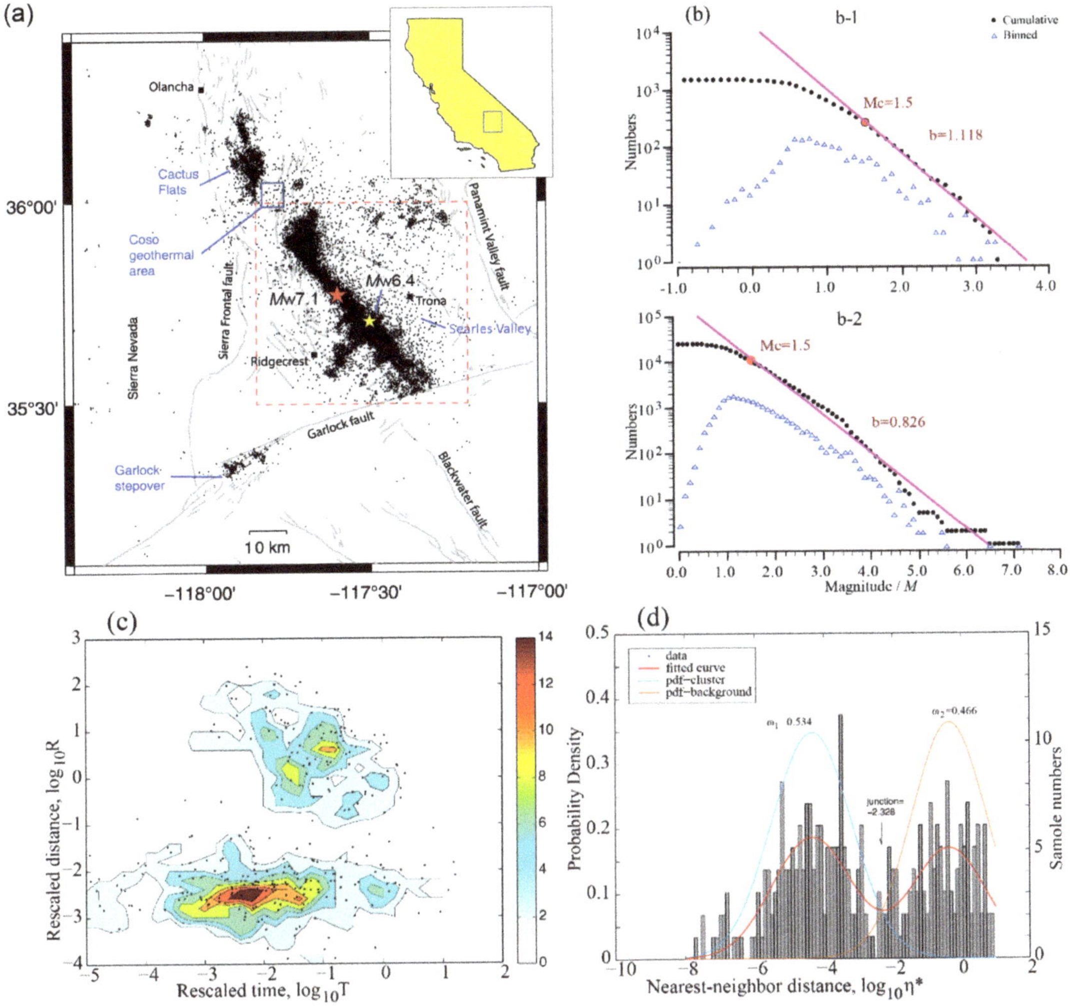

Figure 1. (**a**) Distribution map of the 2019 Ridgecrest sequence and regional seismic activities. The dashed red rectangle denotes the select range of the Ridgecrest sequence, which is studied next in this paper. Events that occurred in Cactus Flats and the Coso geothermal area are not included in the sequence, mainly because the activities in these areas have been proven to be non-tectonic earthquakes. (**b**) The Gutenberg–Richter (GR) relationship for (**b-1**) regional activities in the first half of 2019 and (**b-2**) the 2019 Ridgecrest sequence. Solid purple lines show the fitting results. (**c**,**d**) Results of the NN algorithm for the catalog of (**b-1**): (**c**) 2D distribution and density contours of re-scaled time (tj) and re-scaled distance (rj) components; (**d**) histogram of re-scaled nearest neighbor distances η* for the ECSZ *M*1.5+ catalogue in the first half of 2019, with the red solid curve denoting the fitted probability density function (PDF). The azure bell-shaped curve represents the clustering part, while the orange bell-curve represents background events.

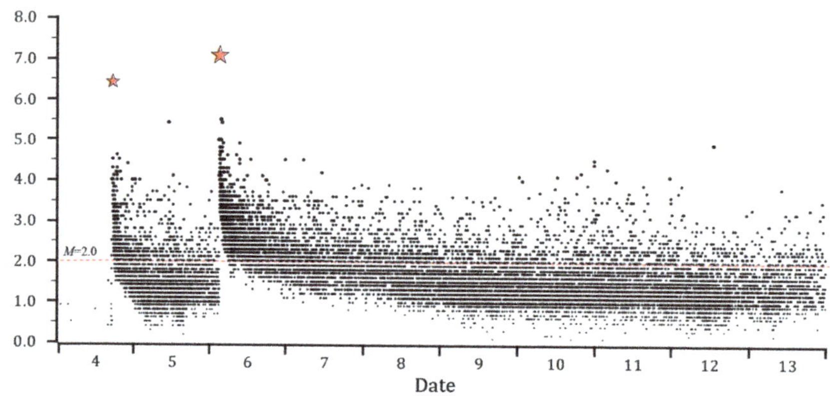

Figure 2. Magnitude–time plot for the first week of the Ridgecrest sequence. The two red stars denote the M_W7.1 mainshock and the M_W6.4 foreshock, respectively. Note the catalog's incompleteness during the short time after the large events and the activities before the M_W6.4 foreshock. The red dashed line denotes $M = 2.0$, and the catalog above this limitation seems more complete.

4. Results

4.1. Family Relations in the Whole Sequence

We applied the NN algorithm to analyze family relations in the 2019 Ridgecrest earthquake sequence. From the histogram of its nearest neighbor distance η^* (Figure 3a), it can be fitted by a single normal probability density function, which implies that most events in the Ridgecrest earthquake sequence belong to clustering earthquakes. This opinion also can be confirmed by the spatiotemporal distribution of η^* (Figure 3b). The data encircle around a horizontal line, as discussed by other researchers [38,45], which indicates that aftershocks are restricted in a limited spatial area and extend only to the time domain.

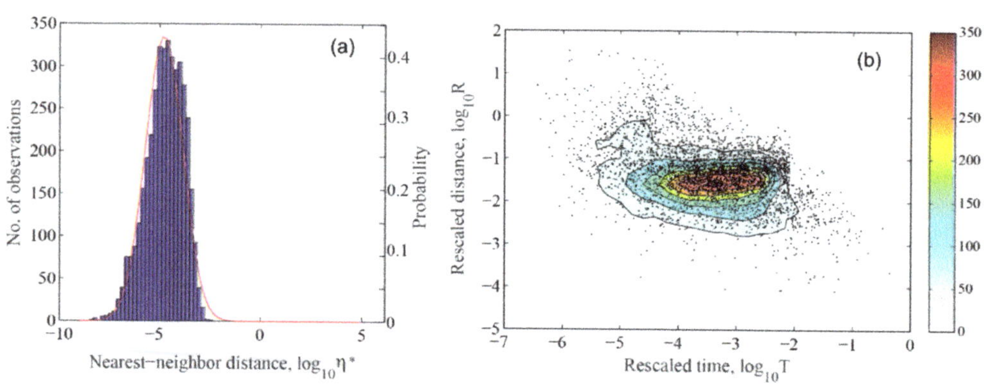

Figure 3. Statistical results of the nearest neighbor distance η^* for the Ridgecrest M_W7.1 earthquake sequence. (**a**) Nearest neighbor distance η^* statistical histogram with normal distribution fit; (**b**) contour plot of the two-dimensional spatiotemporal distribution density.

We connect each $M \geq 2.0$ event in the Ridgecrest sequence to its nearest neighbor (as in Figure 2 in [38]), which can be seen as its parent event, according to the distance η^* (see Figure 4). The logarithmic coordinate is applied on the horizontal time axis in Figure 4b to demonstrate the structures of the foreshock sequence more clearly.

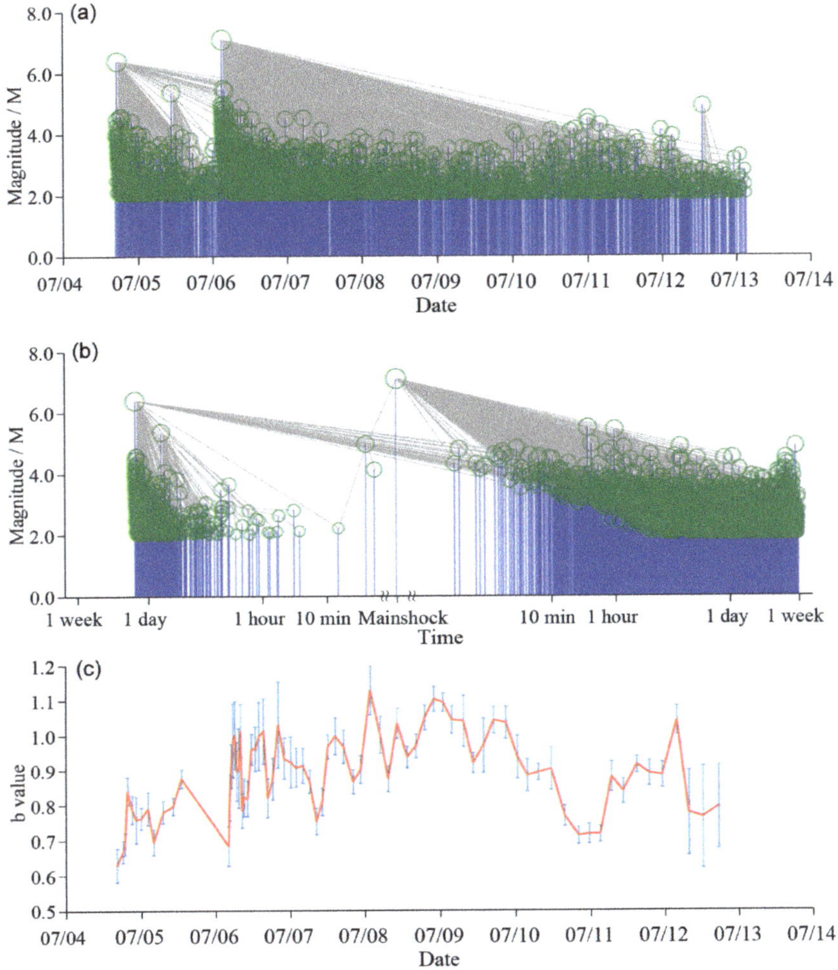

Figure 4. Magnitude–time plot of $M \geq 2.0$ events in the Ridgecrest sequence (**a**). Panel (**b**) is the same as (**a**), but the logarithmic time coordinate is applied. Green circles and blue lines in (**a**,**b**) denote earthquakes, while gray lines are links. (**c**) shows the time variation of the *b*-value.

It is obvious that the M_W7.1 mainshock plays a dominant role in the aftershock activities of the sequence. Most aftershocks are physically intimately related to it and are its offspring events. However, its influence gradually weakens with passage of time. After a few days, some larger aftershocks also have their own aftershocks (Figure 4a). It is also noted in Figure 4 that the impact of the M_W6.4 foreshock does not vanish with the occurrence of the M_W7.1 mainshock. There are still many aftershocks that can be seen as offspring of the M_W6.4 event in the sequence after the M_W 7.1 mainshock. This is also consistent with other studies [3].

The changes in *b*-value in the G-R relationship demonstrate variation in tectonic stress. Figure 4c shows the *b*-value time series along with the Ridgecrest sequence. Here, the *b*-values were calculated with equal event numbers; specifically, the window size is 240, and the step size is 30. The *b*-value increases within the first few days. At the start of the sequence, the *b*-value is significantly lower (<0.7) and then rises to nearly 0.8. Throughout the entire foreshock sequence, the *b*-values remain below 0.8. Aftershocks following the

M_W7.1 mainshock showed elevated b-values compared to foreshocks, yet remained below background levels (1.118, as mentioned above). This is consistent with previous results from other studies [52]. The foreshock sequences always have lower b-values [53], as observed before many large earthquakes (e.g., [54–56]), as well as in laboratory observations [57]. This seismic pattern reveals shifting stress dynamics throughout the earthquake sequence, hinting at complex tectonic interactions beneath the surface.

4.2. M_W6.4 Foreshock Sequence

The M_W6.4 foreshock occurred in ECSZ on the side of the California plate boundary. The rupture began on a northwest-striking right-lateral fault and then continued on a southwest-striking fault with mainly left-lateral slip [3,58]. The M_W6.4 foreshock sequence might have triggered the M_W7.1 Ridgecrest mainshock. However, if we refer to the nearest neighbor link in Figure 4, the M_W6.4 event is probably not the immediate cause of the rupture of the M_W7.1 mainshock. From Figure 4a,b, the parent event of the Ridgecrest M_W7.1 mainshock, or, in other words, the direct foreshock, is an M_W5.0 event that occurred at 03:16 a.m., which is about 3 min and 20 s before the mainshock. This is the 'ancestor' event to the mainshock by means of statistical significance. We then examine the activities of the M_W6.4 foreshock sequence.

The relocated catalogue of the M_W6.4 foreshock sequence shows that the rupturing process can be divided into two parts: a northwest-striking fault and a southwest-striking fault (see Figure 5a). Notably, all the $M \geq 5.0$ events occurred on the northwest-striking fault, suggesting that this fault is the main rupturing fault.

It can be derived from Figure 5c,d that the M_W6.4 event invoked aftershocks in both faults. But, compared to the northwest-striking fault (BB'), the cracks were more evenly distributed on the southwest-striking fault's plane (AA'). The biggest aftershock of the M_W6.4 foreshock was a M_W5.4 event. This event and its own aftershocks were clustered on the northwest-striking fault (BB'). In the left section of Figure 5d (i.e., in the northwest direction of the M_W6.4 event), all aftershocks, except a small group, appear to be halted by a line, particularly in the shallower areas. These phenomena of earthquake migration and seismicity quiescence have already been discussed in [59]. This indicates that there might be a barrier on the fault. The M_W5.4 event and its own aftershocks took place at the edge of the barrier, but did not break it. Finally, the M_W5.0 event took place at the end part of the quiescence area, and then the M_W7.1 mainshock.

In other words, the M_W5.4 event is classical aftershock of the M_W6.4 event, while the M_W5.0 event, which occurred after the M_W6.4 and M_W5.4 events, is not aftershock of either of them. It has a much closer relationship with the M_W7.1 mainshock (as can also be seen in Figure 4b). We finally give the nearest neighbor for $M \geq 5.0$ events in the 2019 Ridgecrest M_W7.1 sequence (Table 1).

Table 1. Nearest neighbors of $M > 5.0$ events in the 2019 Ridgecrest sequence.

Event No.	$M \geq 5.0$ Earthquakes (yyyy-mm-dd HH:MM:SS.s)	Nearest Neighbours
1	2019-07-04 17:33:48.6 M_W6.4	2019-07-04 17:02:55.4 M4.0
2	2019-07-05 11:07:53.2 M_W5.4	2019-07-04 17:33:48.6 M_W6.4
3	2019-07-06 03:16:32.1 M_W5.0	2019-07-06 03:12:41.0 M2.2
4	2019-07-06 03:19:52.3 M_W7.1 [1]	2019-07-06 03:16:32.1 M_W5.0
5	2019-07-06 03:47:53.0 M_W5.5	2019-07-06 03:19:52.3 M_W7.1 [1]
6	2019-07-06 04:18:55.4 M_W5.4	2019-07-06 03:19:52.3 M_W7.1 [1]

[1] Mainshock.

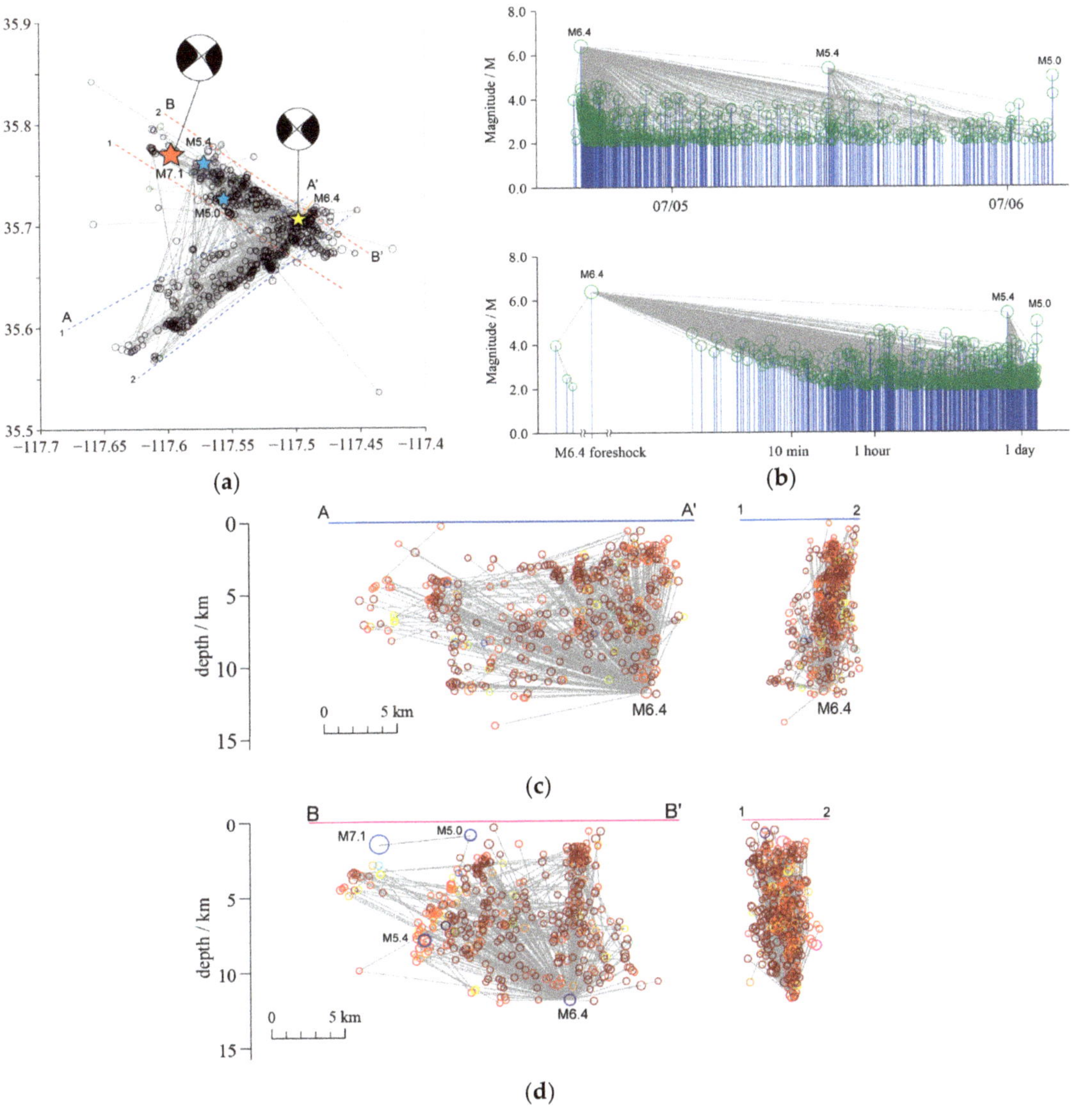

Figure 5. Distribution of the M_W6.4 foreshock sequence. (**a**) shows the epicenters of the sequence, where the red star denotes the M_W7.1 mainshock, while the yellow star is the M_W6.4 foreshock, and the blue stars indicate two $M \geq 5$ events; (**b**) shows the NN results for $M \geq 2.0$ events in the M_W6.4 foreshock sequence, here the M_W6.4 event is seen as a mainshock. Green circles and blue lines denote earthquakes, while gray lines are links. Events with epicenters located between two NE–SW-trending solid blue lines are projected on an AA′ profile (**c**), and (**d**) is the profile of events between two dashed red lines. Different colors of circles in panel (**c**,**d**) denote the time order of these events.

4.3. Foreshocks of the M_W6.4 Foreshock

We examined the catalogues from White et al. [49] and SCSN. No earthquakes took place in the epicenter area of the oncoming M_W6.4 event, at least in June (Figure 6a). Moving into July, two small events with M = 1.5 occurred on 1st July in the rupture area of the coming M_W7.1 earthquake. So, what is the relationship between these two microshocks and the M_W6.4 or M_W7.1 event? Are they the pre-ruptures of the fault? From our calculation, the distance between the latter one and its nearest events in the Ridgecrest sequence $\eta^* \approx 3.343$, which is much larger than the $J_X = -2.328$ in Figure 1. This indicates that these two weak events do not belong to clustering events, and therefore should be seen as background activities. Another piece of evidence is that there were also two $M > 1.0$ events almost at the same location in January 2019. We therefore did not include them in the Ridgecrest sequence.

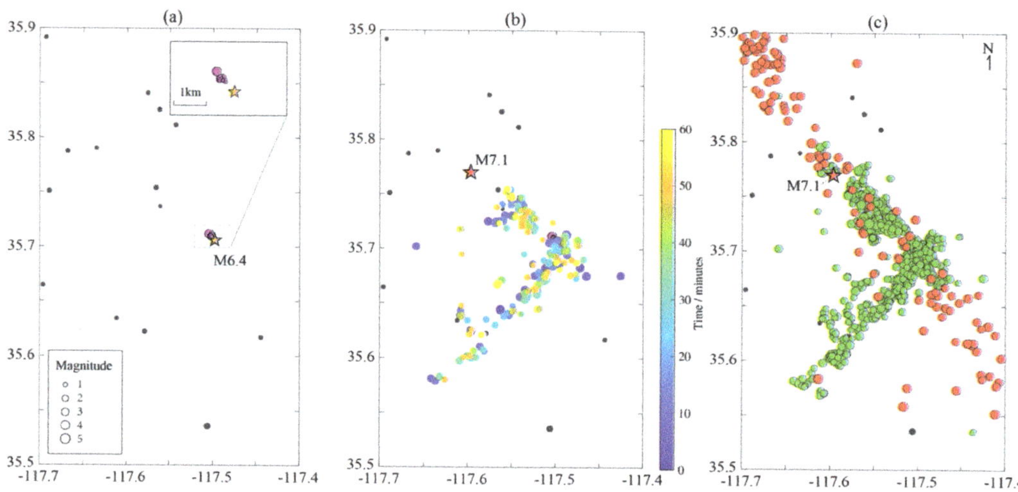

Figure 6. The distribution maps of earthquakes in different periods in the Ridgecrest area. (**a**) Gray dots are earthquakes that occurred in June 2019, and filled purple circles are earthquakes that occurred from 1st July to 17:33 on 4 July, before the M_W6.4 event in the Ridgecrest sequence. The small figure in the upper right corner is an enlargement of the dashed box in this panel; (**b**) circles filled with a gradually changing color from blue to yellow are aftershocks which occurred in the 1 h after the M_W6.4 event; (**c**) green circles represent the M_W6.4 foreshock sequence, while red circles represent aftershocks in the 1 h after the M_W7.1 mainshock. Note that the whole M_W6.4 foreshock sequence did not expand any more than its beginning time, as shown in panel (**b**).

Following this, 3.5 days later, the Ridgecrest sequence begins. A small set of weak earthquakes arrived ahead of the M_W6.4 event, with the biggest $M = 4.0$ event being at 17:02 on 4 July (Figure 6a). From the NN algorithm (Figure 7), the M4.0 earthquake is the parent event of the M_W6.4 earthquake. Statistically, the M4.0 event at 17:02 is the foreshock of the M_W6.4 event, while the M1.5 event at 16:13 is the foreshock of the M4.0 event, and the M0.4 event at 16:07 is the foreshock of M1.5 event.

The M_W6.4 earthquake is seen as conjugate faulting [1,50,60,61]. In the foreshock sequence, the M_W6.4 event triggers simultaneous activities in both the northeast and northwest faults. As shown in Figure 6b, aftershocks form a 'T' shape just minutes after the M_W6.4 event. Subsequent activities remained within this area until the M_W7.1 mainshock outbreak (Figure 6c). The M4.0 foreshock sequence extended in the northwest direction (Figure 6a). Our analysis suggests that the initial rupture of the M_W6.4 event likely originated from the northwest faults. This is also in agreement with other studies [51,60,61].

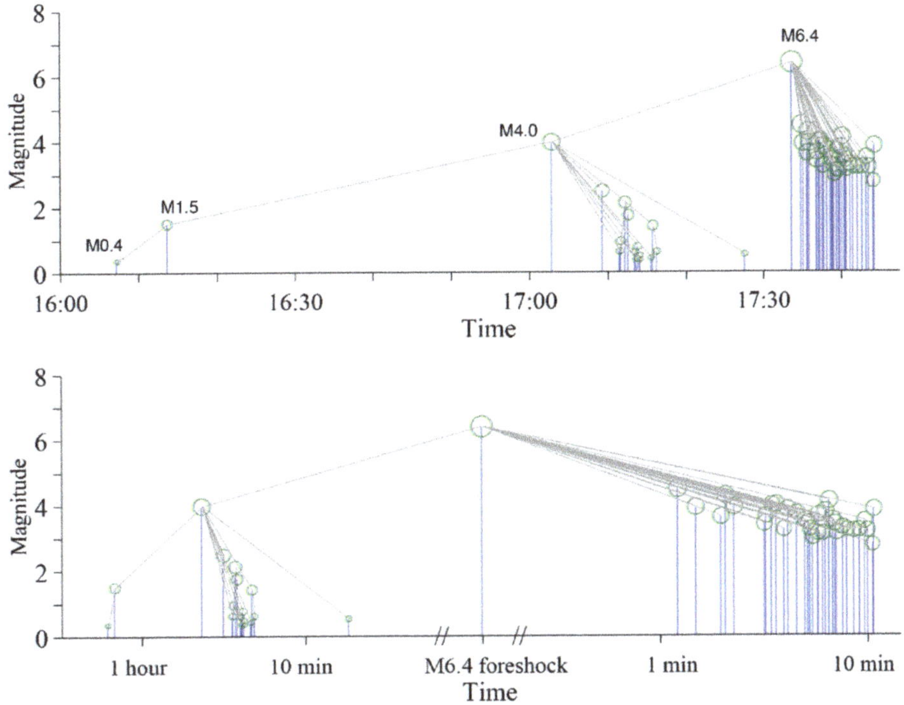

Figure 7. Family links of the events before and after the $M_W6.4$ foreshock. Green circles and blue lines indicate earthquakes and gray lines correspond to parent links. The **upper** panel shows the family links of magnitude over time. The **lower** panel is almost the same, but the horizontal coordinate is in logarithmic scale.

5. Conclusions and Discussion

Large earthquakes can occur in a more complex fault system than commonly assumed. A series of ruptures occur in a web of interconnected faults, with rupturing faults triggering other faults. The stress changes and interactions during the earthquake sequence are intricate and complicated. The 2019 Ridgecrest $M_W7.1$ earthquake sequence occurred in these exact tectonic conditions. In addition to numerous studies on this sequence based on many aspects, e.g., focus kinematics and dynamics, this paper employs statistical techniques to elucidate the relationships between each event within it.

The Ridgecrest $M_W7.1$ earthquake has a foreshock sequence characterized by a significant $M_W6.4$ event. However, the results presented in this paper indicate that the $M_W6.4$ event is not the foreshock of the $M_W7.1$ mainshock, as is generally supposed. Instead, a $M_W5.0$ event in the foreshock sequence, which occurred about 3 min and 20 s before the $M_W7.1$, is the direct foreshock of the mainshock. This event occurred in a quiescence area along the northwest-striking fault in the foreshock sequence, and also with a shallower focus, just like the mainshock. It was located about 6km southeast of the initial rupture point of $M_W7.1$ mainshock. We suppose that this mid–strong event may be linked to barriers that generated the $M_W7.1$ mainshock.

The $M_W6.4$ event triggered aftershocks in both the NW- and SW-direction faults, even several minutes after it. The SW-striking fault ruptured fairly significantly, while subsequent aftershocks on it did not exceed the initial range formed at the beginning. In contrast, the ruptures on the NW-striking fault seem to be restricted or hindered. With the development of the M_W6.4 sequence, aftershocks gradually extended beyond its initial limitations in the NW direction, ultimately leading to the occurrence of the M_W7.1 mainshock.

Before the M_W6.4 earthquake, there was still a small group of events in the sequence. The biggest event in the sequence is a M4.0 medium-strength earthquake, which occurred about 30 min before the M_W6.4 event. This small cluster occurred at a place between the M_W7.1 and M_W6.4 events, northwest of M_W6.4 and also on the NW-striking fault. From this paper, the M4.0 event is the direct foreshock of M_W6.4. This implies that NW fault activity dominates the whole sequence. Small fractures emerge on the NW faults and then trigger conjugated fault slips. Barriers on the NW faults retard the development of ruptures, and a much larger rupture takes place at last.

Based on the nearest neighbor distance algorithm, we analyze the rupture process of the 2019 Ridgecrest sequence. Our findings lead to similar conclusions to those in works focused on other aspects. These findings indicate that statistical approaches with physical meanings can also receive the same understanding in seismology. The results shown in this paper are only from statistical analysis. As demonstrated by other works, foreshocks might have lower stress drops [14,62], higher waveform similarity [57], and other source features [63–65]. We hope that the direct 'foreshocks' recognized in this paper may have some different features which can be derived from their waveforms or other observations. Multidisciplinary studies and more elaborate works on this topic are thus required in the future.

Author Contributions: Conceptualization and investigation, J.Z.; methodology, X.L.; resources and data curation, Z.Z. All authors have read and agreed to the published version of the manuscript.

Funding: This research was funded by the Science and Technology Innovation Team of the Shandong Earthquake Agency.

Institutional Review Board Statement: Not applicable.

Data Availability Statement: Third-part data.

Acknowledgments: We are grateful to Malcolm White for making the relocated catalog publicly available. We thank the three anonymous reviewers for their constructive comments.

Conflicts of Interest: Author Jianchang Zheng, Zhengshuai Zhang and Xiaohan Li were employed by Shandong Earthquake Agency, China Earthquake Administration. The authors declare that the research was conducted in the absence of any commercial or financial relationships that could be construed as a potential conflict of interest.

References

1. Ross, Z.E.; Idini, B.; Jia, Z.; Stephenson, O.L.; Zhong, M.; Wang, X.; Zhan, Z.; Simons, M.; Fielding, E.J.; Yun, S.-H.; et al. Hierarchical interlocked orthogonal faulting in the 2019 Ridgecrest earthquake sequence. *Science* **2019**, *366*, 346–351. [CrossRef]
2. Hardebeck, J.L. A stress-similarity triggering model for aftershocks of the Mw6.4 and 7.1 Ridgecrest Earthquakes. *Bull. Seismol. Soc. Am.* **2020**, *110*, 1716–1727.
3. Lomax, A. Absolute location of 2019 Ridgecrest seismicity reveals a shallow Mw 7.1 hypocenter, migrating and pulsing Mw 7.1 foreshocks, and duplex Mw 6.4 ruptures. *Bull. Seismol. Soc. Am.* **2020**, *110*, 1845–1858. [CrossRef]
4. Chuang, L.Y.; Peng, Z.; Lei, X.; Wang, B.; Liu, J.; Zhai, Q.; Tu, H. Foreshocks of the 2010 Mw 6.7 Yushu, China earthquake occurred near an extensional step-over. *J. Geophys. Res. Solid Earth* **2023**, *128*, e2022JB025176. [CrossRef]
5. Marsan, D.; Enescu, B. Modeling the foreshock sequence prior to the 2011, M_W9.0 Tohoku, Japan, earthquake. *J. Geophys. Res. Solid Earth* **2012**, *117*, B06316. [CrossRef]
6. Cesca, S.; Grigoli, F.; Heimann, S.; Dahm, T.; Kriegerowski, M.; Sobiesiak, M.; Tassara, C.; Olcay, M. TheM_w8.1 2014 Iquique, Chile, seismic sequence: A tale of foreshocks and aftershocks. *Geophys. J. Int.* **2016**, *204*, 1766–1780. [CrossRef]
7. Sheng, S.; Meng, L. Stress field variation during the 2019 Ridgecrest earthquake sequence. *Geophys. Res. Lett.* **2020**, *47*, e2020GL087722. [CrossRef]
8. Reasenberg, P.A. Foreshock occurrence before large earthquakes. *J. Geophys. Res. Solid Earth* **1999**, *104*, 4755–4768. [CrossRef]

9. Zaccagnino, D.; Vallianatos, F.; Michas, G.; Telesca, L.; Doglioni, C. Are foreshocks fore-shocks? *J. Geophys. Res. Solid Earth* **2024**, *129*, e2023JB027337. [CrossRef]
10. Agnew, D.C.; Jones, L.M. Prediction probabilities from foreshocks. *J. Geophys. Res. Solid Earth* **1991**, *96*, 11959–11971. [CrossRef]
11. McGuire, J.J.; Boettcher, M.S.; Jordan, T.H. Foreshock sequences and short-term earthquake predictability on East Pacific Rise transform faults. *Nature* **2005**, *434*, 457–461. [CrossRef] [PubMed]
12. Apostol, B.; Cune, L.C. On the relevance of the foreshocks in forecasting seismic mainshocks. *Ann. Geophys.* **2023**, *66*, SE635. [CrossRef]
13. Helmstetter, A.; Sornette, D. Foreshocks explained by cascades of triggered seismicity. *J. Geophys. Res. Solid Earth* **2003**, *108*, 2457. [CrossRef]
14. Chen, X.; Shearer, P.M. California foreshock sequences suggest aseismic triggering process. *Geophys. Res. Lett.* **2013**, *40*, 2602–2607. [CrossRef]
15. Chen, X.; Shearer, P.M. Analysis of foreshock sequences in California and implications for earthquake triggering. *Pure Appl. Geophys.* **2016**, *173*, 133–152. [CrossRef]
16. Dodge, D.A.; Beroza, G.C.; Ellsworth, W.L. Foreshock sequence of the 1992 Landers, California, earthquake and its im-plications for earthquake nucleation. *J. Geophys. Res. Solid Earth* **1995**, *100*, 9865–9880. [CrossRef]
17. Dodge, D.A.; Beroza, G.C.; Ellsworth, W.L. Detailed observations of California foreshock sequences: Implications for the earthquake initiation process. *J. Geophys. Res. Solid Earth* **1996**, *101*, 22371–22392. [CrossRef]
18. McLaskey, G.C.; Kilgore, B.D. Foreshocks during the nucleation of stick-slip instability. *J. Geophys. Res. Solid Earth* **2013**, *118*, 2982–2997. [CrossRef]
19. Nishikawa, T.; Ide, S. Recurring slow slip events and earthquake nucleation in the source region of the M7 Ibaraki-Oki earthquakes revealed by earthquake swarm and foreshock activity. *J. Geophys. Res. Solid Earth* **2018**, *123*, 7950–7968. [CrossRef]
20. Yoon, C.E.; Yoshimitsu, N.; Ellsworth, W.L.; Beroza, G.C. Foreshocks and mainshock nucleation of the 1999 Mw7.1 Hector Mine, California, Earthquake. *J. Geophys. Res. Solid Earth* **2019**, *124*, 1569–1582. [CrossRef]
21. Console, R.; Murru, M.; Alessandrini, B. Foreshock statistics and their possible relationship to earthquake prediction in the Italian region. *Bull. Seismol. Soc. Am.* **1993**, *83*, 1248–1263. [CrossRef]
22. Helmstetter, A.; Sornette, D.; Grasso, J.R. Mainshocks are aftershocks of conditional foreshocks: How do foreshock sta-tistical properties emerge from aftershock laws. *J. Geophys. Res. Solid Earth* **2003**, *108*, 2046. [CrossRef]
23. Lippiello, E.; Godano, C.; de Arcangelis, L. The relevance of foreshocks in earthquake triggering: A statistical study. *Entropy* **2019**, *21*, 173. [CrossRef]
24. Petrillo, G.; Lippiello, E.; Landes, F.P.; Rosso, A. The influence of the brittle-ductile transition zone on aftershock and foreshock occurrence. *Nat. Commun.* **2020**, *11*, 3010. [CrossRef]
25. Trugman, D.T.; Ross, Z.E. Pervasive foreshock activity across southern California. *Geophys. Res. Lett.* **2019**, *46*, 8772–8781. [CrossRef]
26. Ende, M.P.A.v.D.; Ampuero, J. On the statistical significance of foreshock sequences in Southern California. *Geophys. Res. Lett.* **2020**, *47*, e2019GL086224. [CrossRef]
27. Moutote, L.; Marsan, D.; Lengliné, O.; Duputel, Z. Rare occurrences of non-cascading foreshock activity in southern Cal-ifornia. *Geophys. Res. Lett.* **2021**, *48*, e2020GL091757. [CrossRef] [PubMed]
28. Wetzler, N.; Brodsky, E.E.; Chaves, E.J.; Goebel, T.; Lay, T. Regional characteristics of observable foreshocks. *Seism. Res. Lett.* **2022**, *94*, 428–442. [CrossRef]
29. Console, R.; Murru, M.; Lombardi, A.M. Refining earthquake clustering models. *J. Geophys. Res. Solid Earth* **2003**, *108*, 2468. [CrossRef]
30. Dzwinel, W.; Yuen, D.A.; Boryczko, K.; Ben-Zion, Y.; Yoshioka, S.; Ito, T. Nonlinear multidimensional scaling and visu-alization of earthquake clusters over space, time and feature space. *Nonlin. Process. Geophys.* **2005**, *12*, 117–128. [CrossRef]
31. Console, R.; Murru, M.; Catalli, F. Physical and stochastic models of earthquake clustering. *Tectonophysics* **2006**, *417*, 141–153. [CrossRef]
32. Cho, N.F.; Tiampo, K.F.; Mckinnon, S.D.; Vallejos, J.A.; Klein, W.; Dominguez, R. A simple metric to quantify seismicity clustering. *Nonlinear Process. Geophys.* **2010**, *17*, 293–302. [CrossRef]
33. Jacobs, K.M.; Smith, E.G.C.; Savage, M.K.; Zhuang, J. Cumulative rate analysis (CURATE): A clustering algorithm for swarm dominated catalogs. *J. Geophys. Res. Solid Earth* **2013**, *118*, 553–569. [CrossRef]
34. Lasocki, S. Transformation to equivalent dimensions—A new methodology to study earthquake clustering. *Geophys. J. Int.* **2014**, *197*, 1224–1235. [CrossRef]
35. Baiesi, M.; Paczuski, M. Scale-free networks of earthquakes and aftershocks. *Phys. Rev. E* **2004**, *69*, 066106. [CrossRef] [PubMed]
36. Zaliapin, I.; Gabrielov, A.; Keilis-Borok, V.; Wong, H. Clustering analysis of seismicity and aftershock identification. *Phys. Rev. Lett.* **2008**, *101*, 018501. [CrossRef] [PubMed]

37. Zaliapin, I.; Ben-Zion, Y. Earthquake clusters in southern California I: Identification and stability. *J. Geophys. Res. Solid Earth* **2013**, *118*, 2847–2864. [CrossRef]
38. Zaliapin, I.; Ben-Zion, Y. Earthquake clusters in southern California II: Classification and relation to physical properties of the crust. *J. Geophys. Res. Solid Earth* **2013**, *118*, 2865–2877. [CrossRef]
39. Moradpour, J.; Hainzl, S.; Davidsen, J. Nontrivial decay of aftershock density with distance in Southern California. *J. Geophys. Res. Solid Earth* **2014**, *119*, 5518–5535. [CrossRef]
40. Peresan, A.; Gentili, S. Seismic clusters analysis in Northeastern Italy by the nearest-neighbour approach. *Phys. Earth Planet. Inter.* **2018**, *274*, 87–104. [CrossRef]
41. Bayliss, K.; Naylor, M.; Main, I.G. Probabilistic identification of earthquake clusters using rescaled nearest neighbour distance networks. *Geophys. J. Int.* **2019**, *217*, 487–503. [CrossRef]
42. Martínez-Garzón, P.; Ben-Zion, Y.; Zaliapin, I.; Bohnhoff, M. Seismic clustering in the Sea of Marmara: Implications for monitoring earthquake processes. *Tectonophysics* **2019**, *768*, 228176. [CrossRef]
43. Zaliapin, I.; Ben-Zion, Y. A global classification and characterization of earthquake clusters. *Geophys. J. Int.* **2016**, *207*, 608–634. [CrossRef]
44. Zheng, J. Clustering features and seismogenesis of the 2014 M6.6 Jinggu earthquake in Yunnan Province, China. *Front. Earth Sci.* **2023**, *11*, 1177821. [CrossRef]
45. Li, X.; Zheng, J.; Zhang, H.; Cui, H.; Li, C. Study on the sequence activities of the 2021 Yangbi MS 6.4 earthquake in Yunnan. *Front. Earth Sci.* **2023**, *11*, 1168043. [CrossRef]
46. Walter, A.W.; Weaver, C.S. Seismicity of the Coso Range, California. *J. Geophys. Res. Solid Earth* **1980**, *85*, 2441–2458. [CrossRef]
47. Feng, Q.; Lees, J.M. Microseismicity, stress, and fracture in the Coso geothermal field, California. *Tectonophysics* **1998**, *289*, 221–238. [CrossRef]
48. Schoenball, M.; Davatzes, N.C.; Glen, J.M.G. Differentiating induced and natural seismicity using space-time-magnitude statistics applied to the Coso Geothermal field. *Geophys. Res. Lett.* **2015**, *42*, 6221–6228. [CrossRef]
49. White, M.C.; Fang, H.; Catchings, R.D.; Goldman, M.R.; Steidl, J.H.; Ben-Zion, Y. Detailed traveltime tomography and seismic catalogue around the 2019 Mw7.1 Ridgecrest, California, earthquake using dense rapid-response seismic data. *Geophys. J. Int.* **2021**, *227*, 204–227. [CrossRef]
50. Kaven, J.O. Seismicity rate change at the Coso geothermal field following the July 2019 Ridgecrest earthquakes. *Bull. Seismol. Soc. Am.* **2020**, *110*, 1728–1735. [CrossRef]
51. Chen, K.; Avouac, J.-P.; Aati, S.; Milliner, C.; Zheng, F.; Shi, C. Cascading and pulse-like ruptures during the 2019 Ridgecrest earthquakes in the Eastern California Shear Zone. *Nat. Commun.* **2020**, *11*, 22. [CrossRef]
52. Huang, K.; Tang, L.; Feng, W. Spatiotemporal Distributions of b Values Following the 2019 Mw7.1 Ridgecrest, California, Earthquake Sequence. *Pure Appl. Geophys.* **2023**, *180*, 2529–2542. [CrossRef]
53. Molchan, G.; Kronrod, T.; Nekrasova, A. Immediate foreshocks: Time variation of the b-value. *Phys. Earth Planet. Inter.* **1999**, *111*, 229–240. [CrossRef]
54. Tamaribuchi, K.; Yagi, Y.; Enescu, B.; Hirano, S. Characteristics of foreshock activity inferred from the JMA earthquake catalog. *Earth Planets Space* **2018**, *70*, 90. [CrossRef]
55. Gulia, L.; Wiemer, S. Real-time discrimination of earthquake foreshocks and aftershocks. *Nature* **2019**, *574*, 193–199. [CrossRef] [PubMed]
56. Yao, D.; Huang, Y.; Peng, Z.; Castro, R.R. Detailed investigation of the foreshock sequence of the 2010 Mw7.2 El Mayor-Cucapah earthquake. *J. Geophys. Res. Solid Earth* **2020**, *125*, e2019JB019076. [CrossRef]
57. Goebel, T.H.W.; Schuster, V.; Kwiatek, G.; Pandey, K.; Dresen, G. A laboratory perspective on accelerating preparatory processes before earthquakes and implications for foreshock detectability. *Nat. Commun.* **2024**, *15*, 5588. [CrossRef] [PubMed]
58. Wang, K.; Dreger, D.S.; Tinti, E.; Bürgmann, R.; Taira, T. Rupture process of the 2019 Ridgecrest, California Mw6.4 foreshock and Mw7.1 earthquake constrained by seismic and geodetic data. *Bull. Seismol. Soc. Am.* **2020**, *110*, 1603–1626. [CrossRef]
59. Marsan, D.; Ross, Z.E. Inverse migration of seismicity quiescence during the 2019 Ridgecrest sequence. *J. Geophys. Res. Solid Earth* **2021**, *126*, e2020JB020329. [CrossRef]
60. Barnhart, W.D.; Hayes, G.P.; Gold, R.D. The July 2019 Ridgecrest, California, earthquake sequence: Kinematics of slip and stressing in cross-fault ruptures. *Geophys. Res. Lett.* **2019**, *46*, 11859–11867. [CrossRef]
61. Li, S.; Chen, G.; Tao, T.; He, P.; Ding, K.; Zou, R.; Li, J.; Wang, Q. The 2019 Mw 6.4 and Mw 7.1 Ridgecrest earthquake sequence in Eastern California: Rupture on a conjugate fault structure revealed by GPS and InSAR measurements. *Geophys. J. Int.* **2020**, *221*, 1651–1666. [CrossRef]
62. Kim, W.-Y.; Seo, M.-S.; Park, J.Y.; Han, S.; Son, Y.O.; Kim, Y. The 28 October 2022 Mw 3.8 Goesan earthquake sequence in central Korea: Stress drop, aftershock triggering, and fault interaction. *Bull. Seismol. Soc. Am.* **2023**, *113*, 2416–2431. [CrossRef]
63. Boore, D.M.; Atkinson, G.M. Source spectra for the 1988 Saguenay, Quebec, earthquakes. *Bull. Seismol. Soc. Am.* **1992**, *82*, 683–719.

64. Calderoni, G.; Rovelli, A.; Di Giovambattista, R. Stress drop, apparent stress, and radiation efficiency of clustered earthquakes in the nucleation volume of the 6 April 2009, Mw 6.1 L'Aquila earthquake. *J. Geophys. Res. Solid Earth* **2019**, *124*, 10360–10375. [CrossRef]
65. Castro, R.R.; Colavitti, L.; Pacor, F.; Lanzano, G.; Sgobba, S.; Spallarossa, D. Temporal variation of S-wave attenuation during the 2009 L'Aquila, Central Italy, seismic sequence. *Geophys. J. Int.* **2025**, *240*, 317–328. [CrossRef]

Disclaimer/Publisher's Note: The statements, opinions and data contained in all publications are solely those of the individual author(s) and contributor(s) and not of MDPI and/or the editor(s). MDPI and/or the editor(s) disclaim responsibility for any injury to people or property resulting from any ideas, methods, instructions or products referred to in the content.

entropy

MDPI

Article

Mathematical Theory of Seismic Activity and Its Specific Cases: Gutenberg–Richter Law, Omori Law, Roll-Off Effect, and Negative Binomial Distribution

Roumen Borisov and Nikolay K. Vitanov *

Institute of Mechanics, Bulgarian Academy of Sciences, Academician Georgi Bonchev Street, Block 4, 1113 Sofia, Bulgaria; r.borisov@outlook.com

* Correspondence: vitanov@imbm.bas.bg

Abstract: We discuss a model of seismic activity that is based on the concept of energy in a cluster of sources of seismic activity. We show that specific cases of the studied model lead to the Gutenberg–Richter relationship and the Omori law. These laws are valid for earthquakes that happen in a single cluster of sources of seismic activity. Further, we discuss the distribution of earthquakes for several clusters containing sources of seismic activity. This distribution contains, as a specific case, a version of the negative binomial distribution. We show that at least a part of the roll-off effect connected to the parameter b of the Gutenberg– Richter law occurs because one records earthquakes that happen in more than one cluster of sources of seismic activity.

Keywords: seismic activity; earthquakes; energy-based model; Gutenberg–Richter law; Omori law; negative binomial distribution; roll-off effect

1. Introduction

Earthquakes are complicated and interesting space-time events. One reason for the large research interest in earthquakes is that the destruction potential of an earthquake can be very large. Because of this, it is very important for us to have methods for forecasting the probability that an earthquake will occur. This can help us make decisions in the case of emergencies that are connected to an earthquake [1].

Another reason for the research interest in earthquakes is the hypothesis that earthquakes are specific members of the class of critical phenomena [2–4]. A reason for this hypothesis is that the frequency of earthquakes has a power law relationship to quantities which are characteristic of the size and energy of an earthquake [5].

A standard test for evaluating models is to compare the number of forecast events to the number of real events for the tested period of time. To perform this task, one has to know the relationship for the probability distribution of earthquakes. A discussion of several discrete distributions can be found in [6], where the Poisson distribution, the geometric distribution, the logarithmic distribution, and the negative binomial distribution are discussed. Of these distributions, the negative binomial distribution is the only one that has two parameters. Kagan [6] assumes the possibility that the second parameter in the negative binomial distribution could describe the clusterization of the process.

Several empirical relationships are well-known in seismology. The Gutenberg–Richter law [7] gives a relationship between the magnitude and the number of earthquakes in a region for an interval of time:

$$\log_{10} \mathcal{N} = a - bM. \quad (1)$$

where M is the magnitude of the earthquake and $\mathcal{N}$ is the number of earthquakes with a magnitude equal to or larger than M. The magnitude of an earthquake reflects its strength, and it is measured through the magnitude recorded by seismometers. The parameter a depends on the total number of events and describes the seismic productivity of the region under consideration. The parameter b gives information about the ratio between strong and weak earthquakes in the region. The magnitude M reflects the size of an earthquake, but it is different from the strength of the quake (the energy E freed by the quake) and its seismic moment M_0. Empirically, the relationships between the magnitude, energy, and seismic moment of an earthquake are

$$\begin{aligned} \log_{10} M_0 &= \alpha_0 + \beta_0 M, \\ \log_{10} E &= \alpha + \beta M, \end{aligned} \tag{2}$$

where $\alpha_0, \alpha, \beta_0, \beta$ are empirical constants and $\beta \approx \beta_0 = 1.5$ [8]. Then

$$\mathcal{N} \propto M_0^{-} B_0, \quad \mathcal{N} \propto E^{-B}, \tag{3}$$

where $B_0 = 2b/3$, and it is analogous to the parameter b from the Gutenberg–Richter law [5,8,9].

In all empirical catalogs of earthquakes, a noticeable decline can be observed in the value of b for earthquakes of small magnitudes. This is referred to as the "roll-off" effect of the value of b. In the logarithmic plot of the Gutenberg–Richter law, the roll-off effect is seen as an almost horizontal curve in the region of small magnitudes. This may be a result of the incompleteness of the data in the area of small magnitudes due to a decrease in the experimentally recorded amplitude in relation to the amplitude of the noise [10]. Some recent models of earthquake dynamics lead to the roll-off effect as a natural consequence of the model [11,12].

In addition, due to the finite size of the regions of seismic activity, the Gutenberg–Richter law should be constrained from above. In other words, a maximum amplitude M_{max} should exist for the considered space-time interval [13,14]. The value of M_{max} is an important characteristic, as it is necessary for the evaluation of the risk associated with large earthquakes in the region under consideration. Thus, various methodologies for the determination of M_{max} are available [15–17]. In order to account for the above-mentioned phenomena, some authors modify the Gutenberg–Richter law [18].

Another famous law in seismology is the Omori law of aftershocks [19]. The Omori law states that after a strong earthquake, the frequency of aftershocks (the underground shocks that follow the main shock) decays with time, on average, according to the hyperbolic law [20,21]:

$$N^*(t) = \frac{k}{c+t}, k > 0, c > 0. \tag{4}$$

Nowadays, one uses the formula [22,23]

$$N^*(t) = \frac{k}{(c+t)^p}, k > 0, c > 0, \tag{5}$$

and p can be larger than 1 or smaller than 1.

In this article, we discuss a simple model of seismic activity. The model does not contain assumptions about the mechanics of seismic events, such as the consideration of fractures. Instead, we base the model on considerations connected to energy. Our goal is to show that specific cases of the model lead to several well-known relationships and distributions in seismology such as the Gutenberg–Richter relationship, the Omori law, and the negative binomial distribution.

The text below is organized as follows. In Section 2, we formulate a model based on several assumptions about the motion of energy in a volume containing a cluster of sources of seismic activity. In Section 3, we discuss several results for specific cases of the model. Section 4 is devoted to the discussion of the energy–frequency distributions that occur on the basis of the model. In Section 5, we discuss the magnitude–frequency distributions and the conditions for the occurrence of the Gutenberg–Richter relationship. Section 6 is devoted to a discussion of the relationship between the model and the Omori law. We show in Section 7 that the negative binomial distribution of earthquakes can be connected to the recording of earthquakes from several regions of seismic activity containing different clusters of sources of seismic activity. A short discussion of the results is presented in Section 8. Several concluding remarks are summarized in Section 9.

2. Mathematical Formulation of the Problem

There are many studies on earthquakes based on an assumption of clustering and on stochastic point processes [24–31]. We mention, especially, the models based on branching processes [32–38]. Such models can reproduce the Gutenberg–Richter relationship and the Omori law. We also note the negative binomial distribution, which was used to approximate the earthquake numbers in catalogs [36–42]. We show below that a simple model of seismic activity can lead to similar results as those obtained by the models mentioned above. We have already studied models of this kind and have applied them to various problems connected to the motion of substances in networks [43–49].

Let us consider some volume below the surface of the Earth. In this volume, we assume the existence of a cluster of sources of seismic activity. We note the difference between the source of seismic activity and the seismic source. An earthquake is a seismic source. As a source of seismic activity, we understand a volume which contains a potential seismic source. Thus, below, we understand the energy of the source of seismic activity to be internal energy stored in the corresponding volume and connected to the potential seismic source.

Our model is simple. It is based only on the internal energy connected to a source of seismic activity. We do not consider below the complicated mechanics connected to the seismic sources [50]. We assume that the source of seismic activity may arise from an inflow of energy into the considered cluster. The energy of a source of seismic activity may increase or decrease. At some point, the energy can be released, and we observe a seismic event (an earthquake).

In our model, we collect the sources of seismic activity into groups with respect to the internal energy of the source. Let E_i be the maximum internal energy of the i-th group of sources. Then, the sources from the initial group of sources have internal energy smaller than E_0. We denote this group of sources as the 0-th group of sources. The sources of the next group have internal energy larger than E_0 and smaller than or equal to E_1. This is the first group of sources of seismic activity. We further define the second group of sources (sources with internal energy up to $E_2 > E_1$), etc. The intervals between E_i and E_{i+1} can be chosen to be small enough. Thus, we can have numerous intervals.

Several processes connected to the internal energy of the sources of seismic events are taken into account in the model. A source of seismic activity may arise or vanish in each of the groups. The reason for this is energy, which arrives from (or moves to) the environment. The sources of seismic activity can move from one group of sources to another group of sources. We assume that this motion is only between the neighboring groups of sources (as we discuss short intervals of time). The sources can move from group i to group $i+1$. Such sources of seismic activity gain energy. Other sources can move from group i to group

$i-1$. Such sources of seismic activity lose energy. Finally, in each of the groups, a source of seismic events can release its energy and produce an earthquake.

The processes connected to our model are described mathematically as follows:

1. Arising of new sources of seismic activity: In the considered cluster for unit time, we observe the birth of $\sigma_i(t)N_i(t)$ new sources of seismic activity, where $N_i(t)$ is the number of sources in the i-th group in the time t (the number of sources of internal energy between E_{i-1} and E_i). $\sigma_i > 0$ corresponds to arising of new sources. $\sigma_i < 0$ corresponds to the vanishing of sources.
2. Changes in the internal energy of the existing sources of seismic activity: Part $f_i(t)N_i(t)$ of the sources of seismic activity from the i-th group of sources of seismic activity moves to the $i+1$-st group of sources of seismic activity. Such changes lead to sources of seismic activity with greater internal energy.
3. Changes in the internal energy of the existing sources of seismic activity: Part $g_i(t)N_i(t)$ of the sources of seismic activity from the i-th group of sources of seismic activity moves to the $i-1$-st group of sources of seismic activity. These changes lead to sources of seismic activity with smaller internal energy.
4. Release of energy of sources of seismic activity: Part $\gamma_i(t)N_i(t)$ of sources of seismic activity from the i-th group of sources of seismic events releases its energy and an earthquake occurs. The seismic energy of this earthquake is assumed to be proportional to the internal energy of the corresponding source. We note that in the presented theory, the earthquakes are seismic sources. The energy released by an earthquake can move to other sources of seismic activity from the cluster and may create new sources of seismic activity.

We assume that changes in the energy occur continuously over time. The corresponding model equations are

$$\begin{aligned}
\frac{dN_0}{dt} &= \sigma_0(t)N_0(t) - [f_0(t)+\gamma_0(t)]N_0(t) + g_1(t)N_1(t), \\
\frac{dN_i}{dt} &= \sigma_i(t)N_i(t) + f_{i-1}(t)N_{i-1}(t) - [f_i(t)+\gamma_i(t)]N_i(t) + g_{i+1}(t)N_{i+1}(t) - g_i(t)N_i(t), i = 1,\ldots.
\end{aligned} \tag{6}$$

The model (6) is a complicated one and can be treated numerically. It has an important specific case that can be treated analytically. In this case, $g_i(t)$ is very small, and because of this, these terms can be neglected. In other words, we assume that the probability that a source of seismic activity loses internal energy for reasons other than an earthquake is very small in comparison to the probabilities of occurrence for the other processes described in the model. In this case, the corresponding model equations become

$$\begin{aligned}
\frac{dN_0}{dt} &= \sigma_0(t)N_0(t) - [f_0(t)+\gamma_0(t)]N_0(t), \\
\frac{dN_i}{dt} &= \sigma_i(t)N_i(t) + f_{i-1}(t)N_{i-1}(t) - [f_i(t)+\gamma_i(t)]N_i(t), i = 1,\ldots.
\end{aligned} \tag{7}$$

The solution of the model system of Equation (7) is as follows:

$$\begin{aligned}
N_0(t) &= C_0 \exp\left[\int dt(\sigma_0(t) - f_0(t) - \gamma_0(t))\right], \\
N_i(t) &= \exp\left[-\int dt\ [f_i(t) - \sigma_i(t) + \gamma_i(t)]\right]\left\{C_i + \int dt\ f_{i-1}(t)N_{i-1}(t)\exp\left(\left[\int dt\ [f_i(t) - \right.\right.\right. \\
&\left.\left.\left.\sigma_i(t) + \gamma_i(t)]\right]\right)\right\},
\end{aligned} \tag{8}$$

where C_0 and C_i are constants of integration. By means of this model, we can discuss many situations in the studied cluster of sources of seismic activity.

We note that we can also write equations for the finite number of groups $i = 0, 1, \dots, I$. In this case, we have again (7), and the second equation of this system is for $i = 1, \dots, I-1$. For $i = I$, we have an additional equation. In this equation, we have to account for the fact that there is no next group, and because of this, $f_I = 0$. The additional equation becomes

$$\frac{dN_I}{dt} = f_{I-1}(t)N_{I-1}(t) + [\sigma_I(t) - \gamma_I(t)]N_I(t) - g_I(t)N_I(t). \quad (9)$$

As we assume that $g_I(t)$ has small values, (9) becomes

$$\frac{dN_I}{dt} = f_{I-1}(t)N_{I-1}(t) + [\sigma_I(t) - \gamma_I(t)]N_I(t). \quad (10)$$

Next, we show that specific cases of the above model lead to the Gutenberg–Richter law and the Omori law, which are well known in seismology.

3. Several Specific Cases of the Model

First, we consider the specific case where the model coefficients are time-independent. In this case, the model system (7) becomes

$$\begin{aligned}
\frac{dN_0}{dt} &= \sigma_0 N_0(t) - [f_0 + \gamma_0]N_0(t), \\
\frac{dN_i}{dt} &= \sigma_i N_i(t) + f_{i-1}N_{i-1}(t) - [f_i + \gamma_i]N_i(t),\ i = 1, \dots. \quad (11)
\end{aligned}$$

The solution is a specific case of the solution to the case of time-dependent coefficients

$$\begin{aligned}
N_0(t) &= C_0 \exp[(\sigma_0 - f_0 - \gamma_0)t], \\
N_i(t) &= \exp\left[(\sigma_i - f_i - \gamma_i)t\right]\left\{C_i + f_{i-1}\int dt\ N_{i-1}(t)\exp\left([f_i + \gamma_i - \sigma_i]t\right)\right\}, \quad (12)
\end{aligned}$$

where C_0 and C_i are constants of integration.

We will consider an even simpler specific case. This is a stationary case with time-independent model coefficients. In this case, the number of sources of seismic activity in each interval of energy does not change despite the changes in internal energy of the sources of seismic activity. The model equations are

$$\begin{aligned}
\sigma_0 N_0 - [f_0 + \gamma_0]N_0 &= 0, \\
\sigma_i N_i + f_{i-1}N_{i-1} - [f_i + \gamma_i]N_i &= 0, i = 1, \dots. \quad (13)
\end{aligned}$$

We use this specific case in the discussion below in the text.

In the stationary case, we have

$$\sigma_0 - f_0 - \gamma_0 = 0,$$

and N_0 is a free parameter. For the case of an infinite number of groups

$$N_i = \frac{f_{i-1}}{f_i + \gamma_i - \sigma_i} N_{i-1}, i = 1, \dots$$

N_{i-1} and N_i must be constants because of $\frac{dN_i}{dt} = 0$. Then, we can set $f_{i-1} = \kappa_i[f_i + \gamma_i - \sigma_i]$, where κ_i is a parameter. We note that $\kappa_i < 1$ for the case $N_i < N_{i-1}$. For N_i, we obtain

$$N_i = N_0 \prod_{j=1}^{i} \kappa_j = N_0 \prod_{j=1}^{i} \frac{f_{j-1}}{f_j + \gamma_j - \sigma_j}, i = 1, \ldots . \tag{14}$$

For the case of a finite number of groups, we obtain

$$N_i = N_0 \prod_{j=1}^{i} \kappa_i = N_0 \prod_{j=1}^{i} \frac{f_{j-1}}{f_j + \gamma_j - \sigma_j}, i = 1, \ldots, I-1$$

and

$$N_I = -\frac{f_{I-1}}{\delta_I} N_{I-1} = -\frac{f_{I-1}}{\sigma_I - \gamma_I} N_0 \prod_{j=1}^{I-1} \kappa_j = \frac{f_{I-1}}{\gamma_I - \sigma_I} N_0 \prod_{j=1}^{I-1} \frac{f_{j-1}}{f_j + \gamma_j - \sigma_j}. \tag{15}$$

Next, we can calculate the number of earthquakes in our system for the considered case of stationary-state and time-independent coefficients. For the case when the number of groups is infinite, the number of events by group i is

$$\mathcal{N}_i = \gamma_i N_i = \gamma_i N_0 \prod_{j=1}^{i} \kappa_j = \gamma_i N_0 \prod_{j=1}^{i} \frac{f_{j-1}}{f_j + \gamma_j - \sigma_j}, i = 1, \ldots . \tag{16}$$

For the case of a finite number of groups, we have again (16), but in this case, i changes from 1 to $I-1$. For $i = I$, we can use (16), keeping in mind that $f_I = 0$.

We note that for the case $\kappa_i = \kappa$, (16) reduces to

$$\mathcal{N}_i = \gamma_i N_i = \gamma_i N_0 \kappa^i, i = 1, \ldots . \tag{17}$$

In this case, $\kappa = \frac{f_{j-1}}{f_j + \gamma_j - \sigma_j}$.

Let us consider another specific case. This specific case would be of use for us in Section 7 when we discuss the relationships of the number of earthquakes arising from several regions. In this specific case, $\sigma_i = 0, i = 1, \ldots$ for the case of an infinite number of groups. This means that energy arrives at the system only through the smallest sources of seismic activity, which are in group 0. The model Equation (11) become

$$\begin{aligned} \frac{dN_0}{dt} &= \sigma_0 N_0(t) - [f_0 + \gamma_0] N_0(t). \\ \frac{dN_i}{dt} &= f_{i-1} N_{i-1} - [f_i + \gamma_i] N_i(t), i = 1, \ldots . \end{aligned} \tag{18}$$

Let us consider the specific case when all sources of seismic activity of a group are active, and they either supply energy to the next group or release energy by an earthquake. Then $f_i + \gamma_i = 1$ and we can write $f_i = q_i$ and $\gamma_i = 1 - q_i$. Then $\kappa_i = q_i$. We obtain from the model equations for the case of an infinite number of groups

$$\begin{aligned} \frac{dN_0}{dt} &= \sigma_0 N_0(t) - N_0(t). \\ \frac{dN_i}{dt} &= q_{i-1} N_{i-1} - N_i(t), i = 1, \ldots, \end{aligned} \tag{19}$$

For the stationary case, N_0 is a free parameter and $\sigma_0 = 1$. Further, we obtain for this case

$$N_i = q_{i-1} N_{i-1} = N_0 \prod_{j=0}^{i-1} q_j \tag{20}$$

For the case when all $q_i = q$, this reduces to

$$N_i = N_0 q^i. \tag{21}$$

The number of earthquakes in the case of different q_i is

$$\mathcal{N}_i = \gamma_i N_i = (1 - q_i) N_0 \prod_{j=0}^{i-1} q_j. \tag{22}$$

For the case of all $q_i = q$, this reduces to

$$\mathcal{N}_i = \gamma_i N_i = (1 - q) q^i N_0. \tag{23}$$

Let us now obtain the corresponding relationships for the case of a finite number of groups. In this case, the model equations are

$$\begin{aligned} \frac{dN_0}{dt} &= \sigma_0 N_0(t) - N_0(t), \\ \frac{dN_i}{dt} &= q_{i-1} N_{i-1} - N_i(t), i = 1, \ldots, I-1, \\ \frac{dN_I}{dt} &= q_{I-1} N_{I-1} - (1 - q_I) N_I(t). \end{aligned} \tag{24}$$

Then, for the stationary case, we have again N_0 as a free parameter and (21) till $i = I - 1$. For $i = I$, one obtains

$$N_I = \frac{q_{I-1}}{1 - q_I} N_0 \prod_{j=0}^{I-2} q_j. \tag{25}$$

In the case $q_i = q$, this leads to

$$N_I = \frac{q^I}{1 - q} N_0. \tag{26}$$

The total number of earthquakes from category I in the case of a finite number of groups is

$$\mathcal{N}_I = (1 - q_I) \frac{q_{I-1}}{1 - q_I} N_0 \prod_{j=0}^{I-2} q_j. \tag{27}$$

In the case $q_i = q$, this leads to

$$\mathcal{N}_I = q^I N_0. \tag{28}$$

The last results will be used in Section 7, where we will discuss earthquakes from more than one area and the connection of this situation to the negative binomial distribution.

4. Energy-Frequency Distribution

Let us return to the case of an infinite number of groups. We start from (14). We assume that the quantities connected to the exchange of energy depend on the internal energy, which is characteristic of the corresponding group. Let us assume the following relationships:

$$f_i = f_i^* E_i^{-s}; \quad \gamma_i = \gamma_i^* E_i^{-s}; \quad \sigma_i = \sigma_i^* E_i^{-s}. \tag{29}$$

Above, f_i^*, γ_j^*, and σ_j^* are constant parameters. s is also a parameter (we assume that this parameter has positive value). From (14), we obtain

$$N_i = N_0 \prod_{j=1}^{i} \frac{f_{j-1}^*}{f_j^* + \gamma_j^* - \sigma_j^*} \left(\frac{E_{i-1}}{E_i} \right)^{-s} \tag{30}$$

Let us denote

$$\chi_i(E_i, E_{i-1}) = \prod_{j=1}^{i} \frac{f_{j-1}^*}{f_j^* + \gamma_j^* - \sigma_j^*} \left(\frac{E_{i-1}}{E_i} \right)^{-s}.$$

Then, for the number of earthquakes of category i, we obtain

$$\mathcal{N}_i = \gamma_i N_i = \gamma_i^* N_0 \chi_i(E_i, E_{i-1}) E_i^{-s}. \tag{31}$$

Note that if $\chi_i(E_i, E_{i-1})$ does not depend much on i and it is close to a constant, then $\mathcal{N}_i \propto E_i^{-s}$.

We can choose different relationships for the relation between E_i and E_{i-1}. For example, we can assume

$$E_i = \epsilon E_{i-1}, \quad \epsilon > 1.$$

Then we have $\chi_i(E_i, E_{i-1}) = \epsilon^s \prod_{j=1}^{i} \frac{f_{j-1}^*}{f_j^* + \gamma_j^* - \sigma_j^*} = \epsilon^s \chi_i^*$.

Thus, from (30), we obtain

$$N_i = N_0 \chi_i^* \epsilon^s.$$

For the total number of earthquakes of category i, we obtain

$$\mathcal{N}_i = \gamma_i N_i = N_0 \epsilon^s \chi_i^* \gamma_i^* E_i^{-s}. \tag{32}$$

We note that we can consider another relationship between E_i and E_{i-1}. For example, we can assume $E_i = E_{i-1} + \Delta$ where Δ is some constant.

Then $\chi_i(E_i, E_{i-1}) = \chi_i(E_i) = \epsilon^s \prod_{j=1}^{i} \frac{f_{j-1}^*}{f_j^* + \gamma_j^* - \sigma_j^*} \left(1 - \frac{\Delta}{E_i}\right)^{-s}$ and

$$\mathcal{N}_i = \gamma_i N_i = N_0 \chi_i(E_i) \gamma_i^* E_i^{-s}. \tag{33}$$

For small $\frac{\Delta}{E_i}$ from (33), we have again that $\mathcal{N}_i \propto E_i^{-s}$.

5. Magnitude–Frequency Distribution. Gutenberg–Richter Law

The magnitude of the earthquake is proportional to the released energy. Thus, as magnitude $M > M_i$, we understand an earthquake with energy $E > E_i$.

Let us discuss the conditions for the occurrence of the Gutenberg–Richter law in our model. We begin with (17). Thus, we have made all the assumptions which lead to (17) and, in addition, $\kappa < 1$. We can calculate

$$\mathcal{N}_i = \gamma N_0 \sum_{j=i}^{\infty} \kappa^i = \gamma N_0 \left(\sum_{j=0}^{\infty} \kappa^i - \sum_{j=0}^{i-1} \kappa^i \right) = \gamma N_0 \frac{\kappa^{i-1}}{1-\kappa} \tag{34}$$

Let us set $\epsilon = 10^{\delta\beta}$, and we remember that $\kappa = \kappa^* \epsilon^{-s}$. Then from (34), we have

$$\mathcal{N}(M \geq M_i) = \gamma N_0 \frac{\kappa^{*i-1} \epsilon^{-(i-1)s}}{1 - \kappa^* \epsilon^{-s}}$$

Next, we assume that $\epsilon = 10^{\delta\beta}$. Then from the last relationship, we obtain

$$\mathcal{N}(M \geq M_i) = \gamma N_0 \frac{\kappa^{*i-1} 10^{-\delta\beta(i-1)s}}{1 - \kappa^* 10^{-\delta\beta s}}$$

Let now $M_i = \delta i$. Then,

$$\mathcal{N}(M \geq M_i) = \gamma N_0 \frac{\kappa^{*i-1} 10^{-M_i \beta s}}{10^{-\delta\beta s}[1 - \kappa^* 10^{-\delta\beta s}]}$$

Furthermore, we set $b = \beta s$. In addition, we set $10^a = \gamma N_0 \frac{\kappa^{*i-1}}{10^{-\delta\beta s}[1-\kappa^* 10^{-\delta\beta s}]}$ Then

$$\mathcal{N}(M \geq M_i) = 10^{a - bM_i}. \tag{35}$$

6. The Omori Law

In order to obtain the Omori law, we start from the system (7). We consider the case where $\sigma_i(t) = 0$. This means that we have a large earthquake and that no energy moves to the area under consideration. What happens are aftershocks ($\gamma_i(t) \neq 0$) and changes in energy of the sources of seismic activity. ($f_i(t) \neq 0$). The model system becomes

$$\begin{aligned} \frac{dN_0}{dt} &= -[f_0(t) + \gamma_0(t)]N_0(t). \\ \frac{dN_i}{dt} &= f_{i-1}(t)N_{i-1}(t) - [f_i(t) + \gamma_i(t)]N_i(t), i = 1, \ldots. \end{aligned} \tag{36}$$

Let $N(t) = \sum\limits_{i=0}^{\infty} N_(t)$ be the total number of sources of seismic activity. We sum the equations of the model system. The result is

$$\frac{dN}{dt} = -\sum_{j=0}^{\infty} \gamma_i(t) N_i(t). \tag{37}$$

The key assumption is that $\gamma_i(t) = \gamma(t)$. Then, the last relationship becomes

$$\frac{dN}{dt} = -\gamma(t) N(t). \tag{38}$$

The solution of this equation is

$$N(t) = D \exp[-\int dt \gamma(t)], \tag{39}$$

where D is a constant of integration.

Let us first consider the case $\gamma(t) = \gamma$. Then

$$N(t) = D \exp[-\gamma t].$$

The number of aftershocks at the moment t is

$$N^*(t) = \sum_{j=0}^{\infty} N_i^* = \sum_{j=0}^{\infty} \gamma N_i(t) = \gamma N(t) = \gamma D \exp[-\gamma t]. \tag{40}$$

Thus, for the case of constant γ, we have the exponential decay of aftershocks in the considered time. Note that for small t,

$$N^*(t) \approx \frac{\gamma D}{1+\gamma t},$$

which is the original form of the Omori law.

In order to obtain the Omori law, we have to assume that $\gamma(t)$ has appropriate dependence on t. Then, we have to start from (39). In this case, the number of aftershocks at the time t is

$$N^*(t) = \sum_{j=0}^{\infty} N_i^* = \sum_{j=0}^{\infty} \gamma(t) N_i(t) = \gamma(t) N(t) = \gamma(t) D \exp[-\int dt \gamma(t)].$$

We equate this to the Omori law (5) and obtain an equation for $\gamma(t)$. Let us assume that $\gamma(t) = (d\mu/dt)/\mu$. This leads to the following equation for μ:

$$\frac{d\mu}{dt} = \frac{k}{D(c+t)^p}\mu^2. \tag{41}$$

The solution of this equation is

$$\mu = \frac{D(p-1)(c+t)^{p-1}}{k}.$$

From here,

$$\gamma(t) = \frac{p-1}{c+t}.$$

In order to obtain the Omori law, we have to set the integration constant D to $D = k/(p-1)$. Thus,

$$\gamma(t) = \frac{k}{D(c+t)}. \tag{42}$$

Thus, the Omori law occurs for the specific value of $\gamma(t)$ given by (42).

7. Earthquakes from Different Clusters of Sources of Seismic Activity

Let us consider (17). For the case of two volumes containing clusters of seismic sources—cluster 1 and cluster 2—we obtain

$$\frac{\mathcal{N}_i^{(1,2)}}{N_0^{1,2}} = \gamma_i^{(1,2)} \kappa^{i(1,2)} \tag{43}$$

Below, we demonstrate the occurrence of the negative binomial distribution for the observation of earthquakes happening in several clusters of seismic sources. In order to achieve this, we return to the specific case of the relationship (17) considered above in the text. This specific case leads us to the relationship (23). For the case of two clusters, we obtain from (23)

$$\frac{\mathcal{N}_i^{(1,2)}}{N_0^{(1,2)}} = q^i(1-q) \tag{44}$$

where q is the same for the two regions and i runs from 1 to $n-1$ for region 1 and from 1 to $m-1$ for region 2. We treat the number of earthquakes in the two regions as independent random variables. Under this assumption (that $T = X + Y$ is a sum of two independent random variables), we obtain for the distribution function $f_T = f_{X+Y}(t)$, $t < min(n,m)$.

$$f_T(t) = \sum_x f_X(x) f_Y(t-x) = \sum_{x=0}^{t} q^x(1-q)q^{t-x}(1-q) = \binom{t+1}{t} q^t (1-q)^2.$$

Then, for this process,

$$\frac{\mathcal{N}_i}{N_0} = \binom{i+1}{i} q^i (1-q)^2. \tag{45}$$

However,

$$N_0 = N_0^{(1)} + N_0^{(2)} = \frac{\mathcal{N}_t^{(1)}}{1-q^n} + \frac{\mathcal{N}_t^{(2)}}{1-q^m}.$$

Here, $\mathcal{N}_t^{(1)} = \sum\limits_{j=0}^{n-1} \mathcal{N}_j$ for region 1 and $\mathcal{N}_t^{(2)} = \sum\limits_{j=0}^{m-1} \mathcal{N}_j$ for region 2. Then the number of earthquakes generated in the two regions is

$$\mathcal{N}_i = \binom{i+1}{i} q^i (1-q)^2 \left(\frac{\mathcal{N}_t^{(1)}}{1-q^n} + \frac{\mathcal{N}_t^{(2)}}{1-q^m} \right). \tag{46}$$

For the case of r regions, the corresponding result is

$$\mathcal{N}_i = \binom{i+r-1}{r-1} q^i (1-q)^r \sum_{k=1}^{r} \frac{\mathcal{N}_t^{(k)}}{1-q^{n^{(k)}}}. \tag{47}$$

Thus, the discussed model supports the assumption [1] and the observations [51,52] that the negative binomial distribution can occur as a statistical distribution of earthquake numbers and can describe very well sets of such numbers.

8. Discussion

In this article, we discuss a simple model that leads to several important relationships connected to earthquakes such as the Gutenberg–Richter law and the Omori law. The model uses minimal information about the topology and mechanics of occurrence of earthquakes. Instead, the model is based on the concept of the motion, dissipation, accumulation, and release of energy in a cluster of sources of seismic activity. The sources of seismic activity are distributed in groups according to their internal energy. In the case of an infinite number of groups, we consider a specific form of the model, which is given by the system of Equation (6). This system can be treated numerically. The assumption of a much larger probability of accumulation of internal energy leads us to the system of Equation (7). This system can be solved analytically, and it is the basis for analytical results discussed in this article. In the case of a finite number of groups, we have to add Equation (10). This model can describe various kinds of complicated dynamics. The Gutenberg–Richer law and the Omori law are obtained for specific cases of the model. In order to obtain the Gutenberg–Richter law, we have to assume a specific case where one has a stationary state and time-independent parameters of the model. In addition, we reduced the number of parameters which regulate the motion of energy: we have only three such parameters: γ, σ, and f. We note that the relationships are obtained for a single volume (single cluster of sources of seismic activity). In addition, we note that the model can also lead to relationships that are different from the Gutenberg–Richter relationship. This can happen if the values of some of the parameters γ_i, σ_i, and f_i differ from the values γ, σ, and f or/and the case is not stationary. Thus, the model can explain a part of the differences between the relationship connected to the real situation and the Gutenberg–Richter relationship, which is connected to very specific requirements about the model parameters and about the motion of the energy in the (single) cluster of sources of seismic activity.

The Omori law is obtained for the specific case of the absence of an exchange of energy between the environment and the system of seismic sources after a large earthquake. In addition, a specific value of the parameter $\gamma(t)$, which regulates the release of seismic energy, must be presented, and this parameter has to be the same for the sources of seismic activity with different energies. It is clear that if these requirements are not met, the relationship for the time dependence of the number of aftershocks can differ from the Omori law, and this law can be only an approximation of the relationship corresponding to the real situation.

Finally, we discuss the distribution of earthquakes from several volumes (several clusters of sources of seismic activity). We show that the distribution of earthquakes in this case contains a specific case distribution which is very close to the negative binomial distribution. The obtained distribution has two parameters. The first parameter r is characteristic of the number of volumes (clusters of sources of seismic activity), and the second parameter q can be connected to the parameter b of the Gutenberg–Richter law. The occurrence of a distribution that is close to the negative binomial distribution leads to a natural explanation of the roll-off effect and the possibility for the occurrence of characteristic earthquakes (large-magnitude earthquakes which occur more frequently as predicted by the Gutenberg–Richter law). Thus, the model supports the hypothesis that the negative binomial distribution occurs because of the consideration of earthquakes from more than one cluster of sources of seismic activity.

Further information about the application of the theory to real data can be seen in Appendix A.

9. Conclusions

In this article, we present a simple mathematical theory which leads to several well-known relationships such as the Gutenberg–Richer law, Omori law, etc. The theory is based on the concept of energy. This allows us to obtain the corresponding relationships without the use of considerations connected to the mechanics of seismic events. We do not use details of seismic sources or equations of motion, and we do not consider the different kinds of waves traveling at the surface and in the interior of the Earth. We do not use details about kinematics or about the dynamics of the seismic sources. However, we have shown that a simple model, linear with respect to $N(t)$ and with time-dependent coefficients in general, is capable of leading to important laws and relationships in seismology. We note that research based on energy considerations has also been conducted by other authors [53].

We think that our approach will point to new research questions. One of these questions is about the connections between the presented theory and the characteristics of the mechanical vibrations of the Earth caused naturally by earthquakes. Other questions are connected to the relationship between the presented theory and the aspects of the mechanics of seismic events, mentioned above. Research results on some of these questions will be presented elsewhere.

Author Contributions: Conceptualization: N.K.V. and R.B.; methodology, N.K.V. and R.B.; software, R.B.; validation, N.K.V. and R.B.; formal analysis, N.K.V. and R.B.; resources, N.K.V.; data curation, R.B.; writing—original draft preparation, N.K.V.; writing—review and editing, N.K.V.; visualization, R.B.; supervision, N.K.V.; project administration, R.B.; funding acquisition, N.K.V. All authors have read and agreed to the published version of the manuscript.

Funding: This research received no external funding .

Data Availability Statement: He original contributions presented in the study are included in the article, further inquiries can be directed to the corresponding author..

Conflicts of Interest: The authors declare no conflicts of interest.

Appendix A. Notes About the Application of the Model (6) to Real Data

The model (6) and its truncated versions (6), (9), can fit very well into any real data set because of the flexibility of the model parameters. To show this, we present below a Lemma and a Theorem that prove the last statement for a single cluster of sources of seismic activity (the Lemma) and any set of clusters of sources of seismic activity (the Theorem).

Lemma A1. *Let us have a cluster of sources of seismic activity, and let us measure the changes in the internal energy of the sources over time. Let the internal energy of the sources in the group i be between E_{i-1} and $E_i > E_{i-1}$, $i = 1, 2, \ldots$. Let us record the following: the rise of new sources of seismic activity, changes in the internal energy of existing sources, and the release of internal energy by means of earthquakes. Then, the model (6) describes the time evolution of the number of sources of seismic activity in each group of sources of seismic activity.*

Proof. Let us consider the groups of sources of seismic activity that occur from sorting the sources in a cluster of sources of seismic activity according to their internal energy, as described in the text of the Lemma. Then, we consider the following:

1. One observes the birth of some number of new sources of seismic activity in each group. This change is described in the model by the term $\sigma_i(t)N_i(t)$. Let the number of the newborn sources be $N_i^*(t)$. Then we can set $\sigma_i(t) = N_i^*(t)/N_i(t)$. Thus, the model (6) captures correctly the number of new sources of seismic activity arising in each group i at any moment t.
2. The internal energy of the sources of seismic activity from group i can increase and decrease in time and some of these sources can leave group i. The model gives the number of sources of seismic activity that increase their internal energy and leave group i as $f_i(t)N_i(t)$ and the number of sources of seismic activity that decrease their energy and leave group i as $g_i(t)N_i(t)$. Let the number of sources of seismic activity that increase their internal energy and leave group i be $I_i(t)$. Let the number of sources of seismic activity that decrease their internal energy and leave group i be $D_i(t)$. We can set $f_i(t) = I_i(t)/N_i(t)$ and $g_i(t) = D_i(t)/N_i(t)$. Thus, the model (6) captures correctly any changes in the number of the existing sources of seismic activity in group i which are a consequence of an increase or decrease in the internal energy of the sources, which leads to the transfer of sources of seismic activity to other groups.
3. Finally, the number of sources of seismic activity in group i can decrease because of the release of energy by the sources in the form of earthquakes. The model describes this change as $\gamma_i(t)N_i(t)$. Let the number of earthquakes from the i-th group be $Q_i(t)$. Then we can set $\gamma_i(t) = Q_i(t)/N_i(t)$. Thus, the model (6) captures correctly any changes in the number of the existing sources of seismic activity in group i which are a consequence of the release of internal energy in the form of earthquakes.

Thus, we have shown that the model (6) can capture correctly the birth, deaths, and changes in the number of sources of seismic activity with a specified internal energy in a cluster of sources of seismic activity using the appropriate setting of the functions $\sigma_i(t)$, $f_i(t)$, $g_i(t)$, and $\gamma_i(t)$, which are parametric functions of the model. □

Theorem A1. *Let us have a set of clusters of sources of seismic activity. Let us measure the changes of the internal energy of these sources over time. Let us group the sources of seismic activity from any cluster k ($k = 1, 2, \ldots$) in groups, and let the internal energy of the sources in group i be between $E_{k_{i-1}}$ and $E_{k_i} > E_{k_{i-1}}$, $i = 1, 2, \ldots$. Let us record the following: the rise of new sources of seismic activity, changes in the internal energy of the existing sources, and the release of internal energy through earthquakes in any of the clusters. Then, the model (6) describes the time evolution* *of the number of sources of seismic activity in each group of such sources in the entire set of clusters of sources of seismic activity.*

Proof. According to the Lemma above, the model (6) describes the time evolution of the number of sources of seismic activity in each group of such sources in any of the clusters of sources of seismic activity. This holds for any cluster from the sets of clusters. Thus, the model (6) describes the time evolution of the number of sources of seismic activity in each group of energy sources in any cluster of the entire set of clusters of sources of seismic activity. □

We note that a similar Lemma and Theorem can be formulated also for the truncated version of the model (6), which includes Equations (6) and (9). Thus, the model discussed in the main text is very flexible for describing the corresponding class of experimental sets of data connected with seismic activity.

References

1. Kagan, Y.Y. Statistical distributions of earthquake numbers: Consequence of branching process. *Geophys. J. Int.* **2010**, *180*, 1313–1328. [CrossRef]
2. Bak, P.; Tang, C.; Wiesenfeld, K. Self-organized criticality: An explanation of the 1/f noise. *Phys. Rev. Lett.* **1987**, *59*, 381–384. [CrossRef] [PubMed]
3. Ito, K.; Matsuzaki, M. Earthquakes as self-organized critical phenomena. *J. Geophys. Res. Solid Earth* **1990**, *95*, 6853–6860. [CrossRef]
4. Chen, K.; Bak, P.; Obukhov, S.P. Self-organized criticality in a crack-propagation model of earthquakes. *Phys. Rev. A* **1991**, *43*, 625–630. [CrossRef] [PubMed]
5. Turcotte, D.L. *Fractals and Chaos in Geology and Geophysics*; Cambridge University Press: Cambridge, UK, 1997; ISBN 978-1-139-17469-5.
6. Kagan, Y.Y. *Earthquakes: Models, Statistics, Testable Forecasts*; John Wiley & Sons: Hoboken, NJ, USA, 2013; ISBN 978-1-118-63789-0.
7. Gutenberg, B.; Richter, C.F. Frequency of earthquakes in California. *Bull. Seismol. Soc. Am.* **1944**, *34*, 185–188. [CrossRef]
8. Scholz, C.H. *The Mechanics of Earthquakes and Faulting*; Cambridge University Press: Cambridge, UK, 2019; ISBN 978-1-316-68147-3.
9. Kagan, Y.Y. Seismic moment distribution revisited: I. Statistical results. *Geophys. J. Int.* **2002**, *148*, 520–541. [CrossRef]
10. Schwartz, D.P.; Coppersmith, K.J. Fault behavior and characteristic earthquakes: Examples from the Wasatch and San Andreas fault zones. *J. Geophys. Res. Solid Earth* **1984**, *89*, 5681–5698. [CrossRef]
11. Bhattacharya, P.; Chakrabarti, B.K.; Samanta, D. Fractal models of earthquake dynamics. In *Reviews of Nonlinear Dynamics and Complexity*; Schuster, H.G., Ed.; Wiley: Hoboken, NJ, USA, 2009; Volume 2, Charpter 4. [CrossRef]
12. Pelletier, J.D. Spring-block models of seismicity: Review and analysis of a structurally heterogeneous model coupled to a viscous asthenosphere. *Geocomplex Phys. Earthq.* **2000**, *120*, 27–42. [CrossRef]
13. Main, I.G.; Burton, P.W. Information theory and the earthquake frequency-magnitude distribution. *Bull. Seismol. Soc. Am.* **1984**, *74*, 1409–1426. [CrossRef]
14. Geffers, G.M.; Main, I.G.; Naylor, M. Accuracy and precision of frequency—Size distribution scaling parameters as a function of dynamic range of observations: Example of the Gutenberg–Richter law b-value for earthquakes. *Geophys. J. Int.* **2023**, *232*, 2080–2086. [CrossRef]
15. Kijko, A.; Singh, M. Statistical tools for maximum possible earthquake magnitude estimation. *Acta Geophys.* **2011**, *59*, 674–700. [CrossRef]
16. Beirlant, J.; Alves, I.F.; Gomes, I. Tail fitting for truncated and non-truncated Pareto-type distributions. *Extremes* **2016**, *19*, 429–462. [CrossRef]
17. Beirlant, J.; Kijko, A.; Reynkens, T.; Einmahl, J.H.J. Estimating the maximum possible earthquake magnitude using extreme value methodology: The Groningen case. *Nat. Hazards* **2019**, *98*, 1091–1113. [CrossRef]
18. Kramer, S.L. *Geotechnical Earthquake Engineering*; Prentice Hall: Hoboken, NJ, USA, 1996; ISBN 978-0-133-74943-4.
19. Omori, F. On the aftershocks of earthquakes. *J. Coll. Sci. Imp. Univ. Tokyo* **1894**, *7*, 111–200.
20. Guglielmi, A.V. Omori's law: A note on the history of geophysics. *Physics-Uspekhi* **2017**, *60*, 319–324. [CrossRef]
21. Guglielmi, A.V.; Zavyalova, A.D. The Omori Law: The 150-Year Birthday Jubilee of Fusakichi Omori. *J. Volcanol. Seismol.* **2018**, *12*, 353–358. [CrossRef]
22. Utsu, T. A statistical study on the occurrence of aftershocks. *Geophys. Mag.* **1961**, *30*, 521–605.
23. Utsu, T.; Ogata, Y.; Matsuura, R.S. The centenary of the Omori formula for a decay law of aftershock activity. *J. Phys. Earth* **1995**, *43*, 1–33. [CrossRef]

24. Vere-Jones, D. Stochastic models for earthquake occurrence (with discussion). *J. Roy. Stat. Soc.* **1970**, *B32*, 1–45. [CrossRef]
25. Ogata, Y. Statistical models for earthquake occurrences and residual analysis for point processes. *J. Am. Stat. Assoc.* **1988**, *83*, 9–27. [CrossRef]
26. Reasenberg, P.A.; Jones, L.M. Earthquake hazard after a mainshock in California. *Science* **1989**, *243*, 1173–1176. [CrossRef] [PubMed]
27. Kagan, Y.Y.; Jackson, D.D. Long-term earthquake clustering. *Geophys. J. Int.* **1991**, *104*, 117–133. [CrossRef]
28. Ogata, Y. Space-time point-process models for earthquake occurrences. *Ann. Inst. Stat. Math.* **1988**, *50*, 379–402. [CrossRef]
29. Zhuang, J.; Ogata, Y.; Vere-Jones, D. Stochastic declustering of space-time earthquake occurrences. *J. Am. Stat. Assoc.* **2002**, *97*, 369–380. [CrossRef]
30. Console, R.; Murru, M.; Lombardi, A.M. Refining earthquake clustering models. *J. Geophys. Res.* **2003**, *108*, 2468. [CrossRef]
31. Sornette, D. *Critical Phenomena in Natural Sciences*; Springer: Berlin/Heidelberg, Germany, 2002; ISBN 978-3-540-30882-9.
32. Vere-Jones, D. A branching model for crack propagation. *Pure Appl. Geophys.* **1976**, *114*, 711–725. [CrossRef]
33. Kagan, Y.Y.; Knopoff, L. Stochastic synthesis of earthquake catalogs. *J. Geophys. Res.* **1981**, *86*, 2853–2862. [CrossRef]
34. Kagan, Y.Y. Stochastic model of earthquake fault geometry. *Geophys. J. Roy. Astr. Soc.* **1982**, *71*, 659–691. [CrossRef]
35. Kagan, Y.Y. Observational evidence for earthquakes as a nonlinear dynamic process. *Phys. D* **1994**, *77*, 160–192. [CrossRef]
36. Kagan, Y.Y.; Jackson, D.D. Probabilistic forecasting of earthquakes. *Geophys. J. Int.* **2000**, *143*, 438–453. [CrossRef]
37. Saichev, A.; Sornette, D. Anomalous power law distribution of total lifetimes of branching processes: Application to earthquake aftershock sequences. *Phys. Rev. E* **2004**, *70*, 046123. [CrossRef]
38. Marzocchi, W.; Lombardi, A.M. A double branching model for earthquake occurrence. *J. Geophys. Res. Solid Earth* **2008**, *113*, B08317. [CrossRef]
39. Dionysiou, D.D.; Papadopoulos, G.A. Poissonian and negative binomial modelling of earthquake time series in the Aegean area. *Phys. Earth Planet. Inter.* **1992**, *71*, 154–165. [CrossRef]
40. Kagan, Y.Y. Comment on "The Gutenberg-Richter or characteristic earthquake distribution, which is it?" by Steven G. Wesnousky. *Bull. Seismol. Soc. Amer.* **1996**, *86*, 274–285. [CrossRef]
41. Jackson, D.D.; Kagan, Y.Y. Testable earthquake forecasts for 1999. *Seism. Res. Lett.* **1999**, *70*, 393–403. [CrossRef]
42. Taroni, M.; Spassiani, I.; Laskin, N.; Barani, S. How many strong earthquakes will there be tomorrow? *Front. Appl. Math. Stat.* **2023**, *9*, 1152476. [CrossRef]
43. Vitanov, N.K.; Vitanov, K.N. Box model of migration channels. *Math. Soc. Sci.* **2016**, *80*, 108–114. [CrossRef]
44. Vitanov, N.K.; Vitanov, K.N. On the motion of substance in a channel of a network and human migration. *Phys. A* **2018**, *490*, 1277–1294. [CrossRef]
45. Vitanov, N.K.; Vitanov, K.N. Discrete-time model for a motion of substance in a channel of a network with application to channels of human migration. *Phys. A* **2018**, *509*, 635–650. [CrossRef]
46. Vitanov, N.K.; Vitanov, K.N. Statistical distributions connected to motion of substance in a channel of a network. *Phys. A* **2019**, *527*, 121174. [CrossRef]
47. Borisov, R.; Dimitrova, Z.I.; Vitanov, N.K. Statistical characteristics of stationary flow of substance in a network channel containing arbitrary number of arms. *Entropy* **2020**, *22*, 553. [CrossRef] [PubMed]
48. Vitanov, N.K.; Vitanov, K.N.; Kantz, H. On the motion of substance in a channel of a network: Extended model and new classes of probability distributions. *Entropy* **2020**, *22*, 1240. [CrossRef] [PubMed]
49. Vitanov, N.K.; Borisov, R.; Vitanov, K.N. On the motion of substance in a channel and growth of random networks. *Phys. A* **2021**, *581*, 126207. [CrossRef]
50. Aki, K.; Richards, P.G. *Quantitative Seismology*; University Science Books: Sansalito, CA, USA, 2002; ISBN 0-935792-96-2.
51. Rao, N.M.; Kaila, K.L. Application of the negative binomial to earthquake occurrences in the Alpide-Himalayan belt. *Geophys. J. R. Astron. Soc.* **1986**, *85*, 283–290. [CrossRef]
52. Mohamed, N.A.; Hisam, M.N.F. Introduction to worldwide earthquake probability distributions. *AIP Conf. Proc.* **2021**, *2905*, 080008. [CrossRef]
53. Barani, S.; Taroni, M.; Zaccagnino, D.; Harris, P.A.; Petrillo, G. A Physics-informed stochastic model for long-term correlation of earthquakes. *Prepr. Res. Sq.* **2024**. [CrossRef]

Disclaimer/Publisher's Note: The statements, opinions and data contained in all publications are solely those of the individual author(s) and contributor(s) and not of MDPI and/or the editor(s). MDPI and/or the editor(s) disclaim responsibility for any injury to people or property resulting from any ideas, methods, instructions or products referred to in the content.

entropy

MDPI

Article

Statistical Characteristics of Strong Earthquake Sequence in Northeastern Tibetan Plateau

Ying Wang [1], Rui Wang [2,3,*], Peng Han [2,3,4], Tao Zhao [1], Miao Miao [2,5], Lina Su [1], Zhaodi Jin [1] and Jiancang Zhuang [6]

1 Shaanxi Earthquake Agency, Xi'an 710068, China; wy200543@163.com (Y.W.); zhaotaowy@163.com (T.Z.); sulinawhu@163.com (L.S.); jinxiaoyu991150@163.com (Z.J.)
2 Department of Earth and Space Science, Southern University of Science and Technology, Shenzhen 518055, China; hanp@sustech.edu.cn (P.H.); miaom@sustech.edu.cn (M.M.)
3 Key Laboratory of Earthquake Forecasting and Risk Assessment, Ministry of Emergency Management, Southern University of Science and Technology, Shenzhen 518055, China
4 Guangdong Provincial Key Laboratory of Geophysical High-Resolution Imaging Technology, Southern University of Science and Technology, Shenzhen 518055, China
5 China Nuclear Power Engineering Co., Ltd., Shenzhen 518172, China
6 Institute of Statistical Mathematics, Tokyo 190-8562, Japan; zhuangjc@ism.ac.jp
* Correspondence: wangr9@sustech.edu.cn

Abstract: As the forefront of inland extension on the Indian plate, the northeastern Tibetan Plateau, marked by low strain rates and high stress levels, is one of the regions with the highest seismic risk. Analyzing seismicity through statistical methods holds significant scientific value for understanding tectonic conditions and assessing earthquake risk. However, seismic monitoring capacity in this region remains limited, and earthquake frequency is low, complicating efforts to improve earthquake catalogs through enhanced identification and localization techniques. Bi-scale empirical probability integral transformation (BEPIT), a statistical method, can address these data gaps by supplementing missing events shortly after moderate to large earthquakes, resulting in a more reliable statistical data set. In this study, we analyzed six earthquake sequences with magnitudes of $M_S \geq 6.0$ that occurred in northeastern Tibet since 2009, following the upgrade of the regional seismic network. Using BEPIT, we supplemented short-term missing aftershocks in these sequences, creating a more complete earthquake catalog. ETAS model parameters and b values for these sequences were then estimated using maximum likelihood methods to analyze parameter variability across sequences. The findings indicate that the b value is low, reflecting relatively high regional stress. The background seismicity rate is very low, with most mainshocks in these sequences being background events rather than foreshock-driven events. The p-parameter of the ETAS model is high, indicating that aftershocks decay relatively quickly, while the α-parameter is also elevated, suggesting that aftershocks are predominantly induced by the mainshock. These conditions suggest that earthquake prediction in this region is challenging through seismicity analysis alone, and alternative approaches integrating non-seismic data, such as electromagnetic and fluid monitoring, may offer more viable solutions. This study provides valuable insights into earthquake forecasting in the northeastern Tibetan Plateau.

Keywords: earthquake sequence; statistical analysis; ETAS model; b value; bi-scale transformation

1. Introduction

Earthquakes are among the most devastating natural disasters worldwide. The largest and most destructive seismic events typically occur at plate boundaries. Notable examples

https://doi.org/10.3390/e27020174

include the 1960 $M_W9.5$ Valdivia earthquake in Chile, the 2010 $M_W8.8$ Maule earthquake in Chile, the 2011 $M_W9.0$ Tohoku earthquake in Japan, and the 2007 $M_W8.5$ Sumatra earthquake, among others [1–5]. However, accurate earthquake prediction remains an unsolved challenge. To advance this field, many researchers have concentrated on seismically active regions, including Sichuan-Yunnan in China, Japan, California in the United States, and New Zealand, and conducted extensive observations. Utilizing a wealth of data from these regions, researchers have developed various statistical and physical methods to identify patterns of seismic activity, which has led to improvements in prediction efficiency. Examples of such methods include the b value, the Epidemic-Type Aftershock Sequence (ETAS) model, as well as methods for earthquake identification and localization [6–12]. However, these methods are not applicable in certain regions, making earthquake prediction in these areas particularly challenging.

The Tibetan Plateau is a region of particular geological significance, characterized by its highly complex geological structure. The northeastern section of the plateau represents the frontal region, extending into the mainland [13,14]. Due to the extension of the plateau, stress continuously accumulates; however, the strain rate is approximately 2 mm/year [15], significantly lower than that observed in subduction zones, and the earthquake frequency is relatively low [16]. This discrepancy results in a high level of stress within the region. The high stress levels combined with the complex geological conditions make this region one of the areas with the highest earthquake hazard, contributing to its complex seismicity. Historically, the region has experienced numerous large earthquakes, one of the most notable being the 1920 $M8^1/_2$ Haiyuan earthquake, renowned as one of the most destructive events in seismic history. In recent years, significant seismic events have occurred, including the $M_S7.4$ earthquake in Maduo in 2021; the $M_S6.9$ earthquake in Menyuan, Qinghai Province, in 2022; and the Maerkang $M_S6.0$ earthquake swarm in Sichuan Province in 2022. These events suggest increased seismic activity in the northwestern part of the Qinghai–Tibet Plateau, highlighting the region's substantial earthquake hazard and drawing considerable attention from seismologists. A clear understanding of seismicity characteristics in this area is essential for effective earthquake prevention and disaster response efforts. With the comprehensive upgrade of the seismic network since 2009, earthquake monitoring capabilities have significantly improved, providing an invaluable opportunity to investigate seismicity characteristics through statistical approaches.

The ETAS model is a widely used tool for simulating the temporal evolution of seismicity rates. As one of the most realistic time series models, the ETAS model has been employed by researchers to analyze earthquake sequences across different regions, yielding insights into the characteristics of seismic activity. In China, some scholars [17,18] have utilized the ETAS model to investigate the distribution characteristics of earthquake sequence parameters. As a method based on statistics, the ETAS model relies heavily on earthquake catalogs as its data source. However, the effectiveness of earthquake monitoring can decline significantly following a major earthquake, both within the affected area and potentially in surrounding regions, due to the difficulty of detecting smaller earthquakes amidst the occurrence of numerous moderate to large earthquakes [19,20]. Consequently, a significant amount of post-earthquake data remain unrecorded, resulting in an increase in the number of incomplete magnitude readings. This scarcity can severely undermine the accuracy and stability of parameters fitting within the ETAS model. One relatively straightforward approach to mitigate this issue is to select a higher threshold magnitude; however, a low number of recorded earthquakes can also lead to unstable results [21,22]. Alternative methods aim to address catalog completeness. The template matching technique and other earthquake recognition methods are frequently employed to identify smaller earthquakes, but they require an extensive earthquake observation system [23–27]. The complex terrain of the northeastern Tibetan Plateau complicates the establishment of a dense seismic network, making the application of template matching in this region challenging. The bi-scale empirical probability integral transformation (BEPIT) method proposed by Zhuang et al. [28,29] can be applied to seismic sequences with sparse seismic stations and weak early monitoring ability based on the statistical law of aftershock attenuation. This method has been proven to help estimate stable attenuation parameters and obtain parameter information of early post-earthquake aftershock sequences [30,31]. Consequently, this method is employed in the present investigation to replenish the catalog of earthquake events immediately following the main shock.

In this study, we investigate the statistical characteristics of strong earthquake sequences ($M_S \geq 6.0$) in the northeastern Tibetan Plateau since 2009. Prior to analysis, we apply a seismic event replenishment technique based on statistical seismology to address the low seismicity rate and the incompleteness of the earthquake catalog following major earthquakes. Our analysis focuses on the seismic sequence parameters of these events, utilizing the ETAS model and the b value to elucidate the characteristics of seismicity in the region. Subsequently, we discuss the implications and potential applications of these findings in earthquake forecasting. This study seeks to contribute meaningful insights toward improving earthquake forecasting in the northeastern Tibetan Plateau.

2. Materials and Methods

2.1. Study Area and Data Selection

Six earthquake sequences with $M_S \geq 6.0$ have occurred on the northeastern Tibetan Plateau since 2009 and were selected for investigation. In the study region, seismic station coverage is sparse; as shown in Figure 1, there are four or fewer seismic stations within 100 km of each mainshock epicenter. Figure 1 displays the locations of these seismic events, which include the following: the 2013 M_S6.6 earthquake sequence in Minxian, Gansu Province; the 2016 M_S6.4 earthquake sequence in Menyuan, Qinghai Province; the 2017 M_S7.0 earthquake sequence in Jiuzhaigou, Sichuan Province; the 2021 M_S7.4 earthquake sequence in Maduo, Qinghai Province; the 2022 M_S6.9 earthquake sequence in Menyuan, Qinghai Province; and the 2022 M_S6.0 earthquake cluster in Maerkang, Sichuan Province. The earthquake data utilized in this study were obtained from the China Earthquake Networks Center (CENC). Only events with $M_L \geq 0.0$ are included in the data set. In selecting earthquake sequences, priority is given to intensive aftershock areas that develop within one month following each main event. The data retained for analysis also include the period preceding the main earthquake, enabling an examination of background seismic activity based on the level of seismicity and magnitude of the main event within the selected region.

Complete seismic samples are the basis of reliable results. The complete magnitude of completeness (M_C) is the smallest magnitude at which an earthquake can be completely monitored. It is an index to evaluate the quality of an earthquake catalog. In this study, the maximum curvature (MAXC) method is applied to estimate the temporal M_C of the sequence catalog [32]. This approach aids in estimating a new empirical distribution function based on fully recorded seismic data. However, previous studies indicate that the complete magnitude calculated by the MAXC method tends to be relatively low [33]. Therefore, in this study, we adjusted the MAXC result by adding 0.2 to define the complete magnitude. Using a moving time window, we conducted a temporal M_C. The higher M_C before and after the main shock are set to be the thresholds of magnitude for replenishing to ensure the completeness of the earthquake catalog for most of the time except for immediately after the mainshock. The M_C after supplementing is shown in Table 1.

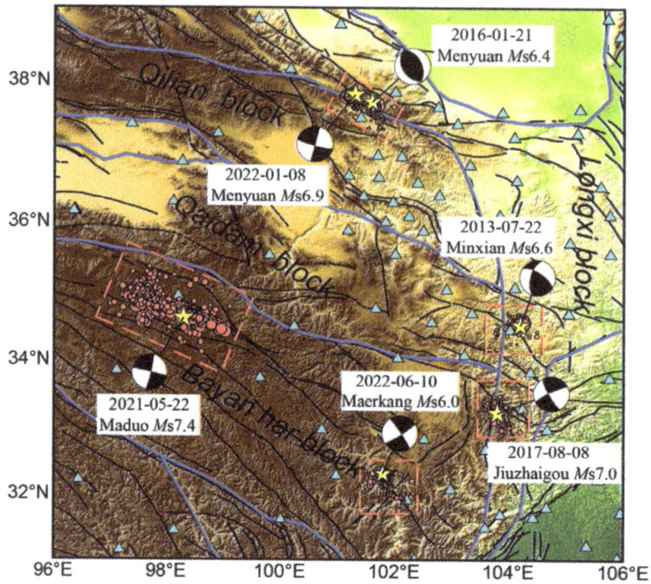

Figure 1. The spatial distribution of six earthquake sequences with a mainshock of $M_S \geq 6.0$ in the northeastern Tibetan Plateau since 2010. The seismic events are represented by red dots, scaled according to their magnitudes. The mainshocks of each sequence are distinguished by yellow five-pointed stars, and the individual focal mechanisms of the mainshocks are marked. Tectonic blocks are delineated by solid blue lines, while tectonic fractures are depicted by solid black lines. Additionally, observation stations are denoted by light blue triangles in the diagram. The focal mechanism results were obtained from the Global CMT Catalog (www.globalcmt.org).

Table 1. The M_C and the supplementary results of six seismic sequences.

Time (dd-mm-yyyy)	Region	M_S	Mc Before Supplementing	Mc After Supplementing
22 May 2021	Maduo	7.4	2.9	1.5
22 July 2013	Minxian	6.6	2.4	1.0
22 January 2016	Menyuan	6.4	1.5	0.8
8 August 2017	Jiuzhaigou	7.0	2.1	1.5
8 January 2022	Menyuan	6.9	2.0	1.5
10 June 2022	Maerkang	6.0	2.0	0.6

2.2. Seismic Event Supplement Technique Based on Statistical Seismology

Randomly occurring seismic events are commonly regarded as marking point processes [34–37]. Based on this framework, Zhuang et al. [28,29] proposed a novel algorithm, the BEPIT, employing a two-scale transformation technique. This algorithm was designed to supplement missing seismic events in incomplete records.

Suppose $N = \{(t_i, m_i) : i = 1, 2, \ldots, n\}$ is a temporal marked point process in a time–magnitude domain $[0, T] \times M$, where M is the space of marks. Using the following BEPIT, the empirical distribution function of time and magnitude is defined:

$$\Gamma_N : [0, T] \times M \rightarrow [0, 1] \times [0, 1] \tag{1}$$

$$(t, m) \rightarrow (t', m') = \left\{ \frac{1}{n} \sum_{j=1}^{n} I(t_j < t), \frac{1}{n} \sum_{j=1}^{m} I(m_j < m) \right\} \tag{2}$$

where I is a logical function. It is defined as $I(x) = 1$ if x is true or as $I(x) = 0$ if x is false.

BEPIT is used to convert the non-uniform mode generated by the actual point process into a uniform mode, and then the missing aftershock events are filled in. The method comprises the following five main steps (for a detailed description of the method, see Zhuang et al. [28,29]):

Step 1. Seismic events are transformed to a [0, 1] × [0, 1] range using the BEPIT point processing technique, and the approximate time–magnitude range is established for missing events, S.

Step 2. Based on the seismic events within the time–magnitude range that should be fully observed, a new empirical distribution function is obtained by searching for the uniform distribution of events through an iterative process and adjusting the missing event region, S.

Step 3. Based on the empirical distribution function of the previous step, independent and uniformly distributed events are generated in the missing event region.

Step 4. Since the missing region will also contain some real seismic events, the supplementary data set needs to be adjusted. Duplicate events in the synthetic data set can be avoided by deleting the most recent supplementary data point for each real event.

Step 5. By means of linear interpolation, the magnitude of each supplementary event is assigned based on the observed relationship between magnitude and time.

2.3. ETAS Model

Ogata [38] extended the Omori–Utsu law by applying the Hawkes point process, positing that aftershocks exhibit self-similarity and that each earthquake has the potential to generate aftershocks. This leads to a cascading series of direct and indirect aftershocks following a main event. He introduced the ETAS model, characterized by a branching point process structure.

The intensity function of the seismic series $\{(t_i,\ M_i); i = 1, 2, \ldots, N\}$ in the subsequent observation period [0, T] with parameters $[\mu, A, c, \alpha, p]$ can be expressed as follows [34,38]:

$$\lambda(t) = \mu + \sum\nolimits_{t_i<t} A e^{\alpha(M_i - M_0)} \frac{p-1}{c} \left(\frac{t - t_i}{c} + 1 \right)^{-p} \quad M_i > M_0 \tag{3}$$

where t represents the elapsed time after the initial zero time. M_i and t_i refer to the magnitude and onset time of the ith event, respectively. M_0 is the reference magnitude, which is usually taken as the cutoff magnitude that is equal to or greater than the complete magnitude M_C. The background seismicity rate is denoted by μ and is caused by the loading of regional stress, but it is usually negligible when compared to the aftershock sequence. The p value indicates how quickly the sequence decays; the larger this value is, the faster the decay, and vice versa. The length of time during which the frequency of aftershocks reaches its peak after the main earthquake is represented by c. A represents the average number of earthquakes triggered by an earthquake of magnitude M_C. α indicates the ability to trigger aftershocks. When it comes to swarm-type sequences, α is generally less than 1; if there is no obvious stimulated aftershock in the earthquake sequence, α is generally greater than 1 [39].

The ETAS model parameters are estimated using the maximum likelihood method, with the likelihood function L taking the form in $[S, T]$ in the fitting time range.

$$\ln L = \sum_{i:S \le t_i < T} \ln \lambda(t_i) - \int_S^T \lambda(t) dt \tag{4}$$

We perform the maximum likelihood estimation of parameters [μ, A, c, α, p] by bringing Equation (3) into Equation (4) and maximizing Equation (4).

2.4. b Value

The Gutenberg–Richter (G-R) law indicates the frequency–magnitude distribution of earthquakes [40,41] as follows:

$$lgN = a - bM \; (M \geq M_C) \tag{5}$$

where N is the number of earthquakes with a magnitude greater than or equal to M, a is the earthquake productivity, and b is the slope indicating the relative proportion of large and small earthquakes. Research has demonstrated that the b value is inversely related to the underground stress level [42–47]. As such, the b value serves as an indicator of geological structure and stress conditions and is widely used in earthquake forecasting and related research [10,48,49].

3. Results

Supplemental Data on Missing Earthquakes

To address the shortage of short-term aftershock data following an earthquake, we employed the BEPIT method. Using a moving time window, we conducted a temporal Mc analysis for each of the six sequences, and the maximum Mc values are summarized; the resulting M_C values are shown in Table 1. In the immediate aftermath of the main earthquake, some aftershock signals were obscured by large-amplitude tail waves [50,51], leading to a temporary increase in M_C. As monitoring capabilities in the aftershock region gradually improved, M_C began to decrease. However, with the reduction in mobile observation stations, M_C gradually increased again, eventually stabilizing at levels similar to those observed prior to the main event.

The BEPIT method was applied to supplement missing earthquake data immediately following the main shock. Figures 2–7 illustrate the results of this supplementation for the early aftershock data of six sequences. The findings show a significant increase in the number of recorded seismic events shortly after the main earthquake, highlighting the effectiveness of this supplementation technique. The enhanced seismic catalog provides a more comprehensive primary data set for subsequent research, enabling the derivation of more stable parameters.

The ETAS model parameters for the six seismic sequences are estimated using maximum likelihood estimation based on a relatively complete catalog. To facilitate comparison and analysis across the six sequences, a unified M_C = M_L1.7 is selected for calculation. Table 2 presents the estimated model parameters. Additionally, the maximum likelihood method is employed to estimate the b values of each seismic sequence (Figure 8).

An analysis of six earthquake sequences in the northeastern Tibetan Plateau revealed that although these sequences occur within the same tectonic region and share some general characteristics, they also display distinct parameter differences. As shown in Table 2, the μ values for all six sequences are low, indicating generally low seismic activity in these areas, with few earthquakes occurring before the main shock, particularly in sequences 2, 4, 5, and 6. Observational records confirm that no significant earthquakes occurred near the epicenters in the months preceding the 2013 Minxian M_S6.6, 2017 Jiuzhaigou M_S7.0, 2022 Menyuan M_S6.9, and 2022 Maerkang M_S6.0 earthquakes, making it challenging to assess earthquake hazards through foreshock activity. Sequence 3, however, has a relatively higher μ value, suggesting that background seismic activity in this region was higher than in the other sequences.

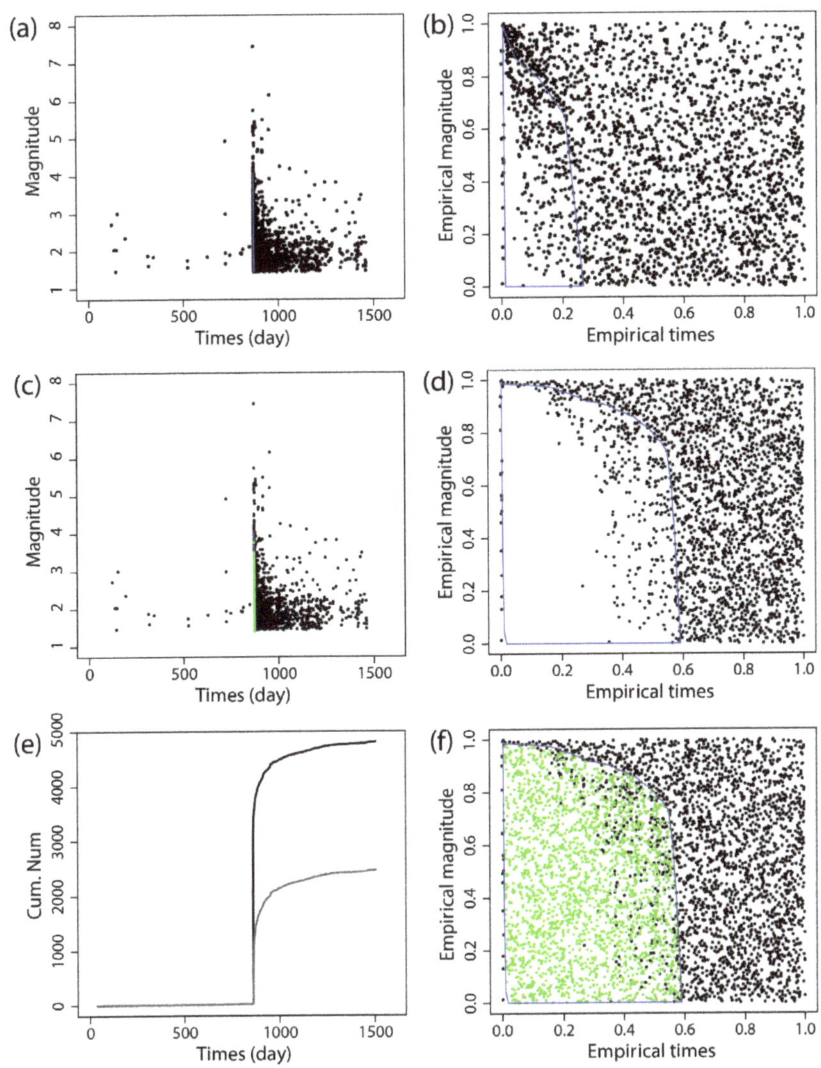

Figure 2. The supplementary results of the aftershock data of the 2021 M_S7.4 Maduo earthquake obtained by using BEPIT. (**a**) shows the magnitude and occurrence time of actual seismic events and missing event ranges; (**b**) shows the empirical distribution of magnitude and the event occurrence time after the double-scale transformation technique (Step 1); (**c**) shows the magnitude and occurrence time of actual and supplementary seismic events (Step 5); (**d**) shows the empirical distribution of magnitude and the event occurrence time outside of the missing event range after the double-scale transformation technique (Steps 2 and 3); (**e**) shows the cumulative number of earthquakes in the original data set (gray curve) and the supplementary data set (black curve); and (**f**) shows the empirical distribution of the magnitude and timing of actual and supplementary seismic events (Step 4). The blue polygon on (**a**,**b**,**d**,**f**) is the region where the missing event is located, and its corresponding mapping and the green dots on (**c**,**f**) are the supplementary events. The x-axis and y-axis in (**b**,**d**,**f**) are the empirical time and empirical magnitude transformed from time and magnitude by BEPIT.

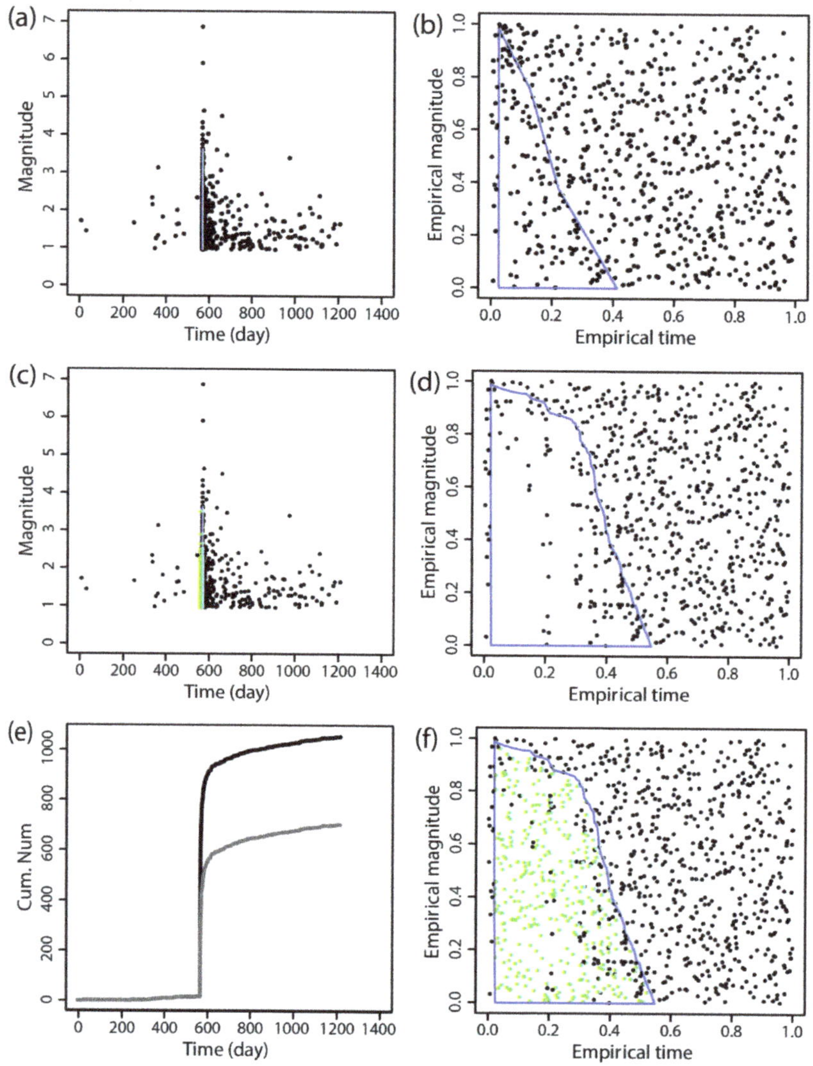

Figure 3. The supplementary results of the aftershock data of the 2013 M_S6.6 Minxian earthquake obtained by using BEPIT. (**a**) shows the magnitude and occurrence time of actual seismic events and missing event ranges; (**b**) shows the empirical distribution of magnitude and the event occurrence time after the double-scale transformation technique (Step 1); (**c**) shows the magnitude and occurrence time of actual and supplementary seismic events (Step 5); (**d**) shows the empirical distribution of magnitude and the event occurrence time outside of the missing event range after the double-scale transformation technique (Steps 2 and 3); (**e**) shows the cumulative number of earthquakes in the original data set (gray curve) and the supplementary data set (black curve); and (**f**) shows the empirical distribution of the magnitude and the timing of actual and supplementary seismic events (Step 4). The blue polygon in (**a**,**b**,**d**,**f**) is the region where the missing event is located, and its corresponding mapping and the green dots in (**c**,**f**) are the supplementary events. The x-axis and y-axis in (**b**,**d**,**f**) are the empirical time and empirical magnitude transformed from time and magnitude by BEPIT.

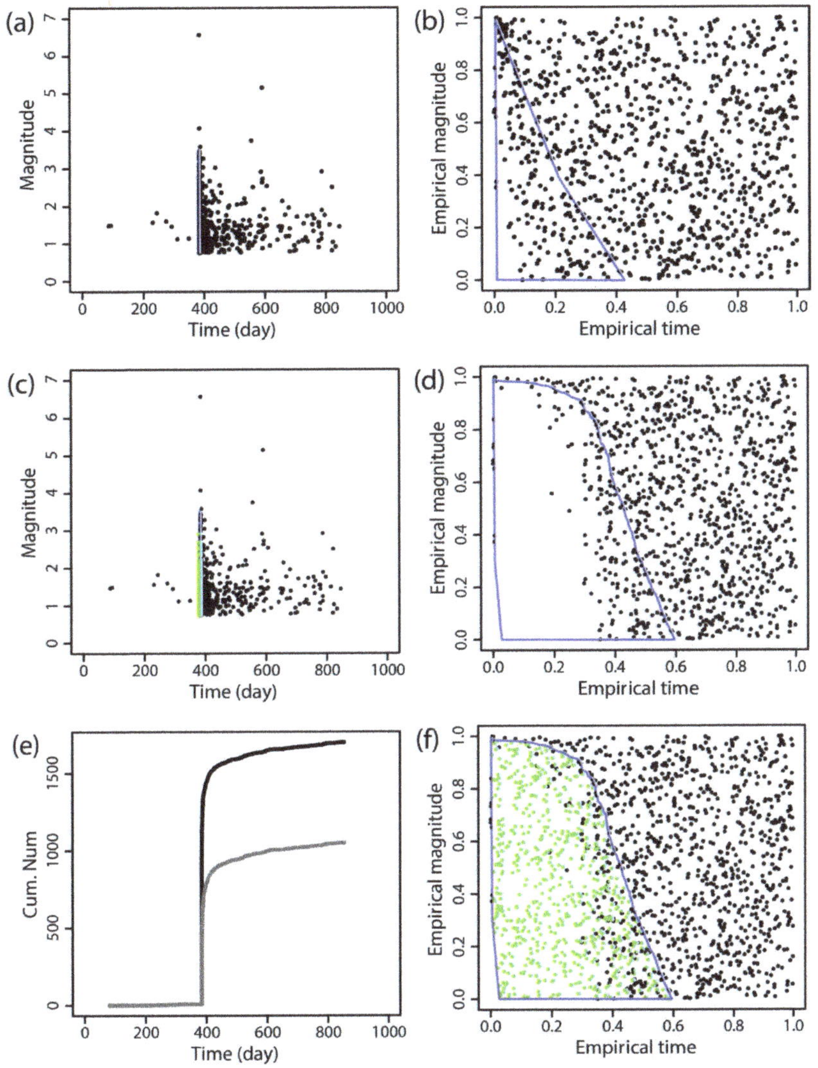

Figure 4. The supplementary results of aftershock data of the 2016 M_S6.4 Menyuan earthquake obtained by using BEPIT. (**a**) shows the magnitude and occurrence time of actual seismic events and missing event ranges; (**b**) shows the empirical distribution of magnitude and the event occurrence time after the double-scale transformation technique (Step 1); (**c**) shows the magnitude and occurrence time of actual and supplementary seismic events (Step 5); (**d**) shows the empirical distribution of magnitude and the event occurrence time outside of the missing event range after the double-scale transformation technique (Steps 2 and 3); (**e**) shows the cumulative number of earthquakes in the original data set (gray curve) and the supplementary data set (black curve); and (**f**) shows the empirical distribution of the magnitude and the timing of actual and supplementary seismic events (Step 4). The blue polygon in (**a**,**b**,**d**,**f**) is the region where the missing event is located, and its corresponding mapping and the green dots in (**c**,**f**) are the supplementary events. The x-axis and y-axis in (**b**,**d**,**f**) are the empirical time and empirical magnitude transformed from time and magnitude by BEPIT.

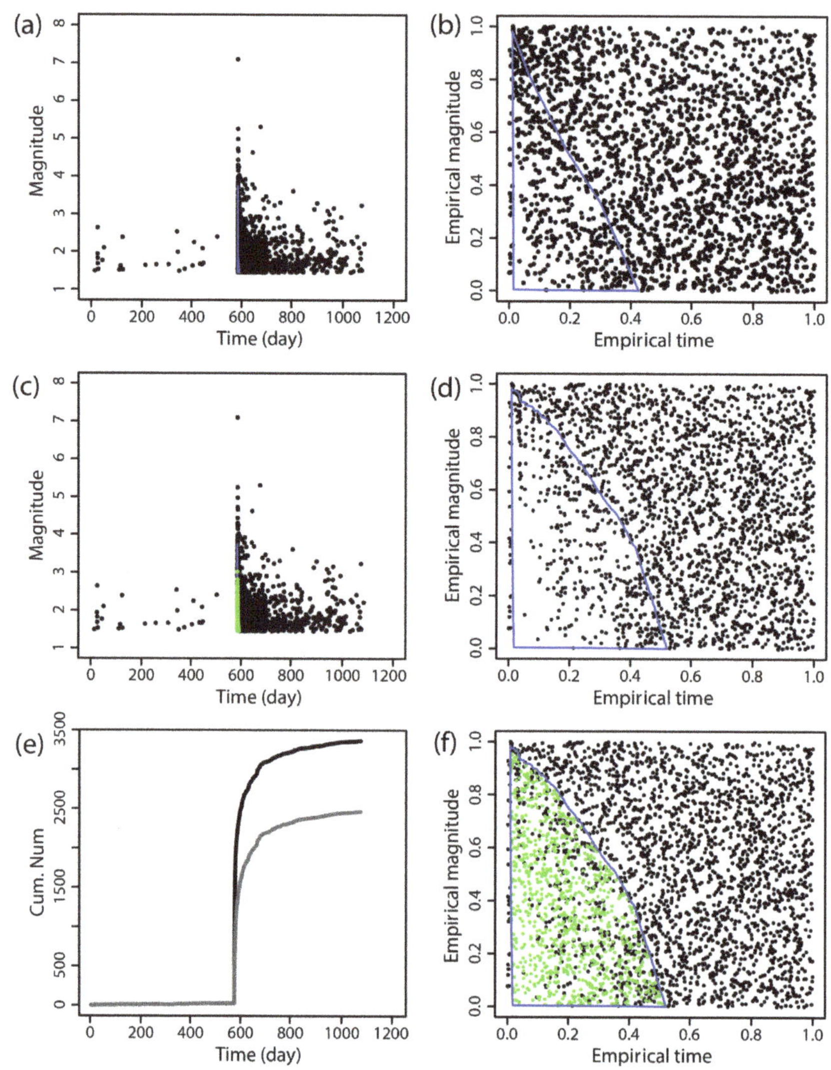

Figure 5. The supplementary results of aftershock data of the 2017 M_S7.0 Jiuzhaigou earthquake obtained by using BEPIT. (**a**) shows the magnitude and occurrence time of actual seismic events and missing event ranges; (**b**) shows the empirical distribution of magnitude and the event occurrence time after the double-scale transformation technique (Step 1); (**c**) shows the magnitude and occurrence time of actual and supplementary seismic events (Step 5); (**d**) shows the empirical distribution of magnitude and the event occurrence time outside of the missing event range after the double-scale transformation technique (Steps 2 and 3); (**e**) shows the cumulative number of earthquakes in the original data set (gray curve) and the supplementary data set (black curve); and (**f**) shows the empirical distribution of the magnitude and timing of actual and supplementary seismic events (Step 4). The blue polygon in (**a**,**b**,**d**,**f**) is the region where the missing event is located, and its corresponding mapping and the green dots in (**c**,**f**) are the supplementary events. The x-axis and y-axis in (**b**,**d**,**f**) are the empirical time and empirical magnitude transformed from time and magnitude by BEPIT.

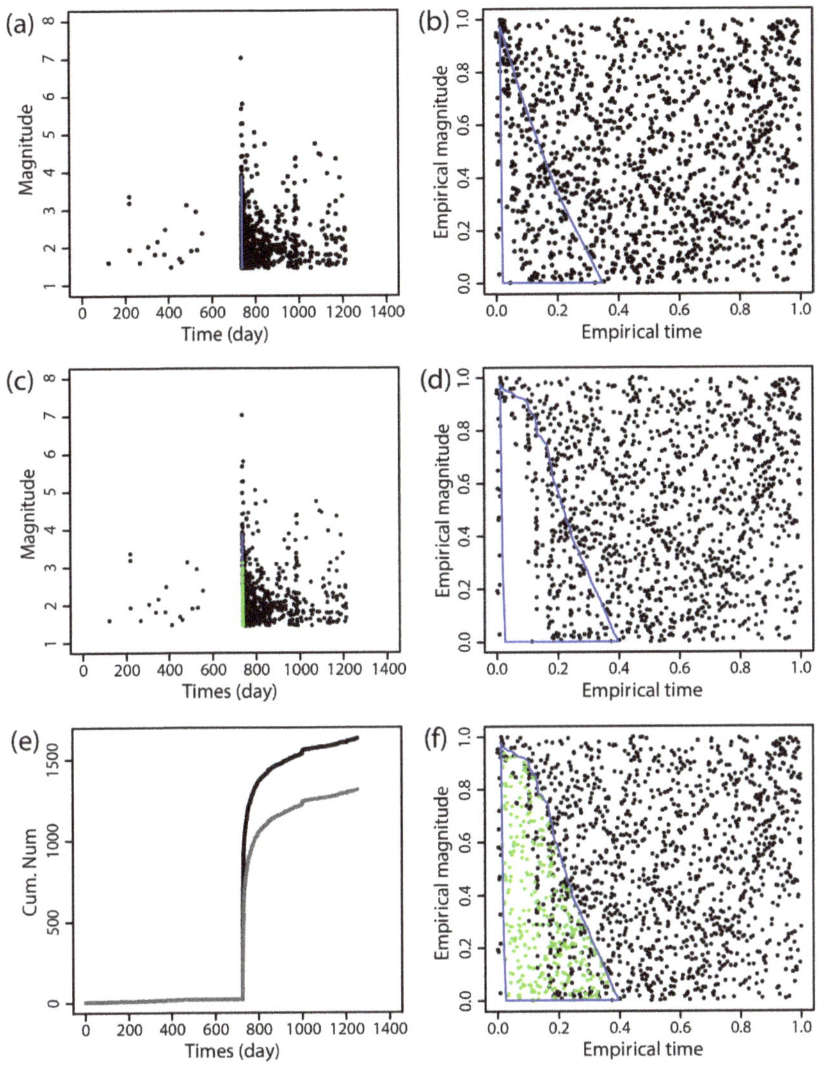

Figure 6. The supplementary results of aftershock data of the 2022 M_S6.9 Menyuan earthquake obtained by using BEPIT. (**a**) shows the magnitude and occurrence time of actual seismic events and missing event ranges; (**b**) shows the empirical distribution of magnitude and the event occurrence time after the double-scale transformation technique (Step 1); (**c**) shows the magnitude and occurrence time of actual and supplementary seismic events (Step 5); (**d**) shows the empirical distribution of magnitude and the event occurrence time outside of the missing event range after the double-scale transformation technique (Steps 2 and 3); (**e**) shows the cumulative number of earthquakes in the original data set (gray curve) and the supplementary data set (black curve); and (**f**) shows the empirical distribution of the magnitude and timing of actual and supplementary seismic events (Step 4). The blue polygon in (**a**,**b**,**d**,**f**) is the region where the missing event is located, and its corresponding mapping and the green dots in (**c**,**f**) are the supplementary events. The x-axis and y-axis in (**b**,**d**,**f**) are the empirical time and empirical magnitude transformed from time and magnitude by BEPIT.

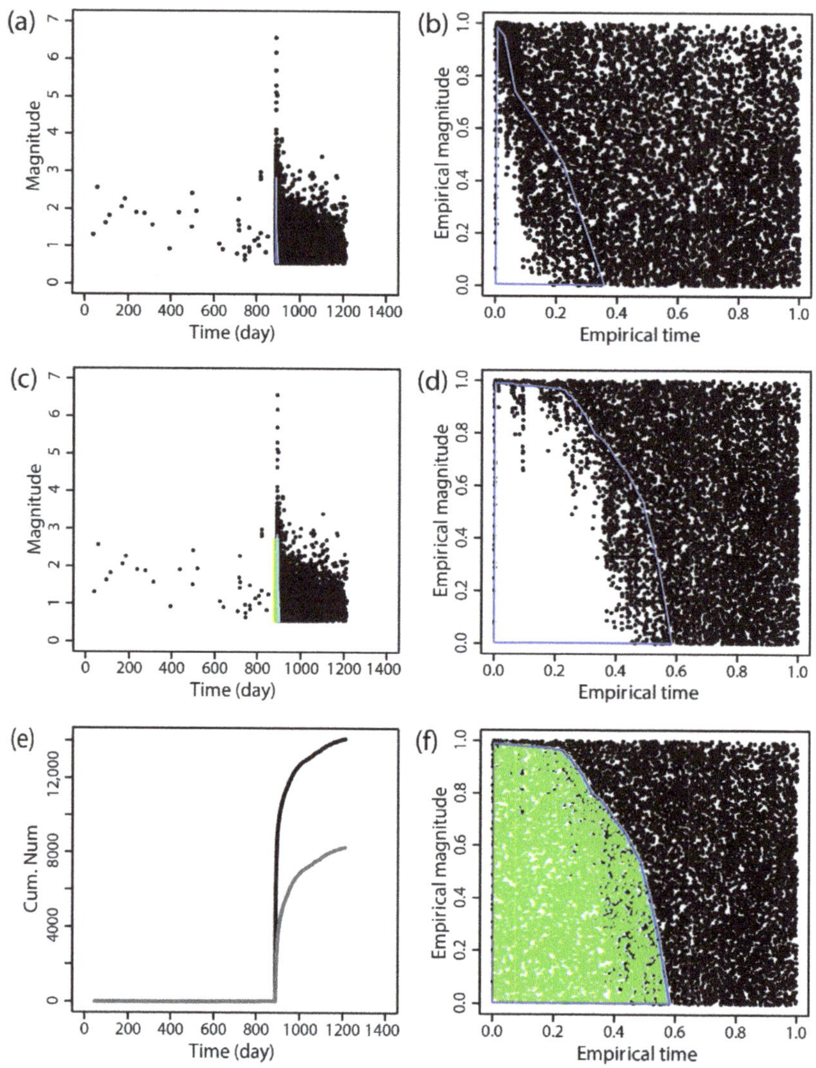

Figure 7. The supplementary results of aftershock data of the 2022 M_S6.0 Maerkang earthquake obtained by using BEPIT. (**a**) shows the magnitude and occurrence time of actual seismic events and missing event ranges; (**b**) shows the empirical distribution of magnitude and the event occurrence time after the double-scale transformation technique (Step 1); (**c**) shows the magnitude and occurrence time of actual and supplementary seismic events (Step 5); (**d**) shows the empirical distribution of magnitude and the event occurrence time outside the missing event range after the double-scale transformation technique (Steps 2 and 3); (**e**) shows the cumulative number of earthquakes in the original data set (gray curve) and the supplementary data set (black curve); and (**f**) shows the empirical distribution of the magnitude and timing of actual and supplementary seismic events (Step 4). The blue polygon in (**a**,**b**,**d**,**f**) is the region where the missing event is located, and its corresponding mapping and the green dots in (**c**,**f**) are the supplementary events. The x-axis and y-axis in (**b**,**d**,**f**) are the empirical time and empirical magnitude transformed from time and magnitude by BEPIT.

Table 2. ETAS model parameter, *b* values and background earthquake probability of main earthquake of six seismic sequence.

Index	Seismic Sequence			Sequence Type	Fault Type	μ	A	α	c	p	b	Background Earthquake Probability of Main Earthquake
	Time (dd-mm-yyyy)	Region	M_S									
1	22 May 2021	Maduo	7.4	M-A	strike-slip	0.0182	0.2711	1.0767	0.0823	1.1842	0.9073 ± 0.015	0.7625
2	22 July 2013	Minxian	6.6	M-A	strike-slip and thrust	0.0001	0.0032	2.2439	0.0121	1.1032	0.7700 ± 0.042	0.7522
3	22 January 2016	Menyuan	6.4	M-A	thrust	0.0328	0.0005	2.6892	0.1087	1.2776	1.0598 ± 0.060	1.0000
4	8 August 2017	Jiuzhaigou	7.0	M-A	strike-slip	0.0002	0.0738	1.9214	0.0291	1.1547	1.1139 ± 0.025	0.2853
5	8 January 2022	Menyuan	6.9	M-A	strike-slip	0.0022	0.0173	2.2601	0.0051	1.0388	0.8691 ± 0.026	0.9241
6	10 June 2022	Maerkang	6.0	S	strike-slip	<0.0001	0.2689	1.7713	0.0071	1.0576	1.2792 ± 0.027	<0.001

M-A: mainshock–aftershock type; S: earthquake swarm type.

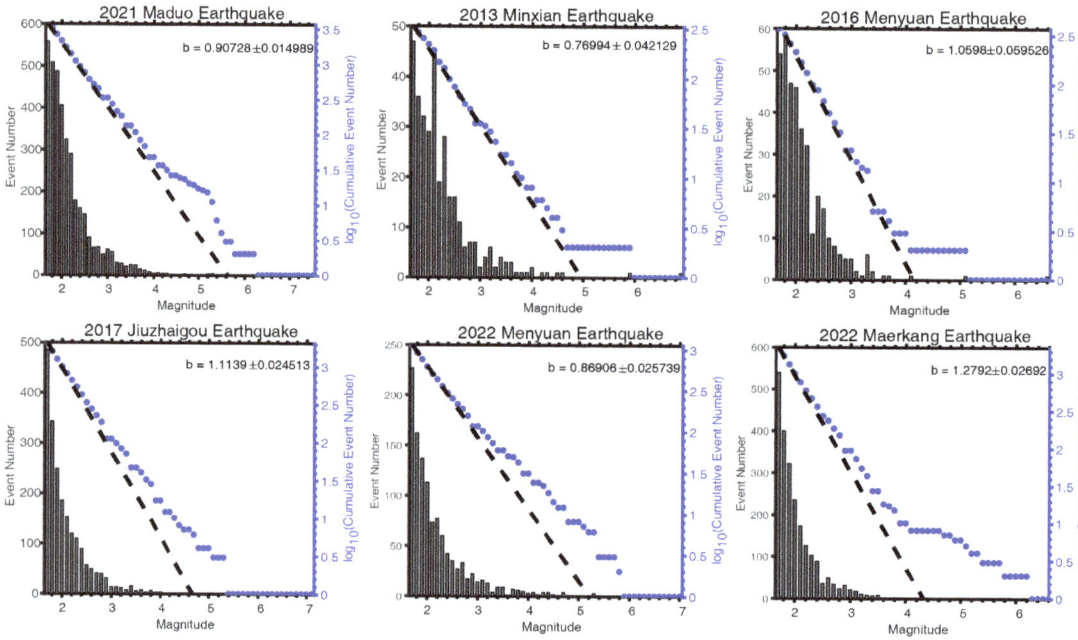

Figure 8. The b values of the six seismic sequences. The histogram represents the magnitude–frequency distribution of the sequence, the blue dots represent the magnitude–frequency distribution under the logarithmic relationship, and the black dashed lines represent the results of fitting using the G-R.

Parameters A and α collectively reflect aftershock productivity [52,53]. Specifically, parameter A represents the number of aftershocks triggered by an earthquake of magnitude M_C, while parameter α indicates the relationship between an earthquake's magnitude and its potential to generate aftershocks [7,54]. A high α suggests that a significant portion of aftershocks are triggered by larger earthquakes, primarily the mainshock. In sequences 2, 3, and 5, the high α value indicates a lower proportion of high-order aftershocks, with most aftershocks primarily being triggered by the mainshock.

The statistical decay of aftershocks is governed by parameters c and p. Sequence 5 exhibits the smallest c value, indicating a shorter time for the aftershock frequency to peak. A larger p value suggests a faster decay rate. Utzu et al. [55], in their analysis of over 200 global seismic sequences, reported an average p of 1.1. In the six sequences presented in Table 2, sequences 1–4 display a p value exceeding this average, suggesting that aftershocks decay rapidly following large earthquakes, potentially reducing the relative damage from aftershock sequences. The b value reveals that aside from sequence 6, overall, the b values are lower, reflecting regional seismic statistical characteristics and indicating high stress levels in the northeastern Tibetan Plateau [56–58].

4. Discussion

4.1. ETAS Parameter

The effect of different cutoff magnitudes on seismic sequence parameters is analyzed using the 2017 Jiuzhaigou M_S7.0 earthquake sequence as a case study, and the results are presented in Table 3. By varying the cutoff magnitudes to M_L 1.7, 1.8, and 1.9, parameters μ, A, and c gradually decrease while α increases, and p remains largely unchanged. These results align with the typical parameter variation characteristics of the ETAS model, indicating that the supplementary catalog is relatively stable. Furthermore, the b value decreases slightly as the cutoff value increases, remaining within the margin of error, which suggests the stability of b and the suitability of the chosen cutoff magnitudes. Therefore, when examining seismic sequence parameters, the selection of the cutoff magnitude should be carefully considered.

Table 3. ETAS model parameter and b values of 2017 Jiuzhaigou M_S7.0 earthquake sequence at different cutoff magnitudes.

Cutoff Magnitude	μ	A	α	c	p	b
M_L1.7	0.000192	0.073782	1.921365	0.029117	1.154718	1.1139 ± 0.025
M_L1.8	0.000293	0.020183	2.230346	0.016399	1.178645	1.0088 ± 0.032
M_L1.9	0.000255	0.018494	2.257887	0.009518	1.168921	1.0089 ± 0.035

Among the six seismic sequences analyzed in this study, five are mainshock–aftershock types, with sequence 6 exhibiting a swarm-type clustering pattern. As shown in Table 2, the ETAS model parameters vary significantly across these sequence types. The swarm-type sequence (sequence 6) demonstrates a higher b value, lower α value, and reduced c value and p value compared to the five mainshock–aftershock sequences. These parameter differences suggest that swarm sequences may feature relatively frequent aftershocks, slower attenuation rates post-event, and a heightened capacity to trigger second-order aftershocks. After a major earthquake, determining the sequence type is essential for assessing post-earthquake trends. The parameter characteristics observed here provide valuable insights for post-earthquake sequence classification and trend assessment.

The six seismic sequences examined in this study are situated on the Tibetan Plateau and represent continental intraplate earthquakes. Compared with subduction zone earthquakes, such as those in Japan, these intraplate sequences exhibit higher p and lower c values [7,59,60]. Consequently, the p and c values can also serve as indicators of tectonic environments.

4.2. Implication on Earthquake Forecasting

To investigate this further, we analyzed the probability of each mainshock being a background event [36], and the findings are presented in Table 2. With the exception of the 2022 M_s6.0 Maerkang earthquake, most of the primary earthquakes exhibit a high probability of being background events, indicating limited foreshock activity and suggesting that these main events were not foreshock-triggered. Indeed, none of these significant earthquakes were preceded by foreshocks. Furthermore, due to the sparse earthquake activity before the main events, it is challenging to observe the long-term decline in the b value that has been observed before some major earthquakes, such as the Wenchuan earthquake, the Tohoku earthquake in Japan, and the Sumatra earthquake [48,49,61,62]. This scarcity of pre-event seismicity complicates earthquake risk assessment based solely on precursor activity.

Due to the low incidence of background earthquakes in the northeastern Tibetan Plateau, seismicity-based prediction methods are challenging to apply in this area. In addition to statistical seismicity modeling, other effective earthquake prediction approaches rely on non-seismic precursors. Currently, geomagnetic field variations and underground fluid anomalies serve as relatively mature earthquake precursors in this region. Approximately six months prior to the 2022 Menyuan M_S6.9 earthquake, eight underground fluid anomalies were observed, primarily within a 200 km radius of the epicenter [63]. Approximately two months before the Menyuan M_S 6.9 earthquake, anomalously high geomagnetic polarization values exceeding the threshold were detected [64]. These geomagnetic observations, combined with recorded underground fluid anomalies, facilitated a successful prediction of the event [65]. Thus, earthquake forecasting in the northeastern Tibetan Plateau might be enhanced by integrating precursor-based approaches [66–68]. In addition to advancing seismic network capabilities, establishing dedicated precursor observation stations should be prioritized to improve predictive accuracy in this region.

The probability of the mainshock in the 2022 $M_S6.0$ Maerkang earthquake sequence being a background event is nearly zero, indicating that it was triggered by preceding foreshock activity. Consistent with previous findings, this sequence exhibited a concentration of foreshocks across multiple faults prior to the mainshock, likely attributable to the region's complex seismogenic environment. The $M_S6.0$ Maerkang earthquake, the largest event in this swarm, was preceded by an $M_S5.8$ foreshock and was followed by an $M_S5.2$ event, resulting in three earthquakes being above $M_S5.0$. This earthquake swarm occurred at the intersection of the Songgang and Longriba faults within the Bayan Har block, an area characterized by a complex epicentral structure. Studies on the precise location of the sequences suggest that the Maerkang swarm is influenced by multiple parallel and small-scale conjugate faults in proximity to the epicenter [69–71]. These three $M_S5.0+$ earthquakes took place on distinct fault sections, forming a swarm driven by multi-fault planes [72]. Compared to single-fault systems, such complex, multi-fault structures can yield more intricate earthquake sequences. Thus, in regions with similarly complex fault systems, the possibility of subsequent moderate to large earthquakes following an initial significant event should be anticipated.

4.3. Constraints and Challenges

As this research progressed, constraints in the application of certain methods also became apparent. One notable limitation pertains to the Gutenberg–Richter (G-R) law. Beyond the requirement that earthquakes used for a b value analysis must have magnitudes equal to or greater than the completeness magnitude, the G-R law may not hold for large-magnitude earthquakes, as illustrated in Figure 8. To address this issue, some studies have introduced derivative forms of the G-R law based on statistical methods, but their practical application remains limited [73]. From the perspective of physical properties, the statistical analysis of seismic energy has been shown to yield more accurate fits and robust results [74,75].

Another limitation involves the determination of the missing event range in the BEPTI algorithm. In Step 2 of BEPTI, the time–magnitude range for missing events, SS, must be manually estimated. This range should encompass the entire region where earthquakes are missing and extend beyond it. However, the manual estimation of this range introduces subjectivity, which may affect the results, as discussed by Zhuang et al. [29]. While it has been suggested that the selection of this range is not highly sensitive to the final outcomes, the development of an algorithm for the objective determination of missing earthquakes is necessary to improve the method's reliability and objectivity.

5. Conclusions

This study examined six $M_S \geq 6.0$ earthquake sequences that have occurred in the northeastern Tibetan Plateau since 2009. Using the BEPIT method, missing earthquakes from the short-term period following major events were supplemented, resulting in a more comprehensive seismic sequence catalog. The findings confirm that BEPIT is a highly efficient method suitable for supplementing any earthquake sequence initially affected by limited early monitoring, facilitating the assessment of missing data impacts and the correction of related biases. A subsequent analysis of the ETAS model parameters for these six sequences yielded the following conclusions.

The μ values for the six seismic sequences in the northeastern Tibetan Plateau are uniformly low, suggesting a generally low background seismicity rate with few foreshocks preceding major earthquakes. This underscores the challenges in forecasting earthquakes in this region solely through seismic activity analysis and foreshock observations, providing critical insights for the strategic planning of earthquake prediction efforts. The findings of this research provide valuable reference points for designing seismic monitoring strategies prior to large earthquakes and for analyzing changes in regional seismic sequence parameters. Additionally, they can contribute to improving the scientific accuracy of early assessments of post-earthquake trends.

The parameters of the six earthquake sequences in the northeastern Qinghai–Tibet Plateau examined in this study differ from those observed in previous earthquake cases within mainland China and subduction zones [59,60,76]. These differences arise from variations in regional stress conditions, seismogenic structures, and crustal medium properties.

It is important to note that the study area experienced a limited number of strong earthquakes after the upgrade of the seismic network, resulting in the selection of only six earthquake sequences for analysis. Consequently, the findings of this study may capture only a subset of statistical characteristics. Further research incorporating a larger set of earthquake cases is needed for a more comprehensive and in-depth analysis.

Author Contributions: Conceptualization, Y.W., R.W. and P.H.; methodology, Y.W., R.W. and J.Z.; software, Y.W. and R.W.; validation, Y.W., R.W. and P.H.; formal analysis, Y.W. and R.W.; investigation, R.W. and P.H.; resources, L.S.; data curation, T.Z. and Z.J.; writing—original draft preparation, Y.W.; writing—review and editing, R.W., M.M. and P.H.; visualization, Y.W. and R.W.; supervision, P.H. and J.Z. All authors have read and agreed to the published version of the manuscript.

Funding: This research was funded by the National Key R&D Program of China, grant number 2023YFC3012005; the Special Fund of the Institute of Geophysics, China Earthquake Administration, grant number DQJB24Z014; the National Natural Science Foundation of China, grant number 42304004, 42404063; and the Earthquake Science and Technology Spark Program, grant number XH23038A.

Institutional Review Board Statement: Not applicable.

Data Availability Statement: The catalog in this study was provided by the China Earthquake Networks Center from 2009 to June 2023.

Acknowledgments: We would like to thank the anonymous reviewers who helped to improve the manuscript. We thank Wessel et al. for providing the Generic Mapping Tools (GMT6.5.0) used to plot some of the figures [77].

Conflicts of Interest: Author Miao Miao was employed by the China Nuclear Power Engineering Co., Ltd. The remaining authors declare that the research was conducted in the absence of any commercial or financial relationships that could be construed as a potential conflict of interest.

References

1. Chapron, E.; Ariztegui, D.; Mulsow, S.; Villarosa, G.; Pino, M.; Outes, V.; Juvignié, E.; Crivelli, E. Impact of the 1960 major subduction earthquake in northern patagonia (Chile, Argentina). *Quat. Int.* **2006**, *158*, 58–71. [CrossRef]
2. Elnashai, A.S.; Gencturk, B.; Kwon, O.S.; Hashash, Y.M.A.; Kim, S.J.; Jeong, S.H.; Dukes, J. The maule (Chile) earthquake of february 27, 2010: Development of hazard, site specific ground motions and back-analysis of structures. *Soil Dyn. Earthq. Eng.* **2012**, *42*, 229–245. [CrossRef]
3. Marsan, D.; Enescu, B. Modeling the foreshock sequence prior to the 2011, M_W9.0 Tohoku, Japan, earthquake. *J. Geophys. Res. Solid Earth* **2012**, *117*, B06316. [CrossRef]
4. Muda, L.A.; Akinori, H.; Toshinori, S. Analysis of afterslip distribution following the 2007 september 12 southern sumatra earthquake using poroelastic and viscoelastic media. *Geophys. J. Int.* **2013**, *192*, 18–37. [CrossRef]

5. Tsang, L.L.H.; Hill, E.M.; Barbot, S.; Qiu, Q.; Feng, L.; Hermawan, I.; Banerjee, P.; Natawidjaja, D.H. Afterslip following the 2007 M_W8.4 Bengkulu earthquake in Sumatra loaded the 2010 M_W7.8 Mentawai tsunami earthquake rupture zone. *J. Geophys. Res. Solid Earth* **2016**, *121*, 9034–9049. [CrossRef]
6. Lengliné, O.; Enescu, B.; Peng, Z.; Shiomi, K. Decay and expansion of the early aftershock activity following the 2011, M_W9.0 Tohoku earthquake. *Geophys. Res. Lett.* **2012**, *39*, L18309. [CrossRef]
7. Harte, D.S. Bias in fitting the ETAS model: A case study based on New Zealand seismicity. *Geophys. J. Int.* **2013**, *192*, 390–412. [CrossRef]
8. Ross, Z.E.; Trugman, D.T.; Hauksson, E.; Shearer, P.M. Searching for hidden earthquakes in southern California. *Science* **2019**, *364*, 767–771. [CrossRef]
9. Long, F.; Zhang, Z.; Qi, Y.; Liang, M.; Ruan, X.; Wu, W.; Jiang, G.; Zhou, L. Three dimensional velocity structure and accurate earthquake location in Changning–Gongxian area of southeast Sichuan. *Earth Planet. Phys.* **2020**, *4*, 163–177. [CrossRef]
10. Wang, R.; Chang, Y.; Miao, M.; Zeng, Z.; Chen, H.; Shi, H.; Li, D.; Liu, L.; Su, Y.; Han, P. Assessing earthquake forecast performance based on *b* value in Yunnan Province. China. *Entropy* **2021**, *23*, 730. [CrossRef]
11. Manganiello, E.; Herrmann, M.; Marzocchi, W. New physical implications from revisiting foreshock activity in southern California. *Geophys. Res. Lett.* **2022**, *50*, e2022GL098737. [CrossRef]
12. Kumazawa, T.; Ogata, Y.; Tsuruoka, H. Characteristics of seismic activity before and after the 2018 M6.7 Hokkaido Eastern Iburi earthquake. *Earth Planets Space* **2019**, *71*, 130. [CrossRef]
13. Zhang, P.; Deng, Q.; Zhang, G.; Ma, J.; Gan, W.; Min, W.; Mao, F.; Wang, Q. Active tectonic blocks and strong earthquakes in the continent of China. *Sci. China Ser. D-Earth Sci.* **2003**, *46*, 13–24. [CrossRef]
14. Zhang, P.; Deng, Q.; Zhang, Z.; Li, H. Active faults, earthquake hazards and associated geodynamic processes in continental China. *Sci. Sin. Terrae* **2013**, *43*, 1607–1620. [CrossRef]
15. Song, X.; Jiang, Y.; Shan, X.; Gong, W.; Qu, C. A fine velocity and strain rate field of present-day crustal motion of the northeastern Tibetan Plateau inverted jointly by InSAR and GPS. *Remote Sens.* **2019**, *11*, 435. [CrossRef]
16. Fukahata, Y. Estimate of the contraction rate of central Japan through the deformation of the Philippine Sea slab. *Prog. Earth Planet. Sci.* **2019**, *6*, 4. [CrossRef]
17. Jiang, H.; Zheng, J.; Wu, Q.; Qu, Y.; Li, Y. Earlier statistical features of ETAS model parameters and their seismological meanings. *Chin. J. Geophys.* **2007**, *50*, 1778–1786. [CrossRef]
18. Jiang, C.; Han, L.; Guo, L. Parameter characteristics in the early period of three earthquake sequences in Yutian, Xinjiang since 2008. *Acta Seismol. Sin.* **2014**, *36*, 165–174. [CrossRef]
19. Enescu, B.; Mori, J.; Miyazawa, M.; Kano, Y. Omori-Utsu law c-values associated with recent moderate earthquakes in Japan. *Bull. Seismol. Soc. Am.* **2009**, *99*, 884–891. [CrossRef]
20. Sawazaki, K.; Enescu, B. Imaging the high-frequency energy radiation process of a main shock and its early aftershock sequence: The case of the 2008 Iwate-Miyagi Nairiku earthquake, Japan. *J. Geophys. Res. Solid Earth* **2014**, *119*, 4729–4746. [CrossRef]
21. Lippiello, E.; Cirillo, A.; Godano, C.; Papadimitriou, E.; Karakostas, V. Post seismic catalog incompleteness and aftershock forecasting. *Geosciences* **2019**, *9*, 355. [CrossRef]
22. Omi, T.; Ogata, Y.; Shiomi, K.; Enescu, B.; Sawazaki, K.; Aihara, K. Implementation of a real-time system for automatic aftershock forecasting in Japan. *Seismol. Res. Lett.* **2018**, *90*, 242–250. [CrossRef]
23. Peng, Z.; Zhao, P. Migration of early aftershocks following the 2004 Parkfield earthquake. *Nat. Geosci.* **2009**, *2*, 877–881. [CrossRef]
24. Kato, A.; Nakagawa, S. Multiple slow-slip events during a foreshock sequence of the 2014 Iquique, Chile M_W8.1 earthquake. *Geophys. Res. Lett.* **2014**, *41*, 5420–5427. [CrossRef]
25. Zhang, M.; Wen, L. An effective method for small event detection: Match and Locate (M&L). *Geophys. J. Int.* **2015**, *200*, 1523–1537. [CrossRef]
26. Liu, M.; Li, H.; Zhang, M.; Wang, T. Graphics processing unit-based Match and Locate (GPU-M&L): An improved Match and Locate method and its application. *Seismol. Res. Lett.* **2020**, *91*, 1019–1029. [CrossRef]
27. Zhou, Y.; Yue, H.; Fang, L.; Zhou, S.; Li, Z.; Ghosh, A. An earthquake detection and location architecture for continuous seismograms: Phase picking, association, location, and matched filter (PALM). *Seismol. Res. Lett.* **2022**, *93*, 413–425. [CrossRef]
28. Zhuang, J.; Ogata, Y.; Wang, T. Data completeness of the Kumamoto earthquake sequence in the JMA catalog and its influence on the estimation of the ETAS parameters. *Earth Planets Space* **2017**, *69*, 36. [CrossRef]
29. Zhuang, J.; Wang, T.; Kiyosugi, K. Detection and replenishment of missing data in marked point processes. *Stat. Sin.* **2020**, *30*, 2105–2130. [CrossRef]
30. Seif, S.; Mignan, A.; Zechar, J.D.; Werner, M.J.; Wiemer, S. Estimating ETAS: The effects of truncation, missing data, and model assumptions. *J. Geophys. Res. Solid Earth* **2017**, *122*, 449–469. [CrossRef]
31. Zheng, Y.; Enescu, B.; Zhuang, J.; Yu, C. Data replenishment of five moderate earthquake sequences in Japan, with semiautomatic cluster selection. *Earthq. Sci.* **2021**, *34*, 310–322. [CrossRef]

32. Wiemer, S.; Wyss, M. Minimum magnitude of complete reporting in earthquake catalogs: Examples from Alaska, the Western United States, and Japan. *Bull. Seismol. Soc. Am.* **2000**, *90*, 859–869. [CrossRef]
33. Woessner, J.; Wiemer, S. Assessing the quality of earthquake catalogues: Estimating the magnitude of completeness and its uncertainty. *Bull. Seismol. Soc. Am.* **2005**, *95*, 684–698. [CrossRef]
34. Ogata, Y.; Zhuang, J. Space–time ETAS models and an improved extension. *Tectonophysics* **2006**, *413*, 13–23. [CrossRef]
35. Werner, M.J.; Helmstetter, A.; Jackson, D.D.; Kagan, Y.Y. High-resolution long-term and short-term earthquake forecasts for California. *Bull. Seismol. Soc. Am.* **2011**, *101*, 1630–1648. [CrossRef]
36. Zhuang, J.; Ogata, Y.; Vere-Jones, D. Stochastic declustering of space-time earthquake occurrences. *J. Am. Stat. Assoc.* **2002**, *97*, 369–380. [CrossRef]
37. Zhuang, J.; Ogata, Y.; Vere-Jones, D. Analyzing earthquake clustering features by using stochastic reconstruction. *J. Geophys. Res.* **2004**, *109*, B05301. [CrossRef]
38. Ogata, Y. Statistical models for earthquake occurrences and residual analysis for point processes. *J. Am. Stat. Assoc.* **1988**, *83*, 9–27. [CrossRef]
39. Ogata, Y. Increased probability of large earthquakes near aftershock regions with relative quiescence. *J. Geophys. Res.* **2001**, *106*, 8729–8744. [CrossRef]
40. Gutenberg, B.; Richter, C.F. Frequency of earthquakes in California. *Bull. Seismol. Soc. Am.* **1944**, *34*, 185–188. [CrossRef]
41. Utsu, T. A method for determing the value of b in a formula log N=a-bM showing the magnitude frequency relation for earthquakes. *Geophys. Bull. Hokkaido Univ.* **1965**, *13*, 99–103. (In Japanese)
42. Convertito, V.; Tramelli, A.; Godano, C. *b* map evaluation and on-fault stress state for the Antakya 2023 earthquakes. *Sci. Rep.* **2024**, *14*, 1596. [CrossRef] [PubMed]
43. Scholz, C.H. On the stress dependence of earthquake *b* value. *Geophys. Res. Lett.* **2015**, *42*, 1399–1402. [CrossRef]
44. Schorlemmer, D.; Wiemer, S.; Wyss, M. Variations in earthquake-size distribution across different stress regimes. *Nature* **2005**, *437*, 539–542. [CrossRef]
45. Spada, M.; Tormann, T.; Wiemer, S.; Enescu, B. Generic dependence of the frequency-size distribution of earthquakes on depth and its relation to the strength profile of the crust. *Geophys. Res. Lett.* **2013**, *40*, 709–714. [CrossRef]
46. Tan, Y.J.; Waldhauser, F.; Tolstoy, M.; Wilcock, W.S.D. Axial Seamount: Periodic tidal loading reveals stress dependence of the earthquake size distribution (*b* value). *Earth Planet. Sci. Lett.* **2019**, *512*, 39–45. [CrossRef]
47. Wu, Y.M.; Chen, S.K.; Huang, T.C.; Huang, H.H.; Chao, W.A.; Koulakov, I. Relationship between earthquake *b*-values and crustal stresses in a young orogenic belt. *Geophys. Res. Lett.* **2018**, *45*, 1832–1837. [CrossRef]
48. Nanjo, K.Z.; Hirata, N.; Obara, K.; Kasahara, K. Decade-scale decrease in b value prior to the *M*9-class 2011 Tohoku and 2004 Sumatra quakes. *Geophys. Res. Lett.* **2012**, *39*, 20304. [CrossRef]
49. Xie, W.; Hattori, K.; Han, P. Temporal variation and statistical assessment of the *b* value off the Pacific Coast of Tokachi, Hokkaido, Japan. *Entropy* **2019**, *21*, 249. [CrossRef]
50. Iwata, T. Low detection capability of global earthquakes after the occurrence of large earthquakes: Investigation of the Harvard CMT catalogue. *Geophys. J. Int.* **2008**, *174*, 849–856. [CrossRef]
51. Mignan, A.; Woessner, J. Estimating the Magnitude of Completeness for Earthquake Catalogs. Community Online Resource for Statistical Seismicity Analysis. 2012. Available online: https://episodesplatform.eu/eprints/1587/ (accessed on 10 October 2024).
52. Nandan, S.; Ouillon, G.; Wiemer, S.; Sornette, D. Objective estimationof spatially variable parameters of epidemic type aftershock sequence model: Application to California. *J. Geophys. Res.* **2017**, *122*, 5118–5143. [CrossRef]
53. Dascher-Cousineau, K.; Brodsky, E.E.; Lay, T.; Goebel, T. What controls variations in aftershock productivity? *J. Geophys. Res.* **2020**, *125*, e2019JB018111. [CrossRef]
54. Shebalin, P.; Baranov, S.; Vorobieva, I. Earthquake productivity law in a wide magnitude range. *Front. Earth Sci.* **2022**, *10*, 881425. [CrossRef]
55. Utsu, T.; Ogata, Y.; Matsu'ura, R.S. The centenary of the Omori formula for a decay law of aftershock activity. *J. Phys. Earth* **1995**, *43*, 1–33. [CrossRef]
56. Jiang, J.; Feng, J. Stress state and *b*-value anomalies before the Jiuzhaigou M_S7.0 earthquake in 2017. *Chin. Earthq. Eng. J.* **2021**, *43*, 575–582. [CrossRef]
57. Guo, Y.; Zhu, Y.; Yu, T.; Li, Q.; Zhang, L.; Yu, N. Research on spatio-temporal characteristics of *b*-value before and after the 2022 Menyuan M_S6.9 earthquake. *J. Geod. Geodyn.* **2023**, *43*, 1155–1161. [CrossRef]
58. Hu, N.; Han, P.; Wang, R.; Shi, F.; Chen, L.; Li, H. Spatial heterogeneity of *b* values in northeastern Tibetan Plateau and its interpretation. *Entropy* **2024**, *26*, 182. [CrossRef]
59. Chu, A.; Schoenberg, F.P.; Bird, P.; Jackson, D.D.; Kagan, Y.Y. Comparison of ETAS parameter estimates across different global tectonic zones. *Bull. Seismol. Soc. Am.* **2011**, *101*, 2323–2339. [CrossRef]
60. Zhang, L.; Werner, M.J.; Goda, K. Variability of ETAS parameters in global subduction zones and applications to mainshock-aftershock hazard assessment. *Bull. Seismol. Soc. Am.* **2020**, *110*, 191–212. [CrossRef]

61. Nuannin, P.; Kulhánek, O.; Persson, L. Spatial and temporal b value anomalies preceding the devastating off coast of NW Sumatra earthquake of December 26, 2004. *Geophys. Res. Lett.* **2005**, *32*, L11307. [CrossRef]
62. Shi, H.; Meng, L.; Zhang, X.; Chang, Y.; Yang, Z.; Xie, W.; Hattori, K.; Han, P. Decrease in *b* value prior to the Wenchuan earthquake (Ms8.0). *Chin. J. Geophys.* **2018**, *61*, 1874–1882. [CrossRef]
63. Zhong, J.; Feng, X.; Wang, B.; Zhou, Z.; Yan, R. Analysis on anomalous characteristics of underground fluid before the Menyuan, Qinghai M_S6.9 earthquake in 2022. *J. Seismol. Res.* **2022**, *45*, 308–317. [CrossRef]
64. Fan, W.; Feng, L.; Li, X.; He, C.; Liao, X.; Yao, X. Characteristic of geomagnetic vertical intensity polarization anomalies before the Menyuan, Qinghai $\mathbf{M}_S$6.9 earthquake on January 8, 2022. *Chin. Earthq. Eng. J.* **2022**, *44*, 744–750. [CrossRef]
65. Feng, L.; Li, X.; Zhao, Y.; Zhang, P. A short-term prediction practice on the Menyuan *M*6.9 earthquake on January 8, 2022. *Earthq. Res. China* **2022**, *38*, 12–20. [CrossRef]
66. Han, P.; Hattori, K.; Zhuang, J.; Chen, C.H.; Liu, J.Y.; Yoshida, S. Evaluation of ULF seismo-magnetic phenomena in Kakioka, Japan by using Molchan's error diagram. *Geophys. J. Int.* **2017**, *208*, 482–490. [CrossRef]
67. Qiu, L.; Zhu, Y.; Liu, Q.; Guo, M.; Song, D.; Wang, A. Response law and indicator selection of seismic wave velocity for coal seam outburst risk. *Adv. Geo-Energy Res.* **2023**, *9*, 198–210. [CrossRef]
68. Song, D.; Liu, Q.; Qiu, L.; Zhang, J.; Khan, M.; Peng, Y.; Zhao, Y.; Wang, M.; Guo, M.; Hong, T. Experimental study on resistivity evolution law and precursory signals in the damage process of gas-bearing coal. *Fuel* **2024**, *362*, 130798. [CrossRef]
69. Long, F.; He, C.; Yi, G.; He, X.; Li, L.; Shi, F.; Yue, C.; Peng, L. Seismogenic structures and spatiotemporal seismicity patterns of the 2022 M_S6.0 Maerkang earthquake sequence, Sichuan, China. *Front. Earth Sci.* **2023**, *10*, 1049911. [CrossRef]
70. Xu, Y.; Guo, X. Relocation of the 2022 M_S6.0 Maerkang earthquake swarm in Sichuan Province and its seismic fault analysis. *Seismol. Geol.* **2023**, *45*, 1006–1024. [CrossRef]
71. Xiao, Y.; Shan, B.; Xiong, X.; Xie, Z.; Zhou, W. Probing into the mechanism of earthquake swarms: A case study of the 2022 Barkam earthquake swarm. *Chin. J. Geophys.* **2024**, *67*, 2159–2174. [CrossRef]
72. Du, F.; Long, F.; Liang, M.; Qi, Y.; Gong, Y.; Wu, J. Characteristics of the Ma'erkang M_S6.0 earthquake-swarm triggered along multiple fault planes in 2022. *Earthq. Res. Sichuan* **2022**, *185*, 1–10. [CrossRef]
73. Utsu, T. Representation and analysis of the earthquake size distribution: A historical review and some new approaches. *Pure Appl. Geophys.* **1999**, *155*, 509–535. [CrossRef]
74. da Silva, S.L.E.F. κ-generalised Gutenberg–Richter law and the self-similarity of earthquakes. *Chaos Solitons Fractals* **2021**, *143*, 110622. [CrossRef]
75. Sotolongo-Costa, O.; Posadas, A. Fragment-asperity interaction model for earthquakes. *Phys. Rev. Lett.* **2004**, *92*, 048501. [CrossRef] [PubMed]
76. Jiang, H.; Qu, Y.; Li, Y.; Zheng, J.; Hua, A.; Dai, L.; Hou, H. Some statistic features of aftershock sequences in Chinese mainland. *Chin. J. Geophys.* **2006**, *49*, 1110–1117. [CrossRef]
77. Wessel, P.; Luis, J.; Uieda, L.; Scharroo, R.; Wobbe, F.; Smith, W.H.; Tian, D. The generic mapping tools version 6. *Geochem. Geophys. Geosyst.* **2019**, *20*, 5556–5564. [CrossRef]

Disclaimer/Publisher's Note: The statements, opinions and data contained in all publications are solely those of the individual author(s) and contributor(s) and not of MDPI and/or the editor(s). MDPI and/or the editor(s) disclaim responsibility for any injury to people or property resulting from any ideas, methods, instructions or products referred to in the content.

entropy

MDPI

Article

Analysis of Aftershocks from California and Synthetic Series by Using Visibility Graph Algorithm

Alejandro Muñoz-Diosdado, Ana María Aguilar-Molina, Eric Eduardo Solis-Montufar and José Alberto Zamora-Justo *

Unidad Profesional Interdisciplinaria de Biotecnología, Instituto Politécnico Nacional, Mexico City 07340, Mexico; amunozdi@ipn.mx (A.M.-D.); anafrom@hotmail.com (A.M.A.-M.); eric.montufar@gmail.com (E.E.S.-M.)
* Correspondence: jzamoraj@ipn.mx

Abstract: The use of the Visibility Graph Algorithm (VGA) has proven to be a valuable tool for analyzing both real and synthetic seismicity series. Specifically, VGA transforms time series into a network representation in which structural properties such as node connectivity, clustering, and community structure can be quantitatively measured, thereby revealing underlying correlations and dynamics that may remain hidden in traditional linear or spectral analyses. The time series transformation into complex networks with VGA provides a new approach to analyze seismic dynamics, allowing scientists to extract trends and behaviors that may not be possible by classical time-series analysis. On the other hand, many studies attempt to find viable trends in order to identify preparation mechanisms prior to a strong earthquake or to analyze the aftershocks. In this work, the seismic activity of Southern California Earthquake was analyzed focusing only on the significant earthquakes. For this purpose, seismic series preceding and following each earthquake were constructed using a windowing method with different overlaps and the slope of the connectivity (k) versus magnitude (M) graph (k-M slope) and the average degree were computed from the mapped complex networks. The results revealed a significant decrease in these parameters after the earthquake, due to the contribution of the aftershocks from the main event. Interestingly, the study was extended to synthetic seismicity series and the same behavior was observed for both k-M slope and average degree. This finding suggests that the spring-block model reproduces a relaxation mechanism following a large-magnitude event like those of real seismic aftershocks. However, this conclusion contrasts with conclusions drawn by other researchers. These results highlight the utility of VGA in studying events that precede and follow major earthquakes. This technique may be used to extract some useful trends in seismicity, which could eventually be employed for a deeper understanding and possible forecasting of seismic behavior.

Keywords: seismicity series; seismicity from California; spring-block model; visibility graph algorithm; complex networks

1. Introduction

Complex systems comprise numerous elements that interact non-linearly, exchange information with the environment, and continuously modify their internal structure and activity patterns through self-organization, a distinguishing property of these systems. As a result, they are flexible and easily adapt to changing external conditions [1].

Self-organized criticality (SOC) is a concept related to conservation laws in complex systems. It was introduced by Bak, Tang, and Wiesenfeld to describe the appearance of scale invariance in nature. Earthquakes are an example of a self-organized critical (SOC) phenomenon in nature and exhibit power law behavior [2,3]. Power laws describe the behavior of earthquakes and the distribution of their magnitude. The movement of continental plates is caused by convection currents in the Earth's mantle. These currents generate displacements and collisions between the plates, which causes the accumulation of tension at their limits. When the accumulated tension exceeds the resistance of the rocks, it is released abruptly, causing an earthquake. In this process, the release of energy causes a rebound or sudden displacement of the plates, which generates seismic waves that propagate through the Earth. Earthquakes are the result of the dynamic organization of the Earth's crust and the fault system that forms it. The large-scale structure of the crust is the product of a historical accumulation of seismic events that have modified and weakened rocks over time [3,4].

Researchers studying earthquakes seek specific mechanisms underlying large events, frequently describing each occurrence individually and independently of others. Seismic events adhere to a simple distribution known as the Gutenberg-Richter law. This law illustrates the frequency of earthquakes at each magnitude in a region, representing the energy released during seismic events. The Gutenberg-Richter law indicates that large or small earthquakes have the same rules. Therefore, this law serves as evidence that the Earth's crust has self-organized until it reaches a critical state [1,5–7].

Olami, Feder, and Christensen (*OFC*) have studied self-organized criticality (*SOC*) in non-conservative systems using an earthquake model. They showed that a two-dimensional spring-block model for earthquakes is equivalent to a non-conservative continuum cellular automaton model. The model exhibits power-law distributions for the energy released during an earthquake and characteristics similar of real earthquakes: the occurrence of small earthquakes is random, while larger earthquakes appear to be clustered. The simplest test for these models is their ability to reproduce the Gutenberg-Richter law [8,9].

Network analysis, based on concepts from statistical physics and graph theory, can be useful in characterizing the irregular behavior of seismicity time series [10,11]. This approach consists of transforming a discrete set of data into a network consisting of nodes and the links between them. Converting a time series into a network facilitates the exploration of complex system dynamics through analysis of network properties [12,13]. Several methods have been proposed to convert time series into networks and to characterize these series in terms of the parameters that describe the network. For instance, Zhang and Small [14] transformed periodic time series into networks by representing each cycle as a node. Connections between nodes were established based on the similarity or difference between cycles. Marwan et al. [15] constructed univariate recurrence networks by determining whether points in a phase space reconstruction of the time series are proximate to each other. If they are, a link is created between the corresponding nodes. Furthermore, Gao et al. [16] proposed an extension of univariate recurrence networks to multiple time series, linking nodes based on proximity in a high-dimensional phase space.

A key method in this area is the visibility graph algorithm (VGA) [17], which transforms a time series into a complex network while preserving its fundamental characteristics, thereby enabling the application of network theory to characterize the original data. This mapping transforms the dynamic characteristics of the time series into features of the resultant network. In this method, each data point in the time series is treated as a node. Two nodes are connected by an edge if they can "see" each other, meaning there exists a direct line of sight between them that does not intersect any intermediate data points. In VGA, the degree of connectivity represents the number of connections per node. This algorithm has recently been applied to various fields, including heart rate variability analysis [18], medical science [19–22], and particularly real and synthetic seismicity series [12,13,23–28].

For instance, Muñoz-Diosdado et al. [18] identified significant differences in the *k-M* parameter, average degree, and average path length of complex networks derived from heart rate variability series of subjects under various exercise and health conditions.

In seismicity research, Telesca et al. [23] applied the VGA method to analyze sequences of seismic magnitudes, revealing a power-law distribution in the connectivity degrees. This scale-free pattern in connectivity aligns with other scale-invariant features observed in earthquake studies. Earthquakes demonstrate complex spatial and temporal behavior, with numerous seismological laws exhibiting fractal characteristics, as indicated by scale exponents [29,30].

In the visibility graph methodology, the degree of connectivity, k, is defined for each event based on its magnitude M and its position in the time series. The *k-M* parameter represents the slope of the linear regression of the graph plotting k against M. Telesca et al. [12] performed a similar analysis on regional seismicity in Pannonia, proposing that the correlation between these two parameters is nearly universal. Analogous results were obtained when analyzing experimentally derived seismicity time series [12]. Further studies in this direction were conducted by Azizzadeh-Roodpish et al. [27,31] for Southern California and the Alaskan Crustal and Aleutian subduction zones, by Khoshnevis et al. [26] for the seismicity of northern Iran, and by Pérez-Oregon et al. [28] using synthetic earthquake time series. These studies collectively reinforced the notion of a universal linear correlation.

In this study, we analyzed the complex network parameters *k-M* slope and average degree using VGA by using real seismicity data from California and synthetic seismicity generated with the spring-block model. The series were selected based on high-magnitude earthquakes, and windowing was applied to include all events before and after each main earthquake. This approach allowed us to observe how these parameters change within the dynamics of seismicity, particularly during aftershock sequences.

2. Materials and Methods

2.1. Visibility Graph Algorithm

The visibility graph algorithm (VGA) was used to transform the seismicity time series into a complex network. In the undirected visibility graph (VG), two events are connected if they can "see" each other, meaning that no event between them intersects the line connecting them (see Figure 1). By mapping the time series into a graph with interconnected nodes, the resulting complex network retains various properties of the time series [17]. Let $x(i), 1 \leq i \leq N$ be a seismicity time series of length N, and consider each earthquake as a node in the VG. Nodes $x(i)$ and $x(j)$ $(i \neq j)$ are connected only when the following condition is met [17]:

$$\forall l \in [i, j]; x(l) < x(i) - (j - l)\frac{x(j) - x(i)}{j - 1}. \tag{1}$$

Adjacency matrices were constructed for the visibility graph of the seismicity time series. The dimension of the adjacency matrix corresponds to the number of nodes in the network. If there is a connection between the nodes represented by a specific row and column, the matrix element is one; otherwise, it is zero. For an undirected visibility graph, this matrix is symmetric, with the main diagonal elements being zero. Typically, there are ones around the main diagonal since neighboring events are more likely to be visible to each other. The degree of connectivity for each node is determined by summing the number of connections in the corresponding row of the matrix [17].

In seismicity analysis, the *k-M* refers to the slope of the linear regression of the graph plotting the connectivity degree k against the earthquake magnitude M. It is generally observed that periods of lower seismic activity correspond to a low connectivity degree k, while periods of higher seismic activity are associated with a higher connectivity degree. Consequently, the *k-M* slope typically has a positive value [32].

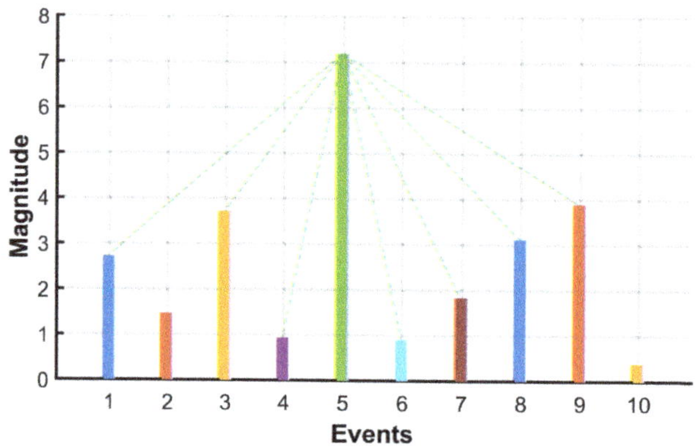

Figure 1. Explanation of the visibility graph algorithm. Each event is represented by a node in the visibility graph. Two nodes are connected if the straight line joining them is not intersected by another event. In this figure, it can be seen the connected events (green dashed line).

2.2. California Seismicity

The first systematic, non-mythical treatment of earthquakes comes from Greece. With the spread of writing, people began to collect descriptions of severe earthquakes. In California, this documentation began around 1800 by the Franciscan Fathers, who documented the development of Spanish missions. By the 19th century, the documentation was quite detailed. Seismographic stations were installed in many parts of the world at the beginning of the 20th century. These sensitive seismographs record small seismic waves [33].

The importance of a global network of seismographs lies in documenting earthquakes worldwide so that they are no longer limited to subjective reports of observed effects. From waves recorded at different seismographic observatories, it is possible to calculate the position of the epicenter of an earthquake, which provides a uniform representation of the distribution of earthquakes.

The seismotectonics of Southern California are shaped by the region's complex tectonic setting, which is dominated by the Pacific and North American plate boundary. This interaction creates a highly active and intricate fault network, making Southern California one of the most seismically active regions in the world. The area is particularly well known for the San Andreas Fault, a transform fault that accommodates much of the relative plate motion and poses a significant seismic hazard [34].

In the Figure 2, it can be observed epicenters of the earthquakes in Southern California with magnitude ≥ 7 between 1980 and 2024.

The southern section of the San Andreas Fault (*SSAF*) is the only historically active segment of the SSAF system, which is believed to represent the greatest seismic risk in California. Concerns about the timing, magnitude, and location of future earthquakes, coupled with the fault's accessibility, have yielded evidence of prehistoric earthquakes [35–37].

It was analyzed the earthquake catalog of Southern California for the period from 1980 to 2024, which was obtained from the website "The Southern California Earthquake Data Center" (*SCEDC*), which operates at the Seismological Laboratory at Caltech and is the primary archive of seismic data for Southern California. The downloaded catalog contains a total of 671,533 events. However, the catalog is complete for magnitudes starting at 1.5, with a total of 284,197 earthquakes remaining in this range. It is important to note that no depth discrimination was performed in this analysis.

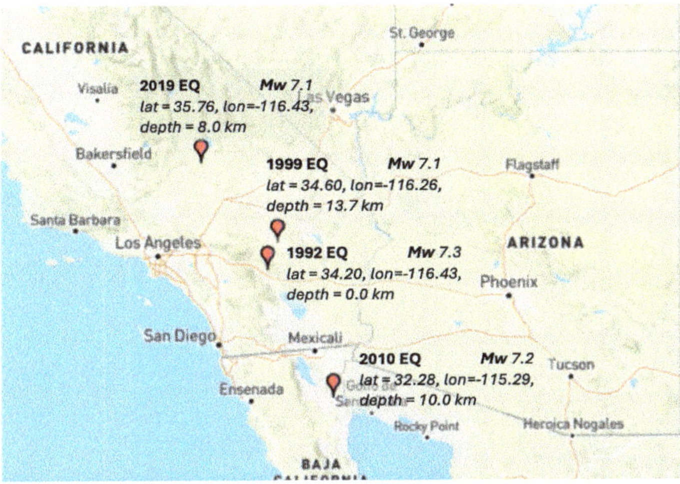

Figure 2. The map showing the locations of earthquakes with a magnitude of 7 or greater from the southern California catalog.

From the Catalog, it was identified earthquakes with a magnitude of 7.0 or greater, finding four such events. The first occurred 10 km north of Yucca Valley, California, on 28 June 1992, with a magnitude of 7.3. The second occurred 16 km southwest of Ludlow, California, on 16 October 1999, with a magnitude of 7.1. The third occurred 12 km southwest of Delta, Baja California, Mexico, on 4 April 2010, with a magnitude of 7.2. Finally, the fourth occurred 18 km west of Searles Valley, California, on 6 July 2019, with a magnitude of 7.1 (see Table 1 and Figure 2 for detailed information on each earthquake). After locating the earthquakes with magnitudes of 7 or greater, we selected 50 windows before and after each event with 2^{10} data. It is worth mentioning that exploration circles of 100 km radius around the main earthquakes were used, helping to exclude distant events.

Figure 3 represents how the windowing process was applied to the seismicity series. The light blue line shows a fragment of this series, where the earthquake (EQ) of great magnitude is located in the middle to perform the windowing. This procedure consists of dividing the series into consecutive windows of 1024 events selected before and after the earthquake. In the figure, the first window before the earthquake is labeled as 1st W-B (First Window-Before), while the first window after the earthquake is labeled as 1st W-A (First Window-After). The double arrow line represents the overlap of 996 events between consecutive windows. To ensure that each window contains exactly 1024 events, the data is completed using adjacent events in the series, i.e., events immediately before or after the current window, if necessary. Subsequent windows are named following the same scheme. For example, the second window before the earthquake is labeled as 2nd W-B (Second Window-Before), and the second window after the earthquake is labeled 2nd W-A (Second Window-After). This procedure is systematically repeated to generate a total of 50 windows before and 50 windows after the selected earthquake. The goal of this method is to analyze the variations in the characteristics of the seismicity series around the main event. This allows for the identification of patterns or anomalies, such as possible seismic precursors, changes in event frequency, or unusual behaviors that could be relevant for the study.

Table 1. The information on earthquakes with a magnitude of 7 or greater from the California catalog for the period from 1 January 1980 to 19 August 2019.

YYY/MM/DD	HH:mm:SS.ss	Magnitude (M_w)	Latitude	Longitude	Depth (km)
1992/06/28	11:57:34.13	7.3	34.20000	−116.43700	0.0
1999/10/16	09:46:44.46	7.1	34.60333	−116.26500	13.7
2010/04/04	22:40:42.36	7.2	32.28617	−115.29533	10.0
2019/07/06	03:19:53.04	7.1	35.76950	−117.59933	8.0

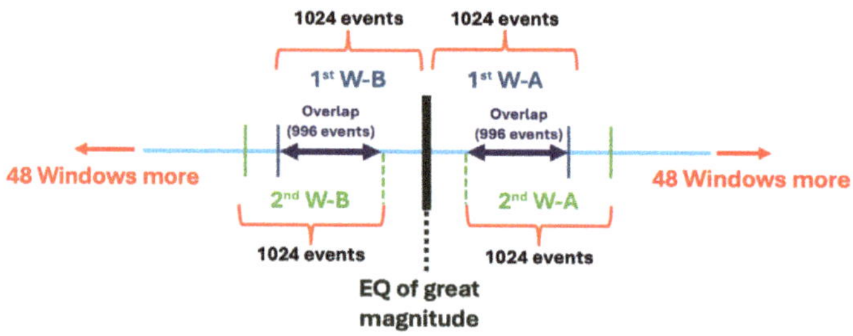

Figure 3. Illustration of the windowing process applied to the seismicity series. The series was divided into overlapping windows of 1024 events before and after the earthquake of great magnitude, with labels 1st W-B and 1st W-A for the first windows before and after the event, and 2nd W-B and 2nd W-A for the second windows before and after.

It is worth mentioning that in this study initially the overlap of the windows was varied, however, the one that yielded the best results was with 996 data.

Figure 4 illustrates some events occurred before and after the 2019 earthquake, which was considered in the aforementioned windowing process. It can be observed that prior to this earthquake, normal seismic activity in Southern California is observed; however, after the earthquake, aftershocks are evident along the San Andreas Fault.

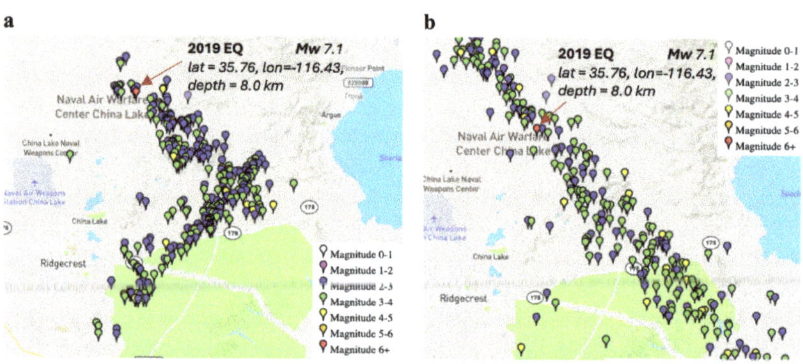

Figure 4. Illustration of the spatial variation of the events included (**a**) before and (**b**) after the 2019 earthquake. Only events with a magnitude of 2.5 or greater are shown.

Finally, the obtained series of each window were analyzed by using VGA and the *k*-*M* slope and average degree were calculated.

2.3. Spring-Block Method

Earthquakes obey the Gutenberg-Richter law, which is the distribution of energy released during an earthquake [5,38]. In 1956 they discovered the relationship [5,38]:

$$\log_{10} N(M > m) = a - bm. \tag{2}$$

where M is magnitude, $N(M)$ is the number of earthquakes of magnitude $\leqq M$, a is a constant related to the overall seismic activity in the region and determines the frequency of earthquakes in that area, and b determines the relative number of earthquakes of different magnitudes. The Equation (2) is the Gutenberg-Richter law. The parameter a and b depend on the location, but b has been observed to vary significantly across different faults. Values of b have been reported ranging from 0.80 to 1.06 for great magnitude earthquakes and from 1.23 to 1.54 for small magnitude earthquakes [5,7,38].

The energy E released during the earthquake increases exponentially with the size of the earthquake as follows [39]:

$$\log_{10} E = c + dm \tag{3}$$

where d is 1 and $3/2$ for small and large earthquakes, respectively [8,38–40]. So, the Gutenberg-Richter law is essentially a power law connecting the frequency distribution function with the energy release E

$$N(E_0 > E) \sim E^{-b/d} = E^{-B} \tag{4}$$

B is in the same range for both small and large earthquakes, namely, 0.80–1.05 [39]. the power law that exhibits the Gutenberg-Richter is related to geometric features of the fault structure and Mandelbrot noted the earthquakes occur on "fractal" self-similar sets [5,38].

The Olami, Feder, and Christensen (OFC) spring-block model [38] is a two-dimensional system of blocks interconnected by springs. Each block is connected to its four nearest neighbors and to a single rigid drive plate by another set of springs, as well as frictionally connected to a fixed rigid plate. The blocks are driven by the relative motion of the two rigid plates. When the force on one of the blocks is greater than the maximum static friction, the block slides.

The OFC model can be mapped to a cellular automaton model that uses an $L \times L$ matrix of blocks identified by their coordinates (i, j), where i,j are integers within the interval $[1, L]$. The displacement of each block from its relaxed position in the grid is denoted as $dx_{i,j}$. The total force exerted by the springs on a given block (i, j) is expressed as:

$$F_{i,j} = K_1[2dx_{i,j} - dx_{i-1,j} - dx_{i+1,j}] + K_2[2dx_{i,j} - dx_{i,j-1} - dx_{i,j+1}] + K_L dx_{i,j} \tag{5}$$

where K_1, K_2 and K_L represent the spring constants.

When the two rigid plates move relative to each other, the total force on each block increases uniformly at a rate proportional to $K_L V$, where V is the relative velocity between the two plates. This increase continues until a site reaches a threshold value, at which point the relaxation process begins, triggering a synthetic earthquake.

The redistribution of stress after a local slip at position (i, j) is described by the following relations:

$$\begin{aligned} F_{i\pm1,j} &\to F_{i\pm1,j} + \delta F_{i\pm1,j}, \\ F_{i,j\pm1} &\to F_{i,j\pm1} + \delta F_{i,j\pm1}, \\ F_{i,j} &\to 0 \end{aligned} \tag{6}$$

where the increments in the forces of the nearest-neighbor blocks are given by:

$$\delta F_{i\pm1,j} = \frac{K_1}{2K_1 + 2K_2 + K_L} F_{i,j} = \beta_1 F_{i,j}$$
$$\delta F_{i\pm1,j} = \frac{K_1}{2K_1 + 2K_2 + K_L} F_{i,j} = \beta_1 F_{i,j} \quad (7)$$

For simplicity, the elastic redistribution coefficients are denoted as β_1 and β_2, respectively, although the isotropic case is generally considered, that is, $\beta_1 = \beta_2 = \beta$. If we assume that all elastic constants are on the same scale ($K_1 \approx K_2 \approx K_L$) then $\beta = 0.2$.

The total number of slips following a single initial slip event is a measure of the size (seismic moment) of the earthquake. *OFC* measure the probability distribution of the size (the total number of relaxations) of the earthquakes, which is proportional to the energy released during an earthquake. We used the *OFC* model to generate a time series of 10,000,000 data with a conservation level of $\beta = 0.2$ for a 100×100 blocks. The series contains data on the number of earthquakes and the number of relaxed blocks. To model the relationship between magnitude and event frequency, the following expression was used:

$$log_3 N = M \quad (8)$$

where N is the number of events and M is the magnitude.

This relationship allows for the adjustment of the magnitude distribution in the synthetic series. Earthquakes with magnitudes greater than 7.0 were excluded from the analysis because synthetic seismicity produces a large number of events of that magnitude, making it challenging to identify specific patterns due to their high frequency. We focused on earthquakes with magnitudes greater than 8.0, which represent the largest and least frequent events. In this case, it was found only three earthquakes of that magnitude, allowing for a more detailed analysis of their characteristics. It is worth mentioning that these identified synthetic earthquakes are well-separated from each other, ensuring no overlap between them. Similarly, for California seismicity, we analyzed the most significant recorded earthquakes, enabling comparisons between the behavior of extreme events in both synthetic and real scenarios, identifying similarities and differences in the distribution and dynamics of these events.

Therefore, we were interested in studying the dynamics that occur before and after an earthquake, as well as the behavior of aftershocks in real seismicity and synthetic seismicity. Then, once the earthquakes with a magnitude of 8.0 or greater were located, we constructed 50 windows before and after each earthquake with 2^{10} data by using an overlap of 996 events (see Figure 3). Additionally, in the case of synthetic catalogs, since they are complete, a threshold magnitude is not considered (lines 100), unlike the California catalog where it was set at 1.5. Finally, we applied VGA to these time series and calculate the *k-M* and average degree.

3. Results

3.1. Seismicity from California

The California seismicity series were analyzed using VGA, where the earthquakes were mapped to nodes in a visibility graph. In this approach, each node's connectivity k is obtained by counting how many other nodes (earthquakes) it is directly visible to in the adjacency matrix of the visibility graph. Specifically, each row of the adjacency matrix reflects a node's links to all other nodes, so the degree k is the sum of those links. Figure 5 shows a typical representation of the complex network formed by series before and after the earthquake, respectively. In the visibility graphs of Figure 5a (before the earthquake), we see a higher concentration of highly connected nodes, forming a more compact structure with larger clusters. By contrast, in the Figure 5a (after the earthquake), the average degree clearly decreases: there are more dispersed clusters with fewer nodes in each cluster, and fewer nodes exhibiting very high connectivity. In terms of visibility graphs, this reduction can be explained by the clustering of aftershocks following the main event. Aftershocks tend to occur in rapid succession, which affects the "lines of sight" between seismic events in the time series—many smaller events in a short period often create shorter visibility spans, leading to a noticeable shift in the node degree distribution toward lower connectivity. Thus, the underlying seismic dynamics, dominated by aftershocks, become reflected in a sparser, more fragmented visibility graph structure.

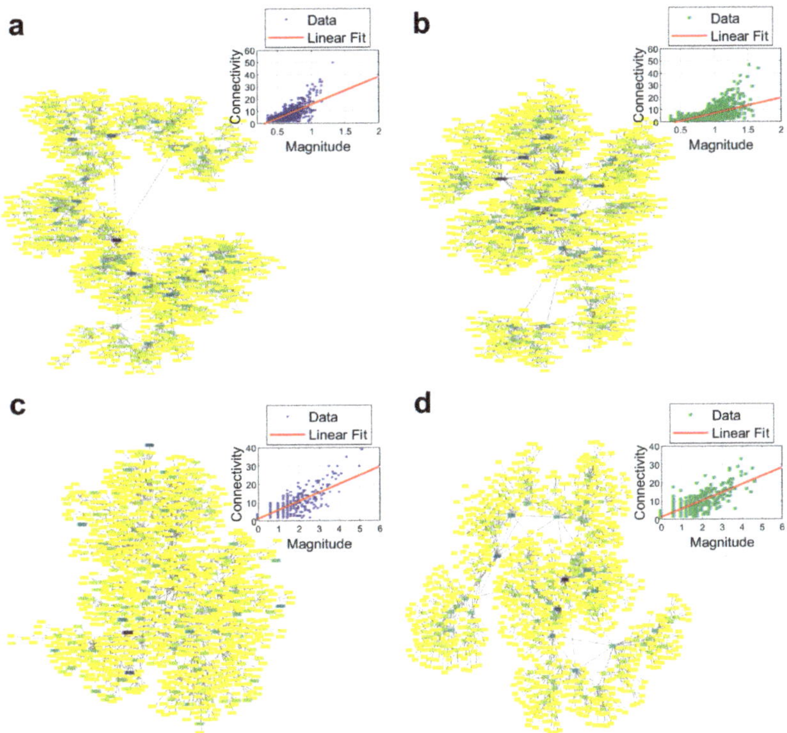

Figure 5. Illustration of the complex network and connectivity vs. magnitude graph formed by the seismicity series from California (**a**) before and (**b**) after a great earthquake, as well as the complex network and *k*-*M* plots formed by synthetic seismicity series (**c**) before and (**d**) after the earthquake. It can be observed that before the earthquake, the networks form fewer clusters of larger size, while those networks after the earthquake form a greater number of clusters with fewer nodes.

First, the slope of the graph of connectivity vs magnitude at each node (*k*-*M* slope) was analyzed. Figure 6 shows the results for the 50 windows before and after the earthquake for the four earthquakes studied. It can be observed that before the earthquake the *k*-*M* values are around 20, however in the following window after the great earthquake these values decrease.

It is noteworthy that for the 2019 earthquake the *k*-*M* actually increases considerably after the great earthquake (Figure 6d), this is attributed to the fact that in window 32 before this great earthquake an event of magnitude 6.4 had already occurred nearby (information about this event: date 2019/07/04 , $M_w = 6.4$, $lat = 35.70533$, $lon = -117.50383$, and $depth = 10.5$ km). Such mid-sequence events can transiently alter connectivity and raise or lower *k*-*M* values as aftershocks subside and the network reconfigures. Furthermore, the aftershocks of a magnitude 6.4 earthquake are smaller in magnitude and fewer in number compared to those generated by a magnitude 7.1 earthquake, so the value of *k-M* will decrease further once a larger magnitude earthquake occurs. This fact is further strengthened by the graph where it can be observed how the *k-M* values decrease in this window and decrease even more after the earthquake of magnitude 7.1.

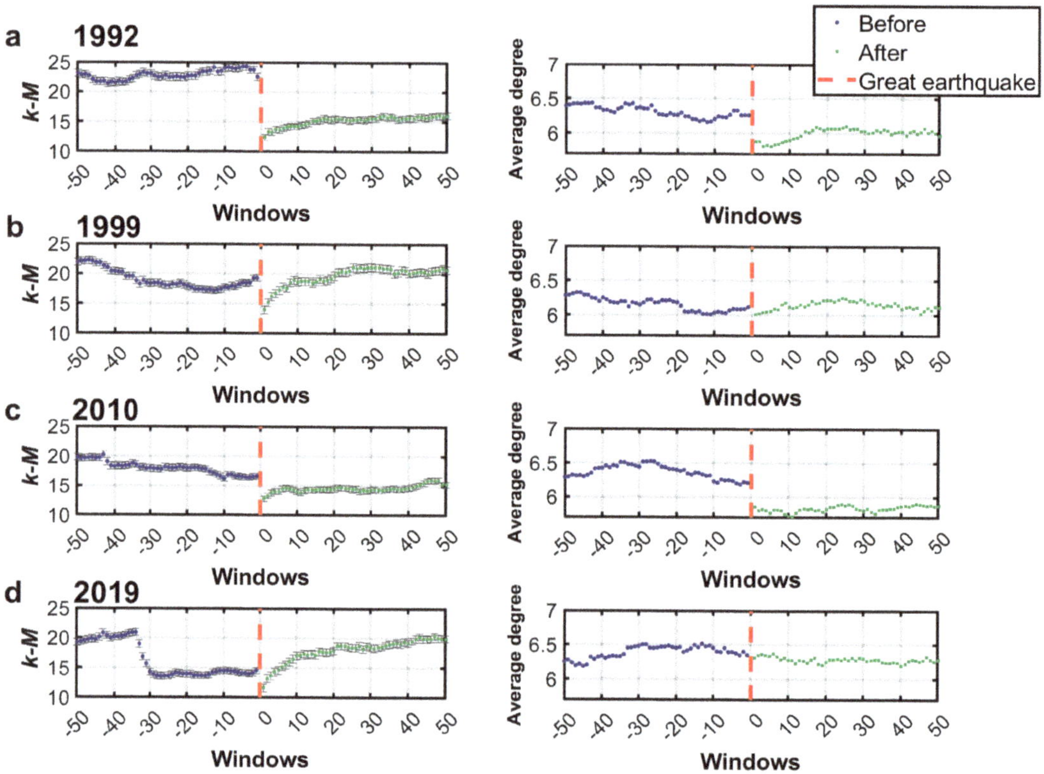

Figure 6. *k-M* slope and average degree values obtained from California seismicity series of the (**a**) 1992, (**b**) 1999, (**c**) 2010, and (**d**) 2019 earthquakes.

Furthermore, Figure 6 shows the error bars corresponding to the calculation of the *k-M* slope from the linear fit by least squares. It can be observed that the errors represent around 2.5% of the calculated *k-M* values, this confirms that the errors in the slope calculation are not significant, which further strengthens the findings described above.

This study was now repeated considering the calculation of the average degree which can be observed in the Figure 6. Here the same trend was observed, that is, the values decrease significantly after the earthquake. It should be noted that the average degree of the second earthquake increases after the earthquake instead of decreasing.

Overall, the observed post-earthquake decrease in *k-M* slope and in average degree suggests a transient disruption in connectivity patterns, likely influenced by the clustering of aftershocks. Over time, these values may recover or even exceed pre-earthquake levels, reflecting how the visibility network reconfigures as seismic activity stabilizes.

3.2. Seismicity from Synthetic Series

Once it was confirmed that in real seismicity there is a significant change in the parameters of complex networks studied for real seismicity, we were interested in verifying whether this trend can also be reproduced by synthetic series of seismicity, so we repeated the same analysis with the series obtained with the OFC model. Especially because we noticed that the representation of the complex networks shown in the insets c and d of Figure 5 also exhibit differences between the series before and after the earthquake. In that figure, it can be observed that before the earthquake the network forms a cluster with many nodes, whereas after the earthquake the network forms smaller clusters.

Figure 7 shows the values of *k-M* and average degree obtained for three synthetic series of seismicity. Although these values were not in the same range than those obtained for the California seismic series, with this analysis it can again be observed that both parameters decrease after the main earthquake. Newly, the error bars for the calculation of *k-M* values are shown in Figure 7. It can be observed that these errors are not significant before or after the earthquake, which suggests that the same behavior observed in real seismicity was reproduced by the OFC model.

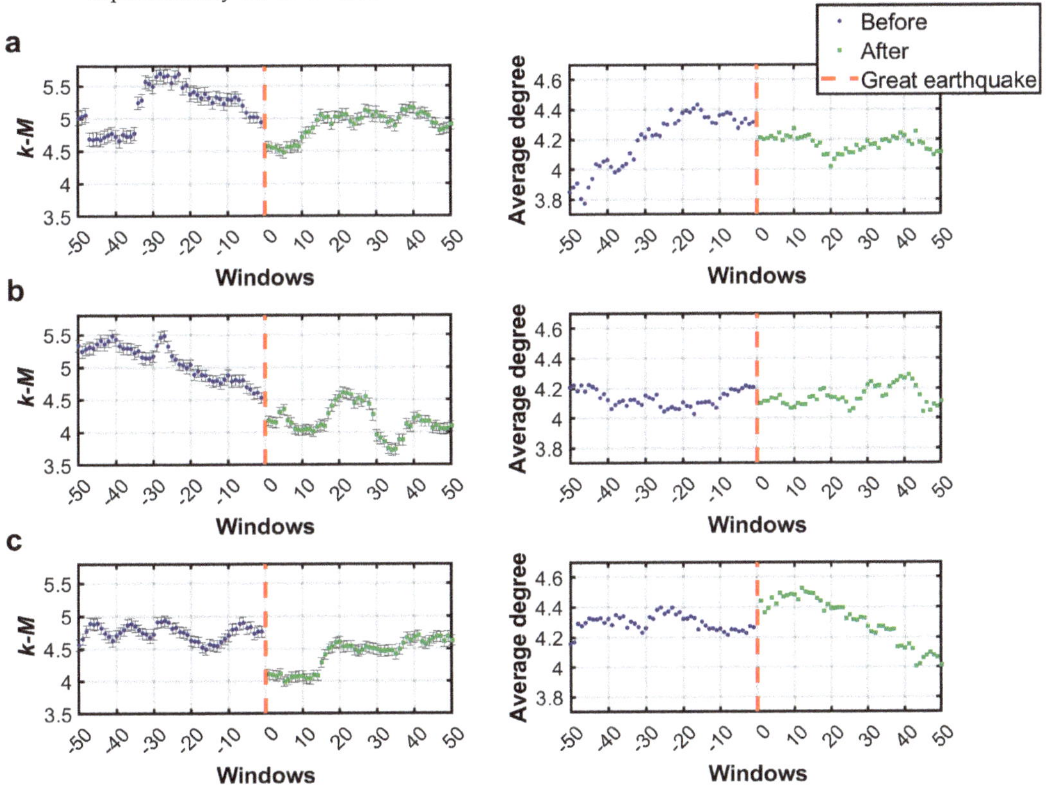

Figure 7. *k-M* slope and average degree values obtained from synthetic seismicity series of the (**a**) earthquake 1, (**b**) earthquake 2, and (**c**) earthquake 3.

4. Discussion

The results suggest that the methods implemented in this work show changes in the dynamics before and after the great earthquake, as reported in [41]. Specially, it was observed that there is a significant change in the *k-M* slope in the windows before and after the three California's earthquakes analyzed. Specifically, the network parameter *k-M* decreases, which is due to a reduction in node connectivity caused by the presence of aftershocks. These aftershocks are more frequent but lower in magnitude, leading to a loss of network connectivity. Additionally, we found that this change is also preserved when analyzing synthetic seismicity using the spring-block model, which suggests that such relaxation mechanisms can also be reproduced by this model, contrary to what has been indicated in other studies [41].

It should be remembered that, in the spring-block model, and specifically in its non-conservative variant Olami–Feder–Christensen (OFC), the aftershock process is not explicitly modeled. However, we observe variations in the results that suggest the possible existence of aftershocks due to the partial redistribution of stresses. The model consists of placing two parallel plates: one mobile and one fixed, to which small blocks are attached by means of springs. When moving the mobile plate, one of the blocks exceeds its threshold force, triggering the continuous movement of the neighboring blocks. During this process, the energy is redistributed towards the adjacent blocks, leaving some of them "loaded" with residual energy. This is manifested in the series of synthetic earthquakes as aftershocks, observed in the graphs and in the multifractal analysis carried out in [38,41].

It is well known that the calculation of the *k-M* slope can be imprecise due to the wide dispersion of points in the connectivity vs. magnitude plot. As a result, after fitting, the correlation coefficient may not be significant. However, to corroborate the aforementioned findings, we also decided to calculate the average degree, which is somewhat related to *k-M* as it helps to measure the average connectivity level of all nodes [17,42]. This analysis revealed that the decrease in the *k-M* slope after the earthquake persists, reaffirming this trend caused by the aftershocks.

Before a large earthquake, *k-M* values correspond to low seismic activity. However, when a large earthquake occurs, the number of aftershocks, which are events of higher magnitude, causes a decrease in connectivity and therefore in *k-M*. Subsequently, after the aftershocks, normal seismic activity is reestablished, causing *k-M* values to rise again. Interestingly, the same pattern was observed in the analysis of synthetic series, once again suggesting that these relaxation mechanisms are also present in the spring-block model.

It is worth mentioning that the initial proposal included the analysis of additional complex network parameters, such as the average path length. However, we found that the differences in the values of these parameters were not significant. This may be because the networks formed from the windowed data exhibit small-world characteristics, which are typically defined by relatively short average path lengths coexisting with high clustering coefficients [43]. In such networks, even when nodes are rearranged or new connections appear, the overall path length may remain consistently short, making it challenging to observe subtle changes in dynamics between events. Consequently, the impact of an earthquake on certain small-world-like properties may be overshadowed by the inherent structural robustness of these networks. Nevertheless, future studies could explore a broader range of parameters to identify new trends that might help detect aftershocks or even preparation mechanisms before a great earthquake occurs.

In addition, the analysis presented highlights a significant similarity in the behavior of the parameters derived from complex networks for both real and synthetic seismicity, particularly in the context of large-magnitude events and their aftershocks. The process of overlapping windowing before and after these earthquakes allows for a detailed evaluation of the evolution of the clustering coefficient *k-M* and the average degree of the networks generated using the visibility algorithm.

The observation of an increase in the *k-M* value in real seismicity, as a consequence of the rise in the number of earthquakes due to aftershocks, is consistent with the physics of the process: the triggering of a secondary seismic sequence enhances the connectivity of the associated networks, reflecting an increase in local interactions between events. The fact that this same behavior is observed in synthetic seismicity generated through the

OFC model suggests that this model adequately captures the essential dynamics of stress generation and relaxation in seismic systems.

The finding of aftershocks in synthetic large-magnitude earthquakes within the OFC model can be interpreted as evidence that the relaxation of blocks following a main event generates near-rupture conditions in some blocks within the affected area. This critical state promotes the occurrence of new events, analogous to aftershocks in natural seismicity. These results strengthen the relevance of the OFC model for studying not only main events but also post-seismic dynamics, paving the way for a more detailed analysis of stress conditions and their evolution after a great earthquake.

5. Conclusions

The largest earthquakes were identified in both synthetic seismicity and real seismicity in Southern California. Taking each of these large-magnitude earthquakes as a reference, a window superposition process was applied before and after the main event. Each window represents a subsequence to which the visibility algorithm was applied and two parameters of the resulting complex networks were calculated, *k-M* and the average degree. This allowed us to observe the evolution of these parameters before and after the earthquake.

There is a difference in the behavior of these parameters in the seismicity of Southern California before and after four earthquakes that were the largest between 1992 and 2019, which is due to the presence of their aftershocks. It is important to note that the same trend is observed in synthetic seismicity, which leads us to propose that there is also aftershock-like behavior in the *OFC* model after large synthetic earthquakes. This is because after a large synthetic earthquake, a significant number of blocks relax. These blocks represent the "rupture zone" of the synthetic earthquake, and it appears that many of these blocks remain in a state of stress very close to the threshold. It is therefore reasonable to expect high activity in the blocks within the synthetic earthquake rupture area after a major event, which is related to aftershocks in real seismicity.

Author Contributions: Conceptualization, A.M.-D.; methodology, A.M.A.-M. and J.A.Z.-J.; software, A.M.A.-M., E.E.S.-M. and J.A.Z.-J.; validation, A.M.-D.; formal analysis, A.M.-D. and J.A.Z.-J.; writing—original draft preparation, A.M.A.-M., E.E.S.-M. and J.A.Z.-J.; writing—review and editing, A.M.-D. and A.M.A.-M.; supervision, A.M.-D. All authors have read and agreed to the published version of the manuscript.

Funding: This research was funded by Secretaría de Investigación y Posgrado (SIP) of the Insituto Politécnico Nacional—México.

Institutional Review Board Statement: Not applicable.

Data Availability Statement: All data used in the present work could be requested to correspondence author.

Conflicts of Interest: The authors declare no conflicts of interest.

Abbreviations

The following abbreviations are used in this manuscript:

EQ	Earthquake
OFC	Olami–Feder–Christensen's model
SCEDF	The Southern California Earthquake Data Center
SSAF	Southern San Andreas Fault
VG	Visibility Graph
VGA	Visibility Graph Algorithm

References

1. Kwapień, J.; Drożdż, S. Physical approach to complex systems. *Phys. Rep.* **2012**, *515*, 115–226. [CrossRef]
2. Smith, J.; Doe, A. Nonconservative earthquake model of self-organized criticality on a random graph. *Phys. Rev. E* **2020**, *102*, 031105.
3. Sornette, A.; Sornette, D. Self-organized criticality and earthquakes. *Tectonophysics* **1990**, *179*, 327–333. [CrossRef]
4. Kanamori, H.; Boschi, E. (Eds.) *Earthquakes: Observation, Theory and Interpretation*; Elsevier: Amsterdam, The Netherlands, 1983.
5. Bak, P.; Tang, C.; Wiesenfeld, K. Self-organized criticality: An explanation of the 1/f noise. *Phys. Rev. Lett.* **1987**, *59*, 381–384. [CrossRef]
6. de Carvalho, J.X.; Prado, C.P.C. Self-Organized Criticality in the Olami-Feder-Christensen Model. *Phys. Rev. Lett.* **2000**, *84*, 4006–4009. [CrossRef]
7. Bak, P. *How Nature Works: The Science of Self-Organized Criticality*; Copernicus: New York, NY, USA, 1996.
8. Christensen, K.; Olami, Z. Variation of the Gutenberg-Richter b values and nontrivial temporal correlations in a Spring-Block Model for earthquakes. *J. Geophys. Res. Solid Earth* **1992**, *97*, 8729–8735. [CrossRef]
9. Bak, P.; Tang, C. Earthquakes as a self-organized critical phenomenon. *J. Geophys. Res.* **1989**, *94*, 15635–15637. [CrossRef]
10. Barabási, A.R. Statistical mechanics of complex networks. *Rev. Mod. Phys.* **2002**, *74*, 47.
11. Newman, M.E.J. *Networks: An Introduction*; Oxford University Press: Oxford, UK, 2010.
12. Telesca, L.; Lovallo, M.; Ramírez-Rojas, A.; Flores-Marquez, L. Relationship between the Frequency Magnitude Distribution and the Visibility Graph in the Synthetic Seismicity Generated by a Simple Stick-Slip System with Asperities. *PLoS ONE* **2014**, *9*, e106233. [CrossRef]
13. Aguilar-SanJuan, B.; Guzmán-Vargas, L. Earthquake magnitude time series: Scaling behavior of visibility networks. *Eur. Phys. J. B* **2013**, *86*, 454. [CrossRef]
14. Zhang, J.; Small, M. Complex network from pseudoperiodic time series: Topology versus dynamics. *Phys. Rev. Lett.* **2006**, *96*, 238701. [CrossRef] [PubMed]
15. Marwan, N.; Carmen Romano, M.; Thiel, M.; Kurths, J. Recurrence plots for the analysis of complex systems. *Phys. Rep.* **2007**, *438*, 237–329. [CrossRef]
16. Gao, Z.K.; Zhang, X.W.; Jin, N.D.; Donner, R.V.; Marwan, N.; Kurths, J. Recurrence networks from multivariate signals for uncovering dynamic transitions of horizontal oil-water stratified flows. *Europhys. Lett.* **2013**, *103*, 50004. [CrossRef]
17. Lacasa, L.; Luque, B.; Ballesteros, F.; Luque, J.; Nuno, J.C. From time series to complex networks: The visibility graph. *Proc. Natl. Acad. Sci. USA* **2008**, *105*, 4972–4975. [CrossRef] [PubMed]
18. Muñoz-Diosdado, A.; Solís-Montufar, E.E.; Zamora-Justo, J.A. Visibility Graph Analysis of Heartbeat Time Series: Comparison of Young vs. Old, Healthy vs. Diseased, Rest vs. Exercise, and Sedentary vs. Active. *Entropy* **2023**, *25*, 677. [CrossRef] [PubMed]
19. Zhu, G.; Li, Y.; Wen, P.P. An efficient visibility graph similarity algorithm and its application on sleep stages classification. In Proceedings of the International Conference on Brain Informatics, Macau, China, 4–7 December 2012; pp. 185–195.
20. Nilanjana, P.; Anirban, B.; Susmita, B.; Dipak, G. Noninvasive alarm generation for sudden cardiac arrest: A pilot study with visibility graph technique. *Transl. Biomed.* **2016**, *7*, 79.
21. Yu, M.; Hillebrand, A.; Gouw, A.A.; Stam, C.J. Horizontal visibility graph transfer entropy (HVG-TE): A novel metric to characterize directed connectivity in large-scale brain networks. *NeuroImage* **2017**, *156*, 249–264. [CrossRef] [PubMed]
22. Bhaduri, A.; Ghosh, D. Quantitative Assessment of Heart Rate Dynamics during Meditation: An ECG Based Study with Multi-Fractality and Visibility Graph. *Front. Physiol.* **2016**, *7*, 44. [CrossRef]
23. Telesca, L.; Lovallo, M. Analysis of seismic sequences by using the method of visibility graph. *Europhys. Lett.* **2012**, *97*, 50002. [CrossRef]
24. Telesca, L.; Lovallo, M.; Ramírez-Rojas, A.; Flores-Marquez, L. Investigating the time dynamics of seismicity by using the visibility graph approach: Application to seismicity of Mexican subduction zone. *Phys. A Stat. Mech. Its Appl.* **2013**, *392*, 6571–6577. [CrossRef]
25. Telesca, L.; Lovallo, M.; Toth, L. Visibility graph analysis of 2002–2011 Pannonian seismicity. *Phys. A Stat. Mech. Its Appl.* **2014**, *416*, 219–224. [CrossRef]
26. Khoshnevis, N.; Taborda, R.; Azizzadeh-Roodpish, S.; Telesca, L. Analysis of the 2005–2016 Earthquake Sequence in Northern Iran Using the Visibility Graph Method. *Pure Appl. Geophys.* **2017**, *174*, 4003–4019. [CrossRef]
27. Azizzadeh-Roodpish, S.; Cramer, C.H. Visibility Graph Analysis of Alaska Crustal and Aleutian Subduction Zone Seismicity: An Investigation of the Correlation between b Value and k–M Slope. *Pure Appl. Geophys.* **2018**, *175*, 4241–4252. [CrossRef]
28. Perez-Oregon, J.; Muñoz-Diosdado, A.; Rudolf-Navarro, A.H.; Angulo-Brown, F. Some Common Features Between a Spring-Block Self-Organized Critical Model, Stick–Slip Experiments with Sandpapers and Actual Seismicity. *Pure Appl. Geophys.* **2019**, *177*, 889–903. [CrossRef]
29. Bak, P.; Christensen, K.; Danon, L.; Scanlon, T. Unified Scaling Law for Earthquakes. *Phys. Rev. Lett.* **2002**, *88*, 178501. [CrossRef] [PubMed]

30. Davidsen, J.; Goltz, C. Are seismic waiting time distributions universal? *Geophys. Res. Lett.* **2004**, *31*, 5. [CrossRef]
31. Azizzadeh-Roodpish, S.; Khoshnevis, N.; Cramer, C.H. Visibility graph analysis of southern California. In Proceedings of the Proceedings Annual Meeting of the Seismological Society of America, Denver, CO, USA, 18–20 April 2017; Volume 10.
32. Pierini, J.O.; Lovallo, M.; Telesca, L. Visibility graph analysis of wind speed records measured in central Argentina. *Physica A* **2012**, *391*, 5041–5048. [CrossRef]
33. Toppozada, T.; Branum, D. California Earthquake History. *Calif. Geol. Surv.* **2024**, *48*, 210–225. [CrossRef]
34. Meade, B.J.; Hager, B.H. Block models of crustal motion in southern California constrained by GPS measurements. *J. Geophys. Res. Solid Earth* **2005**, *110*, B03403. [CrossRef]
35. Weldon, R.J.; Fumal, T.E.; Biasi, G.P.; Scharer, K.M. Past and Future Earthquakes on the San Andreas Fault. *J. Geophys. Res. Solid Earth* **2024**, *129*, 1234–1256. [CrossRef]
36. Hill, R.; Weingarten, M.; Rockwell, T.; Fialko, Y. Major Earthquakes on the Southern San Andreas Fault Modulated by Lake Filling Events. *Geophys. Res. Lett.* **2024**, *51*, 1234–1248.
37. Vavra, E.; Fialko, Y.; Barbot, S. Active Dipping Interface of the Southern San Andreas Fault Revealed by Space Geodetic and Seismic Imaging. *J. Geophys. Res. Solid Earth* **2023**, *128*, e2023JB026346. [CrossRef]
38. Olami, Z.; Feder, H.J.S.; Christensen, K. Self-organized criticality in a continuous, nonconservative cellular automaton modeling earthquakes. *Phys. Rev. Lett.* **1992**, *68*, 1244–1247. [CrossRef] [PubMed]
39. Ekström, G.; Dziewoński, A.M. The moment tensor of earthquakes: Theory and applications to the 1985 Michoacán, Mexico, earthquake. *J. Geophys. Res. Solid Earth* **1988**, *93*, 8049–8084.
40. Pacheco, J.F.; Scholz, C.H.; Sykes, L.R. Changes in frequency–size relationship from small to large earthquakes. *Nature* **1992**, *355*, 71–73. [CrossRef]
41. Aguilar-Molina, A.M.; Muñoz-Diosdado, A.; Salinas Martínez, A.; Angulo-Brown, F. Multifractal Properties of Time Series of Synthetic Earthquakes Obtained from a Spring-Block Model. *Entropy* **2023**, *25*, 773. [CrossRef]
42. Perez-Oregon, J.; Lovallo, M.; Telesca, L. Visibility graph analysis of synthetic earthquakes generated by the Olami–Feder–Christensen spring-block model. *Chaos Interdiscip. J. Nonlinear Sci.* **2020**, *30*, 093111. [CrossRef]
43. Watts, D.J.; Strogatz, S.H. Collective dynamics of 'small-world' networks. *Nature* **1998**, *393*, 440–442. [CrossRef]

Disclaimer/Publisher's Note: The statements, opinions and data contained in all publications are solely those of the individual author(s) and contributor(s) and not of MDPI and/or the editor(s). MDPI and/or the editor(s) disclaim responsibility for any injury to people or property resulting from any ideas, methods, instructions or products referred to in the content.

entropy

MDPI

Article

Earthquake Forecasting Based on *b* Value and Background Seismicity Rate in Yunnan Province, China

Yuchen Zhang [1,2], Rui Wang [2,3], Haixia Shi [4], Miao Miao [2], Jiancang Zhuang [5], Ying Chang [6], Changsheng Jiang [7], Lingyuan Meng [4], Danning Li [8], Lifang Liu [8], Youjin Su [8], Zhenguo Zhang [2] and Peng Han [2,3,*]

[1] Department of Astronautical Science and Mechanics, Harbin Institute of Technology, Harbin 150001, China; 11849527@mail.sustech.edu.cn
[2] Department of Earth and Space Sciences, Southern University of Science and Technology, Shenzhen 518055, China; wangr9@sustech.edu.cn (R.W.); miaom@sustech.edu.cn (M.M.); zhangzg@sustech.edu.cn (Z.Z.)
[3] Key Laboratory of Earthquake Forecasting and Risk Assessment, Ministry of Emergency Management, Southern University of Science and Technology, Shenzhen 518055, China
[4] China Earthquake Networks Center, Beijing 100045, China; shihaixia08@seis.ac.cn (H.S.); menglingyuan@seis.ac.cn (L.M.)
[5] Institute of Statistical Mathematics, Tokyo 190-8562, Japan; zhuangjc@ism.ac.jp
[6] BGRIMM Technology Group, Institute of Mining Engineering, Beijing 100160, China; changy@bgrimm.com
[7] Institute of Geophysics, China Earthquake Administration, Beijing 100081, China; jiangcs@cea-igp.ac.cn
[8] Earthquake Administration of Yunnan Province, Kunming 650224, China; zuni_2001@163.com (D.L.); lifang_l@sina.com (L.L.); suyoujin0818@sina.com (Y.S.)
* Correspondence: hanp@sustech.edu.cn; Tel.: +86-755-8801-5515

Abstract: Characterized by frequent earthquakes and a dense population, Yunnan Province, China, faces significant seismic hazards and is a hot place for earthquake forecasting research. In a previous study, we evaluated the performance of the *b* value for 5-year seismic forecasting during 2000–2019 and made a forward prediction of M $\geq$ 5.0 earthquakes in 2020–2024. In this study, with the forecast period having passed, we first revisit the results and assess the forward prediction performance. Then, the background seismicity rate, which may also offer valuable long-term forecasting information, is incorporated into earthquake prediction for Yunnan Province. To assess the effectiveness of the prediction, the Molchan Error Diagram (MED), Probability Gain (PG), and Probability Difference (PD) are employed. Using a 25-year catalog, the spatial *b* value and background seismicity rate across five temporal windows are calculated, and 86 M $\geq$ 5.0 earthquakes as prediction samples are examined. The predictive performance of the background seismicity rate and *b* value is comprehensively tested and shown to be useful for 5-year forecasting in Yunnan. The performance of the *b* value exhibits a positive correlation with the predicted earthquake magnitude. The synergistic effect of combining these two predictors is also revealed. Finally, using the threshold corresponding to the maximum *PD*, we integrate the forecast information of background seismicity rates and the *b* value. A forward prediction is derived for the period from January 2025 to December 2029. This study can be helpful for disaster preparedness and risk management in Yunnan Province, China.

Keywords: earthquake forecast; *b* value; background seismicity rate; Molchan Error Diagram; Yunnan Province

1. Introduction

The Gutenberg–Richter law (G-R law) describes the relationship between earthquake magnitude (M) and the number of earthquakes (*N*) using the formula $log_{10}(N) = a - bM$, where 'a' and 'b' represent constants for the seismicity and the slope, respectively [1,2].

Several studies have identified the presence of a low b value in the vicinity of the epicenter prior to major seismic events. Notable examples include the 2004 M 9.0 Sumatra earthquake, the 2008 M 8.0 Wenchuan earthquake, and the 2011 M 9.0 Tohoku earthquake [3–7]. These observations suggest a potential relationship between a low b value and the occurrence of significant seismic activity [8–10]. Some studies on natural time analysis of earthquake catalogs emphasize the pivotal role of entropy in assessing earthquake risk and reveal that a decrease in the b value prior to large earthquakes corresponds to an increase in order parameter fluctuations as the system approaches the critical point (i.e., the mainshock) [11–13]. Further analysis from laboratory experiments demonstrates a consistent decrease in b value with increasing stress levels [14]. This finding establishes a clear relationship between the b value and stress differentials, providing robust evidence to support an earthquake prediction methodology that utilizes the b value as a key indicator [15–21].

To quantitatively assess seismic risk using the b value, Wang et al. (2021) partitioned earthquake data from January 2000 to December 2019 into four distinct five-year periods and evaluated forecasting efficiency using the Molchan Error Diagram (MED), Probability Gain (PG), and Probability Difference (PD) [22,23] in Yunnan Province, China. They then utilized the spatial b value from January 2015 to December 2019 to identify high-earthquake-potential regions in Yunnan. As of 2025, the predicted time window has elapsed, allowing a rigorous assessment of the forward prediction performance. On the other hand, the b value has a larger error and is less informative in the regions with very low seismicity. A promising direction for improvement is the incorporation of additional earthquake prediction information, such as background seismicity rate, into the existing framework.

Previous studies suggest that background seismicity rate is a valuable factor for earthquake prediction. According to the rate–state model (RSM), there is a positive correlation between seismicity rate and stress changes, with regional stress loading playing a dominant role in background seismicity rates [24–30]. Numerous studies have established relationships among background seismic rates, strain rates, and underground fluid signals [25,31,32]. And numerical simulations have demonstrated that seismic activity varies with regional stress levels [21,33]. Statistical studies indicate that major earthquakes are more likely to occur in regions with high background seismicity rates [34,35]. The background seismicity rate is a critical reference for middle–long-term earthquake forecasts and is commonly employed to assess earthquake hazards [34–37].

This study aims to identify high-earthquake-potential regions during 2025–2029 for disaster preparedness and risk management in Yunnan Province, China. First, we revisit the previous 5-year forward prediction for 2020–2024. Then, the forecast performance of the spatial b value and background seismicity rate are examined using the data for 2000–2024, and the synergistic effect of combining these two predictors is investigated. Finally, based on the test results, a strategy for integrating the forecast information of background seismicity rates and the b value is proposed, and a forward prediction is derived for 2025–2029.

2. Data

The earthquake catalog used in this study to estimate the b value and background seismicity rate is obtained from the China Earthquake Networks Center (CENC, http://www.ceic.ac.cn). Following the methodology outlined by Wang et al. (2021), our study area is defined by the coordinates 97° E–106.5° E and 21° N–30° N. A magnitude threshold of 3.0 was utilized in accordance with the previous study to ensure the completeness of the earthquake data [23,38].

3. Methods

3.1. b Value Estimation

By the Gutenberg–Richter law (G-R law), the probability density function governing earthquake magnitude can be formally expressed as

$$f(M) = \frac{N(M)}{\int_{M_c}^{\infty} N(M)dM} = \beta e^{-\beta(M-M_c)}, \quad (1)$$

The likelihood function for a specific set of earthquake samples with magnitudes M_1, M_2,......, M_n is defined as

$$L(\beta) = \prod_{i=1}^{n} f_\beta(M_i) = \prod_{i=1}^{n} \beta e^{-\beta(M_i-M_c)}, \quad (2)$$

In this context, M_c represents the complete magnitude. Ogata extends the b value to be contingent upon location and postulates that β is a function of the epicenter coordinates (x_i, y_i), denoted as $\beta = \beta(x_i, y_i)$ [34,39]. Given the inherently positive nature of the b value, $\beta(x_i, y_i)$ can be parameterized as

$$\beta(x, y) = e^{\phi_\theta(x,y)}, \quad (3)$$

Here, ϕ_θ denotes the 2-D B-spline function, while θ represents the coefficients associated with ϕ_θ. Consequently, β can be expressed as a flexible function dependent on spatial coordinates.

In the Hierarchical Space–Time Point-Process Models (HIST-PPM), the study area is partitioned into Delaunay triangles centered on earthquake epicenters. To mitigate the risk of overfitting, Ogata estimated the parameter θ by maximizing the penalized log-likelihood function, formulated as follows [39,40]:

$$R(\theta|w) = lnL(\theta) - Q(\theta|w), \quad (4)$$

Here, $Q(\theta|w)$ represents the penalty term, defined as

$$Q(\theta|w) = w\iint \left\{ \left(\frac{\partial\phi_\theta(x,y)}{\partial x} \right)^2 + \left(\frac{\partial\phi_\theta(x,y)}{\partial y} \right)^2 \right\} dxdy, \quad (5)$$

The weight, denoted as w, is a hyperparameter that can be optimized by the Akaike Bayesian Information Criterion (ABIC) [41,42]. The ABIC is expressed as

$$ABIC = -2max(logL) + 2(number\ of\ \ hyperparameters), \quad (6)$$

By minimizing the ABIC, the optimal set of hyperparameters can be estimated, thereby yielding the best fit to the data.

The computation of the b value at the epicenter is attainable using the optimized parameters θ, as outlined in Equation (3). Furthermore, the b value within the triangular mesh can be estimated through linear interpolation. This process results in a spatial distribution of b values across the entirety of Yunnan Province, with a resolution of $0.1^\circ \times 0.1^\circ$.

3.2. Background Seismicity Rate

Zhuang et al. (2002) proposed an iterative algorithm that can estimate background seismicity rate based on a space–time Epidemic-Type Aftershock Sequence (ETAS) [43]. The conditional intensity functions of spatial–temporal sequences with i earthquakes (t_i, x_i, y_i, M_i) are formulated as follows:

$$\lambda(t,x,y) = \mu(x,y) + \sum_{i;t_i<t} \kappa(M_i) g(t-t_i) f(x-x_i, y-y_i, M_i), \quad (7)$$

Here, $\lambda(t,x,y)$ represents the seismicity rate, indicating the number of earthquakes per unit time and space at time t and coordinates (x,y). The first item on the right side of Equation (7), $\mu(x,y)$, denotes the spatial background seismicity rate. The term $\kappa(M_i)g(t-t_i)f(x-x_i, y-y_i, M_i)$ is the contribution of the i-th earthquake occurring before time t. And $\kappa(M)$ is the mean number of earthquakes directly triggered by an earthquake of magnitude M, expressed as

$$\kappa(M) = Ae^{\alpha(M-M_c)}, \ M \geq M_c, \quad (8)$$

The probability density function for the occurrence times and locations of directly triggered events is given by

$$g(t) = \frac{p-1}{c}\left(1+\frac{t}{c}\right)^{-p}, \ t > 0, \quad (9)$$

$$f(x,y;M) = \frac{q-1}{\pi D e^{\gamma(M-M_c)}}\left(1+\frac{x^2+y^2}{De^{\gamma(M-M_c)}}\right)^{-q}, \quad (10)$$

The parameters $(A,\alpha,c,p,D,q,\gamma)$ can be estimated by maximizing the likelihood function:

$$lnL = \sum_{i:(t_i,x_i,y_i)\in S\times[0,T]} ln\lambda(t_i,x_i,y_i) - \int_0^T \iint_S \lambda(t,x,y)dxdydt \quad (11)$$

Using these parameters, the probability that the i-th earthquake is a background event can be estimated as

$$\varphi_i = \frac{\mu(x_i,y_i)}{\lambda(t_i,x_i,y_i)} \quad (12)$$

With φ_i for all the earthquakes obtained, the $\mu(x,y)$ can be estimated by smoothing the background. Hence, a variable kernel is employed:

$$\hat{\mu}(x,y) = \frac{1}{T}\sum_i \varphi_i Z_{d_i}(x-x_i, y-y_i) \quad (13)$$

Here, Z_d denotes the Gaussian kernel function with bandwidth d, which is calculated as follows: For a given integer n_p, a circle is centered at the i-th earthquake with a radius d_i that exceeds a minimum value ε. This circle must encompass at least n_p earthquakes. In this study, n_p and ε are set to 3 and 0.02, respectively, referring to [37]. By taking the smoothing background in Equation (13) as the background seismicity rate in Equation (7) and then estimating the parameters $(A,\alpha,c,p,D,q,\gamma)$ through maximization as outlined in Equation (11), one can iteratively refine the estimates. This process allows for the determination of the background seismicity rate through multiple iterations. For further details, please refer specifically to [43].

3.3. Evaluation of Forecast Efficiency

The seismic forecast efficiency of the prior investigation is assessed using the MED [22,44,45]. This methodology utilizes a range of values, denoted as *thr*, which serves as a threshold spanning from the minimum to the maximum values observed. In relation to the b value, grid cells with b values lower than *thr* are considered alarmed. For the background seismicity rate, grid cells with rates higher than *thr* are alarmed. The ratio of alarmed grid cells is referred to as the alarming rate τ. An earthquake is considered detected if it occurs within the alarmed grid cells. The ratio of detected earthquakes is referred to as the detecting rate ν, while the rate of missed earthquakes is expressed as the missing rate $1 - \nu$. The curve in the diagram illustrates the relationship between the alarming and missing rates. In the case of a random forecast, the alarming rate is approximately equal to the detecting rate, resulting in a curve that aligns with the diagonal. When the forecasting efficiency exceeds that of a random guess, the alarming rate is lower than the detecting rate, resulting in a curve that falls below the diagonal. Conversely, if the alarming rate exceeds the detecting rate, the curve rises above the diagonal, indicating a less effective forecast than a random guess.

To further quantify forecasting efficiency, the *PG*, defined as the ratio of the detecting rate to the alarming rate, is expressed as follows [46,47]:

$$PG = \frac{\nu}{\tau} \tag{14}$$

PG = 1 indicates that the forecasting efficiency is comparable to that of a random guess. A *PG* value greater than 1 signifies that the prediction outperforms a random guess, with higher *PG* values reflecting superior predictive performance.

Another metric employed to quantify forecasting performance in this study is the *PD*, defined as the difference between the gain (detecting rate) and the cost (alarming rate) [47].

$$PD = \nu - \tau \tag{15}$$

In the context of a random prediction, the estimated *PD* is 0. A *PD* greater than 0 indicates that the prediction strategy outperforms a random forecast. Similar to the *PG*, a higher *PD* reflects superior predictive performance.

4. Results

4.1. Revisit of Earthquake Prediction in 2020–2024

In the study by Wang et al. (2021), the identification of regions with high earthquake potential for the period from January 2020 to December 2024 is based on the b value observed between January 2015 and December 2019 [23]. Table 1 details the 10 earthquakes with M $\geq$ 5.0 and 3 earthquakes with M $\geq$ 5.5 that occurred in Yunnan Province during the forecast period, with their locations illustrated in Figure 1a, including the significant 2021 M6.5 Yangbi earthquake. Notably, on 24 December 2021, an earthquake of magnitude M6.0 occurred near the southern target area (see Figure 8 in the study of Wang et al., 2021 [23]) in Laos. Figure 1b,c display the magnitude–time diagram for earthquakes occurring in 2000–2024 and 2020–2024, respectively.

Table 1. List of earthquakes with M $\geq$ 5.0 in Yunnan Province during 2020–2024.

Serial Number	Time [1]	Location			Magnitude
		Longitude	Latitude	Depth (Km)	
1	2020-05-18 21:48:00	103.17	27.20	8	5.0
2	2021-05-21 21:21:25	99.92	25.65	10	5.6
3	2021-05-21 21:48:35	99.88	25.70	10	6.5
4	2021-05-21 21:55:29	99.89	25.67	10	5.0
5	2021-05-21 22:31:10	99.97	25.62	8	5.2
6	2021-06-10 19:46:07	101.92	24.35	8	5.1
7	2021-06-12 18:00:47	97.88	24.97	16	5.0
8	2022-01-02 15:02:07	100.65	27.79	10	5.5
9	2022-11-19 01:27:34	102.26	23.37	8	5.4
10	2023-05-02 23:27:22	99.28	25.53	10	5.2

[1] Time is given by the date (YYYY-MM-DD) and time (hh:mm:ss).

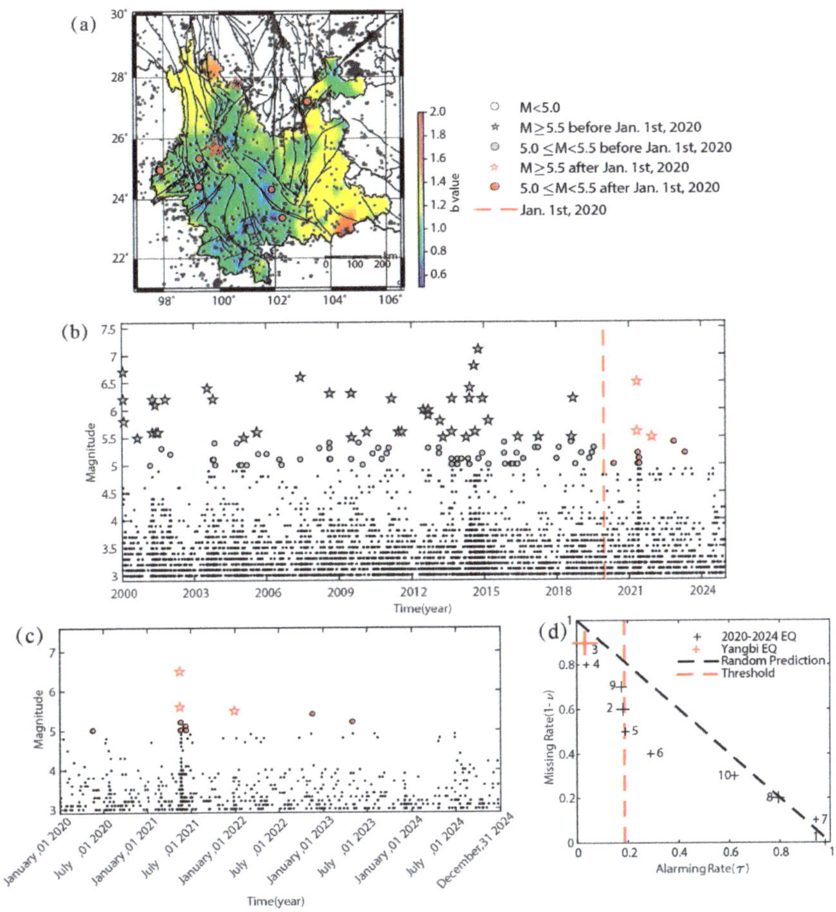

Figure 1. (**a**) The b value from January 2015 to December 2019 and earthquakes with M $\geq$ 5.0 from January 2020 to December 2024. The dot and star are scaled to the magnitude. (**b**) Temporal distribution of earthquakes in Yunnan Province from January 2000 to December 2024. (**c**) Temporal distribution of earthquakes in Yunnan Province from January 2020 to December 2024. (**d**) The MED of forecast performance based on the b value in (**a**). The marked numbers are the serial numbers in Table 1, and the size of the cross markers is scaled to the magnitude.

As detailed in Figure 1d, from January 2020 to December 2024, the observed data show that 2/3 of earthquakes with M $\geq$ 5.5 and 5/10 of those with M $\geq$ 5.0 occurred to the left of the threshold proposed in Wang et al. (2021) [23]. Notably, the 2021 M6.5 Yangbi earthquake (Serial Number 3) occurred at the place with the lowest b value among the ten events and could be predicted at the alarming rate of less than 5%. Although most of the earthquakes are under the diagonal line indicating clear forecast efficiency, the prediction is still far from practical demand. As the b value is hard to estimate and may become less useful if the seismicity is too low, the incorporation of additional earthquake prediction information, such as background seismicity rate, into the existing framework may have to be made.

4.2. *b* Value and Background Seismicity Rate in Yunnan Province

Figure 2 illustrates the *b* values and background seismicity rates across five periods, along with the earthquakes in the subsequent period. From January 2000 to December 2024, the *b* value exhibits significant variability, and its earthquake forecasting performance has been evaluated in prior studies, as noted above. The spatial distribution of background seismicity across the five periods reveals consistent patterns. Notably, there appears to be no discernible correlation between the *b* value and the background seismicity rate. Background seismic activity is notably pronounced in the northwest, west, southwest, and south regions of Yunnan Province, corresponding with the occurrence of moderate to large earthquakes in these areas. In contrast, background seismicity is comparatively low in the central and eastern parts of Yunnan, indicating a spatial variation in seismic activity throughout the province.

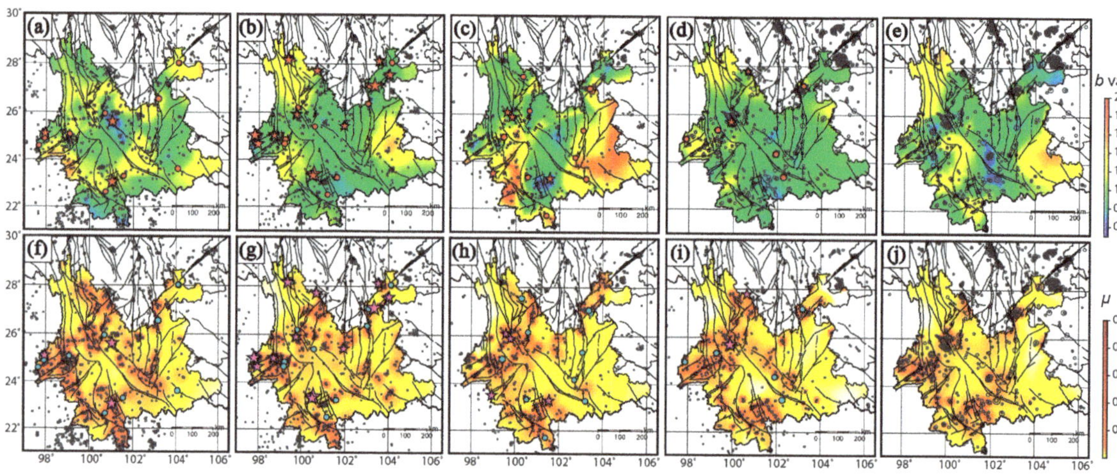

Figure 2. The *b* value and background seismicity rate. (**a**–**e**) *b* value; (**f**,**j**) background seismicity rate. Results in (**a**,**f**) using catalog in 2000–2004 and forecasting moderate–large earthquakes in 2005–2009; (**b**,**g**) using catalog in 2005–2009 and forecasting moderate–large earthquakes in 2010–2014; (**c**,**h**) using catalog in 2010–2014 and forecasting moderate–large earthquakes in 2015–2019; (**d**,**i**) using catalog in 2015–2019 and forecasting moderate–large earthquakes in 2020–2024; (**e**,**j**) using catalog in 2020–2024. A dot represents an earthquake with $5.0 \leq M < 5.5$. A star represents an earthquake with $M \geq 5.5$. The sizes of the dots and stars are scaled to magnitude.

4.3. Comprehensive Forecast Performance

The time–space alarm model is employed to comprehensively evaluate the performance of the spatial *b* value and background seismicity rates. This model encompasses five distinct periods: January 2000 to December 2004, January 2005 to December 2009, January 2010 to December 2014, January 2015 to December 2019, and January 2020 to December 2024. During the interval from January 2005 to December 2024, the anticipated moderate to large earthquakes include 29 events with $M \geq 5.5$ and 86 events with $M \geq 5.0$.

The forecasting performance of *b* values and background seismicity rates from January 2005 to December 2024 is evaluated and tested, as illustrated in Figure 3. In Figure 3a, the forecast efficiency for earthquakes with $M \geq 5.5$ using both the *b* value and background seismicity rate approaches and partially exceeds the 95% significance level. This indicates that both predictors perform better than a random guess. Additionally, as shown in Figure 3d, the forecast efficiency for earthquakes with $M \geq 5.0$ based on the *b* value significantly exceeds that of random predictions, with an alarming rate of less than 0.4.

Furthermore, the forecasting efficiency of the background seismicity rate is significantly better than a random guess and notably higher than that of the *b* value.

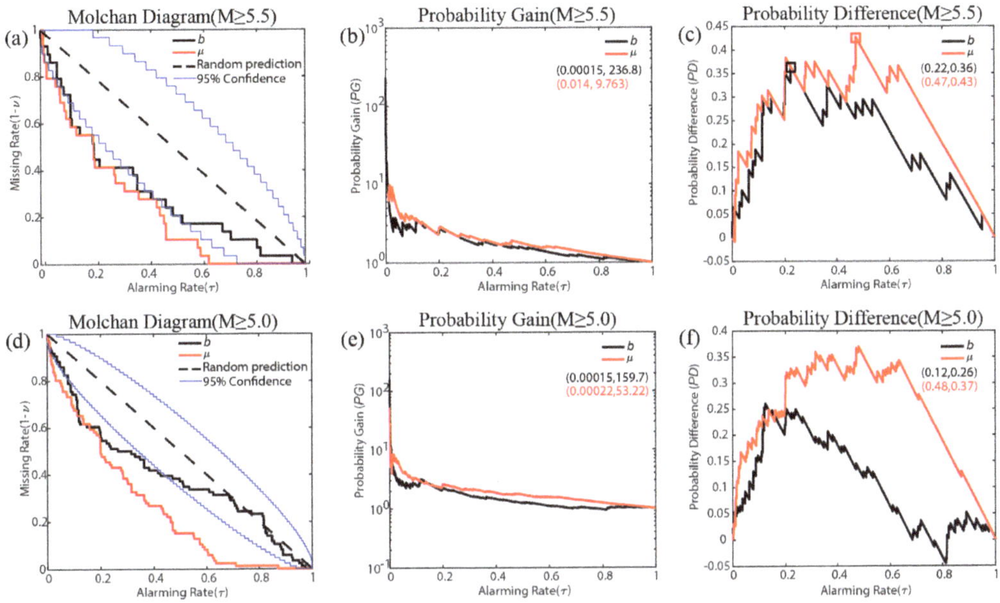

Figure 3. Forecast performance based on *b* value and background seismicity rate during 2005–2024. (**a–c**) show the results of earthquakes with $M \geq 5.5$. (**a**) MED; (**b**) *PG*; (**c**) *PD*. (**d–f**) are the results of earthquakes with $M \geq 5.0$. (**d**) MED; (**e**) *PG*; (**f**) *PD*. The number of earthquake samples is = 29 and $N_{M\geq 5.0} = 86$.

The *PD* for the *b* value and background seismicity rate, as depicted in Figure 3b,e for earthquakes with $M \geq 5.5$ and $M \geq 5.0$, consistently exceeds 1. Specifically, the highest *PG* values for $M \geq 5.5$ are 236.8 and 9.763 for the *b* value and background seismicity rate, respectively, while for $M \geq 5.0$, they are 159.7 and 53.22. All of them are observed at very low alarming rates (below 0.01). In Figure 3c, the *PD* for earthquakes of magnitude $M \geq 5.5$ remains consistently above 0. The highest *PD* values for $M \geq 5.5$ are 0.36 for the *b* value and 0.43 for the background seismicity rate, corresponding to alarming rates of 0.22 and 0.47, respectively. For $M \geq 5.0$, the highest *PD* values are 0.26 and 0.37, with alarming rates of 0.12 and 0.48. In summary, the *b* value demonstrates a higher *PG*, while the background seismicity rate shows a superior *PD*. The above evaluation of forecasting efficiency indicates that both the *b* value and background seismicity rate are effective predictors for middle–long-term earthquake occurrences.

In Figure 3, the *PG* and *PD* for the *b* value appear to increase with the forecasted magnitude, whereas no such trend is observed for the background seismicity rate. This discrepancy likely reflects the differing efficiency of these two factors in earthquake forecasting across varying magnitudes. For further testing, we analyzed the variation in maximum *PG* and *PD* for both the *b* value and background seismicity rate with magnitude, as shown in Figure 4a,b. To quantitatively compare the effectiveness of earthquake forecasts, we employed the modified area score (*S*), which represents the area between the actual prediction curve and the random prediction diagonal line, as depicted in Figure 4c [47]. The maximum *PG*, *PD*, and *S* for the *b* value clearly increase with magnitude. While for the background seismicity rate, the maximum *PG*, *PD*, and *S* have no obvious variation trend.

These results suggest that the b value might be more sensitive to and informative about large earthquakes in the study region.

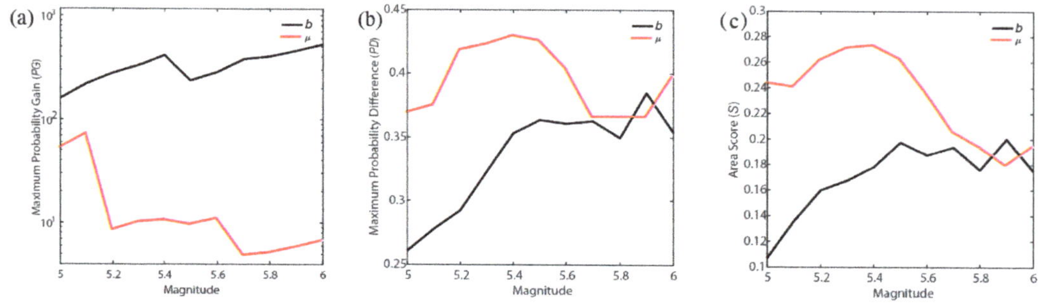

Figure 4. The variation in forecast performance with earthquake magnitude. (**a**) Variation in maximum *PG* with the forecast magnitude; (**b**) variation in maximum *PD* with the forecast magnitude; (**c**) variation in *S* with the forecast magnitude.

To integrate prediction information from both the background seismicity rate and the b value, we conduct a comprehensive evaluation. We establish two thresholds: one for the b value (denoted as thr_b) and another for the background seismicity rate (denoted as thr_μ). Grid cells with a b value below the threshold thr_b and background seismicity rate above thr_μ would be alarmed. These two thresholds change gradually, and as a result, the alarming rates change correspondingly in the range 0–1.0. The overall forecast performance, which integrates both the b value and the background seismicity rate, is illustrated in Figure 5. Table 2 presents the maximum values and their respective locations, along with comprehensive alarming and detecting rates.

Table 2. Maximum *PG* and *PD* marked in Figure 5, their location, alarming rate, and detecting rate.

Magnitude	Type	Maximum Value	Alarming Rate (μ)	Alarming Rate (b)	Comprehensive Alarming Rate	Comprehensive Detecting Rate
$M \geq 5.5$	*PG*	26.68	0.03	0.09	0.0052	0.14
	PD	0.46	0.64	0.54	0.36	0.83
$M \geq 5.0$	*PG*	16.81	0.02	0.01	0.0014	0.023
	PD	0.38	0.48	0.89	0.43	0.81

Effective seismic forecasting must balance both low alarming rates and high detecting rates. As illustrated in Table 2, for maximum *PG*, the alarming rates for earthquakes of $M \geq 5.5$ and $M \geq 5.0$ are 0.0052 and 0.0014, respectively, while the corresponding detecting rates are 0.14 and 0.023. The detecting rates, which fall below 0.2, suggest that using this threshold for reliable earthquake forecasting may result in a high missing rate. Conversely, for maximum *PD*, the alarming rates for $M \geq 5.5$ and $M \geq 5.0$ are 0.36 and 0.43, with detecting rates of 0.83 and 0.81, respectively. Yet the alarming rates exceed 0.3 and may cause large false alarms. Both the maximum *PD* and maximum *PG* fail to establish a suitable threshold for effective earthquake prediction, indicating that further exploration is needed to determine an applicable threshold.

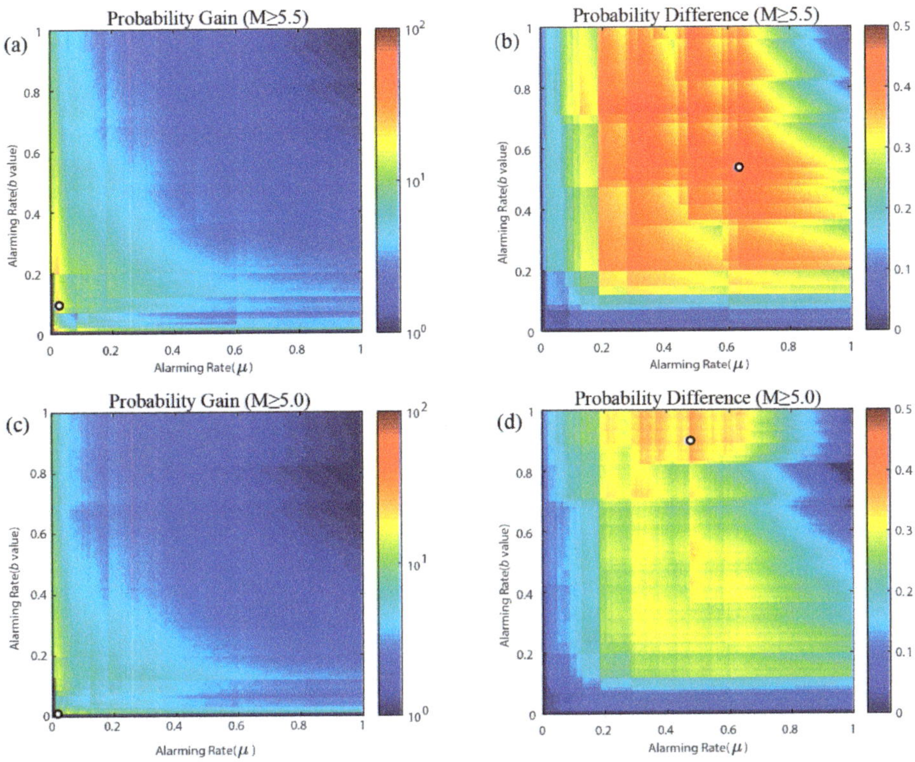

Figure 5. Forecast performance by combining b value and background seismicity rate during 2005–2024. The x-axis is the alarming rate of background seismicity corresponding to thr_{μ}, and the y-axis is the alarming rate of the b value corresponding to thr_b. (**a**) *PG* for $M \geq 5.5$ earthquakes; (**b**) *PD* for $M \geq 5.5$ earthquakes; (**c**) *PG* for $M \geq 5.0$ earthquakes; (**d**) *PD* for $M \geq 5.0$ earthquakes. The location of the maximum value (*PG* or *PD*) in each figure is marked with dots and detailed in Table 2. The cross in (**b**) is located at the alarming rate corresponding to the maximum *PD* in Figure 3c.

5. Implication and Application

Taking a step back, the thresholds used for forecasting are determined based on the *PD* of the b value and background seismicity rate. Using the maximum *PD* for $M \geq 5.5$ in Figure 3c and data from 2000 to 2024, the b value and background seismicity rate corresponding to the maximum *PD* are set as the thresholds, denoted as thr_PD_b and thr_PD_{μ}, respectively, and summarized in Table 3. If earthquake forecasting relies solely on either the b value or the background seismicity rate, the *PG* is 2.64 or 1.91, respectively. However, when integrating the b value and background seismicity rate, the *PG* increases to 3.69. This difference in *PG* suggests that incorporating the background seismicity rate contributes to an improvement in forecasting performance. The earthquake forecast for the period from January 2025 to December 2029 is based on the spatial b value and background seismicity rate data from January 2020 to December 2024, as illustrated in Figure 2e,j. Based on the b value, grid cells with a b value lower than thr_PD_b are alarmed, as shown in red in Figure 6a. Based on the background seismicity rate, grid cells with a background seismicity rate higher than thr_PD_{μ} are alarmed, as shown in red in Figure 6b. When considering both the b value and background seismicity rate, grid cells that are alarmed in both Figure 6a,b are marked for alarm, as shown in Figure 6c. Notably, regions such as Dali, Lijiang, Baoshan, Puer, and Yuxi exhibit higher earthquake potential.

Table 3. The threshold determined by maximum *PD* of M ≥ 5.5 in Figure 3c and its alarming rate, detecting rate, and *PG*.

	Threshold	Alarming Rate	Detecting Rate	*PG*	Comprehensive Alarming Rate	Comprehensive Detecting Rate	Comprehensive *PG*
b	0.9056	0.22	0.58	2.64	0.13	0.48	3.69
μ	0.0033	0.47	0.90	1.91			

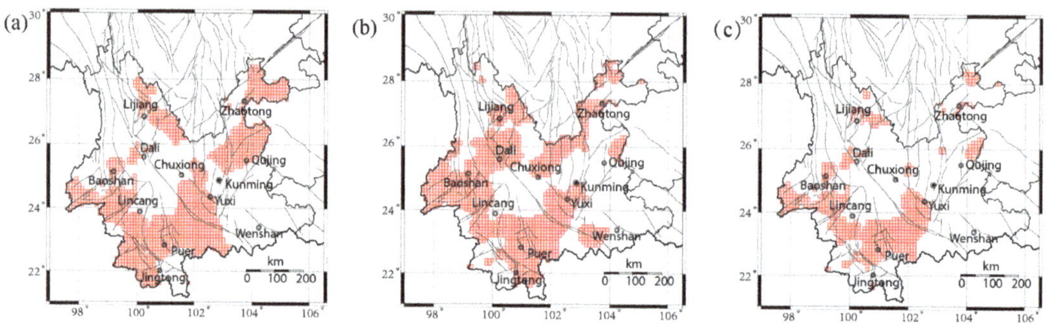

Figure 6. Alarmed regions for the period from January 2025 to December 2029 based on b value and background seismicity rate obtained during 2020–2024. (**a**) Alarmed area based on b value and thr_PD_b, with 0.38 alarming rate; (**b**) alarmed area based on background seismicity rate and thr_PD_μ, with 0.42 alarming rate; (**c**) alarmed area based on b value and background seismicity rate, with 0.20 alarming rate. The red edge squares show the alarmed grid cells.

Based on the maximum *PD*, we first identify potential high-earthquake-risk areas by focusing on regions with low b values, as shown in Figure 6a. Subsequently, the high-risk zones are refined by excluding areas with low background seismicity rates, as shown in Figure 6c. The retrospective analysis of two decades of data (2005–2024) shows that this method reduces the alarming rate and increases *PG* by 40% compared to forecasts based solely on b value, indicating improved forecasting performance by integrating background seismicity rate. Future research will focus on effectively incorporating multiple data sources, as improving observation accuracy and increasing data availability enhanced earthquake forecasting potential. One potential solution is to employ machine learning techniques to assist in decision-making. Compared to direct learning from raw observational data, data that have been effectively processed and preliminarily tested, such as the b value and the background seismicity rate adopted in this study, contain more useful information and may potentially lead to better forecasting outcomes.

The proposed approach involves the formulation of a comprehensive five-year earthquake prediction model that is fundamentally based on patterns of seismic activity. However, accurately determining the timing of earthquake occurrences requires additional validation through short-term prediction techniques. These techniques include the analysis of foreshocks, geophysical anomalies that may signal changes in the Earth's crust, and other recognized earthquake precursors [48–52]. The feasibility of this validation process has been improved due to recent advancements in observational technologies, which allow for more precise monitoring and analysis of seismic phenomena. Moreover, middle–long-term forecasting can provide crucial insights that aid in the systematic organization of high-quality observations in potential fault zones, thus helping to enhance the overall understanding of seismic behavior. In addition, the prediction results can be helpful for regional disaster preparedness and risk management.

6. Conclusions

Using the earthquake catalog from the China Earthquake Networks Center, this study validates the practicality and efficacy of earthquake forecasting based on the *b* value, as proposed in the work of Wang et al. (2021) [23]. The predictive performance of both the background seismicity rate and the *b* value is comprehensively evaluated, demonstrating their effectiveness for 5-year forecasting in Yunnan Province, China. The performance of the *b* value shows a positive correlation with the predicted earthquake magnitude. The synergistic effect of combining these two predictors is also explored. By employing the threshold corresponding to the maximum *PD*, we identify high-earthquake-risk areas based on low *b* values and refine them by excluding regions with low background seismicity rates. A retrospective analysis shows this strategy can reduce the alarming rate and increase *PG* by 40% compared to the *b*-value-only forecast. A forward prediction for the period from January 2025 to December 2029 is finally derived, identifying regions with high earthquake potential, including Dali, Lijiang, Baoshan, Puer, and Yuxi.

Author Contributions: Conceptualization, P.H. and R.W.; methodology, Y.Z., J.Z. and Y.C.; software, J.Z. and Y.C.; validation, Y.Z., R.W., M.M., C.J., L.M., H.S., D.L., L.L., Y.S. and P.H.; formal analysis, Y.Z. and R.W.; investigation, Y.Z., R.W. and P.H.; resources, P.H. and R.W.; data curation, H.S., C.J., L.M., D.L., L.L. and Y.S.; writing—original draft preparation, Y.Z. and R.W.; writing—review and editing, Z.Z. and R.W.; visualization, Y.Z. and R.W.; supervision, P.H., J.Z. and Z.Z. All authors have read and agreed to the published version of the manuscript.

Funding: This research is partly supported by the National Natural Science Foundation of China (Grant No. 42222405, 42404063). J.Z. also thanks the MEXT project for seismology toward research innovation with earthquake data (STAR-E project), Grant No. JPJ010217.

Institutional Review Board Statement: Not applicable.

Data Availability Statement: The catalog in this study was provided by the Earthquake Administration of Yunnan Province, China.

Acknowledgments: We thank Wessel et al. for the Generic Mapping Tools (GMT) used to plot some of the figures [53]. We gratefully acknowledge Ogata et al. for the constructive guidance and Hierarchical Space–Time Point-Process Models software [39]. We thank the three reviewers for their comments and suggestions.

Conflicts of Interest: Author Ying Chang was employed by the company BGRIMM Technology Group. The remaining authors declare that the research was conducted in the absence of any commercial or financial relationships that could be construed as a potential conflict of interest.

References

1. Gutenberg, B.; Richter, C.F. Frequency of Earthquakes in California. *Bull. Seismol. Soc. Am.* **1944**, *34*, 185–188. [CrossRef]
2. Utsu, T. A Method for Determing the Value of b in a Formula Log N=a-BM Showing the Magnitude-Frequency Relation for Earthquakes. *Geophys. Bull. Hokkaido Univ.* **1965**, *13*, 99–103. (In Japanese)
3. El-Isa, Z.H.; Eaton, D.W. Spatiotemporal Variations in the B-Value of Earthquake Magnitude–Frequency Distributions: Classification and Causes. *Tectonophysics* **2014**, *615–616*, 1–11. [CrossRef]
4. Nanjo, K.Z.; Hirata, N.; Obara, K.; Kasahara, K. Decade-Scale Decrease in b Value Prior to the M9-Class 2011 Tohoku and 2004 Sumatra Quakes. *Geophys. Res. Lett.* **2012**, *39*, 20304. [CrossRef]
5. Shi, H.; Meng, L.; Zhang, X.; Chang, Y.; Yang, Z.; Xie, W.; Hattori, K.; Han, P. Decrease in b Value Prior to the Wenchuan Earthquake (Ms8.0). *Chin. J. Geophys.* **2018**, *61*, 1874–1882. [CrossRef]
6. Kulhánek, O. *Seminar on B-Value*; Uppsala University: Uppsala, Sweden, 2005.
7. Nuannin, P. Spatial and Temporal b Value Anomalies Preceding the Devastating off Coast of NW Sumatra Earthquake of December 26, 2004. *Geophys. Res. Lett.* **2005**, *32*, L11307. [CrossRef]
8. Nanjo, K.Z.; Izutsu, J.; Orihara, Y.; Kamogawa, M. Changes in Seismicity Pattern Due to the 2016 Kumamoto Earthquake Sequence and Implications for Improving the Foreshock Traffic-Light System. *Tectonophysics* **2022**, *822*, 229175. [CrossRef]

9. Huang, J.; Turcotte, D.L. Fractal Distributions of Stress and Strength and Variations of B-Value. *Earth Planet. Sci. Lett.* **1988**, *91*, 223–230. [CrossRef]
10. Convertito, V.; Tramelli, A.; Godano, C. B Map Evaluation and On-Fault Stress State for the Antakya 2023 Earthquakes. *Sci. Rep.* **2024**, *14*, 1–7. [CrossRef] [PubMed]
11. Varotsos, P.A.; Sarlis, N.V.; Skordas, E.S. Order Parameter Fluctuations in Natural Time and B-Value Variation before Large Earthquakes. *Nat. Hazards Earth Syst. Sci.* **2012**, *12*, 3473–3481. [CrossRef]
12. Varotsos, P.A.; Sarlis, N.V.; Skordas, E.S. Study of the Temporal Correlations in the Magnitude Time Series before Major Earthquakes in Japan. *J. Geophys. Res. Space Phys.* **2014**, *119*, 9192–9206. [CrossRef]
13. Sarlis, N.V.; Skordas, E.S.; Varotsos, P.A.; Nagao, T.; Kamogawa, M.; Uyeda, S. Spatiotemporal Variations of Seismicity before Major Earthquakes in the Japanese Area and Their Relation with the Epicentral Locations. *Proc. Natl. Acad. Sci. USA* **2015**, *112*, 986–989. [CrossRef] [PubMed]
14. Scholz, C.H. On the Stress Dependence of Earthquake b Value. *Geophys. Res. Lett.* **2015**, *42*, 1399–1402. [CrossRef]
15. Wu, Y.M.; Chen, S.K.; Huang, T.C.; Huang, H.H.; Chao, W.A.; Koulakov, I. Relationship Between Earthquake B-Values and Crustal Stresses in a Young Orogenic Belt. *Geophys. Res. Lett.* **2018**, *45*, 1832–1837. [CrossRef]
16. Spada, M.; Tormann, T.; Wiemer, S.; Enescu, B. Generic Dependence of the Frequency-Size Distribution of Earthquakes on Depth and Its Relation to the Strength Profile of the Crust. *Geophys. Res. Lett.* **2013**, *40*, 709–714. [CrossRef]
17. Schorlemmer, D.; Wiemer, S.; Wyss, M. Variations in Earthquake-Size Distribution across Different Stress Regimes. *Nature* **2005**, *437*, 539–542. [CrossRef]
18. Peng, G.; Lei, X.; Wang, G.; Jiang, F. Precursory Tidal Triggering and b Value Variation before the 2011 Mw 5.1 and 5.0 Tengchong, China Earthquakes. *Earth Planet. Sci. Lett.* **2021**, *574*, 117167. [CrossRef]
19. Ito, R.; Kaneko, Y. Physical Mechanism for a Temporal Decrease of the Gutenberg-Richter b-Value Prior to a Large Earthquake. *J. Geophys. Res. Solid. Earth* **2023**, *128*, e2023JB027413. [CrossRef]
20. Nanjo, K.Z. Were Changes in Stress State Responsible for the 2019 Ridgecrest, California, Earthquakes? *Nat. Commun.* **2020**, *11*, 3082. [CrossRef] [PubMed]
21. Beall, A.; van den Ende, M.; Ampuero, J.P.; Capitanio, F.A.; Fagereng, Å. Linking Earthquake Magnitude-Frequency Statistics and Stress in Visco-Frictional Fault Zone Models. *Geophys. Res. Lett.* **2022**, *49*, e2022GL099247. [CrossRef]
22. Molchan, G. Space—Time Earthquake Prediction: The Error Diagrams. In *Seismogenesis and Earthquake Forecasting: The Frank Evison Volume II*; Springer: Basel, Switzerland, 2010; pp. 53–63.
23. Wang, R.; Chang, Y.; Miao, M.; Zeng, Z.; Chen, H.; Shi, H.; Li, D.; Liu, L.; Su, Y.; Han, P. Assessing Earthquake Forecast Performance Based on b Value in Yunnan Province, China. *Entropy* **2021**, *23*, 730. [CrossRef] [PubMed]
24. Hainzl, S.; Kraft, T.; Wassermann, J.; Igel, H.; Schmedes, E. Evidence for Rainfall-Triggered Earthquake Activity. *Geophys. Res. Lett.* **2006**, *33*. [CrossRef]
25. Hainzl, S.; Ogata, Y. Detecting Fluid Signals in Seismicity Data through Statistical Earthquake Modeling. *J. Geophys. Res. Solid. Earth* **2005**, *110*, 1–10. [CrossRef]
26. Jia, K. Modeling the Spatiotemporal Seismicity Patterns of the Longmen Shan Fault Zone Based on the Coulomb Rate and State Model. *Seismol. Res. Lett.* **2021**, *92*, 275–286. [CrossRef]
27. Heimisson, E.R.; Segall, P. Constitutive Law for Earthquake Production Based on Rate-and-State Friction: Dieterich 1994 Revisited. *J. Geophys. Res. Solid Earth* **2018**, *123*, 4141–4156. [CrossRef]
28. Helmstetter, A.; Shaw, B.E. Afterslip and Aftershocks in the Rate-and-State Friction Law. *J. Geophys. Res. Solid. Earth* **2009**, *114*. [CrossRef]
29. Dieterich, J.H. Earthquake Nucleation on Faults with Rate-and State-Dependent Strength. *Tectonophysics* **1992**, *211*, 115–134. [CrossRef]
30. Nandan, S.; Ouillon, G.; Wiemer, S.; Sornette, D. Objective Estimation of Spatially Variable Parameters of Epidemic Type Aftershock Sequence Model: Application to California. *J. Geophys. Res. Solid. Earth* **2017**, *122*, 5118–5143. [CrossRef]
31. Stevens, V.L.; Avouac, J.P. On the Relationship between Strain Rate and Seismicity in the India–Asia Collision Zone: Implications for Probabilistic Seismic Hazard. *Geophys. J. Int.* **2021**, *226*, 220–245. [CrossRef]
32. Kumazawa, T.; Ogata, Y.; Kimura, K.; Maeda, K.; Kobayashi, A. Background Rates of Swarm Earthquakes That Are Synchronized with Volumetric Strain Changes. *Earth Planet. Sci. Lett.* **2016**, *442*, 51–60. [CrossRef]
33. Bolton, D.C.; Shreedharan, S.; Rivière, J.; Marone, C. Frequency-Magnitude Statistics of Laboratory Foreshocks Vary with Shear Velocity, Fault Slip Rate, and Shear Stress. *J. Geophys. Res. Solid. Earth* **2021**, *126*, e2021JB022175. [CrossRef] [PubMed]
34. Ogata, Y. Prediction and Validation of Short-to-Long-Term Earthquake Probabilities in Inland Japan Using the Hierarchical Space–Time ETAS and Space–Time Poisson Process Models. *Earth Planets Space* **2022**, *74*, 1–12. [CrossRef]
35. Ogata, Y. Statistics of Earthquake Activity: Models and Methods for Earthquake Predictability Studies. *Annu. Rev. Earth Planet. Sci.* **2017**, *45*, 497–527. [CrossRef]

36. Zhuang, J. Long-Term Earthquake Forecasts Based on the Epidemic-Type Aftershock Sequence (ETAS) Model for Short-Term Clustering. *Res. Geophys.* **2012**, *2*, 8. [CrossRef]
37. Xiong, Z.; Zhuang, J.; Zhou, S. Long-Term Earthquake Hazard in North China Estimated from a Modern Catalog. *Bull. Seismol. Soc. Am.* **2019**, *109*, 2340–2355. [CrossRef]
38. Liu, L.; Li, Z.; Jiang, C. Research on Minimum Magnitude of Completeness for Earthquake Catalogue in Yunnan Region. *J. Seismol. Res.* **2012**, *35*, 288–293. [CrossRef]
39. Ogata, Y.; Katsura, K.; Tanemura, M.; Harte, D.; Zhuang, J. Hierarchical Space-Time Point-Process Models (HIST-PPM): Software Documentation. 2020. Available online: https://bemlar.ism.ac.jp/ogata/HIST-PPM-V3/manual.pdf (accessed on 12 January 2025).
40. Ogata, Y.; Imoto, M.; Katsura, K. 3-D Spatial Variation of B-Values of Magnitude-Frequency Distribution Beneath the Kanto District, Japan. *Geophys. J. Int.* **1991**, *104*, 135–146. [CrossRef]
41. Ogata, Y.; Katsura, K. Analysis of Temporal and Spatial Heterogeneity of Magnitude Frequency Distribution Inferred from Earthquake Catalogues. *Geophys. J. Int.* **1993**, *113*, 727–738. [CrossRef]
42. Akaike, H. Likelihood and Bayes Procedure. In *Bayesian Statistics*; Bernardo, J.M., Degroot, M.H., Lindley, D.V., Smith, A.F.M., Eds.; University Press: Valencia, Spain, 1980; Volume 3, pp. 143–166.
43. Zhuang, J.; Ogata, Y.; Vere-Jones, D. Stochastic Declustering of Space-Time Earthquake Occurrences. *J. Am. Stat. Assoc.* **2002**, *97*, 369–380. [CrossRef]
44. Molchan, G.M. Strategies in Strong Earthquake Prediction. *Phys. Earth Planet. Inter.* **1990**, *61*, 84–98. [CrossRef]
45. Molchan, G.M. Structure of Optimal Strategies in Earthquake Prediction. *Tectonophysics* **1991**, *193*, 267–276. [CrossRef]
46. Chen, H.; Han, P.; Hattori, K. Recent Advances and Challenges in the Seismo-Electromagnetic Study: A Brief Review. *Remote Sens.* **2022**, *14*, 5893. [CrossRef]
47. Han, P.; Hattori, K.; Zhuang, J.; Chen, C.H.; Liu, J.Y.; Yoshida, S. Evaluation of ULF Seismo-Magnetic Phenomena in Kakioka, Japan by Using Molchan's Error Diagram. *Geophys. J. Int.* **2017**, *208*, 482–490. [CrossRef]
48. Gulia, L.; Wiemer, S. Real-Time Discrimination of Earthquake Foreshocks and Aftershocks. *Nature* **2019**, *574*, 193–199. [CrossRef]
49. Brgmann, R. Reliable Earthquake Precursors? *Science* **2023**, *381*, 266–267. [CrossRef]
50. Pulinets, S.; Herrera, V.M.V. Earthquake Precursors: The Physics, Identification, and Application. *Geosciences* **2024**, *14*, 209. [CrossRef]
51. Wang, R.; Chang, Y.; Han, P.; Miao, M.; Zeng, Z.; Shi, H.; Li, D.; Liu, L.; Su, Y. Optimized Traffic Light System with AIC and Application to the 2021 M6.7 Yangbi Earthquake Sequence. *Entropy* **2023**, *25*, 759. [CrossRef]
52. Han, P.; Zhuang, J.; Hattori, K.; Chen, C.-H.; Febriani, F.; Chen, H.; Yoshino, C.; Yoshida, S. Assessing the Potential Earthquake Precursory Information in ULF Magnetic Data Recorded in Kanto, Japan during 2000–2010: Distance and Magnitude Dependences. *Entropy* **2020**, *22*, 859. [CrossRef] [PubMed]
53. Wessel, P.; Luis, J.F.; Uieda, L.; Scharroo, R.; Wobbe, F.; Smith, W.H.F.; Tian, D. The Generic Mapping Tools Version 6. *Geochem. Geophys. Geosyst.* **2019**, *20*, 5556–5564. [CrossRef]

Disclaimer/Publisher's Note: The statements, opinions and data contained in all publications are solely those of the individual author(s) and contributor(s) and not of MDPI and/or the editor(s). MDPI and/or the editor(s) disclaim responsibility for any injury to people or property resulting from any ideas, methods, instructions or products referred to in the content.

entropy

MDPI

Article

Quantitative Assessment of the Trigger Effect of Proton Flux on Seismicity

Alexey Lyubushin * and Eugeny Rodionov

Institute of Physics of the Earth RAS, Moscow 123242, Russia; evgeny_980@list.ru
* Correspondence: lyubushin@yandex.ru

Abstract: An estimate of the trigger effect of the proton flux on seismicity was obtained. The proton flux time series with a time step of 5 min, 2000–2024, was analyzed. In each time interval of 5 days, statistics of the proton flux time series were calculated: mean values, logarithm of kurtosis, spectral slope, singularities spectrum support width, wavelet-based entropy, and the Donoho–Johnston wavelet-based index. For each of the used statistics, time points of local extrema were found, and for each pair of time sequences of proton flux statistics and earthquakes with a magnitude of at least 6.5 in sliding time windows, the "advance measures" of each time sequence relative to the other were estimated using a model of the intensity of interacting point processes. The difference between the "direct" measure of the advance of time points of local extrema of proton flux statistics relative to the time moments of earthquakes and the "inverse" measure of the advance was calculated. The maximum proportion of the intensity of seismic events for which the proton flux was a trigger was estimated as 0.28 for using the points of the local minima of the singularities spectrum support width.

Keywords: earthquakes; proton flux; point processes; wavelets; kurtosis; spectral slope; entropy; multifractals

1. Introduction

The influence of solar activity on various processes on Earth has long been the subject of close study, which resulted in the appearance of the term "space weather". The review [1] considers various aspects of the influence of solar activity on the Earth's climate and anthropogenic processes. The ionosphere, as an important component of the concept of space weather, was studied in the works [2–4]. The results of the development of statistical methods for predicting strong solar flares, including using machine learning, are presented in the articles [5–8]. An important issue in the study of space weather is its impact on catastrophic events in the life of society, such as earthquakes. In particular, methods have not yet been developed that allow us to unambiguously answer the question of whether strong solar flares and other electromagnetic events in the ionosphere have a trigger effect on the occurrence of sufficiently strong earthquakes. A lot of research is devoted to this issue [9]. The papers [10,11] present the results of the analysis of correlations between 11 and 12-year cycles of solar activity and time intervals of increasing intensity of seismic events over long periods of time. A comparison of time intervals of high seismic activity with the phases of solar cycles since 1900 is carried out in the paper [12].

The identification of the effects of the delay of strong earthquakes relative to the time intervals of geomagnetic storm maxima was considered in [13,14]. In [15], a similar effect of the delay of seismic events was studied for sunspot numbers. The hypothesis about the occurrence of time anomalies of atmospheric electric fields preceding the occurrence of strong earthquakes, including deep-focus ones, as a result of processes in the source of an impending seismic event was studied in [16]. A similar question about the occurrence of atmospheric and ionospheric electromagnetic signals recorded by spacecraft and preceding moderate seismic events was considered in [17]. In [18,19], the difference between the global seismic process and the Poisson one after excluding aftershocks is explained by the piezoelectric effect in rocks as a result of the impact of the proton flux during solar activity, which has a periodic time structure in addition to the 11–12-year solar cycle. In [20–22], the hypothesis is investigated about the generation of telluric currents in the Earth's crust as a result of the impact of disturbances of ionospheric electromagnetic fields from solar flares and, as a consequence, their trigger effect on the foci of future seismic events. A statistical analysis of the impact of 50 largest solar flares in the time interval 1997–2024 on global seismic activity was performed in [23], as a result of which an increase in seismic activity was discovered within 10 days after the flare compared to 10 days before it. The paper [24] provides an overview of the work in Russia for the period 1995–2020 on the study of the influence of artificial and natural electromagnetic impacts on seismicity and discusses possible ways of using electromagnetic seismicity to reduce seismic hazard. The classification of seismic events with a magnitude of at least 6 as they occur as a result of the impact of a proton flux using a neural network was performed in the paper [25].

The complex dynamics of both the Sun and solar-terrestrial relations requires the use of a set of modern data processing methods based on the use of nonlinear models for the analysis of time series describing interacting systems [26]. In [27,28], the internal dynamics of solar cycles were studied using methods of empirical orthogonal oscillation modes, estimates of their maximum Lyapunov exponents, and entropy flows between the values of various parameters of processes inside the Sun. In [29,30], various estimates of the Hurst exponent and entropy measures were used to analyze data obtained using the Swarm satellite network of the European Space Agency to describe the most intense magnetic storms and to quantitatively study the complexity of processes in the upper ionosphere. In [31], a study was conducted of the structure of currents induced by geomagnetic storms, leading to accidents in electrical networks, by applying information theory and various entropy measures to their time series.

In this paper, a new method is proposed that allows obtaining a quantitative estimate of the influence of various statistics of the proton flux density time series measured by the Solar Heliospheric Observatory (SOHO) [32] on the sequence of earthquakes with a magnitude of at least 6.5. The method is based on the use of estimates of "advance measures" based on a parametric model of the intensities of interacting point processes and on the calculation of wavelet measures of spectral tilt and entropy, as well as on an estimate of the width of the carrier of the multifractal spectrum of singularities of the proton flux density time series.

2. Proton Flux Initial Data

The time series of proton flux values with a time step of 5 min was downloaded from the website [33]. Figure 1 shows a graph of the time series of proton flux density for the time period from the beginning of 2000 to 17 October 2024. The time step is 5 min.

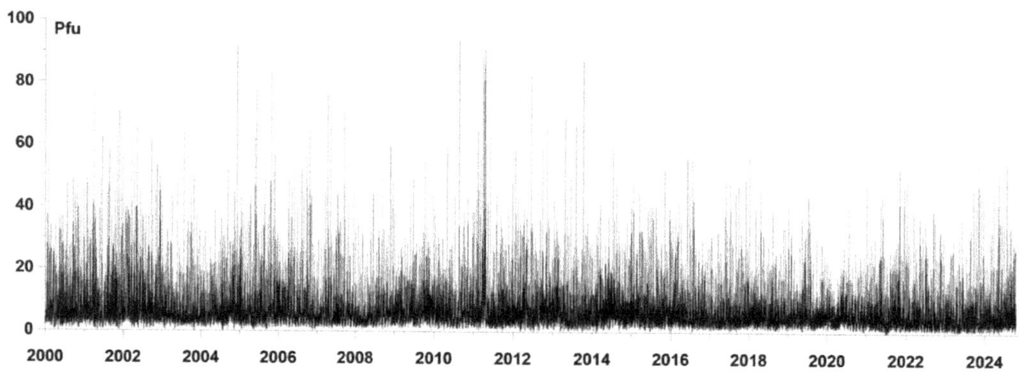

Figure 1. Time series graph of the proton flux from the beginning of 2000 to 17 October 2024 with a time step of 5 min. Proton flux density unit "Pfu" means Particles·cm^{-1}·s^{-1}·steradian^{-1}.

In the future, when analyzing the relationship between the proton flux and earthquakes, we will use various statistics of the proton flux density time series calculated in a time interval of 5 days (1440 readings with a time step of 5 min), taken with an offset of 1 day (288 5-min readings).

We start with the simplest statistics equal to the average value of the flux density in these intervals. From the beginning of 2000 to 17 October 2024, 1136 earthquakes with a magnitude of at least 6.5 occurred. Therefore, we found the 1136 largest local maxima of the average flux density values and present them as a function of the position of the right end of 5-day time windows. These two time sequences of events are shown in Figure 2.

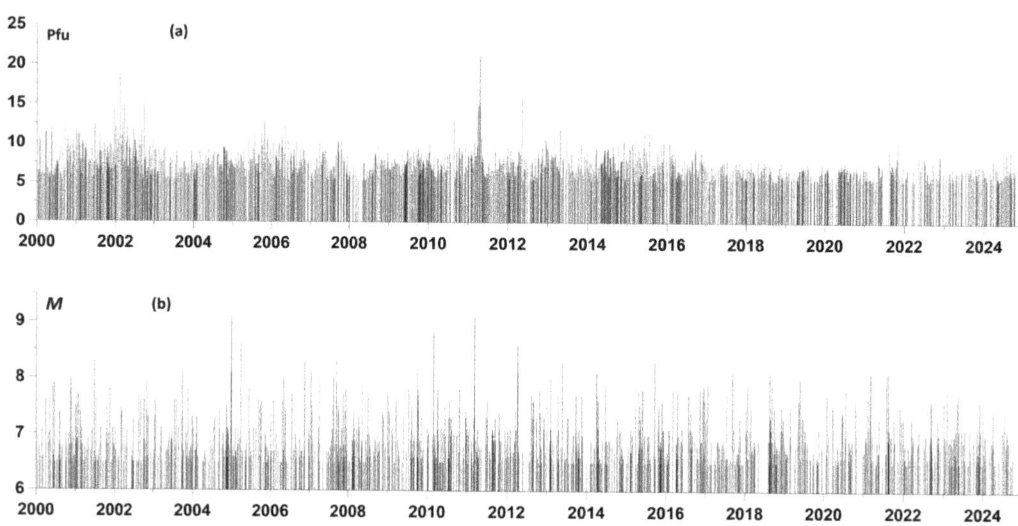

Figure 2. (**a**) Time sequence of 1136 largest local maxima of average values of proton flux density in sliding time windows of 5 days with a shift of 1 day; (**b**) time sequence of earthquakes with a magnitude of at least 6.5; data from the source [34].

The chosen minimum magnitude of 6.5 is representative for the whole world, and the corresponding time sequence does not contain aftershocks, which is important to ensure homogeneity of the time points of seismic events.

3. Periodic Components of the Proton Flux

The proton flux comes from the Sun, for which a number of periodicities are known, the best known of which is the 11–12-year periodicity, which determines the numbering of solar cycles. However, there is also a period due to the rotation of the Sun around its axis, equal to approximately 27 days. This periodicity should be reflected in variations in the proton flux density. Figure 3 shows the spectral composition of the proton flux density after the transition from the original time series to the average daily values. The power spectrum of the proton flux was calculated in a sliding time window of 730 days (2 years) with an offset of 30 days using the autoregressive model of order 70 [35]. The time–frequency diagram of the evolution of the spectrum logarithm is shown in Figure 3a, while the values obtained by averaging the spectral estimates from all time windows are presented as a graph in Figure 3b. This figure highlights four maximum spectral peaks, next to which the values of their periods in days are indicated. It is evident that the maximum spectral peak had a period of 26.95 days, approximately equal to the period of the Sun's rotation. The other periods correspond to its overtones.

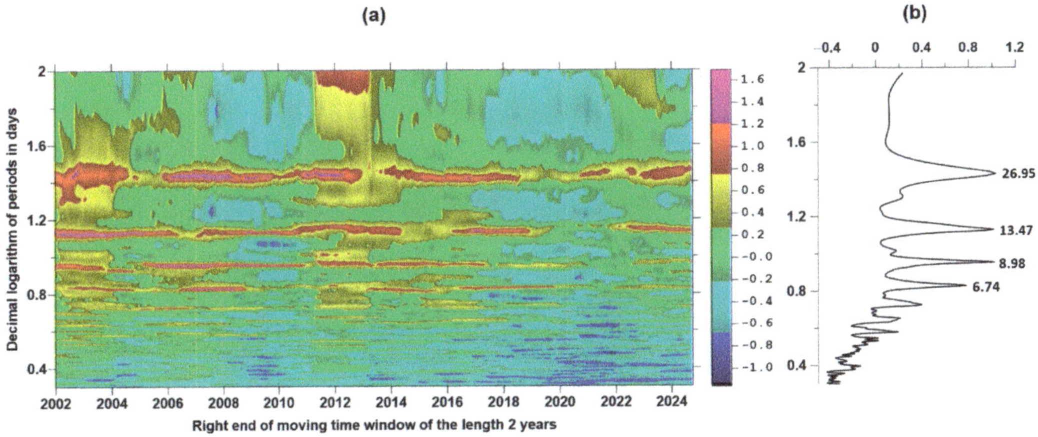

Figure 3. Spectral composition of the proton flux in the low-frequency part of the spectrum: (**a**) time–frequency diagram of the evolution of the logarithm of the power spectrum in a sliding time window of 2 years; (**b**) graph of the average power spectrum from all time windows, where the period in days is shown next to the 4 largest spectral peaks.

4. Periodic Components of the Earthquake Sequence

Of interest is the question of whether the 27-day periodicity of the proton flux shown in Figure 2 is reflected in the periodicity of the intensity of seismic events. To do this, it is necessary to estimate this periodicity, taking into account that the sequence of earthquakes is not a time series with a constant time step, for which classical spectral estimation methods [35] can be applied. Below, the method proposed in [36] is used to estimate the periodic components of the intensity of the sequence of events. In [37], this method was used to calculate the periodic component of the stepwise variations in the time series of the displacement of the earth's surface measured by GPS.

Let t_i, $i = 1, \ldots, N$ be the times of the sequence of events observed on the interval $(0, T]$. Consider the following intensity model containing a periodic component:

$$\lambda(t) = \mu \cdot (1 + a\cos(\omega t + \varphi)) \tag{1}$$

where frequency ω, amplitude a, $0 \le a \le 1$, phase angle φ, and $\varphi \in [0, 2\pi]$ multiplier $\mu > 0$ (describing the Poisson part of the intensity) are parameters of the model. Thus, the

Poisson part of the intensity is modulated by a harmonic oscillation. Let us fix some value of frequency ω. The logarithmic likelihood function [38] in this case for a series of observed events is equal to

$$\begin{aligned}\ln(L) &= \sum_{t_i}\ln(\lambda(t_i)) - \int_0^T \lambda(s)ds = \\ &= N\ln(\mu) + \sum_{t_i}\ln(1 + a\cos(\omega t_i + \varphi)) - \mu T - \frac{\mu a}{\omega}[\sin(\omega T + \varphi) - \sin(\varphi)]\end{aligned} \quad (2)$$

Taking the maximum of expression (2) with respect to the parameter μ, it is easy to find that

$$\ln(L(\hat{\mu}, a, \varphi|\omega)) = \sum_{t_i}\ln(1 + a\cos(\omega t_i + \varphi)) + N\cdot\ln(\hat{\mu}(a, \varphi|\omega)) - N \quad (3)$$

It should be noted that the expression $\hat{\mu}(a = 0, \varphi|\omega) \equiv \hat{\mu}_0 = N/T$ is an estimate of the intensity of the process under the condition that it is Poisson homogeneous (purely random). Thus, the increment of the logarithmic likelihood function due to the consideration of a richer intensity model with a harmonic component with a given frequency ω than for a purely random flow of events is equal to

$$\Delta\ln L(a, \varphi|\omega) = \sum_{t_i}\ln(1 + a\cos(\omega t_i + \varphi)) + N\cdot\ln(\hat{\mu}(a, \varphi|\omega)/\hat{\mu}_0) \quad (4)$$

Let

$$R(\omega) = \max_{a,\varphi}\Delta\ln L(a, \varphi|\omega),\ \ 0 \le a \le 1,\ \varphi \in [0, 2\pi] \quad (5)$$

An important issue when applying this method to real data is determining the statistical significance of the obtained peak values of statistics (5). Let us consider two hypotheses for the same data set $X^{(N)}$ consisting of independent observations:

(1) $X^{(N)}$ distributed by density $p_0(X^{(N)}|\theta_0)$—hypothesis H_0;
(2) $X^{(N)}$ distributed by density $p_1(X^{(N)}|\theta_1)$—hypothesis H_1.

Here, θ_0 and θ_1 are vectors of unknown parameters, having dimensions m_0 and m_1, and the hypothesis H_1 is more "rich": $m_1 > m_0$, and the vector of parameters θ_1 completely include the components of the vector θ_0. Let us consider the difference between the logarithms of the likelihood for these two hypotheses, provided that the vectors of parameters are taken from their maximum likelihood estimates:

$$\Delta\ln L(X^{(N)}) = \ln\left(\max_{\theta_1} p_1(X^{(N)}|\theta_1)\right) - \ln\left(\max_{\theta_0} p_0(X^{(N)}|\theta_0)\right) \quad (6)$$

It is evident that $\Delta\ln L(X^{(N)}) \ge 0$. According to Wilks' theorem [39], if the hypothesis is true, the quantity (6) has an asymptotic distribution:

$$\Delta\ln L(X^{(N)}) \sim \frac{\chi_m^2}{2},\ m = m_1 - m_0,\ N \to \infty \quad (7)$$

In our case, $m = 2$ and therefore, the doubled value (8) has an asymptotic distribution density χ_2^2 equal to $e^{-x/2}/2$, and the value (8) itself is distributed asymptotically as

$$\text{Prob}\{R(\omega) < x\} = 1 - e^{-x},\ N \to \infty \quad (8)$$

provided that the analyzed sequence of time moments is distributed according to the Poisson law with constant intensity. Expression (8) allows us to set thresholds for statistics that allow us to assert that only when they are exceeded does the sequence of time moments differ from the Poisson sequence with a given probability.

For a time sequence of seismic events with a magnitude of at least 6.5 (Figure 2b), we calculated the increments of the logarithmic likelihood function (5) in a sliding time window of 730 days (2 years) with a shift of 30 days for 200 frequency values ω corresponding to the values of periods varying from 10 to 100 days with a uniform step in a logarithmic scale. The resulting time–frequency dependence, similar to the usual spectral time–frequency diagram in Figure 3a, is shown in Figure 4a.

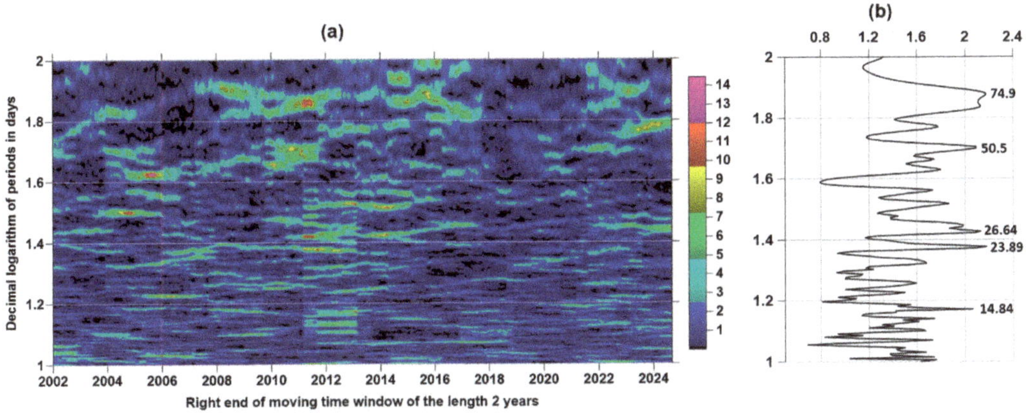

Figure 4. (**a**) Time–frequency diagram of the evolution of the increment of the logarithmic likelihood function in a sliding time window of 2 years; (**b**) graph of the average values of the increment of the logarithmic likelihood function from all time windows, where the period in days is shown next to the 5 largest spectral peaks.

Figure 4b shows the graph of averaging the increments of the logarithmic likelihood function (4) for all time windows and highlights five "spectral" peaks exceeding level 2 with periods of 14.84, 23.89, 26.64, 50.5, and 74.9 days. For them, the peak values of the average increments $\Delta \ln L$ were 2.08, 2.14, 2.15, 2.09, and 2.17, respectively. Using the asymptotic Formula (8), we obtained the following probabilities of difference between the periodic components of the seismic regime with these periods and a purely random Poisson process: 0.875, 0.882, 0.883, 0.863, and 0.886.

Thus, it can be stated that the sequence of time moments of earthquakes with magnitudes not lower than 6.5 contained a periodic component with a period of 26.64 days, close to the period of the Sun's rotation with a probability of not less than 0.883. This fact confirms the hypothesis about the influence of solar activity on the Earth's seismicity.

5. Method for Assessing the Measure of Mutual Advance of Two Streams of Events

In the future, we will be interested in the question of whether there is an advance of the moments of time of the largest local maxima of the average values of the proton flux density (Figure 2a) relative to the moments of time of earthquakes (Figure 2b). Clarification of this question requires also an assessment of the "reverse" advance and calculation of their difference. If the average value of this difference is positive, then there is a trigger effect of the proton flux on seismicity. In addition, the value of the average difference of the advance measures will give a measure of the trigger effect.

To clarify this issue, we applied the influence matrix method proposed in [40] to assess the degree of influence of earthquake sequences on each other in several seismically active regions. In its original implementation, this method is multidimensional. However, below, it is simplified and modified for the practically important situation of two time sequences. This modification was previously used in [41–45] to analyze the relationships between seismic event times and local extremum time points of various microseismic background statistics, magnetic field fluctuations, ground tremor, and meteorological time series properties.

Let $t_j^{(\alpha)},\ j = 1, \ldots, N_\alpha;\ \alpha = 1, 2$ represent the moments of time of two sequences of events. In our case, these are

(1) a sequence of time moments corresponding to the largest local maxima of the average values of the proton flux;
(2) sequence of times of seismic events with magnitude of at least 6.5.

Let us represent their intensities as follows:

$$\lambda^{(\alpha)}(t) = b_0^{(\alpha)} + \sum_{k=1}^{2} b_k^{(\alpha)} \cdot g^{(k)}(t) \tag{9}$$

where $b_0^{(\alpha)} \geq 0, b_\beta^{(\alpha)} \geq 0$ are parameters, $g^{(\beta)}(t)$—function of influence of time moment $t_j^{(\beta)}$ of the sequence with number β:

$$g^{(\beta)}(t) = \sum_{t_j^{(\beta)} < t} e^{-(t - t_j^{(\beta)})/\tau} \tag{10}$$

According to Formula (10), the weight of the event with number j becomes non-zero for times $t > t_j^{(\beta)}$ and decays with characteristic time τ. The parameter $b_\beta^{(\alpha)}$ determines the degree of influence of the flow β on the flow α. The parameter $b_\alpha^{(\alpha)}$ determines the degree of influence of the flow α on itself (self-excitation), and the parameter $b_0^{(\alpha)}$ reflects a purely random (Poisson) component of intensity. Let us fix the parameter τ and consider the problem of determining the parameters $b_0^{(\alpha)}, b_\beta^{(\alpha)}$.

The log-likelihood function for a non-stationary Poisson process is equal to over the time interval $[0, T]$ [38]:

$$\ln(L_\alpha) = \sum_{j=1}^{N_\alpha} \ln(\lambda^{(\alpha)}(t_j^{(\alpha)})) - \int_0^T \lambda^{(\alpha)}(s)ds,\ \alpha = 1, 2 \tag{11}$$

It is necessary to find the maximum of functions (11) with respect to the parameters $b_0^{(\alpha)}, b_\beta^{(\alpha)}$. Taking into account Formula (11), we can write the derivative of the logarithmic likelihood function with respect to the parameters:

$$\frac{\partial \ln(L_\alpha)}{\partial b_0^{(\alpha)}} = \sum_{j=1}^{N_\alpha} \frac{1}{\lambda^{(\alpha)}(t_j^{(\alpha)})} - \int_0^T ds,\quad \frac{\partial \ln(L_\alpha)}{\partial b_\beta^{(\alpha)}} = \sum_{j=1}^{N_\alpha} \frac{g^{(\beta)}(t)}{\lambda^{(\alpha)}(t_j^{(\alpha)})} - \int_0^T g^{(\beta)}(s)ds \tag{12}$$

From where and from Formula (9) it follows:

$$\begin{gathered} b_0^{(\alpha)} \frac{\partial \ln(L_\alpha)}{\partial b_0^{(\alpha)}} + \sum_{\beta=1}^{2} b_\beta^{(\alpha)} \frac{\partial \ln(L_\alpha)}{\partial b_\beta^{(\alpha)}} = \sum_{j=1}^{N_\alpha} \left\{ \frac{b_0^{(\alpha)} + \sum_{k=1}^{2} b_k^{(\alpha)} \cdot g^{(k)}(t)}{\lambda^{(\alpha)}(t_j^{(\alpha)})} \right\} - \\ - \int_0^T (b_0^{(\alpha)} + \sum_{k=1}^{2} b_k^{(\alpha)} \cdot g^{(k)}(s))ds = N_\alpha - \int_0^T \lambda^{(\alpha)}(s)ds \end{gathered} \tag{13}$$

Since the parameters $b_0^{(\alpha)}, b_\beta^{(\alpha)}$ must be non-negative, each term in the leftmost part of this formula is equal to zero at the point of maximum of function (11)—either due to the necessary conditions of the extremum (if the parameters are positive), or, if the maximum is reached at the boundary, then the parameters themselves are equal to zero. Consequently, at the point of maximum of the likelihood function, the equality is satisfied:

$$\int_0^T \lambda^{(\alpha)}(s)ds = N_\alpha \tag{14}$$

Let us substitute the expression $g^{(\beta)}(t)$ from (9) into (14) and divide by T. Then, we get another form of Formula (14):

$$b_0^{(\alpha)} + \sum_{\beta=1}^{2} b_\beta^{(\alpha)} \cdot \overline{g}^{(\beta)} = \lambda_0^{(\alpha)} \equiv N_\alpha / T \tag{15}$$

where

$$\overline{g}^{(\beta)} = \int_0^T g^{(\beta)}(s)ds/T \tag{16}$$

Substituting $b_0^{(\alpha)}$ from (15) into (11), we obtain the following maximum problem:

$$\Psi^{(\alpha)}(b_1^{(\alpha)}, b_2^{(\alpha)}) = \sum_{j=1}^{N_\alpha} \ln(\lambda_0^{(\alpha)} + \sum_{\beta=1}^{2} b_\beta^{(\alpha)} \cdot \Delta g^{(\beta)}(t_j^{(\alpha)})) \to \max \tag{17}$$

Here, $\Delta g^{(\beta)}(t) = g^{(\beta)}(t) - \overline{g}^{(\beta)}$, under restrictions:

$$b_1^{(\alpha)} \geq 0, b_2^{(\alpha)} \geq 0, \sum_{\beta=1}^{2} b_\beta^{(\alpha)} \overline{g}^{(\beta)} \leq \lambda_0^{(\alpha)} \tag{18}$$

Function (17) is convex with negative definite Hessian [40] and, therefore, problem (17)–(18) has a unique solution. Having solved problem (17)–(18) numerically for a given τ, we can introduce the elements of the influence matrix $\kappa_\beta^{(\alpha)}, \alpha = 1,2;\ \beta = 0,1,2$ according to the formulas:

$$\kappa_0^{(\alpha)} = b_0^{(\alpha)} / \lambda_0^{(\alpha)} \geq 0,\ \kappa_\beta^{(\alpha)} = b_\beta^{(\alpha)} \cdot \overline{g}^{(\beta)} / \lambda_0^{(\alpha)} \geq 0 \tag{19}$$

The quantity $\kappa_0^{(\alpha)}$ is a share of the average intensity $\lambda_0^{(\alpha)}$ of the process with number α, which is purely stochastic, the part $\kappa_\alpha^{(\alpha)}$ is caused by the influence of self-excitation $\alpha \to \alpha$ and $\kappa_\beta^{(\alpha)}$, $\beta \neq \alpha$ is determined by the external influence $\beta \to \alpha$. From Formula (15) follows the normalization condition:

$$\kappa_0^{(\alpha)} + \sum_{\beta=1}^{2} \kappa_\beta^{(\alpha)} = 1,\ \alpha = 1,2 \tag{20}$$

As a result, we can determine the influence matrix:

$$\begin{pmatrix} \kappa_0^{(1)} & \kappa_1^{(1)} & \kappa_2^{(1)} \\ \kappa_0^{(2)} & \kappa_1^{(2)} & \kappa_2^{(2)} \end{pmatrix} \tag{21}$$

The first column of matrix (21) is composed of Poisson shares of mean intensities. The diagonal elements of the right submatrix of size 2×2 consist of self-excited elements of mean intensity, while the off-diagonal elements correspond to mutual excitation. The sums of the component rows of the influence matrix (21) are equal to 1. The influence matrices are estimated in a certain sliding time window of length with offset and with a given value of the attenuation parameter τ.

When analyzing variations of the components of influence matrices in sliding time windows corresponding to the mutual influence of the analyzed time sequences, the main attention is paid to their local maxima with their subsequent averaging. Let M_L be the number of windows lengths within limits from $L_{\min}$ up to $L_{\max}$. Thus, the sequence of windows lengths is $L_j = L_{\min} + (j-1)\Delta L$, $j = 1, \ldots, M_L$, where $\Delta L = (L_{\max} - L_{\min})/(M_L - 1)$. Each time window of the length L_j is shifted along time axis with mutual shift Δt. Let $t_k(L_j)$ be the sequence of time moments corresponding to right ends of time windows of the length L_j. The number $K(L_j)$ of time moments $t_k(L_j)$ is defined by mutual shift Δt of time windows of the length L_j. Let $(t_k(L_j),\ c_k^{(1)}(L_j))$ and $(t_k(L_j),\ c_k^{(2)}(L_j))$ be elements $\kappa_2^{(1)}$ and $\kappa_1^{(2)}$ of the matrix (21), corresponding to mutual influences $2 \to 1$ and $1 \to 2$ of analyzed time moments for current position $t_k(L_j)$ of time window of the length L_j. Let $(t_k^*(L_j),\ \hat{c}_k^{(\alpha)}(L_j))$, $\alpha = 1, 2$ be local maxima of $c_k^{(\alpha)}(L_j)$, i.e., $c_{k-1}^{(\alpha)}(L_j)) < \hat{c}_k^{(\alpha)}(L_j) < c_{k+1}^{(\alpha)}(L_j)$.

Let us take some "small" time interval of the length η and for the sequence of time moments $[\nu_m, \nu_{m+1}]$, $\nu_{m+1} - \nu_m = \eta$ of such time fragments, where we will calculate the mean values $G_{2\to1}(\nu_{m+1})$ and $G_{1\to2}(\nu_{m+1})$ of $\hat{c}_k^{(\alpha)}(L_j)$ for which their time marks $t_k^*(L_j)$ belong to these fragments. Averaging is performed over all time window lengths L_j, $j = 1, \ldots, M_L$. These mean values in dependence on the right end of intervals ν_{m+1} gives the measures of the averaged effects of the advance of second sequence of time moments with respect to the first one and vice versa. Our main purpose is calculating the difference $\Delta G(\nu_{m+1}) = G_{2\to1}(\nu_{m+1}) - G_{1\to2}(\nu_{m+1})$. In this formula, the first sequence is the sequence of time moments of earthquakes with a magnitude not less than 6.5, whereas the second sequence is time moments of the largest local maxima of the mean proton flux time series. Thus, if average $< \Delta G(\nu_{m+1}) >$ is positive, it means that there is a trigger effect.

The full set of parameters of the method is the following: τ, $L_{\min}$, $L_{\max}$, M_L, Δt, η. In our calculations, we used $\tau = 0.05$ year (approximately 18 days), $L_{\min} = 0.5$ year, $L_{\max} = 1$ year, $M_L = 100$, $\Delta t = 1$ day, $\eta = 0.1$ year. The calculation results are most sensitive to the choice of parameters τ, $L_{\min}$, $L_{\max}$. The values used were chosen as a result of trial calculations and selection of the best options.

6. Measures of Mutual Advance of Local Maxima of the Average Value of Proton Flux Density and Seismic Event Sequence

In this section of the paper, we apply the method described earlier to the analysis of the relationships between the time sequences presented in Figure 2. Figure 5 presents the results of such an analysis.

From the comparison of the graphs in Figure 5, it is evident that the advance of the moments of time of the largest local maxima of the smoothed proton flux relative to the moments of time of earthquakes with a magnitude of not less than 6.5 was on average significantly greater than the reverse advance. At the same time, the difference between the average values of the advance measures, presented in Figure 5c, had a positive average value equal to 0.17. This value can be interpreted as an estimate of the part of the average intensity of all earthquakes with a magnitude of not less than 6.5 for those seismic events for which the maximum values of the average proton flux density are a trigger. Another numerical characteristic of the trigger effect is the part of the lengths of the time interval for which the difference between the "direct" and "reverse" advance is positive. For the graph in Figure 5c, this part is equal to 0.62.

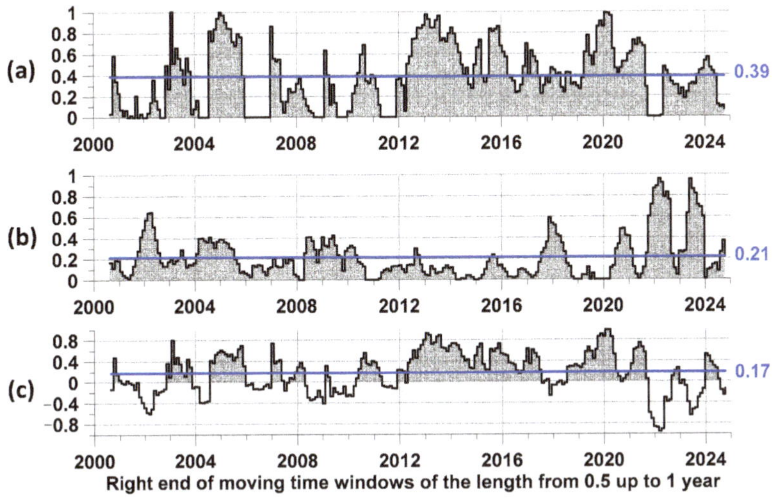

Figure 5. (**a**) Average values of local maxima of the component of influence matrices corresponding to the "direct" influence of the moments of time of the largest local maxima of the averaged values of the proton flux density on the moments of time of earthquakes with a magnitude of at least 6.5; (**b**) average values of local maxima of the component of influence matrices corresponding to the "reverse" influence of the moments of time of earthquakes on the moments of time of the largest local maxima of the averaged values of the proton flux density; (**c**) the difference between the average values of local maxima of the component of influence matrices corresponding to the "direct" influence and corresponding to the "reverse" influence. Blue line—average value; their numerical values are indicated on the right.

7. Proton Flux Density Time Series Statistics

The average proton flux density values used above are the simplest statistics. An idea arises to try other proton time series statistics and to estimate the relationship of the times of their "most expressive" (i.e., largest local maxima or smallest local minima) extreme values with the times of earthquakes using the above model of influence matrices. In addition to the simple average values, we used five different proton flux time series statistics described below. These statistics were estimated in the same time windows of 1440 5 min samples (5 days), taken with an offset of 288 samples (1 day), as before, when calculating the average values.

(1) *The kurtosis* of a time series $x(t)$ is calculated in each time window using the following formula [45]:

$$\kappa =< (x(t) - m_x)^4 > / \left(< (x(t) - m_x)^2 >\right)^2, \; m_x =< x(t) > \tag{22}$$

Here, the angle brackets denote the operation of calculating the mean value. The value κ can be considered as a measure of the difference from the Gaussian distribution, for which $\kappa = 3$. Below, we use the logarithm of the kurtosis coefficient: $\lg(\kappa)$.

(2) *The minimum wavelet-based normalized entropy En* of a time series $x(t)$ is calculated based on the decomposition of the time series within a window into orthogonal wavelets.

$$En = -\sum_k p_k \cdot \log(p_k) / \log(N) \tag{23}$$

In Formula (23), $p_k = c_k^2 / \sum_j c_j^2$, c_k are the wavelet coefficients of the signal $x(t)$, and N is the total number of wavelet coefficients. Seventeen orthogonal Daubechies wavelets were used: 10 ordinary bases with a minimum support with a number of vanishing moments from 1 to 10 and 7 so-called Daubechies symlets [46], with a number of vanishing moments from 4 to 10. For each of the bases, the entropy (23) of the distribution of the squares of the wavelet coefficients was calculated, and then, by enumeration, the optimal basis was found that realized the minimum value in each time window. By construction, $0 \le En \le 1$. The details of calculating the entropy (23) in a sliding time window are described in [47].

(3) *Wavelet-based spectral slope* β. After determining the optimal orthogonal wavelet from the minimum entropy condition, it is possible to calculate the average values S_k of the squares of the wavelet coefficients at each detail level, which is part of the oscillation energy corresponding to the detail level with the number k, which corresponds to the frequency band with the boundary frequencies $f_{\min}^{(k)} = 1/(2^{(k+1)}\Delta s)$ and $f_{\max}^{(k)} = 1/(2^k \Delta s)$, where Δs is the length of the sampling time interval (in our case Δs = 5 min) [46]. Let us consider the values of the periods corresponding to the centers of these frequency bands:

$$T_k = 2/(f_{\min}^{(k)} + f_{\max}^{(k)}) \;=\; 2\Delta s/(2^{-k} + 2^{-(k+1)}) \tag{24}$$

The quantities $S_k = S(T_k)$ are similar to the Fourier power spectra. These quantities are convenient to use when calculating the slope of the graph of the logarithm of the power spectrum as a function of the logarithm of the period. The spectral slope in each time window is found by the least squares method:

$$\textstyle\sum_k (\ln(S(T_k)) - \beta \cdot \ln(T_k)) - c)^2 \to \min_{\beta,c} \tag{25}$$

(4) *The Donoho–Johnston wavelet-based index (DJ-index)* γ is defined as the ratio of the number of "large" wavelet coefficients by absolute value to their total number. By definition, $0 \le \gamma \le 1$. The threshold separating the "large" wavelet coefficients is $T_{DJ} = \sigma\sqrt{2 \cdot \ln N}$. This threshold separates the informative wavelet coefficients from other coefficients that are considered noisy [46,48]. The value σ is an estimate of the standard deviation of noise under the assumption that the noise is most concentrated at the first detail level of the orthogonal wavelet decomposition. To estimate the value, the median estimate of the standard deviation of a normal random variable is used:

$$\sigma = med\left\{\left|c_k^{(1)}\right|,\ k = 1, \ldots, N/2\right\}/0.6745 \tag{26}$$

(5) *The multifractal singularity spectrum support width* $\Delta\alpha$ is an important characteristic of the signal and is considered as a measure of the diversity (complexity) of its stochastic behavior. It is defined as $\Delta\alpha = \alpha_{\max} - \alpha_{\min}$, where $\alpha_{\min}$ and $\alpha_{\max}$ are estimates of minimum and maximum values of the Holder–Lipschitz exponent [49] α, which governs the behavior of the signal at the vicinity of time moment t: $|x(t + \delta/2) - x(t - \delta/2)| \sim |\delta|^{\alpha}$, $\delta \to 0$. For a mono-fractal signal, the Holder–Lipschitz exponent is the same for all time moments t. Otherwise, the signal is multi-fractal, and the concept of the spectrum of singularities $F(\alpha)$ is introduced, equal to the fractal dimension of the time moments with the same value of the Holder–Lipschitz exponent, equal to α [50]. To estimate $\Delta\alpha$ in each time window, we used the method of fluctuation analysis after removing scale-dependent trends [51]. The implementation of the method used is described in detail in [47]. To remove local polynomial trends for the proton flux density time series, we used zero-order polynomials, i.e., we analyzed fluctuations after removing local means.

For a sequence of time intervals of 5 days, taken with a shift of 1 day, we calculated the values of all five statistics of the proton flux density time series. The results of these calculations are presented in the graphs in Figure 6.

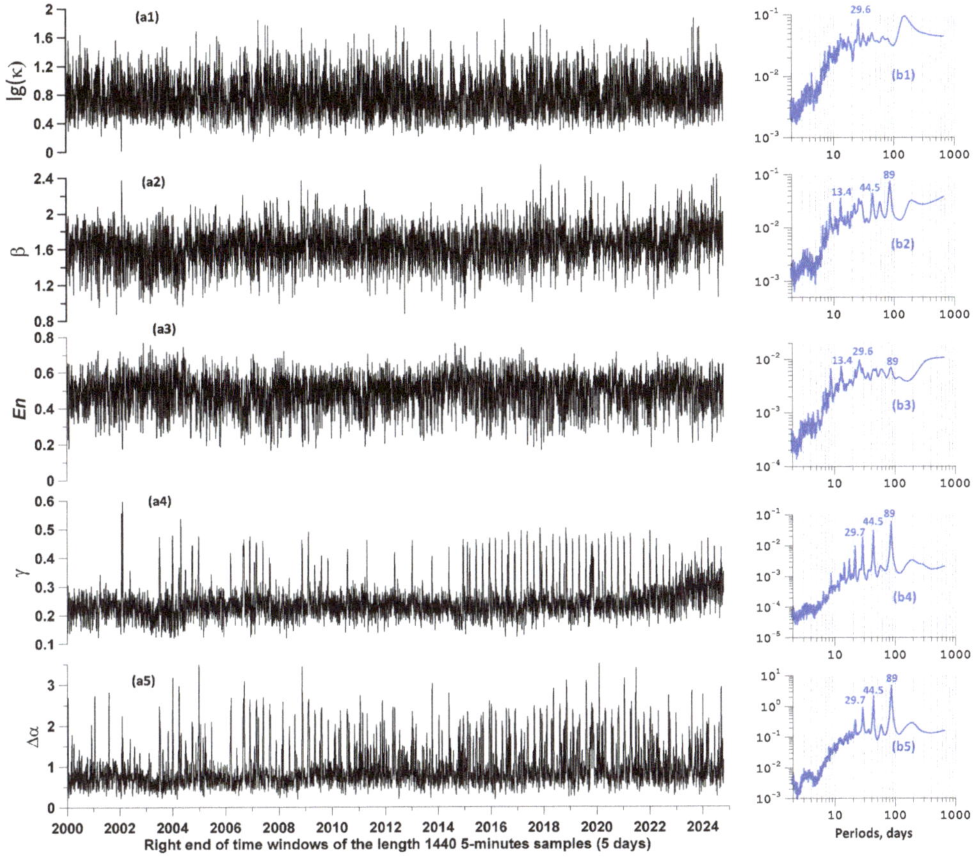

Figure 6. **(a1–a5)** Graphs of time series of 5 proton flux density statistics: logarithm of kurtosis $\lg(\kappa)$, wavelet-based spectral slope β, minimum normalized entropy of wavelet coefficients En, Donoho–Johnstone index γ, and the singularity spectrum support width $\Delta\alpha$, calculated in sliding time windows of 5 days with a shift of 1 day. On the right are graphs **(b1–b5)**, corresponding to the power spectra of time series of proton flux density statistics; for the largest spectral peaks, their periods in days are indicated.

From the graphs of the power spectra of the time series of changes in statistics, it is evident that for all of them, with the exception of $\lg(\kappa)$, there is a periodicity of 89 days, which is especially pronounced for γ and $\Delta\alpha$. It should be noted that the power spectrum of the change in the average values of the proton flux density does not contain a spectral component with a period of 89 days.

Let us consider in more detail the time–frequency structure of the variations in the singularity spectrum support width $\Delta\alpha$ (Figure 6(a5)), for which the 89-day periodicity is most clearly visible. Let us denote $\Delta\alpha(s)$ the dependence of the singularity spectrum carrier width on time (the position of the right end of the 5-day time window with a 1-day offset) s and calculate the Morlet wavelet transform [46]:

$$c_{\Delta\alpha}(t,v) = \frac{1}{\sqrt{v}} \int_{-\infty}^{+\infty} \Delta\alpha(s) \cdot \varphi\left(\frac{s-t}{v}\right) ds,\ v > 0,\ \varphi(t) = \frac{1}{\pi^{1/4}} \exp(-t^2/2 - i\pi t) \quad (27)$$

The values $|c_{\Delta\alpha}(t,v)|^2$ can be interpreted as the energy of signal $\Delta\alpha(s)$ oscillations in the vicinity of a time point t with a period v. Figure 7a shows the Morlet time-frequency diagram of values $\lg|c_{\Delta\alpha}(t,v)|$ for 200 values of periods v varying within the range from 10 to 500 days with a uniform step on a logarithmic scale. For the frequency band with periods from 63 to 158 days (logarithms of periods from 1.8 to 2.2), in which the most intense periodic variations of $\Delta\alpha(s)$ with a central period of 89 days are concentrated, we calculated the maximum values $\max_{v}(\lg|c_{\Delta\alpha}(t,v)|)$. These maximum values are shown in Figure 7b by a black line. The red line in Figure 7b shows the cyclic trend for the maximum values of the logarithms of the Morlet wavelet coefficients in the frequency band highlighted above. The period of this oscillation was determined numerically from the condition of minimum variance of deviations for trial cyclic trends with periods in the range from 1500 to 5500 days. As a result of such calculations, it turned out that the optimal period is equal to 4429 days or approximately 12.13 years, that is, very close to the period of solar cycles.

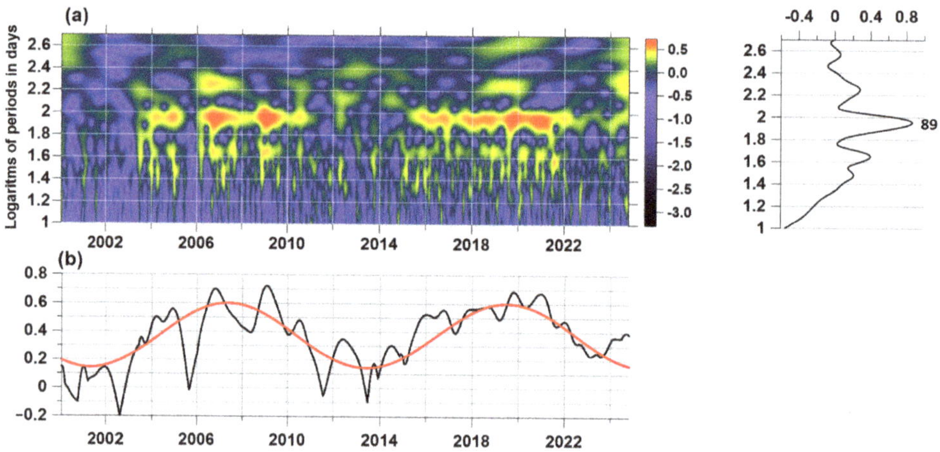

Figure 7. (**a**) Time–frequency diagram of the logarithms of the moduli of the Morlet wavelet coefficients of the variations of the singularity spectrum support width $\Delta\alpha$ for periods from 10 to 500 days; (**b**) the black line represents the maximum values of the logarithms of the moduli of the Morlet coefficients for periods from 63 to 158 days, where the red line is the optimal cyclic trend with a period of 4429 days or 12.13 years.

8. Measures of Mutual Advance of Local Extrema of Proton Flux Density and Seismic Event Sequence Statistics

The further plan of using five statistics of the proton flux density time series consists of assessing the measures of advancement of the time moments of their most expressive local extrema (the largest local maxima and the smallest local minima) relative to the time moments of earthquakes with a magnitude of at least 6.5. In this case, the number of points of the most expressive local extrema will be chosen equal to the number of seismic events, i.e., 1136.

To eliminate the influence of low-frequency components of the change in the values of statistics on the determination of the moments of time of local extremes, the time series, the graphs of which are presented in Figure 6(a1–a5), were subjected to the operation of removing low frequencies using Gaussian kernel smoothing. Let $u(t)$ be a time series with discrete time t. Gaussian kernel averaging of a time series $u(t)$ with radius (scale parameter) $h > 0$ at the moment of time t, is calculated using the following formula [52]:

$$\overline{u}(t|h) = \sum_s u(s) \cdot e^{-\left(\frac{t-s}{h}\right)^2} / \sum_s e^{-\left(\frac{t-s}{h}\right)^2} \quad (28)$$

Calculation of the kernel averaging by Formula (28) for long time series can be effectively implemented using the fast Fourier transform. Then, the average values of the time series for the averaging radius h equal to 2 days were subtracted from the time series of changes in statistics and the most expressive points of local extrema were found for the residuals. These operations are illustrated by the graphs in Figure 8.

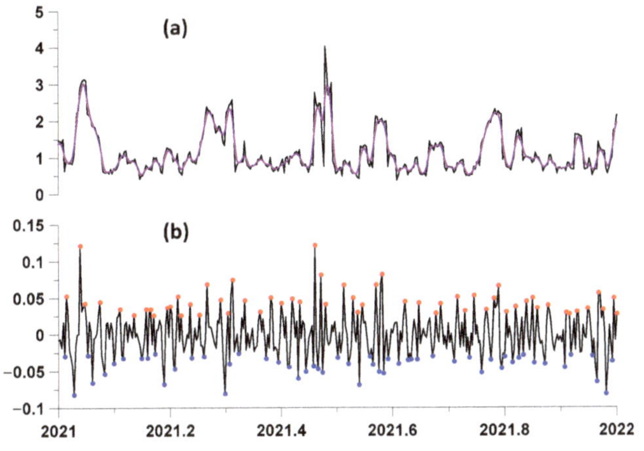

Figure 8. (**a**) The black line shows a graph of a fragment of the time series of changes in singularity spectrum support width $\Delta\alpha$ for the time interval 2021–2022; the purple line is the smoothing of the time series by a Gaussian kernel of radius 2 days. In (**b**), the red and blue dots show the positions of 1136 largest local maxima and minima of the difference between the original changes in statistics $\Delta\alpha$ and the smoothed values (black line) in this time fragment.

When estimating the advance measures by the points of local extrema of the proton flux statistics, we tested both the points of the largest local maxima and the points of the smallest local minima after excluding low frequencies using Gaussian smoothing (28). In this case, the differences between the "direct" and "reverse" lead were calculated. Then, the variant of the largest local maxima and the smallest local minima for which the average value of the difference between the average measures of the "direct" and "reverse" lead was maximum was selected. As a result of such an enumeration of variants, it turned out that the most preferable were the smallest points of local minima for the statistics $\lg(\kappa)$, β, γ, and $\Delta\alpha$, whereas the largest local maxima for the entropy was En. The results of estimating the differences in the lead measures are presented in Figure 9.

It is interesting to note that when analyzing the prognostic properties of low-frequency seismic noise measured by a global network of 229 broadband seismic stations located around the world, it turned out that it is the points of the smallest local minima of statistics γ, $\Delta\alpha$, and the points of the largest local maxima of entropy En that have the maximum prognostic effects relative to the times of the strongest earthquakes with magnitudes of at least 7 [41].

Another characteristic of the difference of average lead measures is the part of interval lengths with positive values of the difference. This characteristic is equal to $\lg(\kappa)_{\min}$—0.78; $\beta_{\min}$—0.75; $\gamma_{\min}$—0.71; $\Delta\alpha_{\min}$—0.83; $En_{\max}$—0.76; $Mean$—0.95, that is, the use of averaging provides a frequent positive value of the lead measure, although it loses out in comparison with the average value of using minima $\Delta\alpha$.

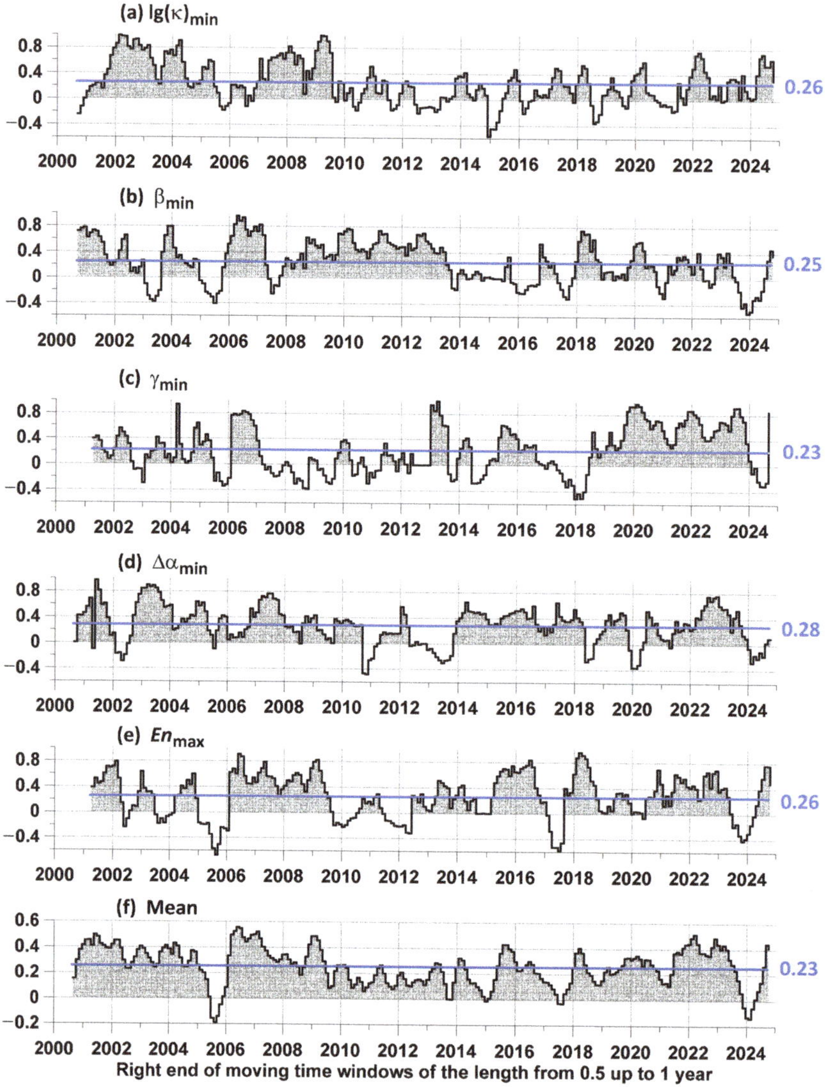

Figure 9. (**a**–**e**) Graphs of differences between average values of local extrema of components of influence matrices corresponding to "direct" advance of time points of local extrema of 5 proton flux density statistics relative to time moments of earthquakes with magnitude not lower than 6.5 and corresponding to "reverse" determination. Graphs (**a**–**d**) were constructed, respectively, for local minima of logarithm of kurtosis $\lg(\kappa)$, spectral slope β, Donoho–Johnstone index γ, and singularity spectrum support width $\Delta\alpha$; graph (**e**) shows points of local maxima of entropy En. Graph (**f**) is the averaging of curves in graphs (**a**–**e**). Blue lines are average values; their numerical values are indicated on the right. From the point of view of the average value of the difference in the advance measures, all these results are noticeably better than using the simplest statistics—the average value of the proton flux density (Figure 5c). In this case, the best result is achieved when using the minimum $\Delta\alpha$ values—the multi-fractal singularity spectrum support width, for which the average value is 0.28.

9. Discussion

The conclusions of the article were obtained as a result of applying a sequence of methods. The first stage consisted of a simple check for the presence of a 27-day period in the seismic event sequence, which dominates the proton flux density time series and is related to the rotation of the Sun. At this stage, the existence of this periodicity in the seismic event stream was confirmed with a probability of 88%. This is an indirect confirmation of the influence of the proton flux on seismicity. At the second stage of the analysis, the hypothesis about the influence of the proton flux on earthquakes was tested by a more "direct" method, based on the influence matrix method. In this method, two time sequences are processed, and the influence of events in each sequence to events in the other stream is directly estimated. In this case, the method allows for the calculating the contribution of a purely random (Poisson) component, the contribution of self-excitation, and the contributions of mutual excitation. In this analysis, one of the event sequences is always a sequence of time moments of earthquakes with a magnitude of at least 6.5. As for the second sequence of times, it varies. The simplest option is to select the time points of the largest local maxima of the average value of the proton flux density. For this option, the proportion of the average intensity of earthquakes for which the maximum values of the proton flux density are a trigger is 17% (Figure 5). However, this result can be significantly improved if, instead of a simple average, we take more sophisticated statistics of the behavior of the time series of the proton flux density. The results for enumerating five variants of statistics are shown in Figure 9. The best result (28%) was obtained when using the time points of the smallest local minima of the multifractal singularity spectrum support width (Figure 9d). But, if we average over the set of all used statistics, we obtain 23% (Figure 9f). Although the second value is less than the first, when averaging, the proportion of time when the trigger effect occurs is 0.95, while for the "record" statistics it is 0.83. In this sense, 23% is a more stable estimate.

An 89-day periodicity in the variations of proton flux statistics has been revealed. One hypothesis is that this periodicity may be related to the modulation of the proton flux density by the motion of Mercury, the planet closest to the Sun with an orbital period of 89 days. The presence of a 12-year periodicity in the change in the maximum values of the logarithms of the modules of the Morlet wavelet coefficients for the singularity spectrum support width confirms the connection of the 89-day periodicity with solar dynamics. Another hypothesis for the origin of this periodicity is the coincidence of 89 days with half the oscillation period of the SOHO satellite, which measures the proton flux density, in the vicinity of the Lagrange libration point L1 [32]. However, the mechanism of such modulation, which is maximum precisely for the Donoho–Johnston index statistics and the singularity spectrum support width, remains unclear.

Author Contributions: A.L.—ideating the research, writing the text, data processing; E.R.—data preparation. All authors have read and agreed to the published version of the manuscript.

Funding: This research received no external funding.

Institutional Review Board Statement: Not applicable.

Informed Consent Statement: Not applicable.

Data Availability Statement: The proton flux data were available from the site https://soho.nascom.nasa.gov/data/data.html, accessed on 1 January 2025. The data of earthquakes sequence are available from the site https://earthquake.usgs.gov/earthquakes/search/, accessed on 2 February 2025.

Acknowledgments: This work was carried out within the framework of the state assignments of the Institute of Physics of the Earth of the Russian Academy of Sciences.

Conflicts of Interest: The authors declare that the research was conducted in the absence of any commercial or financial relationships that could be construed as a potential conflict of interest.

References

1. Singh, A.K.; Bhargawa, A.; Siingh, D.; Singh, R.P. Physics of Space Weather Phenomena: A Review. *Geoscience* **2021**, *11*, 286. [CrossRef]
2. Kokorowski, M.; Seppälä, A.; Sample, J.G.; Holzworth, R.H.; McCarthy, M.P.; Bering, E.A.; Turunen, E. Atmosphere-ionosphere conductivity enhancements during a hard solar energetic particle event. *J. Geophys. Res.* **2012**, *117*, A05319. [CrossRef]
3. Kutiev, I.; Tsagouri, I.; Perrone, L.; Pancheva, D.; Mukhtarov, P.; Mikhailov, A.; Lastovicka, J.; Jakowski, N.; Buresova, D.; Blanch, E.; et al. Solar activity impact on the Earth's upper atmosphere. *J. Space Weather Space Clim.* **2013**, *3*, A06. [CrossRef]
4. Elias, A.G.; de Haro Barbas, B.F.; Zossi, B.S.; Medina, F.D.; Fagre, M.; Venchiarutti, J.V. Review of Long-Term Trends in the Equatorial Ionosphere Due the Geomagnetic Field Secular Variations and Its Relevance to Space Weather. *Atmosphere* **2022**, *13*, 40. [CrossRef]
5. Laurenza, M.; Cliver, E.W.; Hewitt, J.; Storini, M.; Ling, A.G.; Balch, C.C.; Kaiser, M.L. A technique for short-term warning of solar energetic particle events based on flare location, flare size, and evidence of particle escape. *Space Weather* **2009**, *7*, S04008. [CrossRef]
6. Anastasiadis, A.; Papaioannou, A.; Sandberg, I.; Georgoulis, M.; Tziotziou, K.; Kouloumvakos, A.; Jiggens, P. Predicting Flares and Solar Energetic Particle Events: The FORSPEF Tool. *Sol. Phys.* **2017**, *292*, 134. [CrossRef]
7. Aminalragia-Giamini, S.; Jiggens, P.; Anastasiadis, A.; Sandberg, I.; Aran, A.; Vainio, R.; Papadimitriou, C.; Papaioannou, A.; Tsigkanos, A.; Paouris, E.; et al. Prediction of Solar Proton Event Fluence spectra from their Peak flux spectra. *J. Space Weather Space Clim.* **2020**, *10*, 1. [CrossRef]
8. Alberti, T.; Consolini, G.; Marcucci, M.F. Open issues in statistical forecasting of solar proton events: A machine learning perspective. *Space Weather* **2021**, *19*, e2021SW002794. [CrossRef]
9. Pulinets, S.A.; Boyarchuk, K. *Ionospheric Precursors of Earthquakes*; Springer: Berlin/Heidelberg, Germany, 2004.
10. Huzaimy, J.; Yumoto, K. Possible correlation between solar activity and global seismicity. In Proceeding of the 2011 IEEE International Conference on Space Science and Communication (IconSpace), Penang, Malaysia, 12–13 July 2011; pp. 138–141. [CrossRef]
11. Tavares, M.; Azevedo, A. Influences of solar cycles on earthquakes. *Nat. Sci.* **2011**, *3*, 436. [CrossRef]
12. Anagnostopoulos, G.; Spyroglou, I.; Rigas, A.; Preka-Papadema, P.; Mavromichalaki, H.; Kiosses, I. The sun as a significant agent provoking earthquakes. *Eur. Phys. J. Spec. Top.* **2021**, *230*, 287–333. [CrossRef]
13. Sobolev, G.A. The Effect of Strong Magnetic Storms on the Occurrence of Large Earthquakes. *Izv. Phys. Solid. Earth* **2021**, *57*, 20–36. [CrossRef]
14. Ouzounov, D.; Khachikyan, G. Studying the Impact of the Geospace Environment on Solar Lithosphere Coupling and Earthquake Activity. *Remote Sens.* **2024**, *16*, 24. [CrossRef]
15. Saldanha, M.H.J.; Hirata, Y. Solar activity facilitates daily forecasts of large earthquakes. *Chaos Interdiscip. J. Nonlinear Sci.* **2022**, *32*, 061107. [CrossRef] [PubMed]
16. Pulinets, S.; Khachikyan, G. The Global Electric Circuit and Global Seismicity. *Geosciences* **2021**, *11*, 491. [CrossRef]
17. Marchetti, D.; De Santis, A.; Campuzano, S.A.; Zhu, K.; Soldani, M.; D'Arcangelo, S.; Orlando, M.; Wang, T.; Cianchini, G.; Di Mauro, D.; et al. Worldwide Statistical Correlation of Eight Years of Swarm Satellite Data with M5.5+ Earthquakes: New Hints about the Preseismic Phenomena from Space. *Remote Sens.* **2022**, *14*, 2649. [CrossRef]
18. Marchitelli, V.; Harabaglia, P.; Troise, C.; De Natale, G. On the correlation between solar activity and large earthquakes worldwide. *Sci. Rep.* **2020**, *10*, 11495. [CrossRef]
19. Marchitelli, V.; Troise, C.; Harabaglia, P.; Valenzano, B.; De Natale, G. On the Long Range Clustering of Global Seismicity and its Correlation With Solar Activity: A New Perspective for Earthquake Forecasting. *Front. Earth Sci.* **2020**, *8*, 595209. [CrossRef]
20. Novikov, V.; Ruzhin, Y.; Sorokin, V.; Yaschenko, A. Space weather and earthquakes: Possible triggering of seismic activity by strong solar flares. *Ann. Geophys.* **2020**, *63*, PA554. [CrossRef]
21. Novikov, V.A.; Sorokin, V.M. Electromagnetic Trigger Effects in the Ionosphere-Atmosphere-Lithosphere System and Their Possible Use for Short-Term Earthquake Forecasting. *Izv. Phys. Solid. Earth* **2024**, *60*, 879–890. [CrossRef]
22. Sorokin, V.; Yaschenko, A.; Mushkarev, G.; Novikov, V. Telluric Currents Generated by Solar Flare Radiation: Physical Model and Numerical Estimations. *Atmosphere* **2023**, *14*, 458. [CrossRef]
23. Sorokin, V.; Novikov, V. Possible Interrelations of Space Weather and Seismic Activity: An Implication for Earthquake Forecast. *Geosciences* **2024**, *14*, 116. [CrossRef]
24. Zeigarnik, V.A.; Bogomolov, L.M.; Novikov, V.A. Electromagnetic Earthquake Triggering: Field Observations, Laboratory Experiments, and Physical Mechanisms—A Review. *Izv. Phys. Solid. Earth* **2022**, *58*, 30–58. [CrossRef]

25. Altaibek, A.; Nurtas, M.; Zhantayev, Z.; Zhumabayev, B.; Kumarkhanova, A. Classifying Seismic Events Linked to Solar Activity: A Retrospective LSTM Approach Using Proton Density. *Atmosphere* **2024**, *15*, 1290. [CrossRef]
26. Wing, S.; Johnson, J.R. Applications of Information Theory in Solar and Space Physics. *Entropy* **2019**, *21*, 140. [CrossRef]
27. Wing, S.; Johnson, J.; Vourlidas, A. Information theoretic approach to discovering causalities in the solar cycle. *Astrophys. J.* **2018**, *854*, 85. [CrossRef]
28. Consolini, G.; Tozzi, R.; De Michelis, P. Complexity in the sunspot cycle. *Astron. Astrophys.* **2009**, *506*, 1381–1391. [CrossRef]
29. Balasis, G.; Boutsi, A.Z.; Papadimitriou, C.; Potirakis, S.M.; Pitsis, V.; Daglis, I.A.; Anastasiadis, A.; Giannakis, O. Investigation of Dynamical Complexity in Swarm-Derived Geomagnetic Activity Indices Using Information Theory. *Atmosphere* **2023**, *14*, 890. [CrossRef]
30. Papadimitriou, C.; Balasis, G.; Boutsi, A.Z.; Daglis, I.A.; Giannakis, O.; Anastasiadis, A.; De Michelis, P.; Consolini, G. Dynamical Complexity of the 2015 St. Patrick's Day Magnetic Storm at Swarm Altitudes Using Entropy Measures. *Entropy* **2020**, *22*, 574. [CrossRef]
31. Boutsi, A.Z.; Papadimitriou, C.; Balasis, G.; Brinou, C.; Zampa, E.; Giannakis, O. Dynamical Complexity in Geomagnetically Induced Current Activity Indices Using Block Entropy. *Entropy* **2025**, *27*, 172. [CrossRef]
32. Craig, R.E. Long Term Missions at the Sun-Earth Libration Point L1: ACE, SOHO, and WIND. In Proceedings of the AAS 11-485GSFC.CP.4786.2011AAS/AIAA Astrodynamics Specialist Conference, Girdwood, AK, USA, 31 July–4 August 2011. Available online: https://ntrs.nasa.gov/citations/20110008638 (accessed on 1 January 2025).
33. SOHO Data. Available online: https://soho.nascom.nasa.gov/data/data.html (accessed on 2 February 2025).
34. USGS Search Earthquake Catalog. Available online: https://earthquake.usgs.gov/earthquakes/search/ (accessed on 2 February 2025).
35. Marple, S.L., Jr. *Digital Spectral Analysis with Applications*; Prentice-Hall, Inc.: Englewood Cliffs, NJ, USA, 1987.
36. Lyubushin, A.A.; Pisarenko, V.F.; Ruzich, V.V.; Buddo, V.Y. A New Method for Identifying Seismicity Periodicities. *Volcanol. Seismol.* **1998**, *20*, 73–89.
37. Lyubushin, A. Entropy of GPS-measured Earth tremor. In *Revolutionizing Earth Observation—New Technologies and Insights*; IntechOpen: London, UK, 2024. [CrossRef]
38. Cox, D.R.; Lewis, P.A.W. *The Statistical Analysis of Series of Events*; Methuen: London, UK, 1996.
39. Rao, C.R. *Linear Statistical Inference and Its Applications*; John Wiley & Sons, Inc.: Hoboken, NJ, USA, 1965.
40. Lyubushin, A.A.; Pisarenko, V.F. Research on Seismic Regime Linear Model of Intensity of Interacting Point Processes. *Phys. Solid. Earth Engl. Transl.* **1994**, *29*, 1108–1113.
41. Lyubushin, A. Investigation of the Global Seismic Noise Properties in Connection to Strong Earthquakes. *Front. Earth Sci.* **2022**, *10*, 905663. [CrossRef]
42. Lyubushin, A.; Rodionov, E. Wavelet-based correlations of the global magnetic field in connection to strongest earthquakes. *Adv. Space Res.* **2024**, *74*, 3496–3510. [CrossRef]
43. Lyubushin, A.; Rodionov, E. Prognostic Properties of Instantaneous Amplitudes Maxima of Earth Surface Tremor. *Entropy* **2024**, *26*, 710. [CrossRef]
44. Lyubushin, A.; Kopylova, G.; Rodionov, E.; Serafimova, Y. An Analysis of Meteorological Anomalies in Kamchatka in Connection with the Seismic Process. *Atmosphere* **2025**, *16*, 78. [CrossRef]
45. Kendall, M.G.; Stuart, A. *The Advanced Theory of Statistics*; Charles Griffin and Co.: London, UK, 1977; Volume 1.
46. Mallat, S.A. *Wavelet Tour of Signal Processing*, 2nd ed.; Academic Press: Cambridge, MA, USA, 1999.
47. Lyubushin, A. Low-Frequency Seismic Noise Properties in the Japanese Islands. *Entropy* **2021**, *23*, 474. [CrossRef]
48. Donoho, D.L.; Johnstone, I.M. Adapting to unknown smoothness via wavelet shrinkage. *J. Am. Stat. Assoc.* **1995**, *90*, 1200–1224. [CrossRef]
49. Taqqu, M.S. Self-similar processes. In *Encyclopedia of Statistical Sciences*; Wiley: New York, NY, USA, 1988; Volume 8, pp. 352–357.
50. Feder, J. *Fractals*; Plenum Press: New York, NY, USA; London, UK, 1988.
51. Kantelhardt, J.W.; Zschiegner, S.A.; Konscienly-Bunde, E.; Havlin, S.; Bunde, A.; Stanley, H.E. Multifractal detrended fluctuation analysis of nonstationary time series. *Phys. A* **2002**, *316*, 87–114. [CrossRef]
52. Hardle, W. *Applied Nonparametric Regression*; (Biometric Society Monographs, No. 19.); Cambridge University Press: Cambridge, UK, 1990.

Disclaimer/Publisher's Note: The statements, opinions and data contained in all publications are solely those of the individual author(s) and contributor(s) and not of MDPI and/or the editor(s). MDPI and/or the editor(s) disclaim responsibility for any injury to people or property resulting from any ideas, methods, instructions or products referred to in the content.

entropy

Article

Detection of Significant Seismic Quiescence Patterns in the Mexican Subduction Zone Using Extended Schreider Algorithms

Carlos Carrizales-Velazquez [1,*], Jennifer Perez-Oregon [2], Israel Reyes-Ramírez [1], Lev Guzmán-Vargas [1,*] and Fernando Angulo-Brown [3]

[1] Laboratorio de Sistemas Complejos, Unidad Interdisciplinaria en Ingeniería y Tecnologías Avanzadas, Instituto Politécnico Nacional, Ciudad de México 07340, Mexico; ireyesr@ipn.mx
[2] Departamento de Ciencias Básicas, Universidad Autónoma Metropolitana, Azcapotzalco, Ciudad de México 02128, Mexico; jnnfr.po@gmail.com
[3] Departamento de Física, Escuela Superior de Física y Matemáticas, Instituto Politécnico Nacional, Ciudad de México 07738, Mexico; fangulob@ipn.mx
* Correspondence: c.carrizales.v@gmail.com (C.C.-V.); lguzmanv@ipn.mx (L.G.-V.)

Abstract: This study investigates the implementation of Schreider's quiescence algorithm and two variants that utilize spatiotemporal data to identify patterns of seismic quiescence. These patterns are of particular interest as they may serve as precursors to major seismic events, specifically large earthquakes ($M > 7$), within the Mexican subduction zone associated with the Cocos Plate. We identify two characteristic stages: the α-stage, where a notable deviation is observed in the Schreider convolutions, and the β-stage, where the convolutions return to their background levels. In addition, we identify that the Schreider algorithm cannot discern quiescence patterns when earthquakes $M > 7$ are too close in space and time. Consequently, we explore the behavior of the convolutions in three cases where the algorithm is restarted after the mainshocks, and we find apparent advantages for the spatiotemporal variants of the convolutions. The findings contribute to a more profound understanding of the stages preceding large subduction earthquakes and aid in the identification of precursor patterns in this region.

Keywords: seismic precursors; mexican subduction zone; schreider algorithm; seismic quiescence

1. Introduction

Within the context of earth sciences, since several decades ago, the problem of earthquake prediction has attracted the attention of many researchers [1,2]. However, at the present time, no universally accepted method to predict the occurrence of large-magnitude earthquakes currently exists. Nevertheless, efforts to investigate this extraordinarily complex problem continue [3,4]. One of the methods most commonly used is searching for quiescence patterns before the occurrence of great earthquakes using different approaches such as those proposed by Ohtake [5–7] and Schreider [8], among many others [9–16]. In fact, Wyss and Habermann (1988) defined the quiescence pattern formally as follows [10]: "seismic quiescence is a decrease of mean seismicity rate as compared to the background rate in the same crustal volume, judged significant by some clearly defined standard. The rate decrease (α-stage proposed by Ohtake [5]) takes place within part, or all, of the source volume of the subsequent main shock, and it extends up to the time of the mainshock or may be separated from it by a relatively short period of increased seismicity rate (β-stage [5])". For a pedagogical scheme, see the explanation presented online in Section S1 of

 https://doi.org/10.3390/e27090960

the Supplementary Materials. However, the hypothesis of precursory seismic quiescence is not universally accepted, and there exist different approaches to measure, map, and evaluate possible episodes of seismic quiescence [17].

Nonetheless, the pursuit of quiescence patterns is regarded as a promising approach for approximating the forecast of great EQs. In the present article, the Schreider algorithm is employed in its original form and in a modified form. Specifically, this study unveils the existence of quiescence patterns derived from convolution series comprising spatiotemporal information. These patterns are poised to be associated with a series of eight earthquakes of magnitude $M > 7$ that occurred along the Pacific coast of Mexico from 2012 to 2022. Furthermore, we employ a relatively novel method that was published in 2018. This method involves the exploration of a quantity referred to as seismic pseudo-velocity [18]. The present article is organized as follows: Section 2 is dedicated to reviewing the methods we use to study the possible seismic quiescence patterns along the Pacific Mexican Coast in the Latitude interval [10° N, 22° N] and in the Longitude interval [108° W, 87° W] during the period from 1 January 1990 until 1 January 2025. In Section 3, we describe the database used for this paper. In Sections 4 and 5, we show the principal results of the application of the methods described in Section 2 to eight earthquakes ($M > 7$); all of them presented evidence of quiescence patterns before the respective mainshocks. Finally, in Section 6, we present our concluding remarks.

2. Methods

2.1. Schreider Algorithm

The identification of zones of seismic quiescence can be facilitated by employing the Schreider algorithm [8]. The initial step entails the selection of a threshold magnitude, designated as M_{th}, and the delineation of a volumetric region for the study. In this study, cylindrical volumes of radii r are utilized, as previously defined in [14,18]. The focal mechanism of each mainshock is centered in a cylindrical region, with the objective of identifying significant anomalies in the inter-times $\Delta T(n) = t(n) - t(n-1)$ of consecutive earthquakes. In this context, $t(n)$ denotes the occurrence time of the n-th seismic event. Consequently, $\Delta T(n)$ is defined as a measure of seismic frequency, with low (high) seismicity corresponding to large (small) values of ΔT, respectively. To ensure the desired level of smoothness, the Laplace function, denoted by $f(n,s)$, is employed [8]). The definition of this function is as follows:

$$f(n,s) = \frac{1}{s\sqrt{2\pi}} \exp\left[-\frac{n^2}{2s^2} \right], \quad n = 1,2,3,..., \tag{1}$$

where s is the *smoothness* parameter [8]. Subsequently, each k_{th} earthquake can be associated with the convolution through the application of the following formula:

$$\mathcal{T}(k) = \sum_{n=0}^{l} \Delta T(k-n) f(n,s), \tag{2}$$

where the value of l is determined when the function $f(n,s)$ is approximately zero. Consequently, the convolution $\mathcal{T}(k)$ is determined by three parameters, M_{th}, r, and s, which are selected on an arbitrary basis. In order to identify a period of seismic quiescence, it is necessary to ascertain the average value of $\mathcal{T}(k)$ calculated over an extended period of time, under the assumption that this average value is then stabilized. This average value $\overline{\mathcal{T}}$ is as follows:

$$\overline{\mathcal{T}} = \frac{1}{N} \sum_{k=1}^{N} \mathcal{T}(k), \tag{3}$$

where N is the total number of earthquakes with magnitude $M \geq M_{th}$ which fall inside the exploration of the cylindrical region. The standard deviation is calculated as follows:

$$\sigma = \sqrt{\frac{1}{N-1}\sum_{k=1}^{N}\left[\mathcal{T}(k) - \overline{\mathcal{T}}\right]^2}. \tag{4}$$

The temporary convolution function $\mathcal{T}(k)$ follows a Gaussian distribution. Because of this, Schreider assumed that values of $\mathcal{T}(k)$ greater than $\overline{\mathcal{T}} + 3\sigma$ are considered abnormally large. Therefore, cylindrical regions that show this behavior are considered to contain abnormal seismic quiescence [14].

2.2. *Analysis of Spatio-Temporal Series Using the Schreider Algorithm*

The Schreider algorithm focuses exclusively on the temporal characteristics of seismic events, with the objective of identifying periods of seismic quiescence. We hereby propose the inclusion of the inter-distance, denoted here as ΔR, of consecutive earthquakes:

$$\Delta R(n) = \|\vec{R}(n) - \vec{R}(n-1)\|, \tag{5}$$

where $\|\cdot\|$ denotes the euclidean distance. We hereby propose the implementation of the convolution utilized in the Schreider algorithm, albeit employing the product of inter-times and inter-distances, as outlined below:

$$\mathcal{RT}(k) = \sum_{n=0}^{l}\left[\Delta R(k-n) \times \Delta T(k-n)\right] f(n,s). \tag{6}$$

Equation (6) includes the role of seismic frequency and spatial occurrence (distance between consecutive hypocenters) for searching seismic quiescence.

2.3. *Analysis of Pseudo-Velocity Series Using the Schreider Algorithm*

In the aforementioned work [18], the concept of *pseudo-velocity* was introduced with the objective of quantifying multifractal changes associated with major seismic events ($M > 7$). We examine the behavior of this novel variable, which encompasses the temporal and spatial characteristics of seismic events. The pseudo-velocity is defined as the logarithm of the quotient of ΔR and ΔT [18]. Subsequently, the convolution for this new variable is defined as follows:

$$\mathcal{V}(k) = \sum_{n=0}^{l} log\left[\frac{\Delta R(k-n)}{\Delta T(k-n)}\right] f(n,s). \tag{7}$$

The results generated by the Schreider algorithm are typically on the order of $\sim[10^4, 10^5]$, as the inter-times are within these orders [14]. However, the values of pseudo-velocity series are in the lower range of magnitudes $\sim[10^{-5}, 10^1]$ [18]. As is evident, the values differ significantly, and a plot that incorporates both set of results is not visually appealing. Subsequently, the quantities ΔR and ΔT are normalized with their standard deviations $\sigma(\Delta R)$ and $\sigma(\Delta T)$, respectively. For clarity, the following notations will be employed: $\widetilde{\mathcal{T}}(k)$ and $\widetilde{\mathcal{RT}}(k)$ for Equations (2) and (6), respectively, following the normalization procedure outlined herein. A Pipeline Diagram as a summary and complement to this section can be found online in the Section S2 of the Supplementary Materials.

3. Data: Southern Mexican Pacific Seismic Zone

The southern region of Mexico is characterized by a high degree of seismic complexity, which is attributable to the subduction zone where the Cocos, Pacific, and North American plates converge. This dynamic geological setting is a primary source of significant seismic activity in the region. The utilization of seismic data in this study has been facilitated by the National Seismological Service of Mexico (SSN) [19], which has maintained records since the early 20th century. It has been documented that the database is complete from 1990 onwards [18]. An endeavor has been undertaken to categorize the Mexican region based on its seismic dynamics [20].

4. Seismic Quiescence of Mexico Mainshocks, Unmixed Patterns

For the purpose of this study, earthquakes of magnitude $M > 7$ are considered mainshocks within the period from 1 January 2006 to 31 December 2024 (see Table 1). In accordance with the approach outlined in [18], this study focuses on cylinders with radii $R = 200$ km and heights $H = 60$ km. During the period under consideration, eight major seismic events were recorded. Figure 1 presents the epicenters of these seismic events, along with their respective radii and the date and time of occurrence. As observed, such radii exhibit overlapping regions that must be taken into account when interpreting seismic quiescence patterns accurately.

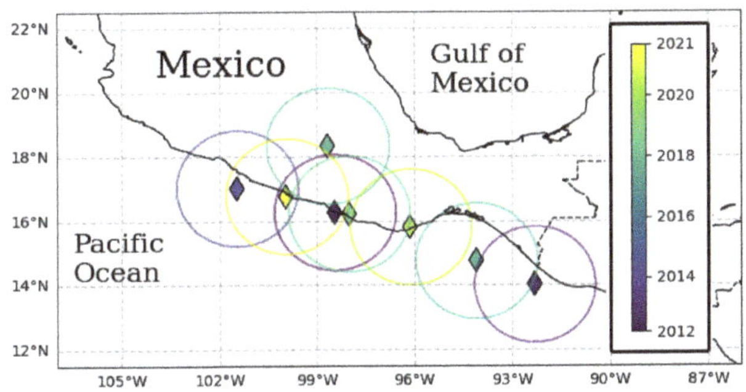

Figure 1. This map shows mainshocks ($EQ > 7$) in Mexico during the period of 2012–2025. The epicenters are shown as diamonds, each with its circular study region.

Table 1. List of mainshocks in Mexico (from 2006 until 2025).

Date	Magnitude	Latitude	Longitude	Depth (km)
20 March 2012	7.5	16.26	−98.46	18.0
7 November 2012	7.3	14.03	−92.32	17.1
18 April 2014	7.2	17.01	−101.46	18.0
7 September 2017	8.2	14.76	−94.10	45.9
19 September 2017	7.1	18.33	−98.67	51.2
16 February 2018	7.2	16.22	−98.01	16.0
23 June 2020	7.4	15.80	−96.13	22.8
17 September 2021	7.1	16.75	−99.95	15.0

4.1. EQ 7.5, 20 March 2012

The seismic event in question occurred in the area between the municipalities of Ometepec-Guerrero and Pinotepa Nacional-Oaxaca. The depth of the cylinder ranges from 0 km to 60 km. Here, we consider a threshold magnitude, $M_{th} = 4.1$. As illustrated in Figure 2, the time series of seismic events within the specified region of study has been examined, along with the outcomes of the Schreider algorithm's implementation on inter-times, pseudo-velocities, and product inter-distance with inter-time series for the EQ7.5.

Figure 2a presents the time series of the magnitudes. As we can see in Figure 2b,d, the values shown for $\widetilde{\mathcal{T}}(k)$ and $\widetilde{\mathcal{RT}}(k)$ do not exceed threshold $\overline{\mathcal{T}} + 3\sigma$ until the beginning of 2008 (where the green shade begins). To determine the intervals at which the convolution consistently exceeds the $\overline{\mathcal{T}} + 3\sigma$ threshold, we used the method that detects the first return to the mean value [21] (see Section S3 of the Supplementary Materials for details). An increase was observed from the beginning of 2008, which lasted two years (considered the α-stage by [5]). The values of the convolution in Figure 2b,d returned to their initial behavior for approximately two years (considered the β-stage by [5]) until the EQ7.5 mainshock occurred. It is important to note that three main shocks occurred during the α-stage, but as they happened after EQ7.5, they possibly did not interfere with the quiescence shown in Figure 2. Regarding pseudo-velocity, as shown in Figure 2c, its values decreased and remained low throughout the entire α-stage period.

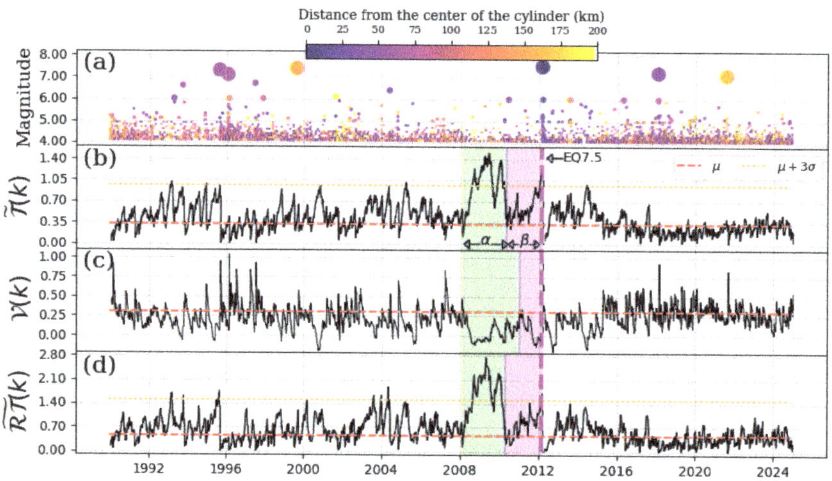

Figure 2. Schreider convolution corresponding to *EQ*7.5, 20 March 2012. (**a**) Time series of earthquake magnitudes in the cylindrical region with a threshold magnitude of $M_{th} = 4.1$. The coloration of the circles is indicative of the distance between the center of the cylinder and the epicenter of each earthquake, while the size of the circles corresponds to the earthquake magnitude. (**b**) Inter-time series $\widetilde{\mathcal{T}}(k)$, (**c**) pseudo-velocity series $\mathcal{V}(k)$, and (**d**) the product of inter-distance with inter-time $\widetilde{\mathcal{RT}}(k)$ series. Red dashed line shows the mean value of the convolution (for each case), orange dotted line is three times the standard deviation for each case, and shaded green and magenta regions correspond to the α and β stages, respectively. The cylinder used has a radius of 200 km and a depth within the range of [0, 60] km.

4.2. *EQ 7.3, 7 November 2012*

This earthquake happened close to the intersection between the Cocos and Caribbean tectonic plates [19]. Its epicenter (14.03 N, 92.32 W) was located in Ciudad Hidalgo-Chiapas at a depth of 17 km. For this case, the cylinder was set from 0 km to a depth of 60 km. The results are shown in Figure 3, using a threshold magnitude of $M_{th} = 4.5$. As we can see, the deviations in the convolutions in Figure 3b–d show an anomaly close to the *EQ*7.3, but their values barely reach the limit 3σ. We identified brief α and β stages, which lasted approximately three years and half of a year, respectively. On the other hand, we observe a peak near the end of 1995 that could be associated with the *EQ*7.1, which occurred on 20 October 1995 at a latitude of 16.81° N and a longitude of 93.47° W. Additionally, an anomaly is observed after the mainshock of this subsection, which could be associated with the *EQ*8.2 on 7 September 2017.

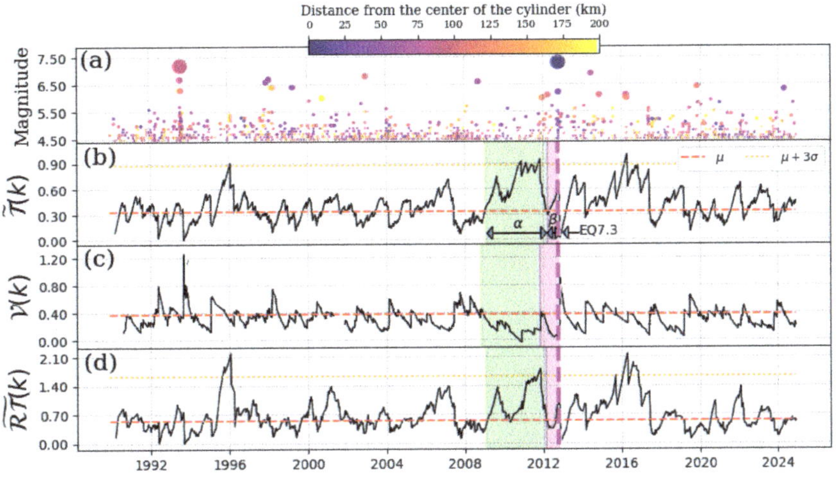

Figure 3. Schreider convolution for *EQ*7.3, 7 November 2012. (**a**) Time series of earthquake magnitudes in the cylindrical region with a threshold magnitude of $M_{th} = 4.5$. The coloration of the circles is indicative of the distance between the center of the cylinder and the epicenter of each earthquake, while the size of the circles corresponds to the earthquake magnitude. (**b**) Inter-time series $\widetilde{\mathcal{T}}(k)$, (**c**) pseudo-velocity series $\mathcal{V}(k)$, and (**d**) the product of inter-distance with inter-time $\widetilde{\mathcal{RT}}(k)$ series. Red dashed line shows the mean value of the convolution (for each case), orange dotted line is three times the standard deviation for each case, and shaded green and magenta regions correspond to the α and β stages, respectively. The cylinder used has a radius of 200 km and a depth within the range of [0, 60] km.

4.3. *EQ 7.2, 18 April 2014*

The mainshock of 18 April 2014 had its epicenter in Petatlán-Guerrero (17 N, 101.46 W). In this case, we also use the same depths for the cylinders as in the previous two reported earthquakes. Figure 4 shows an anomaly that begins at the end of 2011 and disappears at the beginning of 2014 (the α-stage, represented by the green shaded region). The β-stage lasted just a few months until the *EQ*7.2. This behavior was also reported when studying the long-range correlations of the electromagnetic signals of the ground near this epicenter in [22]. Additionally, we observe a significant increase in $\widetilde{\mathcal{T}}(k)$ in 1995, which may be primarily associated with the EQ7.1 (11 January 1997), whose epicenter was located at 189 km.

4.4. *EQ8.2, 7 September 2017*

This is the greatest magnitude earthquake in this work, which had its epicenter in the Tehuantepec's Gulf, Chiapas. In this case, the hypocenter was located at a depth of 46 km, and its cylinder ranged from 30 km to 90 km. This event is one of the cases reported in [18] (threshold magnitude $M_{th} = 4.4$), but here, we provide additional information by applying the Schreider algorithm to the pseudo-velocities and the product $\widetilde{\mathcal{RT}}(k)$ series. Figure 5 shows the possible quiescence presented before the *EQ*8.2. In Figure 5a, we reproduce the behavior reported previously in [18]. Figure 5c shows a more statistically significant pattern where a decreasing behavior is observed in the pseudo-velocities, which also lasted from 2008 until beginning of 2015. This agrees with the so called α-stage showed in Figure 5b (shaded green region). The behavior shown in Figure 5d coincides with Figure 5b.

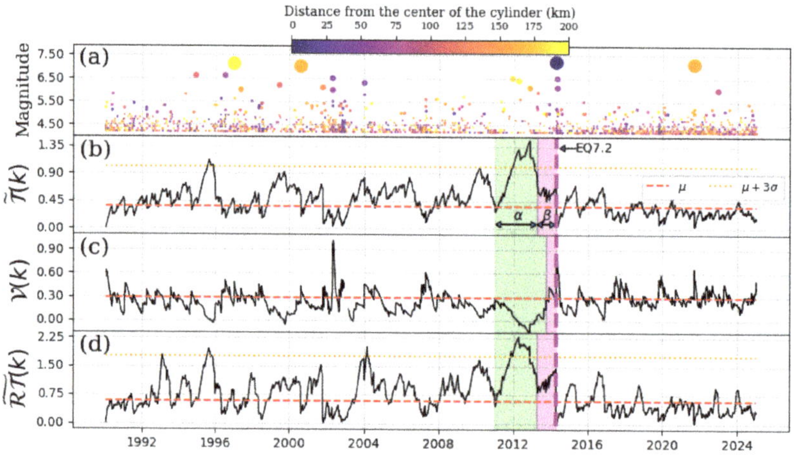

Figure 4. Schreider convolution for $EQ7.2$, 18 April 2014. (**a**) Time series of earthquake magnitudes in the cylindrical region with a threshold magnitude of $M_{th} = 4.2$. The coloration of the circles is indicative of the distance between the center of the cylinder and the epicenter of each earthquake, while the size of the circles corresponds to the earthquake magnitude. (**b**) Inter-time series $\widetilde{\mathcal{T}}(k)$, (**c**) pseudo-velocity series $\mathcal{V}(k)$, and (**d**) the product of inter-distance with inter-time $\widetilde{\mathcal{RT}}(k)$ series. Red dashed line shows the mean value of the convolution (for each case), orange dotted line is three times the standard deviation for each case, and shaded green and magenta regions correspond to the α and β stages, respectively. The cylinder used has a radius of 200 km and a depth within the range of $[0, 60]$ km.

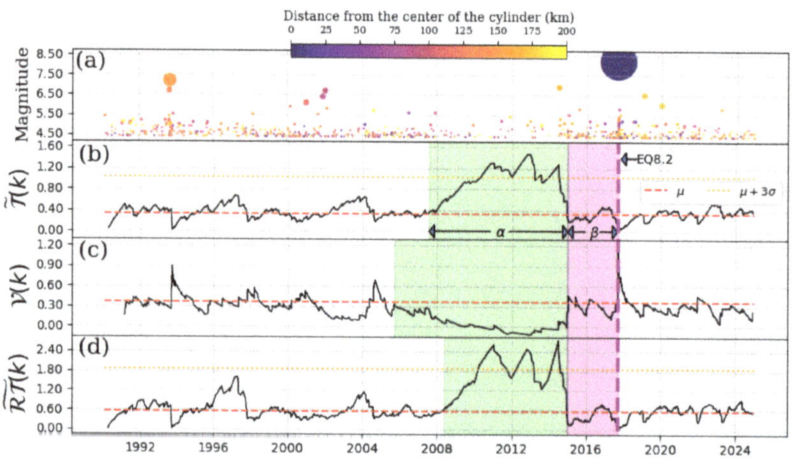

Figure 5. Schreider convolution for $EQ8.2$, 7 September 2017. (**a**) Time series of earthquake magnitudes in the cylindrical region with a threshold magnitude of $M_{th} = 4.4$. The coloration of the circles is indicative of the distance between the center of the cylinder and the epicenter of each earthquake, while the size of the circles corresponds to the earthquake magnitude. (**b**) Inter-time series $\widetilde{\mathcal{T}}(k)$, (**c**) pseudo-velocity series $\mathcal{V}(k)$, and (**d**) the product of inter-distance with inter-time $\widetilde{\mathcal{RT}}(k)$ series. Red dashed line shows the mean value of the convolution (for each case), orange dotted line is three times the standard deviation for each case, and shaded green and magenta regions correspond to the α and β stages, respectively. The cylinder used has a radius of 200 km and a depth within the range of $[30, 90]$ km.

4.5. EQ7.1, 19 September 2017

This earthquake happened on the border of the states of Puebla and Morelos, and its consequences on Mexico City were devastating. It is important to mention that this region was not very seismically active before this EQ; consequently, the seismic rate of this region increased due to the aftershocks, and this zone reached a new seismicity level. The depth of the hypocenter was 51.2 km; that is, the epicenter was far from the so-called Pacific Trench, inland from the continental plate. For this case, we chose a cylinder with depth from 0 km to 90 km. We observe convolutions (see Figure 6) that barely reach $\overline{T} + 3\sigma$ at the beginning of 2012, and it decays at middle of 2015, as observed in Figure 6b, which could be considered as the α-stage. Next, the β-stage lasted two and a half years until the mainshock. Some of this happens when $\widetilde{\mathcal{RT}}(k)$ is combined with other things (see Figure 6d). Actually, for this EQ, the more important quantity was the convolution of pseudo-velocities (see Figure 6c) It is noteworthy that this region typically exhibits low seismic activity, which complicates the discernment of quiescence periods.

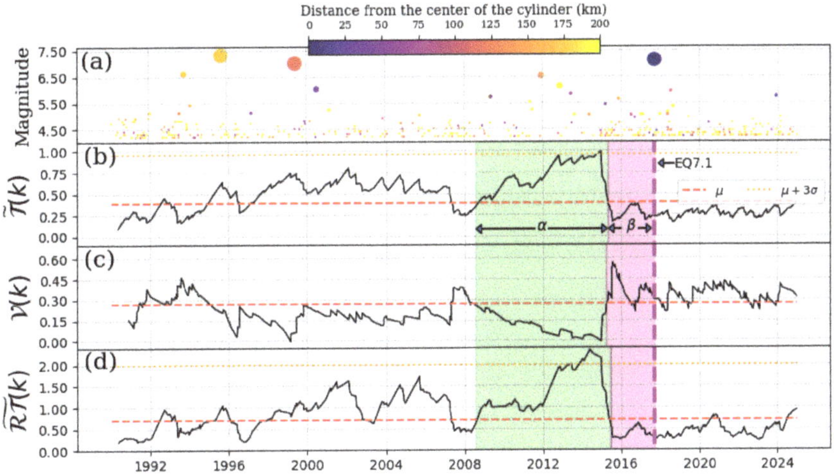

Figure 6. Schreider convolution for *EQ7.1*, 19 September 2017. (**a**) Time series of earthquake magnitudes in the cylindrical region with a threshold magnitude of $M_{th} = 4.2$. The coloration of the circles is indicative of the distance between the center of the cylinder and the epicenter of each earthquake, while the size of the circles corresponds to the earthquake magnitude. (**b**) Inter-time series $\widetilde{\mathcal{T}}(k)$, (**c**) pseudo-velocity series $\mathcal{V}(k)$, and (**d**) the product of inter-distance with inter-time $\widetilde{\mathcal{RT}}(k)$ series. Red dashed line shows the mean value of the convolution (for each case), orange dotted line is three times the standard deviation for each case, and shaded green and magenta regions correspond to the α and β stages, respectively. The cylinder used has a radius of 200 km and a depth within the range of [0, 90] km.

5. Seismic Quiescence of Mexico Mainshocks, Possibly Mixed Patterns

As Figure 1 shows, the last three EQs on the list occurred on dates that were approximately one to two years apart. Additionally, their epicenters were relatively close to each other. This could cause their quiescence patterns to overlap, considering the typical duration of individual quiescence patterns. For this reason, we discuss these three cases separately from the previous ones.

5.1. EQ7.2, 16 February 2018

This earthquake happened near the town Pinotepa Nacional, Oaxaca at a depth of 16 km. We chose a cylinder from 0 km to 60 km in depth. It is important to mention that this event was located at 47.6 km from the $EQ7.5$ of 20 March 2012 (see Figure 1). In consequence, the quiescence of the $EQ7.2$ could be veiled with the quiescence of the $EQ7.5$. Figure 7b–d show the resulting series of convolutions using the Schreider algorithm. As we can see, the most notable deviation pattern is observed from 2008 until 2012; however, this period corresponds to the quiescence of the event $EQ7.5$, as we just commented. Unfortunately, we do not identify important changes in the convolution of $\widetilde{\mathcal{T}}(k)$, but in the convolution of the pseudo-velocity $\mathcal{V}(k)$ and the $\widetilde{\mathcal{RT}}(k)$ series, we observe small changes (α and β regions shown in Figure 7c,d), which could be associated with seismic quiescence of the event $EQ7.2$ on 16 February 2018. Including the spatial aspect in the Schreider convolutions could be an important advantage to recognize possible seismic quiescence just after a mainshock, which could hide changes in the classical convolution for shortly after the mainshocks of inter-times $\widetilde{\mathcal{T}}(k)$. As we assumed, the previous mainshock $EQ7.5$ produces a kind of veil for the quiescence pattern. Then, we decided to re-run the analysis, but beginning after the aftershocks produced by the previous $EQ7.5$ (a few of years after the mainshock). The results of these new calculations are shown in Figure 7f–h. Here, we observe how the 3σ value of the convolution decreases. Consequently, a new seismic quiescence pattern rises, which corresponds to the mainshock in this section ($EQ7.2$, 16 February 2018) becoming clear. The α-stage begins on 20 May 2017 and ends on 10 September 2017 (green shaded region of Figure 7f–h). The β-stage lasted almost 5 months.

5.2. EQ7.4, 23 June 2020

Figure 8 shows similar behavior to that observed in the previous section (see Figure 7). We will then discuss Figure 8f–h, which begin on 1 September 2017. The Schreider convolution of inter-times (Figure 8f) reaches the 3σ values during the 9-month α-stage period (green shaded region in Figure 8f). The β-stage lasted 7 months (magenta shaded region in Figure 8f. In relation to the convolution of pseudo-velocity (Figure 8g), we observe that during the α-stage, this parameter decreases, as expected. In fact, in this α-stage, the decrement below the mean value is more remarkable than that observed in the β-stage. In Figure 8h, during the α-stage, the values of the convolution of $\Delta T \times \Delta R$ exceeded the 3σ-value.

5.3. EQ7.1, 7 September 2021

Another case of possible mixed patterns is the event $EQ7.1$ that occurred on 7 September 2021 (see Figure 9). As we can see, both the α and β stages are thin. We believe that this pattern was affected by the previous events that occurred: $EQ7.5, 2012$; $EQ7.2, 2014$; $EQ7.1, 2017$; and $EQ7.2, 2018$. All of these events had epicenters located almost 200 km from the epicenter of the $EQ7.1$ on 7 September 2021. In particular, the event $EQ7.2, 2018$ is the closest event in time to the $EQ7.1, 2021$. As Figure 9f–h show, before 2018, we can identify notable anomalies in the three convolutions, which correspond to all previous mainshocks. Due to these facts, we again apply the procedure mentioned in the previous subsections, which consists of beginning the analysis just after the last mainshock ($EQ7.2, 2018$). In Figure 9f–h, we can see the results of this procedure. Now, the α and β stages for the EQ7.1, 7 September 2021 mainshock, are more clearly visible for the three convolutions.

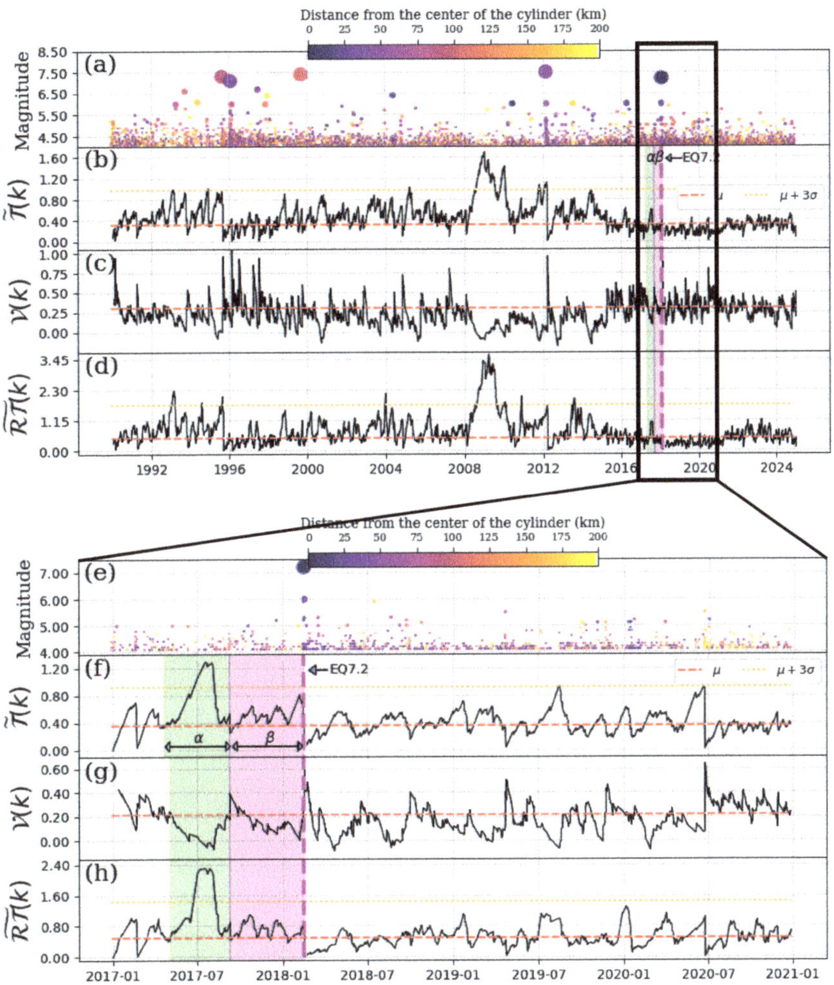

Figure 7. Schreider convolution for *EQ*7.2, 2018-02-16. (**a**) Time series of earthquake magnitudes in the cylindrical region with a threshold magnitude of $M_{th} = 4.1$. The coloration of the circles is indicative of the distance between the center of the cylinder and the epicenter of each earthquake, while the size of the circles corresponds to the earthquake magnitude. (**b**) Inter-time series $\widetilde{\mathcal{T}}(k)$, (**c**) pseudo-velocity series $\mathcal{V}(k)$, and (**d**) the product of inter-distance with inter-time $\widetilde{\mathcal{RT}}(k)$ series. The cylinder used has a radius of 200 km and a depth within the range of [0, 60] km. Panels (**e–h**) zoom in on a segment of the time series shown in panels (**a–d**) (above). The red dashed line shows the mean of the convolution of each series, the orange dotted line is three times the standard deviation of the new segment, the magenta dashed vertical line indicates the date of the mainshock, the shaded green and magenta regions corresponds to the α and β stages, respectively.

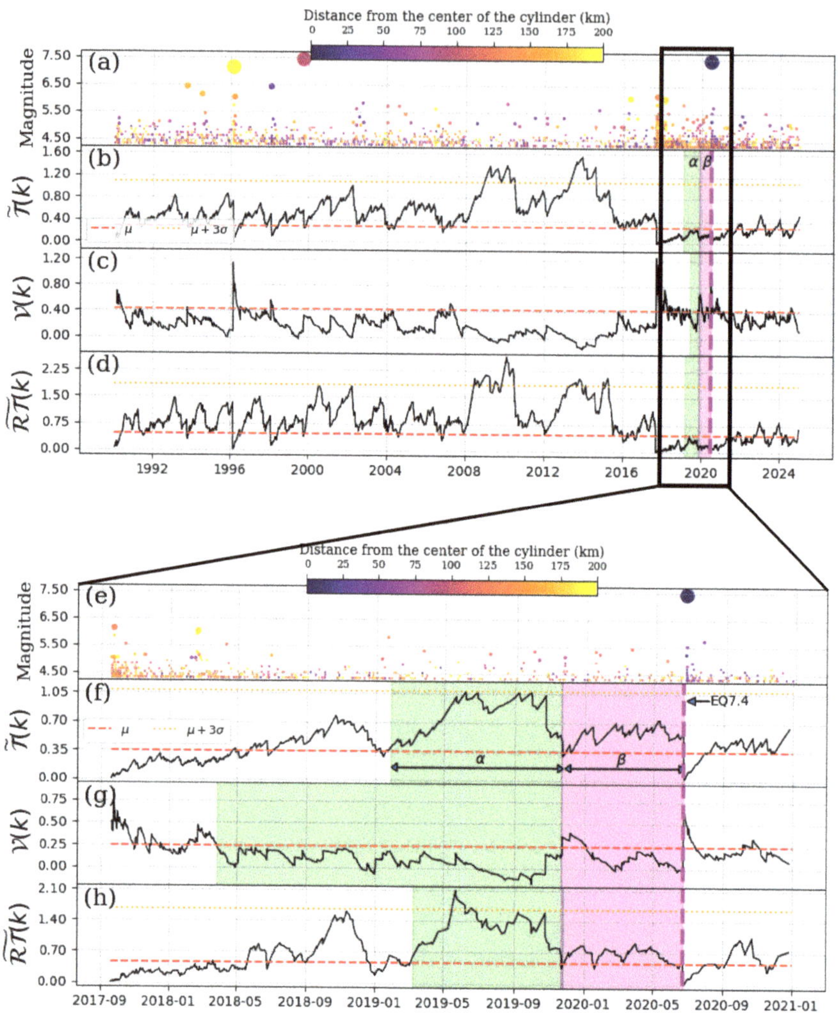

Figure 8. Schreider convolution for *EQ*7.4, 2020-06-23. (**a**) Time series of earthquake magnitudes in the cylindrical region with a threshold magnitude of $M_{th} = 4.3$. The coloration of the circles is indicative of the distance between the center of the cylinder and the epicenter of each earthquake, while the size of the circles corresponds to the earthquake magnitude. (**b**) Inter-time series $\widetilde{\mathcal{T}}(k)$, (**c**) pseudo-velocity series $\mathcal{V}(k)$, and (**d**) the product of inter-distance with inter-time $\widetilde{\mathcal{RT}}(k)$ series. The cylinder used has a radius of 200 km and a depth within the range of [0, 60] km. Panels (**e**–**h**) zoom in on a segment of the time series shown in panels (**a**–**d**). The red dashed line shows the mean of the convolution of each series, the orange dotted line is three times the standard deviation of the new segment, the magenta dashed vertical line indicates the date of the mainshock, the shaded green and magenta regions corresponds to the α and β stages, respectively.

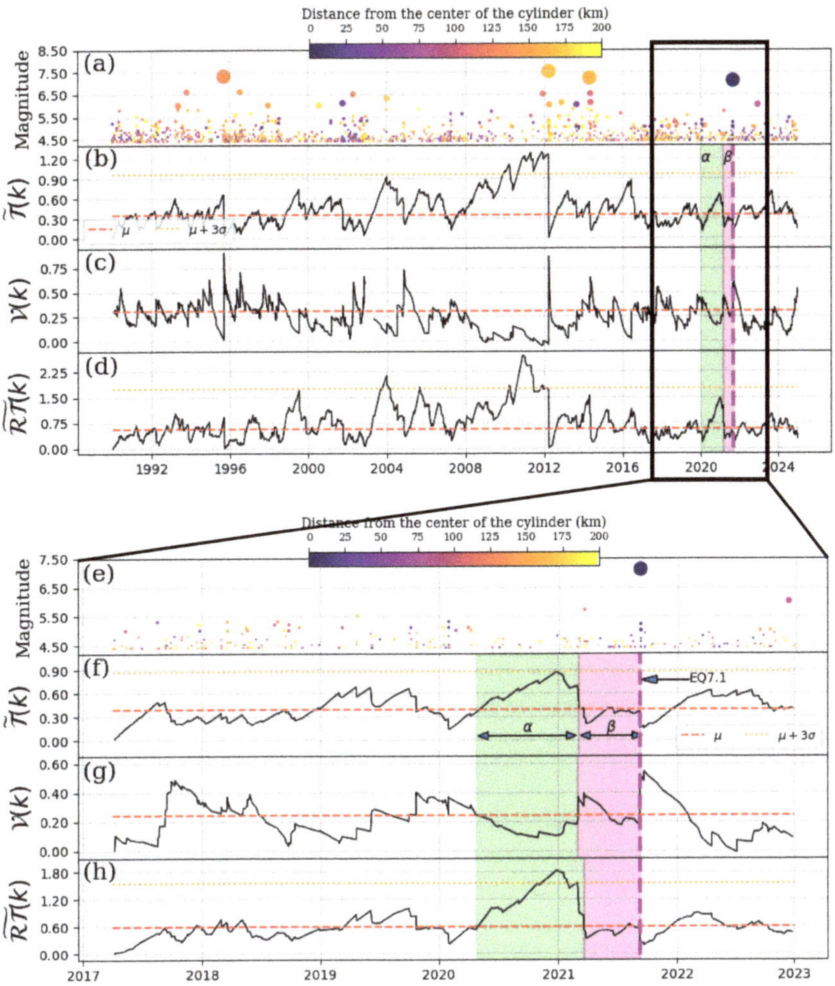

Figure 9. Schreider convolution for *EQ*7.1, 7 September 2021. (**a**) Time series of earthquake magnitudes in the cylindrical region with a threshold magnitude of $M_{th} = 4.4$. The coloration of the circles is indicative of the distance between the center of the cylinder and the epicenter of each earthquake, while the size of the circles corresponds to the earthquake magnitude. (**b**) Inter-time series $\widetilde{\mathcal{T}}(k)$, (**c**) pseudo-velocity series $\widetilde{\mathcal{V}}(k)$, and (**d**) the product of inter-distance with inter-time $\widetilde{\mathcal{RT}}(k)$ series. The cylinder used has a radius of 200 km and a depth within the range of [0, 60] km. Panels (**e**–**h**) zoom in on a segment of the time series shown in panels (**a**–**d**). The red dashed line shows the mean of the convolution of each series, the orange dotted line is three times the standard deviation of the new segment, the magenta dashed vertical line indicates the date of the mainshock, the shaded green and magenta regions corresponds to the α and β stages, respectively.

The eight earthquakes presented in this article were thoroughly analyzed after they occurred. However, the procedure used (based on the Schreider method [8] with modifications proposed by us) can also be applied a priori in seismically active zones. We published a first step with a predictive approach in 2015 [14]. In that article [14], we investigated seismic quiescence over a period of nearly 27 years, observing 19 regions of quiescence, only three of which were significant precursors. In this same paper, however, we proposed a clear criterion to identify false alarms involving quiescence period durations and the level of convolutions considered statistically significant (see [14]).

5.4. Statistical Significance

We also evaluate the significance of our findings using the following method: We generate 1000 surrogates by randomly shuffling the inter-time, pseudo-velocity, and distance-time sequences and calculate the 95% confidence band. A state of persistent quiescence is identified if it exceeds the $\mu + 3\sigma$ threshold and persists for a minimum of three successive intertimes. We confirm that, for randomized data from inter-times from all cases analyzed, the average values of $\widetilde{\mathcal{T}}(k)$ show relatively constant behavior, indicating uncorrelated temporal variation. For reference, see Section S4 of the Supplementary Materials; We observe that, in all cases, the actual data are clearly outside the confidence band, and $\widetilde{\mathcal{T}}(k)$ fully intersect with the confidence band in regions outside the alpha and beta periods. This indicates that these time intervals are indistinguishable from the surrogate distribution. Other details of the statistical analysis performed can be seen online in the Supplementary Materials.

6. Concluding Remarks

Without contradicting the affirmations of seismology that earthquakes cannot be predicted, our results provide evidence of quiescence patterns which were associated with eight earthquakes of magnitude $M > 7$ on the Pacific Coast of Mexico from 2012 until 2022. The new implementation of *pseudo-velocity* $\mathcal{V}$ and *Time-Space* function $\mathcal{RT}$ as series for Schreider convolution provides new features that complement the original Schreider algorithm [8]. Our results regarding temporal convolution are in general agreement with those reported in studies of the Central Iran region [23]. For the case of pseudo-velocity convolution series $\mathcal{V}$, we note that most of the time their values are below the mean $\overline{\mathcal{V}}$ until a quiescence pattern appears. Here, the convolution of pseudo-velocity decreases relative to its mean value $\overline{\mathcal{V}}$, which agrees with the Schreider hypothesis [8] identifying a decreasing seismic rate for a temporal period (the α-stage defined by Ohtake [5]) as a seismic precursor. Then, when the mainshock occurs, a brief increase of $\mathcal{V}$ happens, and its values return to its initial behavior. This feature was consistently observed in all the cases reported in this work, and we also noted that its dynamics were recovered almost instantaneously, showing the fading of the observed anomaly. If we compare this result with the convolutions $\mathcal{T}$ and $\mathcal{RT}$, this could be considered an advantage in discriminating when a seismic quiescence pattern ceases or if an immediate quiescence pattern is observed. On the other hand, the convolution related to time and space $\mathcal{RT}$ shows a generally similar behavior to that observed for the original convolution $\mathcal{T}$. Nevertheless, this new convolution $\mathcal{RT}$ revealed new features such as a (slightly) thinner form of the quiescence pattern, and in some cases, the values of $\mathcal{RT}$ exceeded the level $\mu + 3\sigma$ of this convolution in such a way that it was clearer than that observed for convolution $\mathcal{T}$.

In particular, the benefit of including the Schreider modifications (spatiotemporal variants) is that the threshold value of $\mu + 3\sigma$ is more clearly exceeded by the $\widetilde{RT}(k)$ convolutions for three of the EQs studied here: the EQ7.1, 19 September 2017; the EQ7.4, 23 June 2020; and the EQ7.1, 19 September 2017. On the other hand, by using the criteria of first-passage time [21] in the convolutions of pseudo-velocity, the durations of the α and β stages were larger and shorter, respectively, for the EQ8.2, 7 September 2017 and the EQ7.4, 23 June 2020. A tabular summary is presented online in the Section S3 of the Supplementary Materials. We assume these advantages are also due to the decrease in the seismic activity, where inter-distance ΔR plays an important role in the mechanism that possibly causes the seismic quiescence. In addition, by following the procedure of [18], we calculate the three Schreider algorithm versions presented for magnitude-threshold M_{th} in the range [4.0, 4.5] for a radius of the cylindrical region in the range [150 km, 300 km] and for smooth parameter s in the range [3, 27]. The results can be seen online in Section S5 of the Supplementary Materials; In all cases, the seismic quiescence patterns were observed satisfactorily. It is important to point out that the efficacy of the Schreider algorithm depends strongly on the selection of the threshold magnitude, M_{th}, and the size of the cylinder, which could vary from region to region. Because of this, the ranges of the parameters used in this study may not necessarily apply to other seismic zones in the world. On the other hand, the earthquake magnitude plays a critical role in different studies in the determination of seismic quiescence patterns preceding large events [17,24–29]. For the case of the Schreider algorithm, the earthquake magnitude role is part of the filtration procedure for the detection of seismic quiescence. Given the absence of specification in the seismic catalog utilized in this study regarding the magnitude type reported, a discussion is presented regarding the potential impact of the utilization of disparate magnitude scales on the outcomes of the Schreider algorithm. This discussion is accessible in the Section S7 of the Supplementary Materials; We must emphasize that using the same seismic scale would make the results of different seismic studies more accurate (see [30] for a detailed discussion of the use of different scales). However, this depends on the seismic catalogs, which do not always specify the type of magnitude scale. Nonetheless, we plan to explore the effects of homogenizing magnitude scales in future work. An important point observed in this work is the finding of possibly mixed patterns. The idea of using the Schreider algorithm just after a mainshock has not been sufficiently explored. Here, we proposed to restart the calculation of the Schreider algorithm; however, this implies that the data has an insufficient temporal duration for detecting the new background seismicity level of the studied region. We remark that earthquakes cannot be predicted, in the sense that neither the exact time of occurrence nor the precise location can be predicted. However, this work provides evidence that seismic precursors could be considered as a complement to the evaluation of the short-term seismic hazard. Future work could enhance or strengthen Schreider's algorithm by integrating modern spatiotemporal data mining methods that better capture the complex spatial and temporal dependencies of seismic data. For example, better use of cell-based spatial segmentation combined with time-sequence analysis could allow for more accurate detection of quiescence patterns in distinct regions with significant seismic activity. Seismic precursors have been found in seismic data, electric and magnetic fields, gas/aerosol emissions, outgoing long-wave radiation, air temperature anomalies, geochemical changes, surface deformations, and unusual animal behavior [22,31–41]. Machine learning techniques have been used to identify seismic features for seismic prediction and/or earthquake forecasting [42,43]. The seismic hazard forecast has been explored using spatial and temporal features of earthquake catalogs, with satisfactory results [44]. The main limitation is the data training, which generally has only a few major events (M > 7) [45], and the reported seismic periodicity for large earthquakes is too long [46]. Recent efforts for seismic quiescence have used techniques such as the ZMAP method [47], the Poisson probability map PMAP [48], anomalies using the ETAS model [49], and the RTL method [50,51]. There are also diverse techniques for identifying seismic quiescence [52]. Our findings contribute to these methods for studying seismic hazards.

Supplementary Materials: The following supporting information can be downloaded at: https://doi.org/10.6084/m9.figshare.29874155.v5 last accessed on 10 September 2025. References [53–55] are citied in the Supplementary Materials.

Author Contributions: Conceptualization, C.C.-V., L.G.-V., and F.A.-B.; methodology, C.C.-V. and F.A.-B.; software, C.C.-V.; validation, J.P.-O., I.R.-R., L.G.-V., and F.A.-B.; formal analysis, C.C.-V., L.G.-V., and F.A.-B.; investigation, C.C.-V., J.P.-O., I.R.-R., L.G.-V., and F.A.-B.; resources, C.C.-V. and J.P.-O.; data curation, C.C.-V.; writing—original draft preparation, C.C.-V.; writing—review and editing, C.C.-V., J.P.-O., L.G.-V., and F.A.-B.; visualization, C.C.-V., L.G.-V., and F.A.-B.; supervision, L.G.-V. and F.A.-B.; project administration, L.G.-V. and F.A.-B.; funding acquisition, C.C.-V., J.P.-O., L.G.-V., and F.A.-B. All authors have read and agreed to the published version of the manuscript.

Funding: This research received no external funding.

Data Availability Statement: The data used in this study are available from the official website of the Servicio Sismológico Nacional de la Universidad Nacional Autónoma de México at www.ssn.unam.mx (last accessed date: 6 March 2025). The Python (version 3.12.3) code for the calculation of the original and modified version of the Schreider algorithm presented in this work can be found at: https://github.com/carrizales90/Schreider-Algorithm (last accessed date: 10 September 2025).

Acknowledgments: This work was supported by SECIHTI (México).

Conflicts of Interest: The authors declare no conflicts of interest.

Abbreviation

The following abbreviation is used in this manuscript:

EQ(s) Earthquake(s)

References

1. Richards, P.G.; Simpson, D.W. (Eds.) *Earthquake Prediction: An International Review*; American Geophysical Union: Washington, DC, USA, 1981.
2. Keilis-Borok, V.; Shebalin, P. (Eds.) *Dynamics of the Lithosphere and Earthquake Prediction*; Elsevier: Amsterdam, The Netherlands, 1999; Volume 111, pp. 179–327.
3. Varotsos, P.A.; Sarlis, N.V.; Nagao, T. Complexity measure in natural time analysis identifying the accumulation of stresses before major earthquakes. *Sci. Rep.* **2024**, *14*, 30828. [CrossRef]
4. Zaccagnino, D.; Telesca, L.; Tan, O.; Doglioni, C. Clustering analysis of seismicity in the Anatolian region with implications for seismic hazard. *Entropy* **2023**, *25*, 835. [CrossRef]
5. Ohtake, M.; Matumoto, T.; Latham, G.V. Seismicity gap near Oaxaca, southern Mexico as a probable precursor to a large earthquake. In *Stress in the Earth*; Birkhäuser: Basel, Switzerland, 1977; pp. 375–385.
6. Ohtake, M. Earthquake prediction based on the seismic gap with special reference to the 1978, Oaxaca, Mexico earthquake. *Rept. Natl. Cent. Disaster Prev.* **1980**, *23*, 65–110.
7. Ohtake, M.; Matumoto, T.; Latham, G.V. Evaluation of the forecast of the 1978 Oaxaca, southern Mexico earthquake based on a precursory seismic quiescence. *Earthq. Predict. Int. Rev.* **1981**, *4*, 53–61.
8. Schreider, S.Y. Formal definition of premonitory seismic quiescence. *Phys. Earth Planet. Inter.* **1990**, *61*, 113–127. [CrossRef]
9. Lay, T.; Kanamori, H.; Ruff, L. *The Asperity Model and the Nature of Large Subduction Zone Earthquakes*; Terra Scientific Publishing Company: Tokyo, Japan, 1982.
10. Wyss, M.; Habermann, R.E. Precursory seismic quiescence. *Pure Appl. Geophys.* **1988**, *126*, 319–332. [CrossRef]
11. Chen, C.C.; Wu, Y.X. An improved region—Time—Length algorithm applied to the 1999 Chi-Chi, Taiwan earthquake. *Geophys. J. Int.* **2006**, *166*, 1144–1148. [CrossRef]
12. Huang, Q. Seismicity changes prior to the Ms8.0 Wenchuan earthquake in Sichuan, China. *Geophys. Res. Lett.* **2008**, *35*, L23308. [CrossRef]
13. Rudolf-Navarro, A.H.; Muñoz-Diosdado, A.; Angulo-Brown, F. Seismic quiescence patterns as possible precursors of great earthquakes in Mexico. *Int. J. Phys. Sci* **2010**, *5*, 651–670.
14. Muñoz-Diosdado, A.; Rudolf-Navarro, A.; Angulo-Brown, F.; Barrera-Ferrer, A. Patterns of significant seismic quiescence on the Mexican Pacific coast. *Phys. Chem. Earth Parts A/B/C* **2015**, *85*, 119–130.
15. Mogi, K. Two kinds of seismic gaps. *Pure Appl. Geophys.* **1979**, *117*, 1172–1186. [CrossRef]
16. Mogi, K. *Earthquake Prediction*; Academic Press: Orlando, FL, USA, 1985.
17. Wyss, M.; Sobolev, G.; Clippard, J.D. Seismic quiescence precursors to two M7 earthquakes on Sakhalin Island, measured by two methods. *Earth Planets Space* **2004**, *56*, 725–740. [CrossRef]

18. Carrizales-Velazquez, C.; Rudolf-Navarro, A.; Reyes-Ramírez, I.; Muñoz-Diosdado, A.; Guzmán-Vargas, L.; Angulo-Brown, F. Multifractality of Pseudo-Velocities and Seismic Quiescence Associated with the Tehuantepec M8.2 EQ. *Entropy* **2018**, *20*, 961. [CrossRef] [PubMed]
19. Servicio Sismologico Nacional. Universidad Nacional Autónoma de México. Available online: http://www.ssn.unam.mx/ (accessed on 13 November 2024).
20. Singh, S.; Rodriguez, M.; Esteva, L. Statistics of small earthquakes and frequency of occurrence of large earthquakes along the Mexican subduction zone. *Bull. Seismol. Soc. Am.* **1983**, *73*, 1779–1796.
21. Carretero-Campos, C.; Bernaola-Galván, P.; Ivanov, P.C.; Carpena, P. Phase transitions in the first-passage time of scale-invariant correlated processes. *Phys. Rev. E—Stat. Nonlinear Soft Matter Phys.* **2012**, *85*, 011139. [CrossRef]
22. Guzmán-Vargas, L.; Carrizales-Velazquez, C.; Reyes-Ramírez, I.; Fonseca-Campos, J.; Rosa-Galindo, A.d.l.; Quintana-Moreno, V.O.; Peralta, J.A.; Angulo-Brown, F. A comparative study of geoelectric signals possibly associated with the occurrence of two Ms > 7 EQs in the South Pacific Coast of Mexico. *Entropy* **2019**, *21*, 1225. [CrossRef]
23. Mirabedini, M.S.; Agh-Atabai, M.; Azimmohseni, M.; Zadeh, M.A. Temporal pattern of seismicity in the Zagros belt, SW Iran. *Arab. J. Geosci.* **2021**, *14*, 1707. [CrossRef]
24. Wyss, M.; Wiemer, S. Two current seismic quiescences within 40 km of Tokyo. *Geophys. J. Int.* **1997**, *128*, 459–473. [CrossRef]
25. Wyss, M.; Hasegawa, A.; Wiemer, S.; Umino, N. Quantitative mapping of precursory seismic quiescence before the 1989, M 7.1 off-Sanriku earthquake, Japan. *Ann. Geophys.* **1999**, *42*.. [CrossRef]
26. Huang, Q.; Nagao, T. Seismic quiescence before the 2000 M = 7.3 Tottori earthquake. *Geophys. Res. Lett.* **2002**, *29*, 19–21. [CrossRef]
27. Huang, Q.; Sobolev, G.A.; Nagao, T. Characteristics of the seismic quiescence and activation patterns before the M= 7.2 Kobe earthquake, January 17, 1995. *Tectonophysics* **2001**, *337*, 99–116. [CrossRef]
28. Aden-Antóniow, F.; Satriano, C.; Bernard, P.; Poiata, N.; Aissaoui, E.M.; Vilotte, J.P.; Frank, W.B. Statistical analysis of the preparatory phase of the M w 8.1 Iquique Earthquake, Chile. *J. Geophys. Res. Solid Earth* **2020**, *125*, e2019JB019337. [CrossRef]
29. Derode, B.; Madariaga, R.; Campos, J. Seismic rate variations prior to the 2010 Maule, Chile MW 8.8 giant megathrust earthquake. *Sci. Rep.* **2021**, *11*, 2705. [CrossRef]
30. Das, R.; Das, A. Limitations of Mw and M Scales: Compelling evidence advocating for the das magnitude scale (Mwg)—A critical review and analysis. *Indian Geotech. J.* **2025**, 1–19.. [CrossRef]
31. Bhardwaj, A.; Sam, L.; Martin-Torres, F. The challenges and possibilities of earthquake predictions using non-seismic precursors. *Eur. Phys. J. Spec. Top.* **2021**, *230*, 367–380. [CrossRef]
32. Guo, G.; Wang, B. Cloud anomaly before Iran earthquake. *Int. J. Remote Sens.* **2008**, *29*, 1921–1928. [CrossRef]
33. Eleftheriou, A.; Filizzola, C.; Genzano, N.; Lacava, T.; Lisi, M.; Paciello, R.; Pergola, N.; Vallianatos, F.; Tramutoli, V. Long-term RST analysis of anomalous TIR sequences in relation with earthquakes occurred in Greece in the period 2004–2013. *Pure Appl. Geophys.* **2016**, *173*, 285–303. [CrossRef]
34. Alvan, H.V.; Azad, F.H.; Mansor, S. Latent heat flux and air temperature anomalies along an active fault zone associated with recent Iran earthquakes. *Adv. Space Res.* **2013**, *52*, 1678–1687. [CrossRef]
35. Borghi, A.; Aoudia, A.; Riva, R.E.; Barzaghi, R. GPS monitoring and earthquake prediction: A success story towards a useful integration. *Tectonophysics* **2009**, *465*, 177–189. [CrossRef]
36. Cao, K.; Huang, Q. Geo-sensor (s) for potential prediction of earthquakes: Can earthquake be predicted by abnormal animal phenomena? *Ann. GIS* **2018**, *24*, 125–138. [CrossRef]
37. Paudel, S.R.; Banjara, S.P.; Wagle, A.; Freund, F.T. Earthquake chemical precursors in groundwater: A review. *J. Seismol.* **2018**, *22*, 1293–1314. [CrossRef]
38. Pulinets, S.; Herrera, V.M.V. Earthquake precursors: The physics, identification, and application. *Geosciences* **2024**, *14*, 209. [CrossRef]
39. Picozza, P.; Conti, L.; Sotgiu, A. Looking for earthquake precursors from space: A critical review. *Front. Earth Sci.* **2021**, *9*, 676775. [CrossRef]
40. Mousavi, S.M.; Beroza, G.C. Machine learning in earthquake seismology. *Annu. Rev. Earth Planet. Sci.* **2023**, *51*, 105–129. [CrossRef]
41. Xiong, P.; Tong, L.; Zhang, K.; Shen, X.; Battiston, R.; Ouzounov, D.; Iuppa, R.; Crookes, D.; Long, C.; Zhou, H. Towards advancing the earthquake forecasting by machine learning of satellite data. *Sci. Total Environ.* **2021**, *771*, 145256. [CrossRef]
42. Kong, Q.; Trugman, D.T.; Ross, Z.E.; Bianco, M.J.; Meade, B.J.; Gerstoft, P. Machine learning in seismology: Turning data into insights. *Seismol. Res. Lett.* **2019**, *90*, 3–14. [CrossRef]
43. Kubo, H.; Naoi, M.; Kano, M. Recent advances in earthquake seismology using machine learning. *Earth Planets Space* **2024**, *76*, 36. [CrossRef]
44. Gitis, V.G.; Derendyaev, A.B. Machine learning methods for seismic hazards forecast. *Geosciences* **2019**, *9*, 308. [CrossRef]

45. Johnson, P.A.; Rouet-Leduc, B.; Pyrak-Nolte, L.J.; Beroza, G.C.; Marone, C.J.; Hulbert, C.; Howard, A.; Singer, P.; Gordeev, D.; Karaflos, D.; et al. Laboratory earthquake forecasting: A machine learning competition. *Proc. Natl. Acad. Sci. USA* **2021**, *118*, e2011362118. [CrossRef] [PubMed]
46. Velasco Herrera, V.M.; Rossello, E.A.; Orgeira, M.J.; Arioni, L.; Soon, W.; Velasco, G.; Rosique-De La Cruz, L.; Zúñiga, E.; Vera, C. Long-term forecasting of strong earthquakes in north America, south America, Japan, southern China and northern India with machine learning. *Front. Earth Sci.* **2022**, *10*, 905792. [CrossRef]
47. Katsumata, K. A Long-Term Seismic Quiescence before the 2004 Sumatra (M w 9.1) Earthquake. *Bull. Seismol. Soc. Am.* **2015**, *105*, 167–176. [CrossRef]
48. Katsumata, K.; Zhuang, J. A new method for imaging seismic quiescence and its application to the M w= 8.3 Kurile islands earthquake on 15 November 2006. *Pure Appl. Geophys.* **2020**, *177*, 3619–3630. [CrossRef]
49. Chingtham, P.; Sharma, B. Detection of seismic quiescences before 1991 Uttarkashi (M w 6.8) and 1999 Chamoli M w (6.6) earthquakes and its implications for stress change sensor. *Acta Geophys.* **2022**, *70*, 509–523. [CrossRef]
50. Gentili, S.; Di Giovambattista, R.; Peresan, A. Seismic quiescence preceding the 2016 central Italy earthquakes. *Phys. Earth Planet. Int.* **2017**, *272*, 27–33. [CrossRef]
51. Nagao, T.; Takeuchi, A.; Nakamura, K. A new algorithm for the detection of seismic quiescence: Introduction of the RTM algorithm, a modified RTL algorithm. *Earth Planets Space* **2011**, *63*, 315–324. [CrossRef]
52. Katsumata, K.; Nakatani, M. Testing the seismic quiescence hypothesis through retrospective trials of alarm-based earthquake prediction in the Kurile–Japan subduction zone. *Earth Planets Space* **2021**, *73*, 100. [CrossRef]
53. Aki, K. A probabilistic synthesis of precursory phenomena. *Earthq. Predict. Int. Rev.* **1981**, *4*, 566–574.
54. Perinelli, A.; Ricci, L.; Santis, A.D.; Iuppa, R. Earthquakes unveil the global-scale fractality of the lithosphere. *Commun. Earth Environ.* **2024**, *5*, 146. [CrossRef]
55. Eluyemi, A.A.; Baruah, S.; Baruah, S. Empirical relationships of earthquake magnitude scales and estimation of guttenberg–richter parameters in gulf of guinea region. *Sci. Afr.* **2019**, *6*, e00161. [CrossRef]

Disclaimer/Publisher's Note: The statements, opinions and data contained in all publications are solely those of the individual author(s) and contributor(s) and not of MDPI and/or the editor(s). MDPI and/or the editor(s) disclaim responsibility for any injury to people or property resulting from any ideas, methods, instructions or products referred to in the content.

entropy

MDPI

Article

Physical and Statistical Pattern of the Thiva (Greece) 2020–2022 Seismic Swarm

Filippos Vallianatos [1,2,*], Eirini Sardeli [1], Kyriaki Pavlou [1] and Andreas Karakonstantis [1]

[1] Section of Geophysics-Geothermics, Department of Geology and Geoenvironment, National and Kapodistrian University of Athens, 15784 Athens, Greece; eirsard@geol.uoa.gr (E.S.); kpavlou@geol.uoa.gr (K.P.); akarakon@geol.uoa.gr (A.K.)

[2] Institute of Physics of Earth's Interior and Geohazards, UNESCO Chair on Solid Earth Physics and Geohazards Risk Reduction, Hellenic Mediterranean University Research & Innovation Center, 73133 Chania, Greece

* Correspondence: fvallian@geol.uoa.gr

Abstract: On 2 December 2020, an earthquake with a magnitude of M_w 4.5 occurred near the city of Thiva (Greece). The aftershock sequence, triggered by ruptures on or near the Kallithea fault, continued until January 2021. Seven months later, new seismic activity began a few kilometers west of the initial events, with the swarm displaying a general trend of spatiotemporal migration toward the east–southeast until the middle of 2022. In order to understand the physical and statistical pattern of the swarm, the seismicity was relocated using HypoDD, and the magnitude of completeness was determined using the frequency–magnitude distribution. In order to define the existence of spatiotemporal seismicity clusters in an objective way, the DBSCAN clustering algorithm was applied to the 2020–2022 Thiva earthquake sequence. The extracted clusters permit the analysis of the spatiotemporal scaling properties of the main clusters using the Non-Extensive Statistical Physics (NESP) approach, providing detailed insights into the nature of the long-term correlation of the seismic swarm. The statistical pattern observed aligns with a Q-exponential distribution, with q_D values ranging from 0.7 to 0.8 and q_T values from 1.44 to 1.50. Furthermore, the frequency–magnitude distributions were analyzed using the fragment–asperity model proposed within the NESP framework, providing the non-additive entropic parameter (q_M). The results suggest that the statistical characteristics of earthquake clusters can be effectively interpreted using NESP, highlighting the complexity and non-additive nature of the spatiotemporal evolution of seismicity. In addition, the analysis of the properties of the seismicity clusters extracted using the DBSCAN algorithm permits the suggestion of possible physical mechanisms that drive the evolution of the two main and larger clusters. For the cluster that activated first and is located in the west–northwest part, an afterslip mechanism activated after the 2 September 2021, M 4.0 events seems to predominately control its evolution, while for the second activated cluster located in the east–southeast part, a normal diffusion mechanism is proposed to describe its migration pattern. Concluding, we can state that in the present work the application of the DBSCAN algorithm to recognize the existence of any possible spatiotemporal clustering of seismicity could be helping to provide detailed insight into the statistical and physical patterns in earthquake swarms.

Keywords: Thiva swarm; clusters; seismicity; Tsallis entropy; afterslip; diffusion; DBSCAN

https://doi.org/10.3390/e27090979

1. Introduction

The area of Thiva is located between the Gulf of Corinth and Evia (central Greece), with normal faults oriented in WNW-trending in the eastern part and ENE-trending in the western part [1,2]. Historical records show that this area experienced significant seismic activity in the 19th century. More specifically, a devastating earthquake of magnitude M 7.0 occurred in the Thiva region in 1853 [3], which affected the area between Thiva and Yliki Lake. The next significant seismic event was on 23 May 1893, with a magnitude of M 6.0 [4]. In addition, the earthquake of 17 October 1914, with a magnitude of M_s 6.2, caused severe damage in the city of Thiva and nearby villages [5]. Until 2020, Thiva had not witnessed any significant seismic activity in recent years. However, on 2 December 2020 at 10:54:56 UTC, an earthquake of magnitude 4.5 occurred east of the city of Thiva (Figure 1), initiating a notable series of earthquakes that persisted until June 2022. The 2020 seismic events were concentrated mainly in the eastern part of the study area, occurring along a system of normal faults. The mainshock and the aftershocks were caused by ruptures on or near the Kallithea fault, which dips SW [6,7]. Subsequently, heightened seismic activity commenced on 10 June 2021, with significant events on 11 July 2021, 20 July 2021, and 2 September 2021, of magnitudes M_w 4.3, 4.1, and 4.0, respectively. The seismic activity on 10 July 2021, started at the western part of the swarm, and the following seismic events demonstrated a general trend for spatiotemporal migration towards east–southeast. The final significant event occurred on 10 April 2022, with a magnitude of M_w 4.4.

In the present study, a clustering algorithm is initially applied to the 2020–2022 earthquake sequence of Thiva (Greece) to identify the existence of spatiotemporal clusters and to support the validation of underlying mechanisms that drive seismicity in each cluster. Particularly, the DBSCAN algorithm [8] is utilized, which detects clusters in extensive databases by identifying regions of high point density while treating isolated or sparsely populated points as noise. Nevertheless, a different approach to the DBSCAN algorithm is presented, which intends to identify high-density regions in large datasets while treating isolated events as noise. Our modified approach further allows the recognition of clusters that are correlated in both space and time. Before the clustering algorithm was applied, the hypocenters were relocated using the HypoDD code [9] for a more accurate insight into the seismicity distribution. Furthermore, the frequency–magnitude distribution in terms of Gutenberg–Richter is used to calculate the magnitude of completeness (M_c). The clustering algorithm, including seismic events equal to and above the M_c, is applied to the catalog to ensure more accurate results. Subsequently, we selected the two largest clusters out of the five for further analysis. Afterwards, the spatiotemporal scaling properties of the two largest clusters were analyzed, using the Non-Extensive Statistical Physics (NESP) framework. This innovative approach, as developed by Tsallis [10] and extensively applied in geosciences [11–14] and references therein, aims to provide more detailed insights into the nature of the long-term correlation of the earthquake generation process. Hence, the fragment–asperity model, along with the distribution of inter-event times and distances between the successive events, is analyzed within the framework of Non-Extensive Statistical Physics (NESP), providing the non-additive entropic parameters (q_T, q_D, and q_M) [11]. In addition, possible physical mechanisms that drive the evolution of the two main and larger clusters are suggested. For the first cluster, an afterslip mechanism activated after the 2 September 2021, M 4.0 events seems to control its evolution, while for the second cluster, a normal diffusion mechanism is proposed to describe its migration pattern.

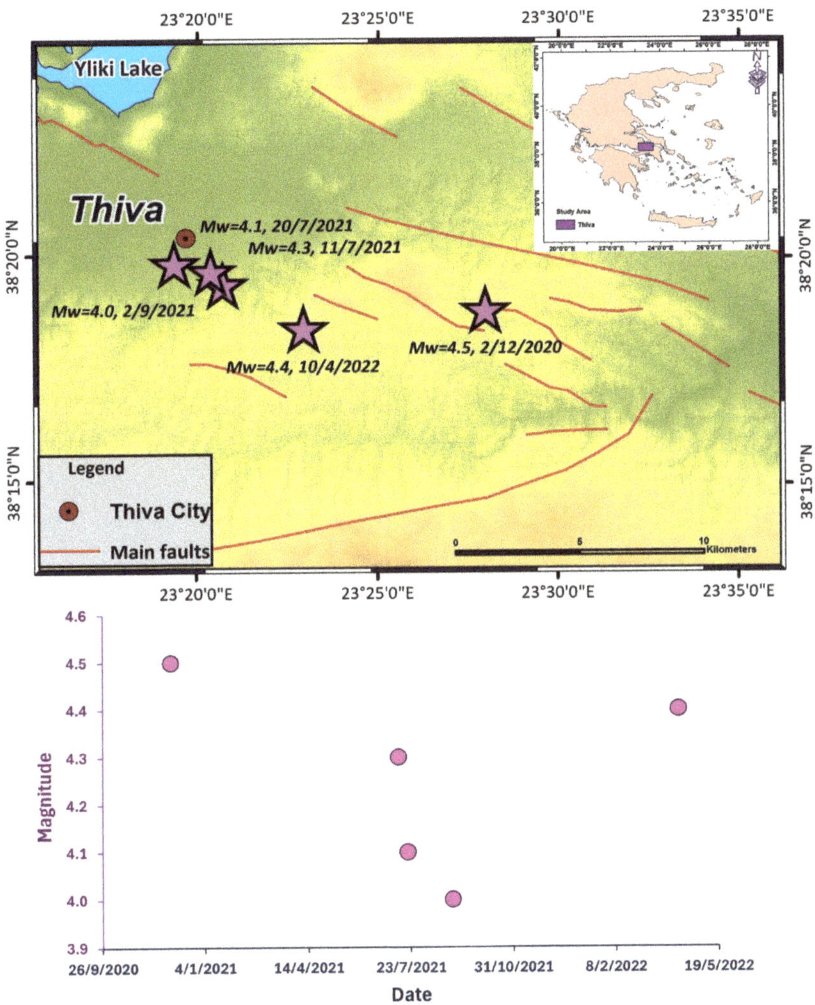

Figure 1. (**Up**) The spatial distribution of major seismic events (purple stars)in Thiva from 25 November 2020 to 1 July 2022. Faults are marked with red lines [7]. (**Down**) The temporal evolution of the major seismic events.

2. Seismological Data

2.1. Relocation Using HypoDD

The earthquake catalog for the 2020–2022 Thiva earthquake swarm was extracted from the Seismological Laboratory of the National and Kapodistrian University of Athens (SL-NKUA) for the period between 25 November 2020 and 13 June 2022. During this period, the catalog includes 4711 events with depths ranging from 0 to 30 km.

The above catalog was used in the relocation procedure. In the first stage of the sequence analysis, hypocenters were located in near real-time using a single-event program, such as HypoInverse [15], along with a custom regional 1D velocity model [16]. The final catalog was processed using HypoDD, a double-difference algorithm [17] that minimizes the double-difference residuals for pairs of earthquakes at each station by weighted least squares, employing the conjugate gradients method (LSQR, [18]).

In the Thiva area, 4182 out of 4711 events of the initial catalog were relocated using HypoDD. The relocated catalog refers to the period between 25 November 2020 and 13 June 2022, consisting of events with a depth distribution between 0 and 30 km and magnitudes of M_w 0–4.5 (Figure 2).

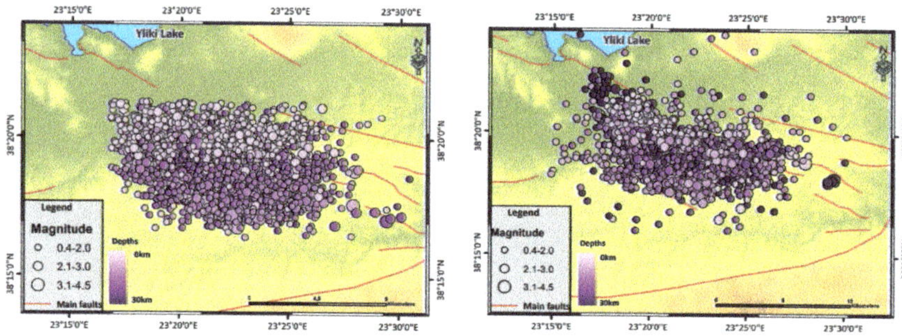

(**a**) (**b**)

Figure 2. (**a**) Initial location of the 2020–2022 Thiva earthquake sequence in comparison with (**b**) the relocated events using HypoDD of the 2020–2022 Thiva earthquake sequence that occurred between 25 November 2020 and 13 June 2022. Faults are marked with red lines [7].

2.2. Catalogue Completeness

The well-known Gutenberg–Richter [19] scaling relation (G-R) indicates a power law behavior and is defined as follows:

$$\log N(> M) = a - bM \quad (1)$$

where $N(> M)$ represents the number of earthquakes with magnitude greater than M, and α and b are positive constants. The α value reflects the total seismicity rate and shows significant variations from one area to another. The parameter b, also known as the b value, is the slope of the frequency–magnitude distribution (FMD) and indicates the proportion of minor to major earthquakes. The b value in Equation (1) can be estimated by maximum likelihood using the equation [20–22] $b = \left(\frac{loge}{\overline{M}-M_{min}}\right)$, where $\overline{M}$ is the observed mean magnitude and Mmin is the minimum magnitude of the given sample.

The magnitude of completeness, M_c, is a crucial parameter in seismicity studies and is obtained after a correction of $Mmin = Mc - \Delta M/2$, where ΔM is the binning width of the catalog (often set to 0.1) [20,22–24]. A correct estimation of the b value depends on M_c. In this study, the magnitude of completeness M_c was estimated using a combination of the maximum curvature method and the goodness-of-fit test with 95% and 90% residuals [24]. The calculation was performed using the Zmap software package, version 7.0 [25].

The FMD for the 2020–2022 Thiva Earthquake Swarm is depicted in Figure 3, along with the fitting according to the G-R scaling relation for the calculated model parameters. The estimated values are α = 4.885, b-value = 0.98 ± 0.02, and M_c = 1.6.

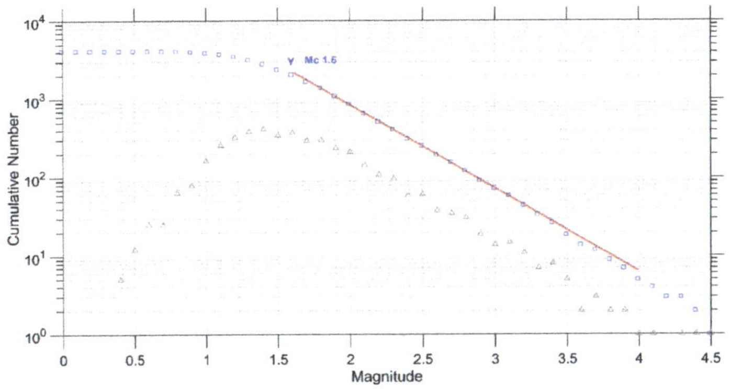

Figure 3. The frequency–magnitude distribution for the 2020–2022 Thiva Earthquake Swarm and the estimated M_c is plotted, showing both the cumulative (blue squares) and the discrete (gray triangles) frequency–magnitude distributions. The red solid line represents the G-R relation.

3. Analysis of Seismicity and Discussion

3.1. The DBSCAN Algorithm Results

DBSCAN (Density-Based Spatial Clustering of Application with Noise) [8] is recognized as one of the most powerful clustering methods, selected for its capability to analyze huge datasets effectively, and has a significant application in seismology [26–28]. The purpose of DBSCAN is to identify clusters of arbitrary shapes in extensive databases containing noise, using a density-based approach. The algorithm is based on the following input parameters: (a) the ε (epsilon value or eps), the distance (radius) around a given point, and (b) MinPoints (minimum number of samples or MinPts), the minimum number of points (including the point itself) that should be within the epsilon distance. These parameters are the same for all clusters.

The value of epsilon (ε) can be determined from the k-distance graph. This graph is constructed by plotting the distance to the kth nearest neighbor for each point in descending order [8]. The point on the graph where maximum curvature (elbow) is observed indicates the optimal value for epsilon. According to Ester et al. [8], the minimum number of points can be set to twice the number of dimensions, i.e., four points for 2D data, six points for 3D data, and eight points for 4D data.

In this study, the DBSCAN was utilized for the spatio-temporal clustering analysis of the 2020–2022 Thiva earthquake swarm. In addition to the three spatial dimensions (latitude, longitude, and depth), a fourth dimension, date–time, was added. The algorithm was applied to the relocated catalog of Thiva, which contains 2079 earthquake events with $M \geq M_c$ between 25 November 2020, and 13 June 2022.

The epsilon value was specified from the k-distance graph [8] (Figure 4a), with the optimal epsilon value for the Thiva earthquake catalog set at 0.044. Furthermore, the value of MinPts was set to 8, and a normalized Euclidean distance was applied to the spatial and temporal width of the four-dimensional data. The temporal outcome of the DBSCAN algorithm is illustrated in Figure 4b, showing the evolution of events with time, counting in days since 2 December 2020. Event distances in Figure 4b are calculated from an initial point at latitude 38.35 N and longitude 23.28 E, which is located at the western edge of the earthquake swarm. In Figure 4c the spatial distribution of clusters is presented, while in Figure 4d the magnitude–date distribution of the events, along with the cluster to which they belong, is demonstrated. The algorithm provided 5 clusters (see Table 1) and detected 366 noise points as a separate cluster, which were not part of any of the clusters due to being either too isolated or not densely connected to other points.

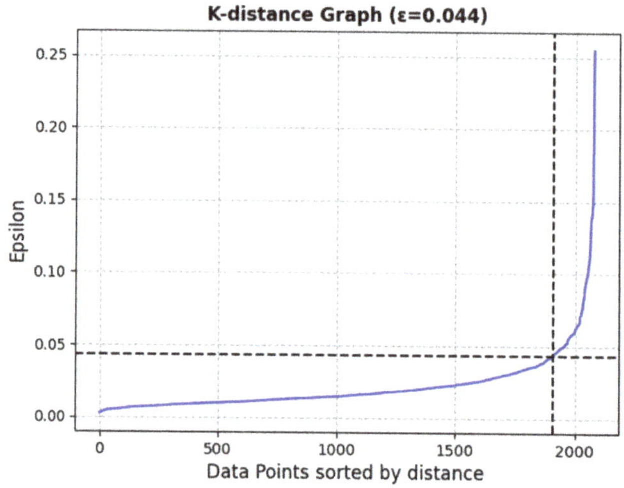

(a)

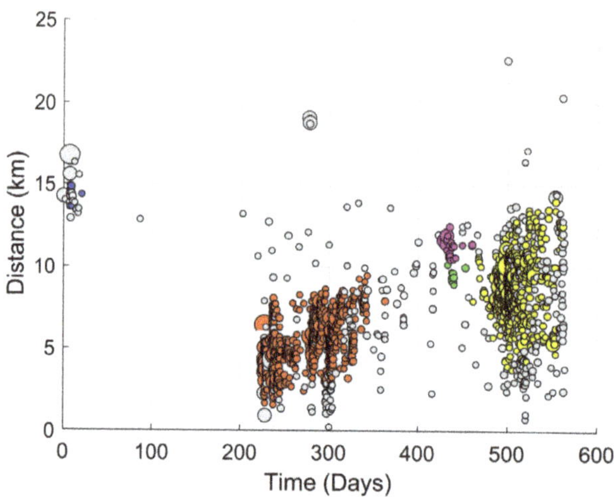

(b)

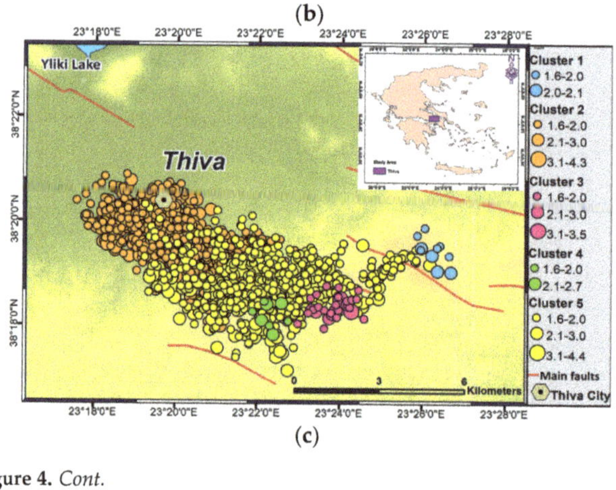

(c)

Figure 4. *Cont.*

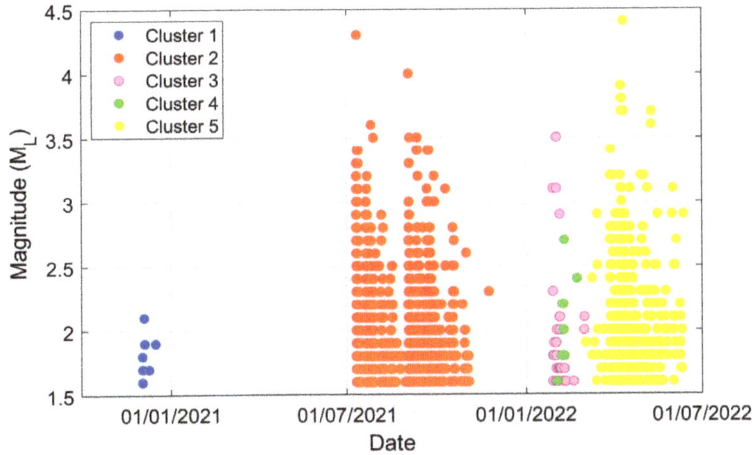

(d)

Figure 4. (**a**) The k-distance graph (k = 4 in our case) for the 2020–2022 Thiva earthquake sequence, with the threshold point indicated by the black dashed lines. (**b**) The distance–time plot showing the five clusters identified by the DBSCAN algorithm. The blue, orange, purple, green, and yellow dots correspond to clusters 1, 2, 3, 4, and 5, respectively. The gray dots represent the noise points. (**c**) Seismicity map of Thiva illustrating the identified earthquake clusters. The seismic events are categorized by size and color based on their magnitude and cluster number. (**d**) The magnitude–date distribution for the different events and the clusters observed.

Table 1. Clusters identified, their duration, and the number of events classified using the DBSCAN algorithm in the Thiva earthquake swarm catalog.

Clusters	Period Time	Events
Cluster 1	2 December2020–15 December 2020	10
Cluster 2	1 July 2021–23 November 2021	1018
Cluster 3	28 January 2022–1 March 2022	32
Cluster 4	1 February 2022–21 February 2022	9
Cluster 5	2 March 2022–10 June 2022	644

Among the five clusters recognized (see Table 1), two of them had a predominant importance since the majority of seismicity was located within these two clusters. Cluster 2 includes 1081 events, while Cluster 5 includes 644.

3.2. A Non-Extensive Statistical Physics Approach (NESP)

Earthquakes exhibit intricate phenomenology characterized by a fractal structure. These complex systems, with strongly correlated elements, typically exhibit power-law behavior. Consequently, the statistical mechanics description of such systems appears better represented by a generalized framework introduced by Tsallis [29,30] known as Non-Extensive Statistical Physics (NESP), which generalizes Boltzmann–Gibbs statistical mechanics.

Non-Extensive Statistical Physics (NESP) offers a more suitable approach for analyzing complex dynamic systems. It is based on a non-additive entropy, denoted as S_q (commonly referred to as Tsallis entropy). This entropy is expressed through the following integral formulation:

$$S_q = k_B \frac{1 - \int_0^\infty p^q(X)dX}{q-1} \tag{2}$$

where k_B represents Boltzmann's constant, while the entropic index q characterizes the degree of non-additivity in the system. This is particularly relevant for complex systems that deviate from the additive nature of classical Boltzmann–Gibbs (BG) entropy. The given expression for S_q applies to a continuous variable X, described by a probability distribution $p(X)$, where $0 \leq p(X) \leq 1$.

3.2.1. Frequency–Magnitude Distribution of Earthquake Clusters in Terms of NESP

Sotolongo-Costa and Posadas [31], based on the fragment–asperity model, proposed a physical model for the earthquake frequency–size distribution. In [31] an energy-distribution function was introduced, and it was illustrated how the size distribution of fragments affects the energy distribution of earthquakes, using the non-extensive formalism (NESP), extracting the Gutenberg–Richter law as a particular case. Long-range interactions between all parts of existing fragments are expected due to the material's severe fragmentation, implying the need for Non-Extensive Statistical Physics. According to Telesca [11], the following modified function that connects the cumulative number of earthquakes with the magnitude was established based on the Non-Extensive Statistical Physics theory:

$$log\left(\frac{N(>M)}{N}\right) = \frac{2-q_M}{1-q_M} log\left(\frac{1-\left(\frac{1-q_M}{2-q_M}\right)\left(\frac{10^M}{A^{2/3}}\right)}{1-\left(\frac{1-q_M}{2-q_M}\right)\left(\frac{10^{M_c}}{A^{2/3}}\right)}\right) \tag{3}$$

where M is the earthquake magnitude, M_c is the completeness magnitude, and A is a parameter proportional to the volumetric energy density. In the fragment–asperity model, the non-extensive parameter q_M indicates the degree of interactions within the system's elements [14,31–33]. As a result, an increase in q_M shows that the physical condition of a seismic region is moving away from equilibrium.

The normalized cumulative magnitude distribution of the Unified Cluster and the two main clusters (Cluster 2 and Cluster 5) is examined using the NESP model of Equation (3), for the entire range of magnitudes above a threshold equivalent to the completeness magnitude. The Unified Cluster involves the 1713 seismic events from the five DBSCAN clusters.

The model satisfactorily describes the observed magnitude distribution for each cluster. In Figure 5, the bold purple line represents the distribution function of Equation (2) for the estimated entropic parameter q_M, while the other two dashed lines show the 95% confidence intervals. The estimated values are presented in Table 2.

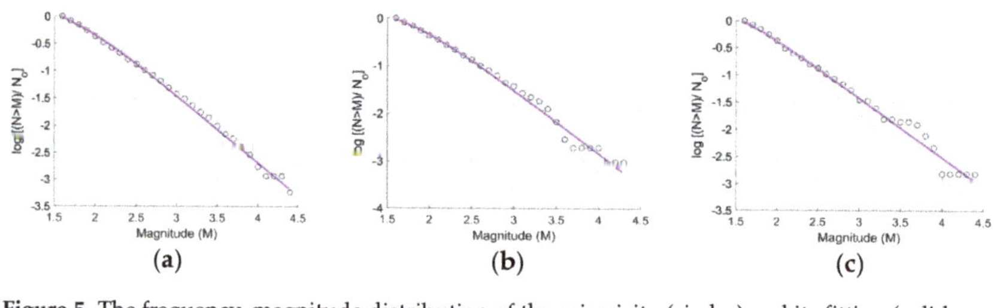

Figure 5. The frequency–magnitude distribution of the seismicity (circles) and its fitting (solid purple line) according to the fragment–asperity model for (**a**) Unified Cluster, (**b**) Cluster 2, and (**c**) Cluster 5 is presented. The 95% confidence intervals are plotted with dashed lines.

Table 2. The estimated entropic parameter q_M for each cluster (for details, see text and [11]).

Clusters	q_M
Unified Cluster	1.65 ± 0.01
Cluster 2	1.63 ± 0.02
Cluster 5	1.68 ± 0.02

3.2.2. Spatiotemporal Scaling Properties of Earthquake Clusters in Terms of NESP

Seismicity is regarded as a point process in time, where the cumulative distribution $P(>T)$ of the inter-event time $Ti = t(i+1) - t(i)$, where $t(i)$ is the time of occurrence of the ith event, and the cumulative distributions $P(>D)$ of inter-event geodetic distance D estimated using the Vincenty inverse formula for ellipsoids between the foci of successive seismic events [34] play a crucial role for the spatiotemporal pattern characterization.

Using the Tsallis entropy, the cumulative distribution function (CDF) $P(>X)$ is estimated using the Q-exponential distribution, defined for $q < 2$, where the constant X may express the inter-event times (T) or inter-event distances (D), respectively:

$$P(>X) = \left[1 - (1-Q)\left(\frac{X}{X_0}\right)\right]^{\frac{1}{1-Q}} \tag{4}$$

The Q-exponential distribution is derived through the maximization of non-additive entropy, S_q, by using the Lagrange multipliers method under relevant constraints [35]. To estimate the values of q and X_0, $q = 2 - (1/Q)$ and $X_q = X_0/Q$ are used [36]. For values of Q greater than 1, the Q-exponential distribution demonstrates asymptotic power-law behavior, while for Q equal to 1, it recovers the ordinary exponential expression.

The inverse of the Q-exponential function leads to the following Q-logarithmic function [35]:

$$ln_Q P(>X) = \frac{P(>X)^{1-Q} - 1}{1-Q} \tag{5}$$

After determining the suitable Q value that best characterizes the distribution of X, the Q-logarithmic distribution displays linearity concerning X. We first fit the observed $P(>X)$ using the Q-exponential distribution (Equation (4)) and then utilize the Q-logarithmic distribution (Equation (5)) as a goodness of linear fit between the observed data and the estimated Q-value (or q-value equivalently), as suggested by Equation (5).

For the Clusters 2 and 5 defined by the DBSCAN algorithm for the Thiva earthquake swarm, the cumulative distributions of the inter-event times $P(>T)$ between the successive earthquakes are quite well described by the Q-exponential distribution, with an entropic parameter q greater than one. The corresponding Q-logarithmic distributions demonstrate linearity with high correlation coefficients, suggesting a strong linear fit between the model and the data (Figure 6) in a wide range of interevent time values.

In Figure 7, the cumulative distributions of the inter-event distances $P(>D)$ between the successive earthquakes are presented, showing a quite good fit with the Q-exponential distribution, characterized by an entropic parameter $q_D < 1$. As Equation (5) suggests, using the proper Q value, the Q-logarithmic function is linearly related with D. In Figure 7, the corresponding Q-logarithmic distributions demonstrate linearity with high correlation coefficients, indicating a strong goodness-of-fit between the model and the data. Table 3 presents the entropic parameters q_T and q_D values for Clusters 2 and 5 along with the q values for the dataset created by the merge of them. We note that the results are in agreement with those presented in [37], indicating that within each cluster of the earthquake swarm, the temporal evolution is described by low degrees of freedom, indicating a high level of organization, hierarchy, and non-additive characteristics.

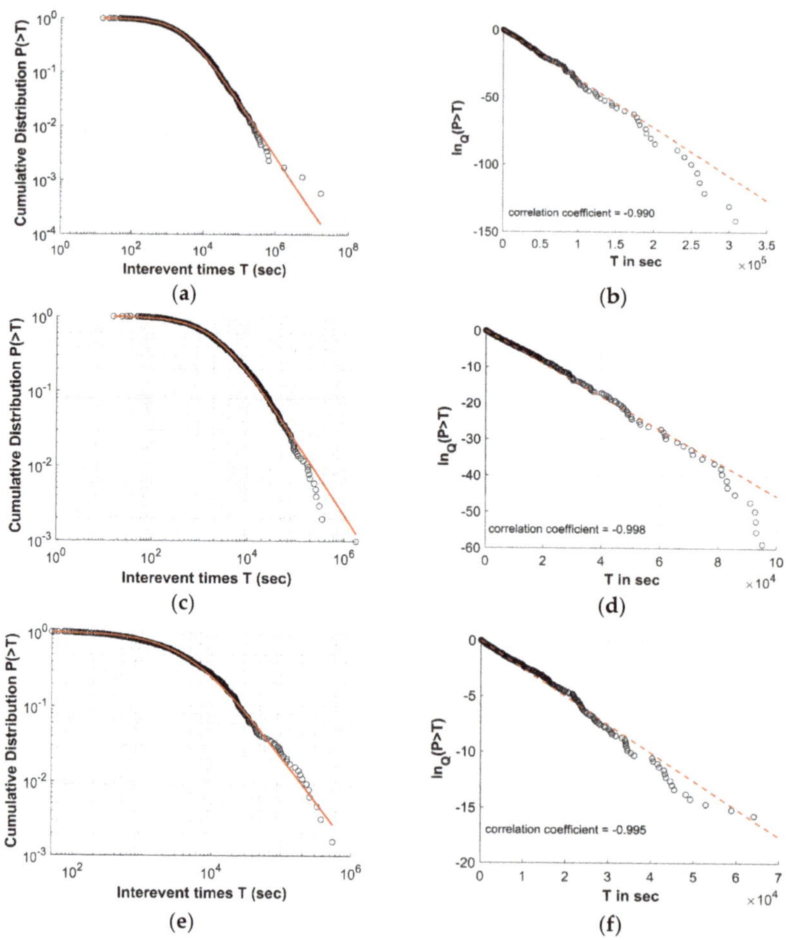

Figure 6. The left panels illustrate the log–log plot of the inter-event times cumulative distribution for the Thiva swarm, showing (**a**) Unified Cluster, (**c**) Cluster 2, and (**e**) Cluster 5. The solid brown line represents the fitting of the *Q*-exponential distribution for the q_T and Tq values. The right panels show the corresponding semi-*q*-log plot of the cumulative distribution of the inter-event times, illustrating (**b**) Unified Cluster, (**d**) Cluster 2, and (**f**) Cluster 5. The *Q*-logarithmic distributions exhibit a correlation coefficient, presented within the panels, while the dashed line is the *Q*-exponential fit.

Table 3. The estimated entropic parameters q_T and q_D, and the generalized scaled interevent time–distance, T_q and D_q, (in analogy with X_0 in Equation (4)) along with their 95% confidence intervals.

Clusters	q_T	Tq (s)	q_D	Dq (km)
Unified Cluster	1.50	1380 ± 4	0.70	2.00 ± 0.01
Cluster 2	1.50	1095 ± 3	0.80	1.45 ± 0.01
Cluster 5	1.44	2210 ± 13	0.78	2.45 ± 0.02

3.3. *Physical Model of Cluster's Evolution*

3.3.1. Coulomb Stress Changes

In recent years, Coulomb stress changes induced by earthquakes have been extensively investigated to assess their role in aftershock sequence evolution and fault interaction [37–44]. These stress variations depend on the earthquake focal mechanism, fault geometry and slip, and the effective friction coefficient, providing a framework to evaluate how major events may trigger subsequent ruptures in the near field. Empirical studies have demonstrated a strong correlation between positive Coulomb stress changes and the spatial distribution of subsequent seismicity [37,45]. Specifically, changes in Coulomb failure stress (ΔCFS) can either advance or delay fault rupture, thereby influencing the timing and spatial evolution of seismic sequences [41,46,47]. Positive ΔCFS promotes failure on a receiver fault, whereas negative ΔCFS tends to inhibit rupture.

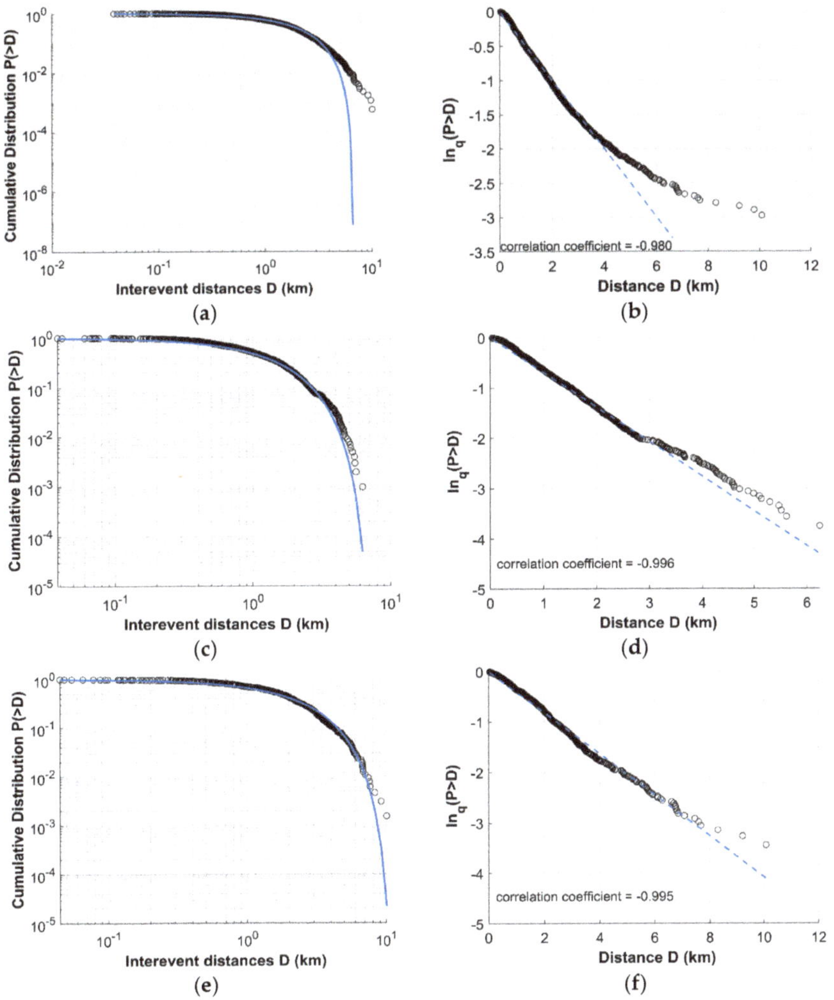

Figure 7. The left panels illustrate the log–log plot of the inter-event distances cumulative distribution for the Thiva swarm: (**a**) Unified Cluster, (**c**) Cluster 2, and (**e**) Cluster 5. The solid blue line indicates the fit of the *Q*-exponential distribution for the values of q_D and Dq. The right panels depict the corresponding semi-*q*-log plot of the cumulative distribution of the inter-event distances: (**b**) Unified Cluster, (**d**) Cluster 2, and (**f**) Cluster 5. The *Q*-logarithmic distributions exhibit a correlation coefficient, presented within the panel, while the dashed line is the *Q*-exponential fit.

Earthquakes occur when the applied stress surpasses the strength of a fault. Under undrained rock conditions, the change in Coulomb Failure Stress (ΔCFS) is evaluated using the Coulomb failure criterion, which quantifies proximity to failure and is expressed as follows [48]:

$$\Delta CFS = \Delta\tau + \mu'\Delta\sigma \tag{6}$$

where $\Delta\tau$ and $\Delta\sigma$ are the static shear stress changes and the product of effective normal stress changes, respectively, while μ' is the coefficient of friction [49]. Moreover, $\Delta\tau$ is positive for increasing shear stress on the observing fault in the direction of relative slip, while $\Delta\sigma$ is positive for increasing tensional normal stress. Failure is encouraged if ΔCFS is positive and it is discouraged if negative.

ΔCFS values were computed using Coulomb 3.3 software [50] within an elastic half-space. Positive ΔCFS, often referred to as stress bright zones, brings a fault closer to failure and increases its likelihood of rupture, whereas negative ΔCFS, or stress shadows [51, 52], moves it further from failure. Accordingly, blue regions indicate negative Coulomb stress changes and reduced rupture potential, while yellow-to-red regions denote positive changes and an elevated likelihood of rupture.

The calculated co-seismic result for the ΔCFS changes for the seismic event on 2 September 2021 of magnitude M_w 4.0 is presented in Figure 8. The focal parameters that were used for the estimation of ΔCFS are as follows: depth of 7 km, strike of 318°, dip of 33°, and rake of −61°, according to the moment tensor solutions of the Institute of Geodynamics, National Observatory of Athens "http://bbnet.gein.noa.gr/ (accessed on 2 July 2025)". The spatial distribution of the ΔCFS reveals a stress decrease towards NE and WS and a stress increase towards NW and SE, coinciding with the location of Clusters 2 and 5 (Figure 8). Notably, the M_w = 4.0 event appears to have played a key role in triggering Cluster 2, as the majority of subsequent earthquakes occurred in regions of positive Coulomb stress changes. This stress transfer brought adjacent fault segments closer to failure, promoting seismic activity. A similar pattern is observed in Cluster 5, which initiated shortly after the M_w = 4.0 event, further supporting the hypothesis of stress-driven activation. The occurrence of earthquakes in areas of increased ΔCFS motivated the investigation of aseismic processes such as afterslip and stress diffusion. We note that the above result is in agreement with that reported in [53] for the major earthquakes that occurred on 2 December 2020, where the same orientation of the positive Coulomb stress changes was observed, suggesting a stable stress transfer direction throughout the sequence.

3.3.2. Evidence of Afterslip Migration of Seismicity in Cluster 2

The spatiotemporal distribution of a swarm seismic sequence is determined by static and dynamic stresses [54] or by fluid diffusion [55]. Here, we examined the expansion of Thiva's Cluster 2 swarm over time. Perfettini et al. [56] proposed an analytical model predicting key features of this migration along strike, attributed to co-seismic deformation. According to their model, aftershock activity is governed by afterslip loading asperities, which in turn controls the seismicity rate. In this approach a fault is modeled with depth-dependent variations in normal stress, stressing rate, and the introduction of a rheological parameter A [45,56–59].

Following this approach (see details in [56,59]), the average migration of the aftershock zone becomes:

$$< \Delta L_a(t) >=< L_a(t) > -< L_a(t_1) >= \zeta A \frac{R}{\Delta\sigma} ln\left(\frac{t}{t_1}\right) \tag{7}$$

where $< \Delta L_a(t) >$ is the mean migration distance between times t_1 and t; ζ is a constant parameter (with a value close to 2.77), which scales the average gradient of the Coulomb stress along the strike; the radius of the coseismic rupture is R; and the mean coseismic stress drop is $\Delta\sigma$.

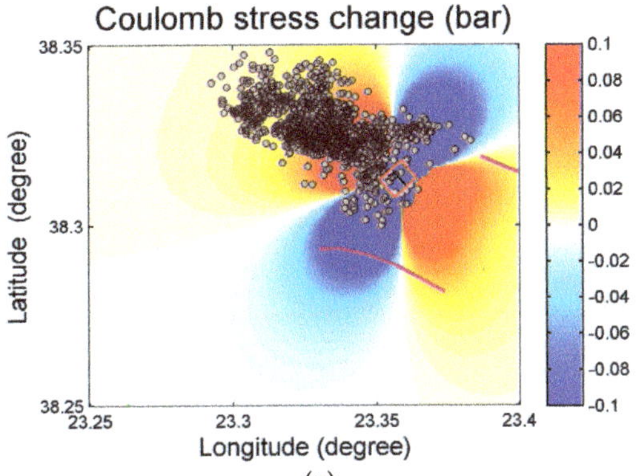

(**a**)

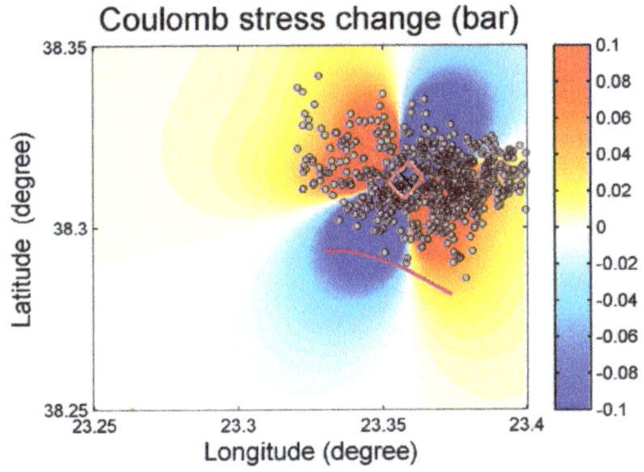

(**b**)

Figure 8. Coulomb stress changes produced by the M_w 4.0 earthquake on 2 September 2021 at a centroid depth of 7 km. The red rectangle shows the fault model for the kinematics of the M_w 4.0 event. The solid purple lines show the area faults [7], while the brown circles are the epicenters of (**a**) Cluster 2 and (**b**) Cluster 5.

Figure 9a shows the migration of seismicity following the 7 July 2021, M 4.3 event. It is obvious that Equation (7) does not describe the mean migration distance observed. In contrast, ten days after the M 4.3 event, a decrease in $< \Delta L_a(t) >$ was characterized by the mean migration distance, which is associated with an increase in microseismic activity; possibly, a forerunner indicated the preparation of a forthcoming event on 2 September 2021, with a similar size (M 4.0). Note that a similar observation is reported for the Cefalonia Island event in [59].

After the 2 September 2021, magnitude M 4.0 earthquake, the mean migration distance is calculated (see Figure 9b). The $< \Delta L_a(t) >$, which occurred a day after the M 4.0 event, presents a logarithmic with-time migration of the seismicity in agreement with Equation (7). The latter implies that the spatiotemporal evolution of Cluster 2 following the M_w = 4.0 event shows a logarithmic migration pattern over time, aligning with theoretical models of aftershock migration driven by afterslip loading asperities. This behavior indicates that the M_w = 4.0 earthquake was not only an isolated rupture but also signaled the beginning of a secondary phase of the swarm governed by aseismic slip.

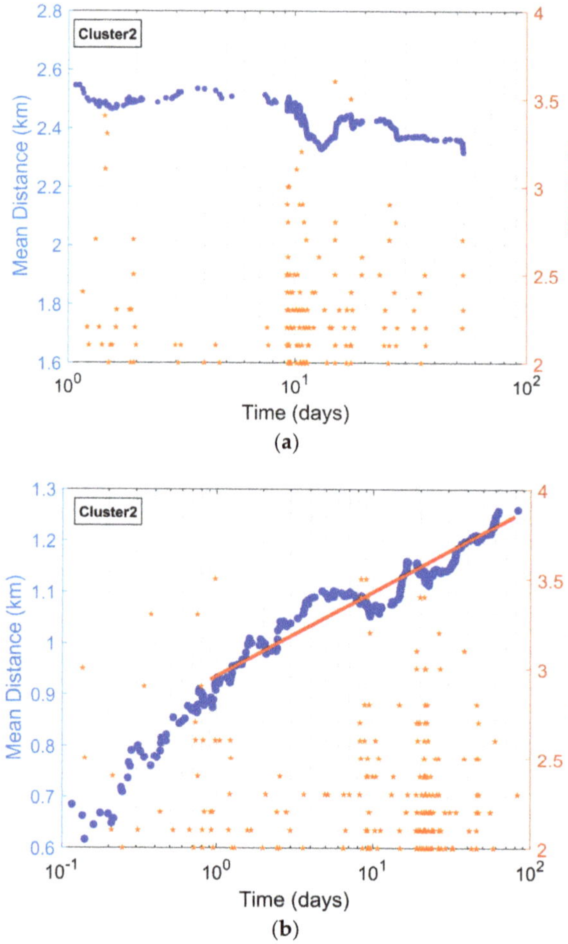

Figure 9. (**a**) The mean migration distance (blue circles in figures) as a function of the logarithm of time for Cluster 2 of Thiva, after the 7 July 2021, *M* 4.3 event. (**b**) The mean migration distance as a function of the logarithm of time for Cluster 2 of Thiva, after the 2 September 2021, *M* 4.0 earthquake. The orange stars illustrate the seismic events of magnitude over 2, while the red line in (**b**) presents the logarithmic trend in the evolution of mean migration distance.

3.3.3. Evidence of a Diffusion Process of Seismicity of Cluster 5

Among the elementary processes that underly seismic phenomena, diffusion is undoubtedly one of the most ubiquitous [60,61]. In a first approximation, diffusion is modeled by Brownian motion. In its simplest version, Brownian motion is a random walker where earthquake hypocenters move at discrete time steps and migrate ("jump") with equal probability [60]. This stochastic process can be readily generalized, with time made continuous by introducing random waiting times between jumps. Finally, the length of each jump can also be chosen at random from a continuous set with a prescribed probability distribution [61].

A typical solution to the Brownian diffusion problem shows that the width of the spatial distribution grows with time as follows:

$$< r^2 > \sim Dt \tag{8}$$

where D is the normal diffusion coefficient [60,61].

This proportionality between mean square distance and time is the fingerprint of normal diffusion, as it can be used to detect this kind of transport mechanism in a given natural process. Despite the fact that diffusion is a well-accepted transport mechanism in natural processes, it is known that at the mesoscopic level diffusion-like mechanisms, which violate Equation (8), exist and are generally referred to as anomalous diffusion [61,62]. More specifically, anomalous diffusion has been devoted to processes where, for large t, the mean square distance varies with time as follows:

$$< r^2 > \sim t^\alpha \tag{9}$$

where α is the dynamic exponent, or random walk fractal dimension, of the transport process [62].

To quantify the rate of earthquake diffusion, we used notions of the random walk theory to estimate the mean squared distance $\langle r^2(t) \rangle$ of seismicity with time. The 3D Euclidean distance r of each event is calculated from the reference point of the swarm and the estimated mean squared distance as follows [63–65]:

$$\langle r^2(t) \rangle = \frac{1}{N(t)} \sum_{n=1}^{N(t)} r_n^2(t) \tag{10}$$

where $r_n(t)$ is the distance of the nth event at time t from the origin and N is the total number of events.

As mentioned, in normal diffusion (Gaussian), the mean squared distance linearly depends on time. However, in complex heterogeneous media, other functions are encountered based on Equation (9) that take the form of a power law [62,66]:

$$\langle r^2(t) \rangle = D_a t^a \tag{11}$$

where D_a is a generalized diffusion coefficient that denotes the instantaneous response of seismicity to the diffusive process, while the diffusion exponent α can provide a quantitative measure of the rate of the triggered earthquake diffusion [67]. Normal diffusion corresponds to $\alpha = 1$. For $\alpha < 1$, the growth rate of the mean square displacement is smaller than in normal diffusion, and transport is consequently said to be subdiffusive. On the other hand, for $\alpha > 1$, the mean square displacement grows relatively faster, and transport is superdiffusive [67–70].

Taking as a reference point the mean position of the first 10 events of Cluster 5, the mean squared distance with time was estimated using Equation (10). The result is shown in Figure 10a in double-logarithmic axes. The mesoscopic scaling behavior can be approximated, for large t, with the power-law relation of Equation (11) (see Figure 10a), yielding the parameter value of $\alpha = 0.94$, with a correlation coefficient of $R^2 = 0.92$. The diffusion exponent α being quite close to 1 suggests that the swarm migration is approximately normal (Gaussian) diffusion in nature. This near-linear growth of mean square distance with time indicates that stress diffusion dominates the process, with only slight deviations from ideal diffusion behavior [63].

The observed diffusion process is usually associated with pressurized fluid migration that could generate earthquakes in the volume behind a triggering front that spreads through the fracture network, increasing pore pressure and reducing the effective normal stress on a fault plane, allowing slip to occur [71]. Within a normal diffusion mechanism, the expanding spherical triggering front of induced seismicity, in an isotropic and homogeneous medium, can be modeled with a parabolic envelope that is characteristic for pore-fluid pressure diffusion, according to the following expression [71–73]:

$$r(t) = \sqrt{4\pi D t} \tag{12}$$

where $r(t)$ is the radius of the propagating triggering front (which is a sphere in a homogenous isotropic medium) caused by pore-fluid pressure diffusion, t is the time since the beginning of the pore-pressure perturbation, and D is the hydraulic diffusivity.

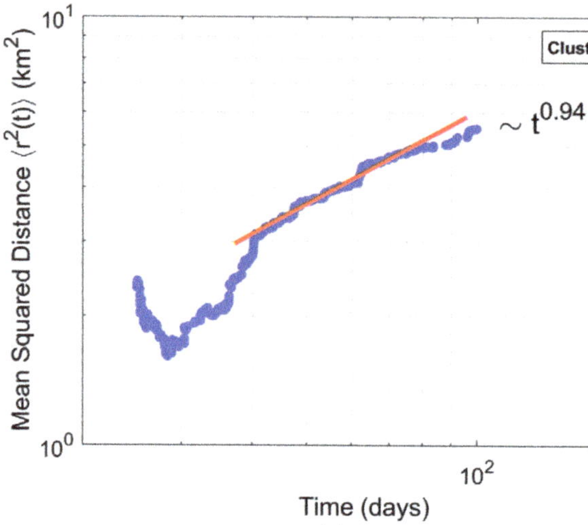

(**a**)

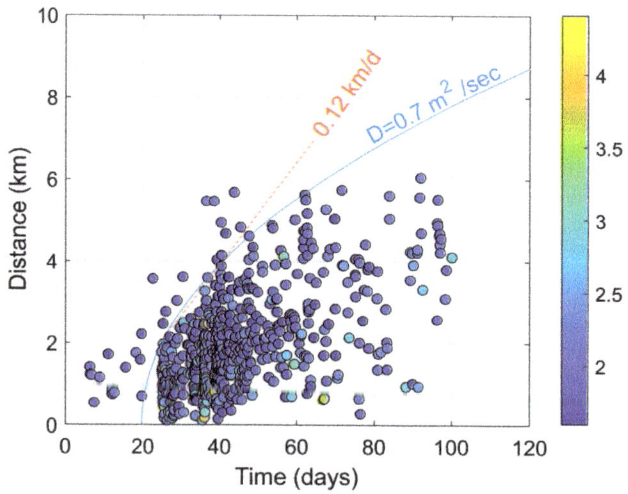

(**b**)

Figure 10. (**a**) Mean square distance $\langle r^2(t) \rangle$ of seismicity (blue circles) with time t in double logarithmic axes, for Cluster 5 of Thiva. The red line indicates the power-law growth of $\langle r^2(t) \rangle$ according to Equation (11). (**b**) Migration of Thiva's Cluster 5 (see details in text). The events are colored according to magnitude. The solid blue line represents the parabolic triggering front with D = 0.7 m^2/s, and the average initial seismicity migration speed, presented in km/day, is drawn by a dashed orange line.

Equation (12) can be considered as an equation for the earthquake triggering by a fluid-related mechanism of earthquake sequences in tectonic environments [73,74].

The diagram in Figure 10b indicates that as seismicity evolved during the first days (from 3 March 2022), the events systematically migrated away from the origin, forming a seismic front with an average initial velocity of 0.12 km/day. In addition, as can be observed, most of the migrating seismicity is located behind the parabolic triggering front envelope of hydraulic diffusivity $D = 0.7\ \mathrm{m}^2/\mathrm{s}$, although some sparse events are located on the outside, possibly triggered due to pore-fluid diffusion following paths of higher hydraulic diffusivity values [53,75,76].

The evolution of the earthquake activity follows the pore-fluid pressure triggering front with hydraulic diffusivity values ranging from 0.01 to 10 m^2/s within the Earth's crust and usually less than 1 m^2/s [75–80]. The seismic front, however, may also be described with a linear triggering front with a constant velocity of the order of 0.1 to 1 km/h. Such migration velocities are consistent with a fluid-related triggering mechanism [75], while faster velocities have been associated with an aseismic slip driving force [77–80].

At this point, we clarify that both clusters were analyzed using both models. Cluster 2 did not provide evidence for a normal diffusion mechanism, while Cluster 5 did not produce meaningful results for an afterslip mechanism.

4. Discussion

The 2020–2022 seismic sequence at Thiva includes the mainshock and aftershock sequence in December 2020 at the Kallithea fault, as well as a seismic swarm from July 2021 to June 2022 near the city of Thiva. The seismic activity began on 10 July 2021, in the western part of the swarm, with subsequent seismic events demonstrating a general trend of spatiotemporal migration towards the east–southeast. The final significant event occurred on 10 April 2022, with a magnitude of M_w 4.4. Consequently, the seismic swarm can be divided into two parts: the western and the eastern clusters (Figure 4c).

To study spatiotemporal scaling properties and seismic energy distributions, we separated the swarm into clusters using the Density-Based Spatial Clustering of Application with Noise (DBSCAN). Specifically, we applied this algorithm to the relocated seismic events of the Thiva earthquake swarm with $M \geq M_c$ and identified five clusters (two main and three smaller clusters) based on space and time. In each main cluster of the Thiva sequence, the ideas of Non-Extensive Statistical Physics (NESP) are applied to the inter-event times and distances as well as the magnitude distributions.

In a number of previous works, it has been demonstrated that the spatiotemporal distribution of seismicity as expressed by the interevent distances [35] and the interevent times [33] distributions follows a q-exponential distribution with $q_D < 1$ and $q_T > 1$, respectively. In our study, the non-additive entropic parameters range from 0.7 to 0.8 for inter-event distances, whereas the corresponding ones for inter-event times range between 1.44 and 1.5. These q-values are in agreement with the q-values found in other studies (see [33,35,53,57,81,82] and references therein).

The entropic parameter estimates strongly suggest that in each cluster of the earthquake swarm, the temporal evolution is described by low degrees of freedom, indicating a high level of organization, hierarchy, and non-additive characteristics in agreement with the results presented in [37].

The spatiotemporal distribution of a swarm seismic sequence is determined by static and dynamic stresses or by fluid diffusion. Here, the expansion of Thiva's Cluster 2 swarm over time was studied. Following [56,58], aftershock activity is governed by afterslip loading asperities, which in turn controls the seismicity rate. In this approach, a fault is modeled with depth-dependent variations in normal stress, stress rate, and the introduction of rheological parameter A, leading to a logarithmic with-time evolution of migration. In Cluster 2, the major earthquakes of the swarm in July 2021 occurred at its western end, and the swarm progressed eastward. There is no significant migration of seismicity after the 7 July 2021, M 4.3 event. In contrast, ten days after the M 4.3 event, a decrease in mean migration distance was observed associated with the increase in microseismic activity, possibly indicating the accumulation of stress and the preparation of the forthcoming event of 9 September 2021, with a similar size (M 4.0). Following a short interval of low seismic activity in the second half of August 2021, a second stage of the swarm was initiated in September 2021. After the 9 September 2021, M 4.0 earthquake, the mean migration distance presents a logarithmic with time migration of the seismicity in agreement with a mechanism of aftershock migration driven by afterslip [56].

Cluster 5, which is located in the east–southeast part of the swarm and starts in March 2022, exhibits diffusion characteristics. The mean squared distance of epicenters scales with time, with a diffusion exponent α being quite close to 1, implying that the swarm migration is approximately normal (Gaussian) diffusion in nature. Furthermore, seismicity evolved during the first days (from 3 March 2022), with events systematically migrating away in the SSE direction with an average initial velocity of 0.12 km/day, presenting a hydraulic diffusivity of $D = 0.7$ m^2/s. The intrusion of fluids through the fracture network can induce seismicity either by localizing stress or by increasing pore pressure, reducing the effective normal stress, and facilitating aseismic creep. The evolution of seismicity in Cluster 5, which seems to be fluid-driven, helps small asperities in the fractured zone to break, transferring static stress to neighboring fault patches where events are triggered in agreement with that presented in [53].

5. Concluding Remarks

In this work, using a relocated catalog of seismicity, we study the physical and statistical pattern of the Thiva swarm activated after the 2 December 2020 earthquake with a magnitude of M_w 4.5 that occurred near the city of Thiva. The swarm displayed a general trend of spatiotemporal migration toward the east–southeast until the middle of 2022.

The DBSCAN clustering algorithm was subsequently applied to the 2020–2022 Thiva earthquake sequence to identify spatiotemporal earthquake clusters. The scaling properties of the main clusters were analyzed using the Non-Extensive Statistical Physics (NESP) approach, providing detailed insights into the nature of the long-term correlation of the seismic swarm. The results of the analysis indicate that the statistical properties of earthquake swarm clusters can be successfully reproduced by means of NESP and confirm the complexity and non-additivity of the spatiotemporal evolution of seismicity.

The entropic parameters were estimated with q_D values ranging from 0.7 to 0.8 and q_T values from 1.44 to 1.50. Furthermore, the frequency–magnitude distributions were analyzed using the fragment–asperity model proposed within the NESP framework, providing the non-additive entropic parameter (q_M). The results suggest that the statistical characteristics of earthquake clusters can be effectively interpreted using NESP, highlighting the complexity, hierarchy, and non-additive nature of the spatiotemporal evolution of seismicity in agreement with a system described by low degrees of freedom.

In addition, possible physical mechanisms responsible for the evolution of the two main and larger clusters are suggested. For Cluster 2, located in the west–northwest part of the activated zone, an afterslip mechanism activated after the 2 September 2021, M 4.0 events seems to control its evolution, while for the second cluster located in the east—south part of the fractured zone (Cluster 5), a normal diffusion mechanism is proposed to describe its migration pattern. Subsurface fluids under pressure seem to have played a significant role in the evolution of the Cluster 5, 2021–2022 seismic swarm, either causing local stress concentrations or facilitating slip by lowering the effective normal stresses or weakening the faults' walls through erosion.

Author Contributions: Conceptualization, F.V.; methodology, F.V., K.P., and E.S.; software, K.P. and E.S.; validation, E.S., K.P., A.K., and F.V.; formal analysis, E.S., K.P., A.K., and F.V.; investigation, E.S., K.P., A.K., and F.V.; resources, E.S., K.P., and A.K.; data curation, E.S., K.P., A.K., and F.V.; writing—original draft preparation, E.S. and F.V.; writing—review and editing, E.S., K.P., and F.V.; visualization, E.S., K.P., and F.V.; supervision, F.V.; project administration, F.V. All authors have read and agreed to the published version of the manuscript.

Funding: This research work of E.S. was supported by the Hellenic Foundation for Research and Innovation (HFRI) under the 5th Call for HFRI PhD Fellowships (Fellowship Number: 20518).

Institutional Review Board Statement: Not applicable.

Data Availability Statement: Data are openly available at the Seismological Laboratory of the National and Kapodistrian University of Athens (SL-NKUA, http://www.geophysics.geol.uoa.gr/) for Thiva (last accessed on 2 July 2025). Seismological waveform data from permanent and temporary stations of the HUSN are available at the European Integrated Data Archive (EIDA) node hosted at GI-NOA (http://eida.gein.noa.gr/; accessed on 2 July 2025).

Acknowledgments: We would like to thank Georgios Michas, Ioannis Spingos, and Davide Zaccagnino for their valuable support, helpful suggestions, and insightful feedback during the preparation of this work.

Conflicts of Interest: The authors declare no conflicts of interest.

References

1. Tsodoulos, I.M.; Koukouvelas, I.K.; Pavlides, S. Tectonic geomorphology of the easternmost extension of the Gulf of Corinth (Beotia, Central Greece). *Tectonophysics* **2008**, *453*, 211–232. [CrossRef]
2. Sboras, S.; Ganas, A.; Pavlides, S. Morphotectonic Analysis of the Neotectonic and Active Faults of Beotia (Central Greece), Using G.I.S. Techniques. *Bull. Geol. Soc. Greece* **2017**, *43*, 1607–1618.
3. Papazachos, B.C.; Papazachou, C. *The Earthquakes of Greece*; Ziti Publications: Thessaloniki, Greece, 2003.
4. Ambraseys, N.N.; Jackson, J.A. Seismicity and Strain in the Gulf of Corinth (Greece) Since 1694. *J. Earthq. Eng.* **1997**, *1*, 433–474. [CrossRef]
5. Ambraseys, N.N.; Jackson, J.A. Seismicity and associated strain of central Greece between 1890 and 1988. *Geophys. J. Int.* **1990**, *101*, 663–708. [CrossRef]
6. Elias, P.; Spingos, I.; Kaviris, G.; Karavias, A.; Gatsios, T.; Sakkas, V.; Parcharidis, I. Combined Geodetic and Seismological Study of the December 2020 Mw = 4.6 Thiva (Central Greece) Shallow Earthquake. *Appl. Sci.* **2021**, *11*, 5947. [CrossRef]
7. Ganas, A.; Oikonomou, I.A.; Tsimi, C. NOAfaults: A digital database for active faults in Greece. *Bull. Geol. Soc. Greece* **2017**, *47*, 518. [CrossRef]
8. Ester, M.; Kriegel, H.-P.; Sander, J.; Xu, X. A Density-Based Algorithm for Discovering Clusters in Large Spatial Databases with Noise. In Proceedings of the Second International Conference on Knowledge Discovery and Data Mining (KDD-96), Portland, OR, USA, 2–4 August 1996; Volume 34, pp. 226–231.
9. Waldhauser, F. *HypoDD-A Program to Compute Double-Difference Hypocenter Locations*; Open-File Report 01-113; U.S. Geological Survey: Menlo Park, CA, USA, 2001.
10. Tsallis, C. Nonextensive Statistical Mechanics and Thermodynamics: Historical Backgroundand Present Status. In *Nonextensive Statistical Mechanics and Its Applications*; Abe, S., Okamoto, Y., Eds.; Springer: Berlin/Heidelberg, Germany, 2001.
11. Telesca, L. Maximum Likelihood Estimation of the Nonextensive Parameters of the Earthquake Cumulative Magnitude Distribution. *Bull. Seismol. Soc. Am.* **2012**, *102*, 886–891. [CrossRef]
12. Vallianatos, F.; Sammonds, P. Evidence of non-extensive statistical physics of the lithospheric instability approaching the 2004 Sumatran–Andaman and 2011 Honshu mega-earthquakes. *Tectonophysics* **2013**, *590*, 52–58. [CrossRef]
13. Papadakis, G.; Vallianatos, F.; Sammonds, P.A. Nonextensive Statistical Physics Analysis of the 1995 Kobe, Japan Earthquake. *Pure Appl. Geophys.* **2015**, *172*, 1923–1931. [CrossRef]
14. Michas, G.; Vallianatos, F.; Sammonds, P. Non-extensivity and long-range correlations in the earthquake activity at the West Corinth rift (Greece). *Nonlinear Process. Geophys.* **2013**, *20*, 713–724. [CrossRef]

15. Klein, F.W. *User's Guide to HYPOINVERSE-2000, a Fortran Program to Solve for Earthquake Locations and Magnitudes*; Open-File Report 2002-171; United States Department of the Interior Geological Survey: Menlo Park, CA, USA, 2002.
16. Karakonstantis, A. 3-D Simulation of Crust and Upper Mantle Structure in the Broader Hellenic Area through Seismic Tomography. Ph.D. Thesis, Department of Geophysics-Geothermics, Faculty of Geology, University of Athens, Athens, Greece, 2017. (In Greek).
17. Waldhauser, F.; Ellsworth, W. A Double-Difference Earthquake Location Algorithm: Method and Application to the Northern Hayward Fault, California. *Bull. Seismol. Soc. Am.* **2000**, *90*, 1353–1368. [CrossRef]
18. Paige, C.C.; Saunders, M.A. LSQR: An Algorithm for Sparse Linear Equations and Sparse Least Squares. *ACM Trans. Math. Softw.* **1982**, *8*, 43–71. [CrossRef]
19. Gutenberg, B.; Richter, C.F. Frequency of Earthquakes in California. *Bull. Seismol. Soc. Am.* **1944**, *34*, 185–188. [CrossRef]
20. Aki, K. Maximum lilkelihood estimate of b in the formula logN=a-bM and its confidence limits. *Bull. Earthq. Res. Inst.* **1965**, *43*, 237–239.
21. Utsu, T. A statistical significance test of the difference in b-value between two earthquakes groups. *J. Phys. Earth* **1966**, *14*, 37–40. [CrossRef]
22. Bender, B. Maximum likelihood estimation of b values for magnitude grouped data. *Bull. Seismol. Soc. Am.* **1983**, *73*, 831–851. [CrossRef]
23. Utsu, T. Representation and analysis of the earthquake size distribution: A historical review and some new approaches. *Pure Appl. Geophys.* **1999**, *155*, 509–535. [CrossRef]
24. Wiemer, S.; Wyss, M. Minimum Magnitude of Completeness in Earthquake Catalogs: Examples from Alaska, the Western United States, and Japan. *Bull. Seismol. Soc. Am.* **2000**, *90*, 859–869. [CrossRef]
25. Wyss, M.; Wiemer, S.; Zuniga, R. Zmap: A Tool for Analyses of Seismicity Patterns, Typical Applications and Uses: A Cookbook. 2001. Available online: https://www.researchgate.net/publication/261170802 (accessed on 2 July 2022).
26. Sabermahani, S.; Frederiksen, A.W. Improved Earthquake Clustering Using a Density-Adaptive DBSCAN Algorithm: An Example from Iran. *Seismol. Res. Lett.* **2023**, *95*, 942–951. [CrossRef]
27. Sharma, A.; Vijay, R.K.; Nanda, S.J. Identification and spatio-temporal analysis of earthquake clusters using SOM–DBSCAN model. *Neural Comput. Applic.* **2023**, *35*, 8081–8108. [CrossRef]
28. Sardeli, E.; Michas, G.; Pavlou, K.; Zaccagnino, D.; Vallianatos, F. Spatiotemporal properties of the 2020–2021 Petrinja (Croatia) earthquake sequence. *J. Seismol.* **2024**, *28*, 899–920. [CrossRef]
29. Tsallis, C. Possible generalization of Boltzmann-Gibbs statistics. *J. Stat. Phys.* **1988**, *52*, 479–487. [CrossRef]
30. Tsallis, C. *Introduction to Nonextensive Statistical Mechanics: Approaching a Complex World*; Springer: Berlin/Heidelberg, Germany, 2009.
31. Sotolongo-Costa, O.; Posadas, A. Fragment-Asperity Interaction Model for Earthquakes. *Phys. Rev. Lett.* **2004**, *92*, 048501. [CrossRef]
32. Matcharashvili, T.; Chelidze, T.; Javakhishvili, Z.; Jorjiashvili, N.; Fra Paleo, U. Non-extensive statistical analysis of seismicity in the area of Javakheti, Georgia. *Comput. Geosci.* **2011**, *37*, 1627–1632. [CrossRef]
33. Papadakis, G.; Vallianatos, F.; Sammonds, P. Evidence of Nonextensive Statistical Physics Behavior of the Hellenic Subduction Zone Seismicity. *Tectonophysics* **2013**, *608*, 1037–1048. [CrossRef]
34. Vincenty, T. Direct and inverse solutions of geodesics on the ellipsoid with application of nested equations. *Surv. Rev.* **1975**, *23*, 88–93. [CrossRef]
35. Vallianatos, F.; Papadakis, G.; Michas, G. Generalized statistical mechanics approaches to earthquakes and tectonics. *Proc. R. Soc. A Math. Phys. Eng. Sci.* **2016**, *472*, 20160497. [CrossRef] [PubMed]
36. Picoli, S., Jr.; Mendes, R.S.; Malacarne, L.C.; Santos, R.P.B. q-distributions in complex systems: A brief review. *Braz. J. Phys.* **2009**, *39*, 468–474. [CrossRef]
37. Sardeli, E.; Michas, G.; Pavlou, K.; Vallianatos, F.; Karakonstantis, A.; Chatzopoulos, G. Complexity of Recent Earthquake Swarms in Greece in Terms of Non-Extensive Statistical Physics. *Entropy* **2023**, *25*, 667. [CrossRef]
38. King, G.C.; Stein, R.S.; Lin, J. Static stress changes and the triggering of earthquakes. *Bull. Seismol. Soc. Am.* **1994**, *84*, 935–953.
39. Stein, R.S.; King, G.C.; Lin, J. Stress triggering of the 1994 M= 6.7 Northridge, California, earthquake by its predecessors. *Science* **1994**, *265*, 1432–1435. [CrossRef] [PubMed]
40. Stein, R.S.; Barka, A.A.; Dieterich, J.H. Progressive failure on the North Anatolian fault since 1939 by earthquake stress triggering. *Geophys. J. Int.* **1997**, *128*, 594–604. [CrossRef]
41. Stein, R.S. The role of stress transfer in earthquake occurrence. *Nature* **1999**, *402*, 605–609. [CrossRef]
42. Harris, R.A.; Simpson, R.W. Suppression of large earthquakes by stress shadows: A comparison of Coulomb and rate-and-state failure. *J. Geophys. Res. Solid Earth* **1998**, *103*, 24439–24451. [CrossRef]
43. Parsons, T.; Toda, S.; Stein, R.S.; Barka, A.; Dieterich, J.H. Heightened odds of large earthquakes near Istanbul: An interaction-based probability calculation. *Science* **2000**, *288*, 661–665. [CrossRef] [PubMed]

44. Toda, S.; Lin, J.; Meghraoui, M.; Stein, R.S. 12 May 2008 M = 7.9 Wenchuan, China, earthquake calculated to increase failure stress and seismicity rate on three major fault systems. *Geophys. Res. Lett.* **2008**, *35*, L17305. [CrossRef]
45. Vallianatos, F.; Pavlou, K. Scaling properties of the Mw7.0 Samos (Greece), 2020 aftershock sequence. *Acta Geophys.* **2021**, *69*, 1067–1084. [CrossRef]
46. Kilb, D.; Gomberg, J.; Bodin, P. Triggering of earthquake aftershocks by dynamic stresses. *Nature* **2002**, *408*, 570–574. [CrossRef]
47. Kilb, D.; Gomberg, J.; Bodin, P. Aftershock triggering by complete Coulomb stress changes. *J. Geophys. Res. Solid Earth* **2002**, *107*, ESE 2-1–ESE 2-14. [CrossRef]
48. Scholz, C.H. *The Mechanics of Earthquakes and Faulting*, 3rd ed.; Cambridge University Press: Cambridge, UK, 2019.
49. Cocco, M. Pore pressure and poroelasticity effects in Coulomb stress analysis of earthquake interactions. *J. Geophys. Res.* **2002**, *107*, 2030. [CrossRef]
50. Toda, S.; Stein, R.S.; Sevilgen, V.; Lin, J. *Coulomb 3.3 Graphic-Rich Deformation and Stress-Change Software for Earthquake, Tectonic, and Volcano Research and Teaching-User Guide*; Open-File Report 2011-1060; U.S. Geological Survey: Menlo Park, CA, USA, 2011; p. 63.
51. Harris, R.A.; Simpson, R.W. In the shadow of 1857, an evaluation of the stress changes generated by the M8 Ft. Tejon, California, earthquake. *Eos Trans. Am. Geophys. Union* **1993**, *74*, 427.
52. Harris, R.A.; Simpson, R.W. In the shadow of the 1857—The effect of the great Ft. Tejon earthquake on the subsequent earthquakes in southern California. *Geophys. Res. Lett.* **1996**, *23*, 229–232. [CrossRef]
53. Kaviris, G.; Kapetanidis, V.; Spingos, I.; Sakellariou, N.; Karakonstantis, A.; Kouskouna, V.; Elias, P.; Karavias, A.; Sakkas, V.; Gatsios, T.; et al. Investigation of the Thiva 2020–2021 Earthquake Sequence Using Seismological Data and Space Techniques. *Appl. Sci.* **2022**, *12*, 2630. [CrossRef]
54. Lippiello, E.; Giacco, F.; Marzocchi, W.; Godano, C.; De Arcangelis, L. Mechanical origin of aftershocks. *Sci. Rep.* **2015**, *5*, 15560. [CrossRef]
55. Shapiro, S.A.; Rothert, E.; Rath, V.; Rindschwentner, J. Characterization of fluid transport properties of reservoirs using induced microseismicity. *Geophysics* **2002**, *67*, 212–220. [CrossRef]
56. Perfettini, H.; Frank, W.B.; Marsan, D.; Bouchon, M. A Model of Aftershock Migration Driven by Afterslip. *Geophys. Res. Lett.* **2018**, *45*, 2283–2293. [CrossRef]
57. Michas, G.; Pavlou, K.; Avgerinou, S.-E.; Anyfadi, E.-A.; Vallianatos, F. Aftershock patterns of the 2021 Mw 6.3 Northern Thessaly (Greece) earthquake. *J. Seismol.* **2022**, *26*, 201–225. [CrossRef]
58. Perfettini, H.; Avouac, J.-P. Postseismic relaxation driven by brittle creep: A possible mechanism to reconcile geodetic measurements and the decay rate of aftershocks, application to the Chi-Chi earthquake, Taiwan. *J. Geophys. Res. Solid Earth* **2004**, *109*, 2003JB002488. [CrossRef]
59. Pavlou, K.; Michas, G.; Vallianatos, F. Scaling Law Analysis and Aftershock Spatiotemporal Evolution of the Three Strongest Earthquakes in the Ionian Sea During the Period 2014–2019. *Geosciences* **2025**, *15*, 84. [CrossRef]
60. Metzler, R.; Klafter, J. The random walk's guide to anomalous diffusion: A fractional dynamics approach. *Phys. Rep.* **2000**, *339*, 1–77. [CrossRef]
61. Metzler, R.; Jeon, J.H.A.; Cherstvy, G.; Barkai, E. Anomalous diffusion models and their properties: Non-stationarity, non-ergodicity, and ageing at the centenary of single particle tracking. *Phys. Chem. Chem. Phys.* **2014**, *16*, 24128–24164. [CrossRef]
62. Bouchaud, J.P.; Georges, A. Anomalous diffusion in disordered media: Statistical mechanisms, models and physical applications. *Phys. Rep.* **1990**, *195*, 127–293. [CrossRef]
63. Michas, G.; Vallianatos, F. Scaling properties and anomalous diffusion of the Florina micro-seismic activity: Fluid driven? *Geomech. Energy Environ.* **2020**, *24*, 100155. [CrossRef]
64. Michas, G.; Vallianatos, F. Modelling earthquake diffusion as a continuous-time random walk with fractional kinetics: The case of the 2001 Agios Ioannis earthquake swarm (Corinth Rift). *Geophys. J. Int.* **2018**, *215*, 333–345. [CrossRef]
65. Michas, G.; Vallianatos, F. Stochastic modeling of nonstationary earthquake time series with long-term clustering effects. *Phys. Rev. E* **2018**, *98*, 042107. [CrossRef]
66. Michas, G.; Vallianatos, F. Stochastic modeling of injection induced seismicity based on the continuous time random walk model. *Sci. Rep.* **2024**, *14*, 4951. [CrossRef]
67. McKernon, C.; Main, I.G. Regional variations in the diffusion of triggered seismicity. *J. Geophys. Res.* **2005**, *110*. [CrossRef]
68. Helmstetter, A.; Ouillon, G.; Sornette, D. Are aftershocks of large Californian earthquakes diffusing? *J. Geophys. Res. Solid Earth* **2003**, *108*, 2483. [CrossRef]
69. Huc, M.; Main, I.G. Anomalous stress diffusion in earthquake triggering: Correlation length, time dependence, and directionality. *J. Geophys. Res. Solid Earth* **2003**, *108*, 2324. [CrossRef]
70. Marsan, D.; Bean, C.J.; Steacy, S.; McCloskey, J. Observation of diffusion processes in earthquake populations and implications for the predictability of seismicity systems. *J. Geophys. Res. Solid Earth* **2000**, *105*, 28081–28094. [CrossRef]
71. Shapiro, S.A.; Huenges, E.; Borm, G. Estimating the crust permeability from fluid-injection-induced seismic emission at the KTB site. *Geophys. J. Int.* **1997**, *131*, F15–F18. [CrossRef]

72. Shapiro, S.A.; Audigane, P.; Royer, J. Large-scale in situ permeability tensor of rocks from induced microseismicity. *Geophys. J. Int.* **1999**, *137*, 207–213. [CrossRef]
73. Parotidis, M.; Rothert, E.; Shapiro, S.A. Pore-pressure diffusion: A possible triggering mechanism for the earthquake swarms 2000 in Vogtland/NW-Bohemia, central Europe. *Geophys. Res. Lett.* **2003**, *30*, 20. [CrossRef]
74. Antonioli, A.; Piccinini, D.; Chiaraluce, L.; Cocco, M. Fluid flow and seismicity pattern: Evidence from the 1997 Umbria-Marche (central Italy) seismic sequence. *Geophys. Res. Lett.* **2005**, *32*, 10. [CrossRef]
75. Michas, G.; Kapetanidis, V.; Spingos, I.; Kaviris, G.; Vallianatos, F. The 2020 Perachora peninsula earthquake sequence (East Corinth Rift, Greece): Spatiotemporal evolution and implications for the triggering mechanism. *Acta Geophys.* **2022**, *70*, 2581–2601. [CrossRef]
76. Kapetanidis, V.; Michas, G.; Kaviris, G.; Vallianatos, F. Spatiotemporal Properties of Seismicity and Variations of Shear-Wave Splitting Parameters in the Western Gulf of Corinth (Greece). *Appl. Sci.* **2021**, *11*, 6573. [CrossRef]
77. Talwani, P.; Chen, L.; Gahalaut, K. Seismogenic permeability, k_s. *J. Geophys. Res.* **2007**, *112*, B07309. [CrossRef]
78. Chen, X.; Shearer, P.M.; Abercrombie, R.E. Spatial migration of earthquakes within seismic clusters in Southern California: Evidence for fluid diffusion. *J. Geophys. Res. Solid Earth* **2012**, *117*, B04301. [CrossRef]
79. Lohman, R.B.; McGuire, J.J. Earthquake swarms driven by aseismic creep in the Salton Trough, California. *J. Geophys. Res. Solid Earth* **2007**, *112*. [CrossRef]
80. Roland, E.; McGuire, J.J. Earthquake swarms on transform faults. *Geophys. J. Int.* **2009**, *178*, 1677–1690. [CrossRef]
81. Abe, S.; Suzuki, N. Law for the distance between successive earthquakes: A New Law for Distance Between Earthquakes. *J. Geophys. Res. Solid Earth* **2003**, *108*. [CrossRef]
82. Abe, S.; Suzuki, N. Scale-free statistics of time interval between successive earthquakes. *Phys. A Stat. Mech. Its Appl.* **2005**, *350*, 588–596. [CrossRef]

Disclaimer/Publisher's Note: The statements, opinions and data contained in all publications are solely those of the individual author(s) and contributor(s) and not of MDPI and/or the editor(s). MDPI and/or the editor(s) disclaim responsibility for any injury to people or property resulting from any ideas, methods, instructions or products referred to in the content.

MDPI AG
Grosspeteranlage 5
4052 Basel
Switzerland
Tel.: +41 61 683 77 34

Entropy Editorial Office
E-mail: entropy@mdpi.com
www.mdpi.com/journal/entropy

MDPI

Disclaimer/Publisher's Note: The title and front matter of this reprint are at the discretion of the Guest Editors. The publisher is not responsible for their content or any associated concerns. The statements, opinions and data contained in all individual articles are solely those of the individual Editors and contributors and not of MDPI. MDPI disclaims responsibility for any injury to people or property resulting from any ideas, methods, instructions or products referred to in the content.

www.ingramcontent.com/pod-product-compliance
Lightning Source LLC
Chambersburg PA
CBHW061519210926
51850CB00008B/1973
* 9 7 8 3 7 2 5 8 6 5 0 0 0 *